MILK STREET

BACKROADS

ITALY

Finding Italy's Forgotten Recipes

CHRISTOPHER KIMBALL AND J.M. HIRSCH

ADDITIONAL WRITING AND EDITING

Michelle Locke, Ari Smolin, Dawn Yanagihara and Matthew Card

RECIPES

Wes Martin, Courtney Hill, Rose Hattabaugh,
Hisham Ali Hassan, Kevin Clark, Diane Unger and the
Milk Street Cooks and Recipe Contributors

ART DIRECTION

Jennifer Baldino Cox

PRINCIPAL TRAVEL PHOTOGRAPHY

Christopher Warde-Jones

VORACIOUS

LITTLE, BROWN AND COMPANY

NEW YORK BOSTON LONDON

Little, Brown and Company
Hachette Book Group
1290 Avenue of the Americas, New York, NY 10104
littlebrown.com

First Edition: April 2025

Voracious is an imprint of Little, Brown and Company,
a division of Hachette Book Group, Inc.

The Voracious name and logo are trademarks of
Hachette Book Group, Inc.

The publisher is not responsible for websites (or their content)
that are not owned by the publisher.

The Hachette Speakers Bureau provides a wide range of authors for
speaking events. To find out more, go to hachettespeakersbureau.com
or call (866) 376-6591.

ISBN 978-0-316-58206-3
LCCN 2024945379

10 9 8 7 6 5 4 3 2 1

IM

Print book interior design by Gary Tooth / Empire Design Studio,
and Ashley Prine / Tandem Books.

Printed in China

Photography Credits: Christopher Warde-Jones, pages vi-vii, 2-3, 7, 10 (bottom), 12, 14, 15, 18-19, 22-23, 26, 32-33, 40-41, 46-47, 54, 55, 60-61, 64, 65, 68, 69, 74, 88-89, 92-93, 96, 97, 100, 101, 104-105, 108-109, 112-113, 120, 121, 128-129, 132, 136, 138, 140, 141, 144-145, 156, 162, 166-167, 168, 172-173, 184, 185, 204-205, 206, 208-209, 218-219, 220, 221, 225, 228-229, 245, 248 (top), 249, 268-269, 276-277, 280-281, 284, 285, 298-299, 304-305, 319, 322 (bottom left), 326, 327, 332, 333, 352-353, 358, 359, 360-361, 366-367, 374, 375, 400; Joe Murphy, pages 1, 5, 6, 9, 10 (top), 24, 29, 30, 36, 37, 38, 43, 44, 57, 63, 66, 71, 77, 78, 90, 95, 107, 111, 114, 117, 122, 123, 127, 131, 137, 139, 147, 152, 155, 165, 180, 181, 183, 187, 188, 190, 191, 199, 203, 211, 231, 234, 236, 243, 247, 251, 259, 263, 265, 267, 271, 274, 275, 287, 289, 290, 292, 295, 296, 297, 301, 302, 303, 308, 309, 310, 311, 313, 314, 331, 335, 343, 349, 351, 355, 356, 363, 369, 377, 381, 384, 385; Connie Miller, pages xvi, 12, 16, 21, 31, 39, 45, 49, 52, 59, 72, 73, 83, 84, 86, 98, 103, 116, 118, 119, 134, 135, 142, 148, 149, 159, 160, 169, 170, 171, 175, 178, 192, 193, 201, 207, 213, 214, 215, 216, 217, 223, 226, 232, 237, 252, 253, 257, 266, 283, 306, 316, 317, 321, 325, 328, 337, 338, 347, 357, 365, 370, 373, 383; J.M. Hirsch, pages ii, viii-ix, 27, 46, 80, 81, 150, 151, 163, 248 (bottom), 318; Christopher Kimball, pages i, iv-v, 50-51, 124-125, 154, 194, 195, 196, 197, 238, 239, 240, 254-255, 260-261, 272-273, 312, 330, 340, 341, 378-379; Erika LaPresto, pages 34, 133, 279; Brian Samuels, page 371; Carlo Gianferro, pages 176-177, 348; Beatrice Melotti, pages 344, 345; Petr Svarc / Alamy Stock Photo, pages 322-323

Food Styling Credits: Wes Martin, pages 1, 5, 6, 9, 10 (top), 24, 29, 30, 34, 36, 37, 38, 43, 44, 52, 57, 63, 71, 77, 78, 90, 95, 107, 111, 114, 117, 122, 123, 127, 131, 133, 137, 139, 147, 152, 155, 165, 180, 181, 183, 187, 188, 190, 191, 199, 203, 211, 231, 234, 236, 247, 251, 259, 263, 265, 267, 271, 274, 275, 279, 287, 289, 290, 292, 295, 296, 297, 301, 302, 303, 308, 309, 310, 311, 313, 314, 335, 343, 349, 351, 355, 356, 363, 369, 377, 381, 384, 385; Christine Tobin, pages xvi, 12, 16, 21, 31, 39, 49, 59, 66, 72, 73, 83, 84, 86, 98, 103, 116, 118, 119, 134, 135, 142, 148, 149, 159, 160, 169, 170, 171, 175, 178, 192, 193, 201, 207, 223, 226, 237, 257, 266, 283, 316, 317, 321, 325, 328, 337, 338, 347, 357, 364, 365, 370, 371, 373, 383; Catrine Kelty, pages 45, 213, 214, 215, 216, 217, 232, 252, 253, 306

CONTENTS

Introduction

My first trip to Italy was in 1967 when I arrived with my family in Rome and we stayed at the Hotel Hassler just above the Spanish Steps. It was a classic tourist trip—three days and then on to Paris and London—only stopping long enough to see the major tourist destinations, consuming the obligatory classics, and never experiencing the heart and soul of our host country.

Since then, I've been back many times, usually guided by cookbook authors and locals. I've visited small eateries in Rome's Jewish quarter, local markets and farms outside Bologna; cooked a white wild boar sauce, ragu bianco de cinghiale, and eaten fried dough for breakfast; I surrendered to the unwashed chaos of Naples, took a walking tour from Ravello to Amalfi through the Valle delle Ferriere (iron works), and spent a week in Umbria cooking my favorite type of cuisine, cucina povera.

A great travel cookbook has to take one off the beaten path, but it also has to immerse you in the soul of a region. You want to meet the people, walk the land, sniff the aromas of wild herbs, sit at the table, and listen to the conversation. Many, many times I have sat at those tables, trying to keep pace with my rudimentary Italian, understanding the rhythm of the back and forth, the feeling of the language, without all of the particulars. A table in Calabria is quite different than one in Bologna, Rome or Bari. And that's what great travel writing is all about, capturing the warp and weft of a culture, not just its food.

For those of you who have been to Rome, you know what I mean. The city is filled with the usual suspects, particularly mediocre pasta dishes. But if you know where to look, one finds the sublime. Antico Falcone for one (the palline al verde —ricotta spinach balls—are divine) or try Le Mani in Pasta, which offers shaved truffles over thin raw slices of branzino.

Or spend time at the Hotel Barbieri in Altomonte, Calabria, where three generations live under the same roof just a hundred yards away from the hotel they built in the 1960s. They still do some of their cooking in a wood-fired oven, including pizzas topped with chopped, seasoned pig offal. You are there for the hospitality as well as the food.

You can use this volume as a cookbook, as an armchair travel experience, or as a planning guide for your next trip to Italy. We cannot hope to cover the entirety of what Italy offers, but we can provide a peek at what lies beneath the typical tourist excursion—recipes that mostly have not crossed the Atlantic and remain connected to the people and places that birthed them.

It's not just a story of cooking, it's the story of many cultures, many regions and many families that somehow, magically, are woven into the fabric of what we call Italy.

—Christopher Kimball

Italian Pantry Essentials

Quality Italian ingredients have become widely available in U.S. grocery stores, from authentic Parmigiano-Reggiano cheese and prosciutto to true aceto balsamico and salt-cured capers. These ingredients make it easier to capture both the flavors and traditions of classic Italian cooking. The following list covers many of the ingredients we like to keep on hand.

Anchovies

In Italian, alici refers to fresh anchovies; acciughe refers to cured anchovies, whether salt-preserved or oil-packed. We often cook with the latter, as they are easy to find and are ready to use right out of the container. Oil-packed anchovies are sold jarred and in tins. Avoid anchovy paste sold in a tube; it tends to be unpleasantly salty and lack umami depth. White anchovies, a Spanish specialty, typically are packed in vinegar and oil; they are meant to be eaten as is and are not intended for cooking. Colatura di alici is an Italian fermented anchovy condiment similar to Southeast Asian fish sauce, but its taste is saltier, smoother and less pungent. Depending on the dish, oil-packed anchovies, rinsed and patted dry, can be a reasonably good substitute for colatura di alici.

Arborio and Carnaroli Rice

Taking its name from a town in the Po Valley of northern Italy's Piedmont region, Arborio rice is a medium-grain variety with a stubby shape, high starch content and ability to absorb large amounts of liquid. It's the best-known rice for making luxuriously creamy risotto. But in our experience, carnaroli rice, which also comes from Piedmont, is more resistant to overcooking, making it our favorite. The two types can be used interchangeably in recipes, but Arborio requires a little more attention when simmering to ensure the proper degree of doneness. Vialone nano is yet another Italian high-starch rice; it's the preferred variety in the Veneto region.

Beans

Nutritious, inexpensive and shelf-stable, dried beans, or fagioli, are co-stars in countless Italian soups, stews and pasta dishes, and often are the featured ingredient. The varieties we cook with most are white, creamy cannellini beans and beige and red-mottled Roman beans, which also are known as cranberry beans or borlotti, in Italian. In addition, chickpeas, or ceci, are a staple legume in the Italian kitchen. No matter the variety, soaking in salted water, then simmering dried beans yields the best taste and texture. But when short on time, canned beans are a terrific option, too. We often drain and rinse canned beans before use, but sometimes we add some or all of the canning liquid to give the dish starchiness and body, so be sure to read the recipe before draining your canned beans. See p. 87 for instructions on cooking dried beans.

Calabrian Chili Paste

Sold in jars, Calabrian chili paste, sometimes referred to as bomba calabrese, is made by crushing fresh red chilies from Italy's Calabria region with oil, salt and vinegar. The vividly hued, coarse-textured condiment is quickly gaining in popularity, as it's an easy way to spike dishes with spiciness, saltiness and a little tang, plus the fruity notes of fresh red chili. The paste is terrific in sauces, soups and stews, as well as on sandwiches and pizzas. Stored in the refrigerator after opening, it will keep for several months.

Capers

To make punchy, pungent capers, the tiny flower buds of a bush that thrives in hot, dry climates are harvested, then preserved. In Italy, salt-packed capers are common, but here in the U.S., capers packed in brine are more common. The term "non-pareil" on jar labels indicates that the capers are of the smallest size on the grading scale (no larger than 7 millimeters). Salted capers should be briefly soaked in water, then rinsed before use. Capers in brine need only to be drained before use, but also can be quickly rinsed to tame their intensity. Caperberries are the flower buds that have matured into fruits. Roughly the dimensions of olives, and with their stems still attached, caperberries also are sold salted and brined. With a milder flavor and a texture that is seedy and slightly pickle-like, caperberries are better on an antipasto platter than used in place of regular capers.

Cheeses

Burrata, a specialty of the Campania region of Southern Italy, is a stark white, ball-shaped soft cheese. It consists of an outer casing of what is essentially fresh mozzarella and a rich, oozy center of cream with mozzarella curds called stracciatella. (The term stracciatella, which translates as "little rags," also refers to a Roman egg-drop soup and to chocolate-chip gelato or ice cream.) Burrata may be made with cow's or buffalo milk, though in the U.S., the former is the more common variety. Either way, it's highly perishable and should be enjoyed soon after purchase.

Fontina is a semi-firm unpasteurized cow's milk cheese made in the Aosta Valley in dairy-loving northern Italy. With a washed rind and small "eyes" that dot the interior, fontina has a rich, buttery, slightly nutty, vaguely truffle-y flavor that's assertive yet approachable. An excellent melting cheese, fontina is a key ingredient in fonduta, Italy's version of Swiss fondue. When shopping, be sure to purchase fontina from Italy, sometimes labeled "fontina Val d'Aosta." Pass on Danish fontina; encased in a tell-tale red-wax rind, this cheese has a rubbery texture and uninspiring flavor.

Gorgonzola, a rich cow's milk blue cheese, is produced in northern Italy, specifically in the dairy-rich regions of Piedmont and Lombardy. Its texture and assertiveness depend on how long it is aged. Gorgonzola dolce is the cheese in its younger stages, when it is luscious and spreadable, with a mellow, subtly sweet flavor. Gorgonzola piccante, often labeled simply as "Gorgonzola," has a creamy yet crumbly consistency and bold, salty pungency. Either type works both in recipes and on cheese boards.

Mozzarella is a household cheese, but the bouncy, rubbery shreds scattered on pizza and chicken Parmesan in the U.S. have little in common with Italian mozzarella. The latter is a fresh, stretched-curd cheese produced with the milk of water buffalo. A specialty from Southern Italy with protected status by the European Union, mozzarella di bufala ideally is eaten the day it is made, as it is highly perishable. If produced with cow's milk, the cheese is called fior di latte—what we in the U.S. refer to as "fresh mozzarella." These days, most supermarkets sell fresh mozzarella, typically packed in whey, and in a variety of sizes, from egg-sized ovoline to diminutive perline. It's also relatively easy to find mozzarella di bufala in specialty markets and grocery stores with sizable cheese departments. Smoked mozzarella has a firmer texture than fresh mozzarella, and is a great way to add woodsy flavor to cheesy dishes.

Parmesan needs little introduction. When we call for the firm, aged, umami-rich cow's milk cheese, we mean Parmigiano-Reggiano, which is produced according to European Union regulations in a handful of provinces within the regions of Emilia-Romagna and Lombardy. Parmesan can be grated or shaved for adding to dishes, or cut into shards for a cheese plate. To taste the full spectrum of rich, nutty flavor notes, purchase Parmesan in chunks that you will use within a few weeks' time. Avoid pre-grated Parmesan, as the cheese loses its character, including its unique crystalline crunchiness, with exposure to air. We prefer to grate Parmesan as needed on a wand-style grater, which yields a finer, fluffier texture than if grated on the small holes of a box grater. Be sure to reserve the rind in a zip-close bag in the freezer. Simmered into soups and stews, even just a small piece of rind will add great depth of flavor.

Pecorino Romano is the best-known member of the pecorino family of cheeses, all made with sheep's milk. A firm, crumbly cheese with assertive salinity, a little spiciness, a touch of tang and a notable but pleasant funkiness, pecorino Romano pairs perfectly with the bold, strong flavors of Central and Southern Italian cooking.

Though the name implies the cheese comes from Rome or its environs—and indeed it does—it also is produced in parts of Tuscany and Sardinia, which is where most pecorino Romano is made. Tuscany also produces pecorino Toscano and Sardinia has pecorino Sardo, but these varieties are more difficult to source in the U.S.

Provolone from Italy is recognizable as the log-, cone- or pear-shaped cheese tied with string and hung from the rafters to age. Originally from the southern part of the country, the northern region of Lombardy now is famed for the production of the semi-firm cow's milk cheese. Other areas of Italy produce different types of provolone. In the U.S., we typically have few options when it comes to imported provolone. Dolce is a softer, mellower, younger version of the cheese, while piccante is a little drier and firmer, with a pleasant sharpness. Provolone stracciatella, a smoked version, is another variety, and a delicious way to work woodsy flavor into a cheesy dish. Domestically produced provolone tends to be liked mainly for its texture, ease of melting and innocuous flavor.

Ricotta, which translates from Italian as "recooked," can be made with buffalo, goat's or sheep's milk, but in the U.S., cow's milk is used most often. Milky, mellow and spoonable, ricotta, like yogurt and sour cream, is equally at home in sweet preparations as it is in savory dishes. In the traditional Italian method of ricotta production, the whey left over from cheesemaking is heated, often with added milk, plus a coagulant, then the curds are salted and drained. In the U.S., commercial ricotta is made more simply by coagulating milk with additives, which results in a blander, more watery cheese. When shopping, look for a brand that does not include stabilizers and preservatives. We typically prefer to drain ricotta cheese before use to remove excess moisture (see p. 247).

Ricotta salata has the same stark-white color as fresh ricotta, but its texture is dry and semi-firm from pressing and aging. Sardinia, in particular, is famous for its ricotta salata. There, it is made with either goat's or sheep's milk; versions produced in the U.S. are likely to be made from cow's milk, which tend to taste more subdued. Still, the flavor is pleasantly salty with just enough sharpness and funkiness to make it interesting. Ricotta salata can be shredded, crumbled or shaved, and is excellent on pasta dishes or on salad. In supermarkets, it typically is sold in plastic-wrapped slabs or wedges at the cheese counter, not alongside the fresh ricotta in the refrigerator case.

Garlic

Garlic, aglio in Italian, is fiery and pungent when raw. Cooking tames its bite, but how the cloves are prepped also impacts its potency. The more cells that are ruptured, the stronger the flavor. In descending order of boldness, garlic can be grated, minced or chopped. Slicing is a good option for eliciting milder flavor, as well as for when you'd like the garlic to have greater visual presence in the dish. For the subtlest notes, simply smash the cloves and sauté them in the oil that will be used to cook other ingredients or simmer them into a soup or stew, then remove and discard them when they've contributed the desired amount of garlickiness.

Lentils

Like dried beans, lentils (lenticchie in Italian), are an important ingredient in the Italian kitchen. The Italian New Year's tradition of eating lentils as soon as the calendar flips is said to bring good luck. Brown and green lentils are commonplace, but Castelluccio lentils, sometimes referred to as Umbrian lentils—so called because they are grown in the village of Castelluccio in the Umbria region of central Italy—are a unique variety. With an earthy golden-green hue, Castelluccio lentils are prized for their nutty, subtly sweet flavor, and though they have thin skins, they hold their shape even when simmered until fully tender. They are worth seeking out in Italian markets, but if they are not available, French lentils du Puy are a reasonably good substitute, though they are darker in color and have a firmer texture when cooked.

Nuts

Almonds (mandorle), hazelnuts (nocciole), pine nuts (pinoli), pistachios (pistacchi) and walnuts (noci) are widely used in Italian cooking and baking, and they even flavor liqueurs such as amaretto, Frangelico and nocino. Sicily, in particular, is famous for its pistachios, and though hazelnuts grow throughout the country, Lombardy is home to the much-loved hazelnut-chocolate combination known as gianduja. Nuts add texture to dishes, but they also are used as thickeners, and since they are high in fat, they also enrich. Their fattiness also means that they easily go rancid, so we recommend purchasing in quantities that can be used within a few months and storing nuts of all varieties in the refrigerator or freezer to keep them fresh for longer.

Olives

Whether brined or oil-cured, olives pack tons of flavor. The most well-known Italian varieties in the U.S. are Castelvetrano olives from Sicily, which are plump and vibrantly green, with a mild, buttery flavor, and similarly smooth, extra-meaty Cerignola (also called Bella di Cerignola) from Puglia. In the U.S., Cerignola are most commonly green, but they also can be black. Gaeta olives from Lazio and Taggiasca from Liguria are two varieties of Italian black olives that are relatively easy to source. (Our recipes sometimes call for Kalamata, which come from Greece, because they are one of the most widely available types of black olives.) These days, many supermarkets feature olive bars that allow you to purchase just the quantity you need. Pitted olives offer the convenience of being ready to use, but if your olives require pitting, smash them with the flat side of the blade of a chef's knife, then use your fingers to pull the pits from the flesh. It can be tedious work, so when you need a large quantity, pitted olives are the way to go.

Olive Oil

We use a lot of olive oil in our cooking. In most cases, we favor full-flavored but moderately priced extra-virgin olive oil that can be used for sautéing garlic for pasta sauce, but also is good enough for making a vinaigrette, or even lending luxuriousness to a cake. Save the expensive, ultra-premium extra-virgin olive oil for use as a finishing drizzle on dishes where its nuances aren't masked by other ingredients or where heat won't degrade its flavor. Regular olive oil—not extra-virgin—and light olive oil are made from subsequent pressings and lack the deeper color and robust flavor of extra-virgin. Both do have higher smoke points, which makes them better for sautéing; light olive oil could even be used in recipes that call for neutral oil.

Pancetta and Guanciale

Pancetta is made by salt-curing fat-rich pork belly, the same cut used to make smoky American bacon. The type most common in the U.S., called pancetta arrotolata, is rolled into a cylinder, though it also is produced as a slab, known as pancetta stesa. In supermarkets, pancetta often is sold thinly sliced in packages, but some deli counters or Italian markets will slice it to order from the whole cylinder. This is an excellent option when a recipe calls for chunky nubs of pancetta for texture, which thin, wispy ribbons cannot provide. Chopped and sautéed, pancetta and its rendered fat create a deeply savory, meaty base for sauces, soups, stews and braises, and the crisped bits lend character to pasta and vegetable dishes. Similar to pancetta but even fattier, guanciale is salt-cured pork jowl. One of guanciale's most famous uses is in classic Roman pasta alla carbonara. In many recipes, pancetta is a fine stand-in for guanciale. Both can be frozen for longer storage.

Pasta

Dried pasta is a staple in our kitchen. Versions made with egg are widely available, but when we cook with dried pasta, it's almost always the type made with semolina, water and little else. Supermarkets offer an array of brands of differing qualities and price points, and specialty markets may offer pricier, lesser-known imports. Our pantry staple tends to be DeCecco, a middle-of-the-road supermarket Italian-made pasta that is produced using bronze dies that leave the noodles with a coarse, floury appearance. Once cooked, pasta that is rough-cut—premium brands may boast "bronze-cut"—has a texture that grips sauces for superior adhesion and integration. They also exude more starch during cooking, which helps thicken sauces. Inexpensive brands use nonstick die to make their pasta, so the noodles have a smooth, slick surface that offers less traction. The drying method also affects the quality of the pasta, with slow-drying at lower temperatures the preferred method over faster drying at higher temperatures.

Fresh pasta, or pasta fresca, usually refers to wheat noodles made with egg. Even in Italy, fresh pasta and dried pasta are considered different ingredients; which one a dish calls for typically comes down to tradition. Fresh pasta cooks quickly and has a rich flavor and a silky, delicate texture, making it a good match for cream- or butter-based sauces (think Alfredo). Supermarkets in the U.S. usually offer fresh pasta in the refrigerator case. Flat, ribbon-like shapes, such as linguine and fettuccine, are common, though well-stocked stores might also offer pasta sheets that can be cut to your preferred width or even filled to make ravioli or tortellini. Not surprisingly, homemade fresh pasta outclasses the typical supermarket offering, as the flavors are cleaner and purer. We like to make ours with a generous amount of egg yolks for an especially rich, elegant taste and texture; see p. 215 for our recipe.

Polenta

The term polenta refers to both the savory (and sometimes sweet) porridge-like dish and the dry cornmeal used to make it. Allowed to cool and set, cooked polenta can be cut into pieces and fried to make polenta fritta. To make polenta (the cornmeal), kernels of yellow flint corn are dried and milled. (In Italy, white cornmeal is mostly used in sweet preparations.) If you have the option, choose cornmeal that has been stone ground; we have found steel-ground grain to be less flavorful. We prefer the hearty, rustic texture of coarsely ground polenta, but medium grind will work, though it will cook more quickly. Read package labels carefully when shopping, as instant polenta looks similar to traditional polenta and sometimes is not clearly marked. Instant polenta is a convenience product of precooked fine cornmeal that reduces an hour-long cooking time to under five minutes, but sacrifices flavor and the robust texture we prefer.

Porcini Mushrooms

Seasonal and highly perishable porcini mushrooms are rarely sold fresh in the U.S.; dried porcini are more common. The fungi are sliced before they're desiccated, and typically sold in small quantities. Fortunately, a little goes a long way, as dried porcini pack an enormous amount of earthy, woodsy umami. They can be pulverized in a spice grinder and used as a seasoning, or can be rehydrated and used in risotto, sauces, braises and soups. The soaking liquid takes on the hue of black tea and is rich with the meaty flavor and aroma of the mushrooms. Strain the liquid to remove any sediment and use it in the recipe in place of water or broth, or refrigerate for use as a flavor booster in vegetarian or vegan dishes.

Prosciutto

In Italian, prosciutto means ham—as in the hind leg of the pig. But when most of us think of prosciutto, we mean the dry-aged, salt-cured, uncooked ham served in paper-thin slices. The rosy meat and streaks of white fat have a flavor that is porky and salty, of course, yet also slightly sweet, with a subtle gaminess and loads of umami. Prosciutto di Parma, from the Emilia-Romagna region, is the most famous of this style of Italian ham, and its production is regulated by the European Union. From the Friuli Venezia-Giulia region, prosciutto di San Daniele, another well-known version, also has been granted protected status. We rarely cook prosciutto, as it truly is meant to be enjoyed raw. Use it in sparing amounts since its taste is intense and cost is high.

Semolina Flour

Milled from high-protein durum wheat and commonly used to make dried pasta, semolina has a pale, creamy yellow color and a granularity akin to fine cornmeal. In Italy and the Middle East, semolina often is used in breads, but its subtly nutty flavor and distinctive texture also have a place in cookies, puddings and other sweets, and its sandiness is ideal for dusting surfaces, such as a baking peel, so dough slides instead of sticks. Semolina flour is available in different grinds, so shopping can be confusing. Domestically produced Bob's Red Mill semolina flour, widely available in supermarkets, has a medium coarseness that works well in many applications, but avoid any labeled "coarse," which is too gritty.

Tomatoes

Canned tomatoes are more than a convenience; they are a great ingredient in their own right, and Italian cooks use them often. When we use canned tomatoes, it's almost always the whole peeled variety, as their flavor and texture are the purest and freshest. For many recipes, we prefer them over diced tomatoes, which tend to remain firm, even after simmered into a sauce, because they are processed with calcium chloride. We also tend to avoid canned pureed, ground and stewed tomatoes because of their heavy, "cooked" taste, which sometimes comes across as tinny.

Fresh tomatoes that are in season and sun-ripened obviously have superior flavor and texture, but we have found that cherry or grape tomatoes are dependably sweet even in non-summer months. Campari tomatoes—sometimes referred to as cocktail tomatoes—are a good choice when larger fruits are needed. When fresh tomatoes are used raw, salting is an effective way to enhance juiciness, heighten flavor and slightly soften the too-firm texture of supermarket tomatoes. Sprinkle ¼ to ½ teaspoon kosher salt per pound of tomatoes that have been prepped. The moisture that is released can be discarded or, in some cases, used in the dressing. Fresh tomatoes are best stored on the counter at room temperature.

Passata is a pantry staple in Italian kitchens but has only recently started to appear in the U.S. Typically bottled in glass jars, passata is a pureed-tomato product with a slightly pulpy consistency, but don't mistake it for the canned tomato puree that's used to make dishes such as all-American chili. Passata's flavor is lighter, brighter and fresher because it is much less cooked. Our recipes do not call for passata because it is not widely available, but we do sometimes blitz canned whole peeled tomatoes in a blender or food processor, which approximates the taste and texture of passata.

Sun-dried tomatoes, or pomodori secchi, are halved tomatoes that are dessicated to remove most of their moisture, making them shelf-stable. In the U.S., they typically are sold oil-packed in jars, though some Italian markets offer them dry. In Italy, we have seen sun-dried tomatoes that are quite plump and tender, and usable straight from the container. In the U.S., dried tomatoes often are leathery and tough. Depending on how they will be used, the tomatoes may require draining (if oil-packed), then rehydrating in water until softened.

Tomato paste is made by cooking tomatoes, straining out skins and seeds, then continuing to cook until it is deep red and ultra-thick. Sold in cans, tubes or jars, the paste, which is rich in umami, is a hardworking pantry staple at Milk Street. We often brown it in a little oil to build a flavor foundation for sauces and stews, or use it as a way to incorporate tomato notes without adding the moisture of the fresh fruits. It's also an easy way to infuse a rusty, warm hue into a dish that needs color. Some brands of tomato paste are double concentrated, so

take a look at the label before using. Our recipes assume regular single-strength paste, so if you're using one that is more intense, you may wish to reduce the amount.

Vinegar

Balsamic vinegar originates in Modena, Italy, but the dark, tangy-sweet ingredient has become a staple ingredient in most home pantries. Traditional balsamic vinegar is made purely from cooked grape must (the fruits that have been pressed with their skins, seeds and stems) that is aged in wood barrels; the longer the aging, the more syrupy the consistency and the more complex and concentrated the flavors—and the higher the price, which can run into the hundreds, and even thousands, of dollars. Traditional balsamic should be used sparingly as a condiment, not as an ingredient in cooking. On the other end of the spectrum are supermarket balsamics that have an acidity of about 6 percent. They are made by combining wine vinegar with cooked grape must, sometimes with added coloring, before aging. Our recipes that call for balsamic vinegar assume a decent supermarket brand.

White balsamic vinegar, sometimes labeled as "white condiment" or "White Italian Condiment," has the sweet-tart notes of regular balsamic, but its flavor and color are lighter and more neutral. The production is similar to that of regular balsamic, but the must is not allowed to develop caramelization during cooking. White balsamic is great for adding bright notes of acidity that are tempered with a little sweetness, but its flavor and golden hue do not try to upstage other ingredients.

Wine vinegars, both red and white, are great pantry staples, as they will keep almost indefinitely. Red wine vinegar is the sharper and more assertive of the two, while white wine vinegar has a softer, more delicate acidity. They both convey notes of fermentation from the wine used to make them.

SALADS
and SIDES

Sweet-and-sour perfection

Plodding diligently, the donkey knowingly navigates the cobblestone maze of Castelbuono. The man trails, matching the clap-clap-clap cadence of hooves. At each home in this tiny Sicilian town, a bag of trash dangles by a rope from the balcony. Wordlessly, he plucks each and tosses it into wooden boxes strapped to the animal's flanks.

They work to a purposeful rhythm—an old solution to an older problem—walking a virtuous circuit as no truck could to green the city, save a breed and create jobs. My own circuit of Sicily, however, has been less productive, and even more plodding.

For days, I've circumnavigated the island, searching for the perfect plate of its iconic dish—caponata. Done well, this stew-like eggplant recipe is prototypical Sicilian cooking, the finest example of the agrodolce—a balance of sweet and sour—that defines so much of the region's cooking, a melding of North African and Mediterranean flavors and influences.

But after dozens of samples, I'm disappointed. Too often, the vegetables are indistinct, victims of overcooking—often in deep slicks of oil—until their textures blur. Or the sugar and acid lack balance, each bite either bracingly sharp or achingly sweet. I begin to consider that perhaps caponata isn't right for Milk Street.

Then I take a table at Sicilia in Tavola, a stone-arched trattoria in Siracusa. Owner Doriana Gesualdi presents her version and I'm wooed. Each bite contains chunks of eggplant, zucchini, pepper and onion that though married, remain true to themselves. The caponata is lighter, yet retains the appealing push and pull of sugar and vinegar. Served at room temperature with hunks of fresh bread to scoop it up, it tastes rich, satisfying and sweetly refreshing.

Gesualdi's secret, it turns out, is all about pacing. Most cooks fry the eggplant in copious oil, then add all remaining ingredients and simmer an hour or more. At Sicilia in Tavola, each vegetable is cooked separately, then stirred together off heat, no further cooking needed. The result: Each is prepared perfectly without over- or undercooking others.

Adapting Gesualdi's approach to Milk Street was simple. We followed her method and most of her ingredients. Our biggest variation was to season the finished dish with fresh basil instead of mint. We felt mint overpowered the other flavors and favored basil's peppery-savory notes. Turns out, plodding along at a donkey's pace could pay off.

—J.M. Hirsch

"Each bite contains chunks
of eggplant, zucchini,
pepper and onion that
though married, remain
true to themselves."

Sicilian Caponata

Start to finish: 45 minutes   Servings: 4

In Siracusa, Doriana Gesualdi taught us to treat each vegetable in caponata individually before marrying them in the pot to create a dish that brings together different flavors and textures. Caponata, a sweet-and-sour eggplant dish from Sicily, gets its distinctive flavor from a blending of the island's Mediterranean and North African influences. Cooking the eggplant, zucchini and onion plus bell pepper separately keeps the caponata bright and full of texture rather than a one-dimensional stew. A tangy-sweet vinegar-sugar glaze, added at the end of cooking, brings the elements together. If you prefer a sweeter caponata, stir in additional sugar when seasoning with salt and pepper. Serve warm or at room temperature with crusty bread as an appetizer or as a side to grilled or roasted meats and seafood.

Don't forget to stir the vegetables while they cook. Occasionally moving them around the pan ensures they cook and brown evenly. To preserve the basil's bright color, don't tear and add the leaves until you are ready to serve.

6 tablespoons extra-virgin olive oil, divided

1 medium eggplant (about 1 pound), trimmed and cut into 1-inch chunks

Kosher salt and ground black pepper

1 medium zucchini, trimmed, halved lengthwise and cut into 1-inch pieces

1 large yellow onion, cut into 1-inch pieces

1 red bell pepper, stemmed, seeded and cut into 1-inch pieces

½ cup red wine vinegar

2 tablespoons white sugar, plus more to serve

1 tablespoon tomato paste

¼ cup lightly packed fresh basil, torn

In a 12-inch nonstick skillet over medium, heat 4 tablespoons of oil until shimmering. Add the eggplant and ½ teaspoon salt, stir, then distribute in an even layer. Cover and cook, stirring occasionally, until the eggplant is browned and a fork inserted in the largest piece meets no resistance, 10 to 15 minutes. Using a slotted spoon, transfer to a large bowl.

In the same skillet over medium-low, heat 1 tablespoon of the remaining oil until shimmering. Add the zucchini and a pinch of salt, stir, then distribute in an even layer. Cover and cook, stirring occasionally, until the zucchini is browned and a fork inserted in the largest piece meets no resistance, 5 to 8 minutes. Transfer to the bowl with the eggplant.

In the same skillet over medium, heat the remaining 1 tablespoon oil until shimmering. Add the onion, bell pepper and a pinch of salt, stir, then spread evenly. Cover and cook, stirring occasionally, until the vegetables are lightly browned and softened, 7 to 10 minutes. Add the vinegar, sugar and tomato paste, then stir until the sugar has dissolved. Cook, stirring, until the liquid turns syrupy, 1 to 2 minutes. Add to the bowl with the eggplant and zucchini and stir. Taste and season with salt, pepper and sugar. Serve warm or at room temperature, stirring in the basil just before serving.

Cipolla Bianca Fritta con Sale al Rosmarino
Fried Onion Strings with Rosemary Salt

Start to finish: 20 minutes Servings: 4

In Bellosguardo, a remote town in southwestern Italy's Campania region, chef Guiseppe Croce showed us how semolina yields feather-light, crisp onion rings. Croce, chef of Tenuta Nonno Luigi, slices onions paper-thin before giving them a toss in semolina then quickly deep-frying them. The result is golden brown and crackling-crisp, but incredibly light. "Onions aren't generally well thought of," Croce told us. "They smell and they make you cry. So I wanted to do something special with them. Now it's the most popular item in the restaurant." We season our version with fresh rosemary, which we grind with salt and sprinkle onto the onion strings after frying. A drizzle of syrupy balsamic also is great, providing a perfect sweet-tart counterpoint. Look for balsamic syrup—also called balsamic glaze or balsamic reduction—in the grocery store's vinegar aisle.

Don't try to slice the onion by hand with a knife. You'll need a mandoline to get slices thin enough to cook and crisp quickly. Make sure to bring the oil back to temperature before frying the second batch.

1 tablespoon fresh rosemary

Kosher salt

2 medium or 1 extra-large yellow onion (about 1 pound), sprout end(s) trimmed, root end(s) intact, peeled

1 cup semolina flour

1 quart sunflower oil or peanut oil

Balsamic syrup, to serve (optional; see headnote)

In a spice grinder, combine the rosemary and 1 teaspoon salt. Pulse until finely ground; transfer to a small bowl and set aside. Adjust the blade of your mandoline to slice $\frac{1}{16}$ inch thick. If the diameter of the onion(s) is larger than the width of the mandoline blade, halve the onion(s) from end to end. Holding the whole or half onion by the root end, slice it into thin rings or half rings, slicing only as far as is safe; discard the base.

In a medium bowl, stir together the semolina and 1 teaspoon salt. Add half of the onion slices and toss with your hands until well coated; set aside. In a large Dutch oven, heat the oil over medium-high until it reaches 350°F. Meanwhile, line a wire rack with paper towels and set it near the stove.

When the oil comes to temperature, lift the coated onion slices out of the semolina mixture and transfer to a fine-mesh strainer. Shake to remove excess semolina, allowing the excess to fall back into the bowl. Tilt the strainer and slide the slices into the oil; cook, stirring often, until golden brown, about 3 minutes. Using a slotted spoon, transfer the fried onion slices to the prepared baking sheet. Immediately sprinkle with half of the rosemary salt; toss gently to coat.

Coat, shake and fry the remaining onion slices in the same way, allowing the oil to return to 350°F before frying. Sprinkle with the remaining rosemary salt and toss to coat. Serve right away, drizzled with balsamic syrup (if using).

Concia di Zucchine

Marinated Zucchini with Garlic and Herbs

Start to finish: 1½ hours (30 minutes active) Makes about 3 cups

Marinated zucchini, or concia di zucchine (sometimes shortened to concia), is part of the cucina tradizionale Giudaico-Romana, or Jewish-Roman cuisine. Concia translates as "tanning" (as in the tanning of leather) but in her book "Portico," a classic of Jewish-Roman cooking, Leah Koenig explains that the term stems from a word from the ancient Roman dialect that referred to hanging clothes out to sun-dry, much as the zucchini slices are laid out for frying, then marinating. The ingredients are simple: zucchini, extra-virgin olive oil, vinegar, garlic, herbs, salt and pepper. We slice our zucchini slightly thicker than most recipes, but marinating still takes as little as 30 minutes at room temperature, or cover and refrigerate it for up to three days (if chilled, let it stand at room temperature for about 30 minutes before serving). Serve concia as an appetizer or side dish, or tuck it into sandwiches. Eggplant also is delicious given this treatment; see recipe facing page

Don't add the zucchini to the skillet until the oil is shimmering. If added when the oil is not yet hot, the slices will absorb too much fat and end up greasy.

Line a large cutting board or baking sheet with paper towels. Lay the zucchini slices in a single layer on the paper towels and sprinkle with ¼ teaspoon salt. Flip the slices and sprinkle the second sides with another ¼ teaspoon salt. Let stand for about 20 minutes.

Meanwhile, in a 9-inch pie plate or medium bowl, stir together the ¼ cup oil, the vinegar, garlic, mint, pepper flakes and ¼ teaspoon each salt and pepper; set aside. Line a large plate with paper towels.

Pat the zucchini dry with paper towels. In a 12-inch skillet over medium, heat 2 tablespoons of the remaining oil until shimmering.

Add half of the zucchini in a single layer. Cook until lightly browned on the bottoms, about 2 minutes. Using tongs, flip the slices and cook until lightly browned on the second sides, 1 to 2 minutes. Transfer to the prepared plate. Add the remaining 1 tablespoon oil to the skillet and cook the remaining zucchini in the same way.

Add the still-warm zucchini to the oil-vinegar mixture and toss to coat. Cover and let stand at room temperature for 1 hour or refrigerate up to 3 days. If refrigerated, let stand at room temperature for about 30 minutes before serving.

3 medium zucchini (about 1½ pounds), sliced ½ inch thick on the diagonal

Kosher salt and ground black pepper

¼ cup plus 3 tablespoons extra-virgin olive oil, divided

2 tablespoons white wine vinegar

1 medium garlic clove, minced

½ cup chopped fresh mint, basil or a combination

¼ teaspoon red pepper flakes

Garlic and Herb Marinated Eggplant

Cut **3 small Italian eggplants** (about 1½ pounds) crosswise into ½-inch rounds. Follow the recipe to salt the eggplant and make the marinade. When the eggplant has been salted for about 20 minutes, cook the slices as directed but in 3 batches to avoid crowding the skillet, adding another **2 tablespoons extra-virgin olive oil** to the pan before each subsequent batch. Marinate the eggplant as directed.

This Italian dip improves anything, especially broccoli

In northwest Italy, the unctuous anchovy-oil sauce bagna càuda is consumed like fondue, a well of garlicky, often butter-enriched oil into which one dips crisp vegetables or crusty bread. Or whatever is on hand.

Bagna càuda means "hot bath" in Italian. It originated in the landlocked Piedmont region, the country's main dairy-producing area, where farmers would trade butter for salted anchovies with fisherman from the Ligurian coast. Farmers would dunk whatever they had into the pungent slurry—often cardoons, a thorny relative of the artichoke.

We agreed the dip improved just about anything, but we decided steamed broccoli, with its sauce-friendly florets, would be especially good. (Of course, our broccoli is just one option for using bagna càuda; try serving it with any number of raw or cooked vegetables, or hunks of bread.)

We gave our bagna càuda deep herbal flavor with bay and rosemary, and added brightness with lemon juice. We used a full tin of anchovies; if you use jarred anchovies, you'll need 4 teaspoons of minced fillets.

Traditional bagna càuda is like a broken sauce, with bits of anchovy and garlic settling on the bottom. We preferred tasting every ingredient's flavor in each bite, so we processed the warm sauce in a blender for a smooth emulsion.

Bagna Càuda with Steamed Broccoli

Start to finish: 30 minutes Servings: 6

We found Italy's answer to fondue in Piedmont's bagna càuda—a buttery, garlicky dip that bathes vegetables, crusty bread—anything, really—with umami-rich flavor. We gave ours a layer of herbal flavor with the addition of bay and rosemary and added some brightness with lemon juice. If you're using oil-packed anchovies from a jar, you'll need about 1 ounce of drained fillets (4 teaspoons minced). Our broccoli is just one serving option; offer any number of raw or cooked vegetables, or even pieces of crusty bread. Bagna càuda can be refrigerated in an airtight container for up to a week; reheat before serving.

Don't season the broccoli with salt; the bagna càuda provides plenty.

In a small saucepan over low, combine the butter, oil, garlic, anchovies, bay leaves, rosemary and pepper flakes. Cook, stirring occasionally, until the garlic is lightly toasted and the anchovies have disintegrated, 15 to 20 minutes.

Remove and discard the herbs and transfer the mixture to a blender. Let cool for about 10 minutes, then blend until smooth, about 30 seconds. Add 2 tablespoons of the lemon juice and the reserved anchovy oil and blend until well combined and lighter in color, about another 30 seconds.

In a large pot fitted with a steamer insert, bring 1 inch of water to a boil. Add the broccoli to the steamer (you may need to cook in 2 batches), then cover and cook until the broccoli is crisp-tender and bright green, about 5 minutes.

Transfer the broccoli to a medium bowl. Drizzle with the remaining 1 tablespoon lemon juice and ½ cup of the bagna càuda. Toss, then transfer to a platter. Serve the broccoli with the remaining bagna càuda and lemon wedges.

8 tablespoons salted butter

¼ cup extra-virgin olive oil

12 garlic cloves, minced

2-ounce can oil-packed anchovies, drained and minced, 2 tablespoons oil reserved

2 bay leaves

2 small sprigs fresh rosemary

¾ teaspoon red pepper flakes

3 tablespoons lemon juice, divided, plus lemon wedges, to serve

2 pounds broccoli, florets cut into 3-inch pieces, stems peeled, quartered and sliced 3 inches thick (about 12 cups)

Insalata di Pollo con Zucchine

Shaved Zucchini and Chicken Salad with Lemon and Almonds

Start to finish: 35 minutes   Servings: 4

A salad we ate at Trattoria Masuelli San Marco, the Milan restaurant that's been in the Masuelli family since 1921, inspired this elevated chicken salad with contrasting textures and flavors. Crunchy celery and salty fried almonds balance smooth, mild shaved zucchini and shredded chicken. We like the richness of Spanish Marcona almonds that have been fried and salted, but toasted regular blanched almonds work, too. For easy prep, use the meat from a store-bought rotisserie chicken; an average-size bird yields about 3 cups, the amount needed for this recipe.

Don't use the cores of the zucchini, as they are watery in flavor and seedy in texture. Stop shaving when you reach the center, rotate the zucchini and continue shaving another side until you're left with only the core, which should be discarded.

In a large bowl, whisk together the oil, allspice, lemon zest and juice and ½ teaspoon each salt and pepper; set aside.

Using a Y-style peeler, shave the zucchini from top to bottom into long, wide ribbons, rotating as you go. Stop shaving when you reach the core; discard the cores. Add the zucchini, almonds, celery and chicken to the dressing, then toss. Taste and season with salt and pepper. Let stand at room temperature for about 15 minutes. Sprinkle with parsley (if using), then serve.

¼ cup extra-virgin olive oil

½ teaspoon ground allspice

2 teaspoons grated lemon zest, plus ¼ cup lemon juice

Kosher salt and ground black pepper

Two 8- to 10-ounce zucchini, trimmed

½ cup Marcona almonds or toasted whole blanched almonds, roughly chopped (see headnote)

2 medium celery stalks, thinly sliced on the diagonal

3 cups shredded cooked chicken (see headnote)

Fresh flat-leaf parsley, roughly chopped or torn, to serve (optional)

In Sicily, a classic orange-fennel salad is at once sweet, savory, crunchy and tender

The salad in front of me was a delicious cacophony of color, flavor and texture—at once sweet-salty-creamy-crunchy-tender. And it all was born of a lack of sardines.

An unlikely origin story for a dish built around oranges, perhaps. But one Doriana Gesualdi clearly relished telling as I sat in the tiny dining room of Sicilia in Tavola, her trattoria in Siracusa, a 2,700-year-old sun-swept seaport in southeastern Sicily.

Sardines, it seems, were long a marker of wealth on the island, where the culinary influences are as much Greek and North African as Italian. Maybe more so.

But Siracusans weren't wealthy enough for sardines. So they sufficed with anchovies. And so Sicily's classic pasta con le sarde became pasta con le acciughe. Ditto for orange and fennel salad with chopped sardines.

"Siracusa is built around cucina povera," Gesualdi offered as we sipped a dry moscato under the restaurant's vaulted stone ceilings hung with jellyfish-shaped lights, walls lined with wine bottles.

The salad—insalata di arance, finocchi e olive siciliane—tasted of anything but poverty. A delicate pile of orange segments punctuated by the island's signature briny green Castelvetrano olives, peppery-anise shavings of fennel, pops of floral salt from plump capers. All tied together by a vinaigrette built on a mash of anchovies and shavings of feta-like ricotta salata. Complex without overwhelming, layered and utterly satisfying.

I couldn't help but think... I wouldn't WANT sardines in this salad. The richness of the anchovies—and their ability to underscore without dominating—made the salad. What Siracusans once considered a mark of making do clearly was a strength.

Back at Milk Street, this salad was easily adapted. Mashed anchovies and olive oil formed the base of our dressing, which we enriched with some of the ricotta salata and capers. As in Siracusa, no additional acid was needed—the orange segments and their juice would provide that. But we did want to bring the orange flavor more to the fore, accomplished by adding some of the zest.

The rest of the salad reflected much of what we had on Gesualdi's plate: freshly sliced orange segments, lightly crisp shavings of fennel bulb, tender Castelvetrano olives and—for sharpness and crunch—thinly sliced red onion.

The result was a layered and robust salad that nonetheless tasted light and fresh. Cucina povera? Perhaps once. But the richness of this salad tells another tale.

—J.M. Hirsch

"Complex without overwhelming, layered and utterly satisfying."

Insalata di Arance, Finocchi e Capperi Siciliane

Orange, Fennel and Caper Salad

Start to finish: 30 minutes   Servings: 8

Savory olives, capers and anchovies temper the sweetness of orange and fennel in this dish we tasted at Sicilia in Tavola in Siracusa. Onions add pungency and the salty yet mild cheese rounds everything out. We liked meaty and mild Castelvetrano olives from Sicily, but any large, firm green olive will do. To pit the olives, simply smash each with the flat side of a chef's knife, then pick out the pit. To make ahead, assemble the salad but hold back the oranges, which discolor if dressed too far in advance. Cover and refrigerate for up to 12 hours. When ready to serve, toss in the oranges, then transfer to a serving bowl or platter with tongs, leaving behind any accumulated liquid.

Don't confuse ricotta salata with fresh ricotta. Ricotta salata is a firm, shreddable salty cheese with a milky flavor, while fresh ricotta is mild, creamy and spoonable. If you can't find ricotta salata, Mexican queso fresco is a good substitute, as the two cheeses are similar in flavor and texture.

2 ounces ricotta salata cheese, crumbled

¼ cup drained capers, chopped

8 anchovy fillets, minced to a paste

2 teaspoons dried oregano

2 teaspoons grated orange zest, plus 2 medium navel oranges

2 tablespoons extra-virgin olive oil, plus more to serve

1 small red onion, halved, root removed and cut lengthwise into ¼-inch slices

3 small fennel bulbs, trimmed

⅓ cup Castelvetrano olives (see headnote), pitted and sliced

Set aside 2 tablespoons of the ricotta salata for garnish. In a large bowl, stir together the remaining ricotta, the capers, anchovies, oregano, orange zest and oil. Add the onion and toss to coat; set aside.

Halve each fennel bulb lengthwise, then cut each half crosswise into thin slices. Alternatively, if you have a mandoline, adjust the blade to slice ¹⁄₁₆ thick. Working one at a time, hold the fennel bulb by the base and thinly slice. Add the sliced fennel to the bowl and toss to combine.

Cut ½ inch off the top and bottom of the oranges. Working one at a time, stand the oranges on a cut end and, slicing from top to bottom, cut away the peel and pith following the contour of the fruit. Cut the orange vertically into quarters, then trim away the seedy core from each quarter. Cut each quarter crosswise into ¼-inch-thick slices. Add the oranges to the bowl and toss.

Transfer to a serving platter or bowl and sprinkle with the reserved ricotta salata and the olives. Drizzle with additional oil and serve.

A story of love and zucchini

A winding, rutted dirt road cuts through a dry landscape, acre upon acre of stark punctuated only by the dark green of grape vines and knotted, leafless olive trees. It makes the blaze of white that is Masseria Potenti that much more stunning, a bold stroke that at once blinds and cools under the intense Puglian sun.

Here in the heel of the Italian boot, masseria are fortified farms, high-walled compounds from another era. When Maria Grazia Di Lauro bought the 14th-century Masseria Potenti outside Manduria, it had been empty 100 years. Today, the bed and breakfast's vibrantly whitewashed arched ceilings and sprawling, lush courtyards give no sign of such neglect.

Di Lauro had invited me for a lesson in Puglian cooking, a hardscrabble variant of cucina povera built from robust pastas, plentiful produce and ample olive oil. She has been cooking since she was 5— "It is impossible to study to be a good chef. You are born."—but ignored her passion for a career in law until she and her husband renovated the masseria.

Standing at a rustic wooden banquet table in an alcove off the main courtyard, Di Lauro kneads dough for what will become a folded and stuffed focaccia while explaining that the masseria was supposed to be a family retreat. But friends and family visited so often for the beauty—and her cooking—it simply made sense to turn it into a business.

As she carefully folds the focaccia dough plumply around a heap of roasted zucchini, peppers, eggplant, raisins, onions and mozzarella, more of her culinary philosophy spills out. "If you have no fantasy, you have no good food." It's easy to fantasize as the aromas of baking bread, melting

"It's an explosion of fresh, bright, herbal and citrus that I can't stop eating."

cheese and savory herbs rise around us.

While we wait for the focaccia, Di Lauro prepares two zucchini dishes, almost as afterthoughts. The first is the simplest of salads. Raw zucchini shredded and tossed with fresh mint, lemon juice, ample extra-virgin olive oil, salt and pepper. That's it. It's an explosion of fresh, bright, herbal and citrus that I can't stop eating.

For the second dish, she slices a zucchini lengthwise into thin strips, wrapping them around a mixture of fresh ricotta, lemon zest, fresh rosemary, olive oil and salt, dipping one end of each roll in sesame seeds, the other in poppy seeds. Topped with fresh mint, they are amazing—salty, crunchy, creamy, minty and fresh.

Back at Milk Street, we were smitten with both of Di Lauro's takes on raw zucchini and decided to combine them into one simple salad. Thinly sliced raw zucchini tossed with herb-flecked lemon juice evoked the freshness of the first dish, while a topping of ricotta with lemon zest, fresh mint and a scattering of seeds and nuts brought in the second.

The result was as bright and wonderful as Masseria Potenti itself. And as for that focaccia? With Di Lauro's words, you can imagine how good it was. "In the kitchen if you give love, the food you prepare gives love."

—J.M. Hirsch

Insalata di Zucchine al Limone e Ricotta

Zucchini Salad with Lemon, Herbs and Ricotta

Start to finish: 35 minutes   Servings: 4

At Masseria Potenti, in Puglia, we tasted an unforgettable starter featuring thin slices of fresh zucchini rolled around a lemony ricotta filling and dipped, cannoli-like, into sesame and poppy seeds. This salad is our deconstructed version of that dish. We seed the zucchini so the soft cores don't release liquid that would dilute the other flavors. Toasted sesame seeds and chopped pistachios add richness along with a crisp, nutty texture to contrast the zucchini and ricotta.

Don't marinate the zucchini for longer than 15 minutes or the slices will turn limp.

In a large bowl, whisk together the lemon juice, rosemary, honey and ½ teaspoon each salt and pepper. Halve the zucchini lengthwise, then use a spoon to scrape out and discard the seeds. Slice the zucchini ⅛ to ¼ inch thick on the diagonal, then toss with the lemon juice mixture. Let stand for 15 minutes, tossing once or twice.

Meanwhile, in an 8-inch skillet over medium, combine the pistachios and sesame seeds. Toast, stirring often, until fragrant, about 2 minutes. Set aside to cool. In a small bowl, stir together the ricotta, oil, lemon zest and ¼ teaspoon salt.

To the zucchini, add the mint and chives, then toss. Taste and season with salt and pepper. Transfer to a serving platter and dollop the ricotta mixture on top. Scatter on the pistachio-sesame mixture, then drizzle with additional oil and sprinkle with flaky sea salt (if using).

2 teaspoons grated lemon zest, plus 2 tablespoons lemon juice

2 teaspoons minced fresh rosemary

1 teaspoon honey

Kosher salt and ground black pepper

2 medium zucchini (about 8 ounces each)

2 tablespoons pistachios, finely chopped

1 teaspoon sesame seeds

½ cup whole-milk ricotta cheese

2 tablespoons extra-virgin olive oil, plus more to serve

½ cup lightly packed fresh mint, roughly chopped

½ cup chives cut into 1-inch lengths

Flaky sea salt, to serve (optional)

In Udine, we learned to transform cauliflower and Parmesan into a toasty-crispy salad

If cauliflower can be repurposed as rice and pizza and mashed "potatoes," asking it to become croutons for a robust salad honestly seems like the least onerous of foods we can ask it to transform itself into. And it doesn't hurt that—unlike some of those other sometimes dubious ideas—cauliflower croutons happen to be delicious.

It helps, of course, when you shower them with Parmesan cheese and crisp them in the oven.

The idea came to us in Udine, a hilltop town in the far reaches of Friuli-Venezia Giulia in northeastern Italy. At Hostaria alla Tavernetta, owner Roberto Romano serves a simple salad of lightly cooked kale, broccoli and beets sprinkled with chopped hazelnuts, all piled over a dollop of romesco sauce, a tangy blend of roasted red peppers, olive oil, almonds and garlic.

Sprinkled over the whole affair was a mix of shaved Parmesan and tiny florets of blanched cauliflower. After several weeks of eating far too much pasta across many regions of Italy, it was a welcome infusion of vegetables. But we suspected it could be even more delicious with a simple tweak inspired by a regional dish.

Friuli is famous for crisply fried frico, a dish built from bits of cheese and vegetables—often potatoes—fried or baked until crisp. And they run a gamut of textures, from tender cheesy hash browns to toasty-crispy croutons.

This gave us the idea of taking those tiny cauliflower florets, tossing them with the cheese, then roasting them until both tender and wonderfully toasted and crisp. Tossed with kale and hazelnuts, and dressed simply with lemon juice and a bit more Parmesan, the result was the perfect cool weather salad.

All without needing to ask cauliflower to awkwardly contort itself into something it shouldn't.

—J.M. Hirsch

"We suspected it could be even more delicious with a simple tweak inspired by a regional dish."

Insalata di Cavolo Nero con Crostini di Cavolfiore

Kale Salad with Crispy Parmesan-Cauliflower Croutons

Start to finish: 1 hour Servings: 4 to 6

A kale and Parmesan salad made for us by Roberto Romano in a northeastern hilltop town served as the springboard for this dish topped with frico, the region's famous toasty cheese topping. Italian frico takes a couple different cheese-centric forms. One resembles a thick pancake that typically consists of potatoes and onions bound with an enormous amount of Montasio, a semi-firm cheese from the Friuli-Venezia Giulia and Veneto regions of northeastern Italy. The other is a light, lacy wafer made by frying a thin layer of shredded or grated cheese until lightly browned and crisped. This salad takes loose inspiration from the latter sort. We roast cauliflower tossed with a modest amount of dried breadcrumbs, then we sprinkle the florets with grated Parmesan, along with chopped hazelnuts, during the final minutes in the oven. The cheese creates a crisp, toasty crust that brings complex taste and texture to shredded kale tossed with a lemon, olive oil and Parmesan dressing. The warmth from the cauliflower softens the leaves just enough, and while the florets cool, they absorb flavor. Serve the salad as a side dish or offer it as a light vegetarian main.

Don't skip the kitchen parchment liner for the baking sheet. It prevents sticking and makes it easy to remove the cauliflower mixture, especially the toasty cheese bits.

2½-pound head cauliflower, trimmed and cut into 1-inch florets

½ cup extra-virgin olive oil, divided

Kosher salt and ground black pepper

¼ cup plain fine breadcrumbs

3 ounces Parmesan cheese, finely grated (1½ cups), divided

½ small red onion, thinly sliced

¼ cup lemon juice

½ cup hazelnuts, roughly chopped

2 small bunches lacinato kale (about 12 ounces total), stemmed, leaves sliced into thin ribbons (about 8 cups)

Heat the oven to 450°F with a rack in the upper-middle position. Line a rimmed baking sheet with kitchen parchment. In a large bowl, toss the cauliflower, ¼ cup oil and ½ teaspoon each salt and pepper. Sprinkle with the breadcrumbs and 1 cup of the Parmesan; toss well. Distribute in an even layer on the prepared baking sheet, then sprinkle on any breadcrumb-cheese mixture remaining in the bowl. Roast until a skewer inserted into the largest florets meets just a little resistance, 15 to 20 minutes. Meanwhile, wipe out the bowl. In it, combine the onion, lemon juice and ¼ teaspoon salt; set aside.

When the cauliflower is almost fully tender, remove the baking sheet from the oven. Using a wide metal spatula, scrape up and flip the cauliflower, then redistribute in an even layer. Sprinkle on the hazelnuts and half (¼ cup) of the remaining Parmesan. Continue to roast until the cheese is nicely browned, 8 to 10 minutes.

Meanwhile, add the remaining ¼ cup oil and the remaining Parmesan to the bowl with the onion. Using a fork, stir to combine. Add the kale, toss until evenly coated and let stand for 15 minutes to allow the kale to soften slightly.

Using tongs, transfer the still-warm cauliflower florets to the kale mixture, leaving the bits of nuts and cheese on the baking sheet. Toss, then taste and season with salt and pepper. Transfer the salad to a platter and sprinkle with the bits remaining on the baking sheet.

Stop frying your eggplant!

It's a look I've come to appreciate, even if it shames me a bit. A look each of the five Vittozzi sisters is a master of—undoubtedly learned from their mother and grandmother, usually cooking nearby. A look slightly scolding, slightly puzzled by the silliness of my questions. A look, nonetheless, followed by a patient explanation of everything I've misunderstood.

I've cooked with the Vittozzi sisters—Rosa, Anna, Veronica, Enza and Elena—repeatedly over the years at La Tavernetta Vittozzi, their cozy back-alley restaurant not far from the Gulf of Naples. It's the sort of Central Casting eatery where most diners are diners who visit daily, where the side dishes are displayed in the window and the menu is handwritten and photocopied fresh.

Each time, I bring new-to-me mysteries from my mission to understand real Italian cooking. How do you make the perfect meatball? How do you get your onions so beautifully caramelized for pasta alla Genovese? What's the real Italian wedding soup and why is it so much better than Italian-American versions? And oh-my-god! Your grandmother's lasagna! Please, teach me!

Hence, the look.

This visit is no different. This time I've come to them to learn Parmigiana di melanzane, or eggplant Parmesan, a dish loved and loathed in the U.S. Loved because it channels the spirit of lasagna, with meaty-rich slabs of eggplant standing in for the noodles, layered and slathered in sweet tomato sauce, herbs and cheese. Loathed because, well... where should I start?

In the U.S., the equation is pretty standard. Slabs of eggplant are dipped in flour, then dipped in egg, then dipped in breadcrumbs. It would be hard to imagine a better-designed culinary sponge. Which is why when those slabs are deep-fried, they sop up ridiculous amounts of oil no amount of tangy tomato sauce can cut through. And don't forget the mozzarella.

Which is to say, in the U.S. eggplant Parmesan too often is a gut-buster of a dish.

It's another matter entirely in Italy, where claims to the dish's origins are debated, though most say the dish dates back at least a few hundred years and center it around southern regions or Sicily.

Here, Parmigiana di melanzane runs a spectrum, some almost as heavy and breaded as back home, some just lightly floured to lend crispness with less heft. Some are coated with nothing at all, creating a dish tender and light in ways that defy its richness.

The version served by the Vittozzi sisters in Naples leans to the latter, and the reason is simple. We think of eggplant Parmesan as a main course. But in and around Naples it often is a side. Sometimes it's even a sandwich filling. The local recipe evolved as it did—with no coating and only gentle frying—because in both cases, lighter is better.

"A subtle difference made all the difference."

more than onion, olive oil, tomatoes and salt. Then she was ready to assemble. And here again, a subtle difference made all the difference.

She didn't merely layer tomato sauce, fresh basil, eggplant and cheese—more on the cheese in a moment—she rotated the pan 90 degrees with each successive layer. The result created an almost thatched structure in the finished dish, making it easier to cut, serve and eat.

As for that cheese... We're used to a blend of Parmesan and stringy mozzarella, the latter generally adding heft without a lot of flavor. But at La Tavernetta Vittozzi, they favor a blend of Parmesan and smoked provolone. I wasn't convinced it would make a difference, assuming the smoky flavors would be lost under the tomato sauce and assertive Parmesan.

As usual, I was wrong. Baked for just about 20 minutes, the eggplant Parmesan emerged bubbling and lightly browned. The taste was phenomenal, rich and savory and sweet. And the most notable flavor was the smoked provolone, a wonderful contrast to the tangy-sweet tomatoes that added tremendous depth.

Our changes to the Vittozzis' recipe were minor. We liked a bit of butter stirred into the tomato sauce; it gave it a wonderful richness—thank you, Marcella Hazan! And with a bit of tinkering, we found that brushing the eggplant with oil and baking it delivered results as good and even a bit lighter, and with less mess.

A result, I suspect, that won't earn me another look from the Vittozzi sisters. Until next time, of course.

—J.M. Hirsch

Each sister specializes in a different dish. Anna's art is Parmigiana di melanzane, so today it was her turn to endure my questions and throw me "the look" when my questions seemed too basic. As ever, during prep time, the kitchen spilled into the dining room and white marble tables were pulled together to create a work area for my lesson.

The ingredients were simple, the method even simpler. Most important, Anna explained, is the way the eggplant are cut. Slice them by hand or with a mandoline—she prefers the control she gets from a knife, cupping each vegetable in her left hand and pulling a short knife through it toward her one slab at a time—but either way make the slices no thicker than ¼ inch, thinner if you can. And leave some of the skin on, which keeps the slices from breaking down too much during cooking.

She then fried the slices, but only in a bare amount of oil and for just shy of a minute, long enough to tenderize and lightly brown the center and begin to crisp the edges. Most importantly, not long enough to absorb much oil, a factor further enhanced by the lack of any coating.

While the slices drained on paper towels, Anna made a spectacularly simple sauce from little

Parmigiana di Melanzane
No-Fry Neapolitan Eggplant Parmesan

Start to finish: 1¾ hours, plus cooling Servings: 6 to 8

At the family-owned trattoria La Tavernetta Vittozzi in Naples, Anna Vittozzi taught us to make a lighter, brighter eggplant Parmesan that still was rich with cheese and tangy with tomato sauce. The secret? Skip the breading. Though the Vittozzi version involved pan-frying eggplant, we found we could achieve similar results by roasting olive oil-brushed slices in the oven. This easier, more hands-off approach yields golden-brown, silky-textured eggplant, perfect for layering with a simple tomato sauce and fresh basil, plus plenty of cheese. In addition to umami-packed Parmesan, Vittozzi used smoked provolone, which added a delicious depth and savoriness to the dish. Smoked mozzarella might be easier to find in the U.S., and it's a fine stand-in, as is scamorza cheese. If none of those are options, opt for low-moisture mozzarella cheese but avoid fresh mozzarella, which contains too much water.

Don't peel off all of the skin from the eggplants. Remove the skin in interval strips so the eggplants look striped. The skin helps hold the flesh together, so if all of it is peeled away, the eggplant slices too easily fall apart after cooking.

Heat the oven to 425°F with racks in the upper- and lower-middle positions. Brush 2 rimmed baking sheets with 2 tablespoons oil each.

Remove half of the skin from each eggplant. To do this, using a vegetable peeler and working from top to bottom, peel off strips of skin about 1 inch apart. Cut the eggplants crosswise into ¼-inch-thick rounds, then arrange in a single layer on the prepared baking sheets, slightly overlapping.

Brush the eggplant with 2 tablespoons of the remaining oil, then sprinkle lightly with salt and pepper. Roast until the slices are spottily browned, the edges are slightly crisped and the moisture has cooked off, 35 to 40 minutes; halfway through, use a wide metal spatula to flip the slices, then switch the positions of the baking sheets. Remove from the oven; leave the oven on.

Meanwhile, in a large saucepan over medium-low, heat the remaining 1 tablespoon oil until shimmering. Add the onion and ½ teaspoon salt; cover and cook, stirring occasionally, until the onion is translucent, 4 to 5 minutes. Stir in the tomatoes, butter, ½ teaspoon pepper and ½ cup water. Bring to a simmer, then reduce to medium-low and cook, stirring occasionally, until the sauce is slightly thickened, 15 to 20 minutes. Remove from the heat and cool for 15 minutes. Taste and season with salt and pepper.

7 tablespoons extra-virgin olive oil, divided

Five 1-pound globe eggplants

Kosher salt and ground black pepper

1 medium yellow onion, finely chopped

28-ounce can crushed tomatoes

3 tablespoons salted butter, cut into 3 pieces

8 ounces smoked provolone, smoked mozzarella or smoked scamorza cheese, shredded (2 cups), divided

2 ounces Parmesan cheese, finely grated (1 cup), divided

1 cup lightly packed fresh basil, torn

Measure 1 cup of the tomato sauce into a 9-by-13-inch baking dish and spread to cover the bottom. Arrange one-third of the eggplant on top of the tomato sauce, overlapping the slices if needed, then sprinkle evenly with 1 cup provolone, ¼ cup Parmesan and about half of the basil. Spoon on another ¾ cup tomato sauce and spread evenly. Layer on half of the remaining eggplant, followed by the remaining provolone, ¼ cup of the remaining Parmesan and the remaining basil. Spoon on another ¾ cup sauce and layer on the remaining eggplant. Cover with the remaining sauce, spreading it evenly, then sprinkle with the remaining Parmesan.

Bake on the lower rack until the edges are bubbling and the cheese is melted, 15 to 20 minutes. Cool for about 10 minutes before serving.

Pancotto

Parmesan-Garlic Crisped Bread with Spicy Greens

Start to finish: 35 minutes Servings: 4

In Campania, home cook Antonietta di Gruttola showed us how to create a tender, almost stuffing-like pancotto melded with spiced greens. Pancotto, also known as pane cotto, translates as "cooked bread," a reference to the stale bread that is torn into pieces and cooked similar to pappa al pomodoro, the much-loved Tuscan tomato-bread soup. In Italy, we learned there is no one way to make pancotto. In fact, the version taught to us by di Gruttola in Ariano Irpino, about 100 kilometers east of Naples, was hardly a soup, and more like a soft, forkable, egg-free "stuffing" that might accompany roasted poultry. She kept the bread chunky and added a generous amount of olive oil as well as wild bitter greens flavored with garlic that melted into the softened bread. For our adaptation of di Gruttola's pancotto, we opted to start with fresh bread and toast the pieces in garlic-infused oil so they offered a chewy crispness in the finished dish. After toasting, we dusted the bread with Parmesan for a flavor boost. Without any foraged greens at hand, we chose escarole, a type of chicory that boasts a pleasant bitterness and a leafiness that becomes silky with heat. We cooked the bread and greens separately, brought the two together at the end and finished the dish with another drizzle of olive oil.

Don't bother to carefully dry the escarole after washing it. Simply allow it to drain in a colander, and shake the colander a couple times to remove the excess. A little water clinging to the leaves is fine, as the added moisture will create more steam during cooking.

In a large Dutch oven over medium-low, combine ½ cup of the oil and the garlic. Cook, stirring often, until the garlic is lightly browned, about 2 minutes. Using a slotted spoon, remove and discard the garlic. Add the bread to the pot and toss to coat with the oil. Cook over medium, stirring, until the bread is well browned and crisp, 5 to 7 minutes. Remove from the heat and transfer the bread to a large bowl; reserve the pot. Add the Parmesan to the bread and toss to combine; set aside.

In the same pot over medium-high, bring the broth and pepper flakes to a simmer. Add the escarole a couple handfuls at a time, stirring to wilt the leaves before adding more. After all the escarole has been added, cook, uncovered and stirring often, until the escarole is tender and most of the liquid has evaporated, about 10 minutes.

Off heat, drizzle in the remaining ¼ cup oil, then return the toasted bread to the pot and stir to combine. Taste and season with salt and black pepper. Serve sprinkled with additional cheese.

¾ cup extra-virgin olive oil, divided, plus more to serve

6 medium garlic cloves, smashed and peeled

8 ounces crusty white bread, cut into ½-inch cubes (about 6 cups)

1 ounce Parmesan cheese, finely grated (½ cup), plus more to serve

½ cup low-sodium chicken broth or vegetable broth

1 teaspoon red pepper flakes

3 large heads escarole (2½ to 3 pounds total), bruised outer leaves discarded, torn into rough 1-inch pieces (about 16 cups)

Kosher salt and ground black pepper

Patate in Umido
Tuscan Braised Potatoes

Start to finish: 1 hour Servings: 4

For richer, more flavorful skillet potatoes, Italian cookbook author Rolando Beramendi gives them the risotto treatment. Beramendi, author of "Autentico," cooks potatoes by incorporating liquid in multiple additions. This concentrates flavors while using the potatoes' natural starch to create a sauce that clings lightly to the chunks. We like the flavor backbone of chicken broth, but you could make this dish vegetarian by substituting vegetable broth. Patate in umido is an excellent accompaniment to roasted chicken, pork or seafood.

Don't use a narrow pot; the wide diameter of a Dutch oven allows for more rapid evaporation of liquid. Also, don't use lower-starch potatoes, such as red, white or Yukon Gold potatoes. Russets are the best choice, as their starchiness gives them a light, tender texture when cooked and lends the sauce a velvety quality.

In a large Dutch oven over medium, combine the oil, onions and garlic. Cook, stirring occasionally, until the onions just begin to brown, 8 to 10 minutes. Add the potatoes and stir to coat with the oil. Cook, stirring occasionally, until the potato starch that coats the bottom of the pot starts to brown, about 5 minutes.

Stir in the tomatoes, 1 cup of broth, the pepper flakes, rosemary and ¼ teaspoon salt. Bring to a simmer over medium-high, then distribute the potatoes in an even layer. Cook, occasionally scraping along the bottom of the pot with a silicone spatula and gently folding the mixture, for 10 minutes; adjust the heat as needed to maintain a steady simmer.

Add ½ cup of the remaining broth and cook, occasionally scraping and folding, for another 10 minutes. Add the remaining 1 cup broth in 2 additions in the same way, cooking for only 5 minutes after the final addition and stirring gently so the potatoes don't break up. Cover the pot, remove from the heat and let stand for 5 minutes.

Stir in half the basil, then taste and season with salt and black pepper. Remove and discard the rosemary, then transfer the potatoes to a bowl, drizzle with additional oil and sprinkle with the remaining basil.

¼ cup extra-virgin olive oil, plus more to serve

2 small red onions, quartered lengthwise and thinly sliced crosswise

3 medium garlic cloves, smashed and peeled

2 pounds russet potatoes, peeled and cut into 1-inch chunks

14½-ounce can whole peeled tomatoes, crushed by hand

2½ cups low-sodium chicken broth, divided

½ teaspoon red pepper flakes

8-inch sprig fresh rosemary

Kosher salt and ground black pepper

½ cup lightly packed fresh basil leaves, roughly chopped

Broccoli rabe meets Italian sausage

Italian cooks understand the allure of bitter greens, those radicchios and arugulas and brassicas that punctuate so many dishes with bracing, fresh flavor. They also seem preternaturally inclined to understand how best to balance those flavors.

Something sweet. Something savory. A bit of heat. A bit of fat. A lot of bitter. It's an equilibrium that, when executed poorly, can leave a dish tasting unpleasantly tannic, a mess of flavors that never meld.

But done properly? It becomes a harmony that works similar to sweet-and-sour, a push-and-pull in your mouth that takes you just to the edge of unexpected, while still grounded solidly in everything delicious that makes you want more.

You see it in orecchiette con cime di rapa, the Puglian pasta dish in which bitter broccoli rabe is balanced by savory anchovies, creamy Parmesan and hits of spicy red pepper flakes. Also in Campania's minestra maritata, a marriage of greens, savory meats, sweet vegetables and—of course—more Parmesan.

I was lucky enough to get a master class in this. Working in a kitchen high atop a terraced lemon grove along Italy's Amalfi Coast, home cook Lina Celia proved herself a pro. She offered to teach me what may well be Italy's platonic form for harnessing bitter greens—broccoli e salsiccia—well-browned Italian sausage tucked into a tangle of tender broccoli rabe.

Her recipe was simple. Ample olive oil, chopped garlic, onion and red pepper flakes went into a large pot. It all cooked slowly, the garlic becoming savory, the onion meltingly tender and sweetly caramelized, the oil drawing out the heat of the pepper. Eventually, robust Italian sausage rich with fennel and fat went into the pot.

Finally, the bitter greens. Broccoli rabe, in this case. Huge bunches of it. Celia knew it would wilt down to become tender-crisp, sweetening slightly as it cooked but retaining its bitter edge. Tossed with all the other ingredients, then finished with—once again, of course—Parmesan, the result was shockingly good.

Perhaps balanced is too simple a word? Bitter and savory and sweet and meaty and spicy all played perfectly together. It needed nothing more than a hunk of bread to sop up whatever didn't cling to my fork. A master class in mastering bitter greens, for sure.

—J.M. Hirsch

"Bitter and savory and sweet and meaty and spicy all played perfectly together."

Broccoli e Salsiccia

Broccoli Rabe and Sausage

Start to finish: 30 minutes Servings: 4 to 6

In a kitchen perched on the Amalfi Coast, home cook Lina Celia showed us how sweet-spicy Italian sausage brings out the best in greens in just minutes. The dish, broccoli e salsiccia—well-browned Italian sausage and tender broccoli rabe—was one of our favorite meals during a trip to Naples. The earthy, pleasantly bitter brassica pairs perfectly with spice-rich sausage. The rendered fat from the sausage works perfectly to sauté and season the sturdy greens. Garlic and red pepper flakes, plus nutty Parmesan and a splash of tangy-bright lemon juice, round out the easy dish. Sweet or hot Italian sausage is great; use whichever you prefer. Serve with thick slices of warm, crusty bread.

Don't worry if the second addition of broccoli rabe crowds the skillet; after a few minutes of covered cooking it will wilt, ensuring everything fits nicely.

In a 12-inch nonstick skillet over medium, heat the oil until barely smoking. Add the sausage, cover and cook, turning occasionally, until well browned and the centers reach 160°F, 6 to 8 minutes. Transfer to a large plate; set aside.

To the skillet, add the garlic and pepper flakes, stirring. Add half the broccoli rabe and ½ cup water; using tongs, toss to combine. Cover and cook, tossing occasionally, until the rabe is wilted, 3 to 4 minutes. Scatter the remaining rabe on top, then cover and cook, tossing occasionally, until the stem pieces are tender, another 3 to 5 minutes.

Add the sausage, half of the Parmesan and the lemon juice; toss. Cook, uncovered and stirring, until the sausage is heated through, about 2 minutes. Taste and season with salt and black pepper. Serve sprinkled with additional Parmesan and lemon wedges on the side.

1 tablespoon extra-virgin olive oil

1 pound sweet or hot Italian sausage, cut into 2½- to 3-inch sections

3 medium garlic cloves, chopped

½ to 1 teaspoon red pepper flakes

2 large bunches (2 pounds) broccoli rabe, trimmed and cut into 1-inch pieces

1 ounce Parmesan cheese, finely grated (½ cup), plus more to serve

2 tablespoons lemon juice, plus lemon wedges to serve

Kosher salt and ground black pepper

Pomodori Ripieni di Riso

Arborio-Stuffed Tomatoes with Potato Wedges

Start to finish: 1¾ hours (1 hour active) Servings: 6

At Panificio Bonci, a renowned bakery in Rome, we encountered pomodori ripieni di riso, a hearty but still bright and summery regional dish of rice-stuffed tomatoes baked with potato wedges tucked between the fruits. The duo of carbs makes the dish satisfying, but the tomato and herb flavors provide lightness. For an especially flavorful filling, after scooping the insides out of the tomatoes, we process the innards then strain the puree so we can use the lump-free tomato liquid to cook the rice. The trick to this dish is getting the starchy, highly absorbent Arborio rice to properly cook in the hollowed-out tomatoes. We needed to use a combination of tomato juices and water as the liquid, and for an evenly tender texture without any mushiness, the grains required a soak in the liquid prior to cooking. The timing is rather persnickety: 30 minutes was sometimes too brief, resulting in underdone rice, and 1 hour too long, resulting in a soft, mushy texture. Forty-five minutes cooking time is ideal—and it's also just the right amount of time for heating the oven and pre-roasting the potatoes so the wedges, nestled into gaps in the baking dish, emerge fully tender with the tomatoes after baking. Served warm or at room temperature—or even lightly chilled—the tomatoes are a terrific side to roasted or grilled meats or seafood, but they're substantial enough to be a light main.

Don't choose tomatoes that are soft and yielding. Select ones that are ripe yet firm enough to hold their shape while being hollowed out otherwise the fruits will oversoften during baking. Also, don't use a blender to puree the tomato guts. We found that it breaks down the ingredients too much, yielding a puree that can alter the finished texture of the rice.

6 ripe but firm 8-ounce beefsteak tomatoes, each about 3½ inches round

Kosher salt and ground black pepper

7 tablespoons extra-virgin olive oil, divided

⅓ cup lightly packed fresh basil, chopped

1 medium garlic clove, finely grated

¼ teaspoon dried oregano

½ cup Arborio rice

3 medium (about 1 pound) Yukon Gold potatoes, peeled and cut into ½-inch wedges

Line a large plate with paper towels. Cut off the top ½ inch of each tomato; set the tops aside. Working over a medium bowl, use a small spoon to scoop out the pulp, core and ribs from each tomato, letting the tomato innards collect in the bowl. Sprinkle the inside of each tomato with salt and pepper, then place upside down on the prepared plate.

In a food processor, puree the tomato innards until as smooth as possible, 1 to 2 minutes. Place a fine-mesh strainer over a measuring cup and strain the puree, pressing on the solids to extract as much liquid as possible; discard the solids. Pour 1 cup of the tomato liquid into a bowl, then add ⅓ cup water, 3 tablespoons oil, the basil, garlic, oregano, ½ teaspoon salt and ¼ teaspoon pepper. Stir in the rice, then set aside at room temperature for 45 minutes, stirring once or twice. Discard any remaining tomato liquid or reserve it for another use.

Meanwhile, heat the oven to 350°F with a rack in the middle position. On a rimmed baking

sheet, toss the potatoes with 2 tablespoons of the remaining oil and ¼ teaspoon each salt and pepper. Distribute in an even layer and roast until a skewer inserted into the largest piece meets little resistance, 18 to 22 minutes; flip the wedges with a metal spatula about halfway through. Set aside to cool; leave the oven on.

Place the hollowed-out tomatoes cut sides up in a 9-by-13-inch baking dish. Spoon the rice mixture into the tomatoes, dividing it evenly, then cover with the tomato tops. Tuck the potato wedges between the tomatoes. Drizzle everything with the remaining 2 tablespoons oil. Bake until the tomatoes are shriveled a bit and the rice is tender, about 1 hour. Cool in the baking dish on a wire rack for at least 30 minutes. Serve warm or at room temperature.

Cipolline in Agrodolce
Agrodolce Red Onions

Start to finish: 30 minutes Makes about 1½ cups

At Ristorante Barbieri in Calabria we found a simple way to create a standout onion side using Italy's agrodolce—sweet and sour—cooking technique. Italian sweet-and-sour onions—called cipolline in agrodolce—typically are small whole onions simmered with sugar and vinegar. But Ristorante Barbieri uses sliced tropea onions, a variety that is a specialty of the region. We apply their technique to standard supermarket red onions. The slices are cooked briefly—just about 15 minutes—to soften them slightly. They will not reduce to a sticky, jammy consistency; these are not caramelized onions. Be sure to use a nonreactive skillet to avoid an interaction between the metal and the vinegar. Agrodolce onions are a great accompaniment to grilled or roasted meats, add them to an antipasto platter or use them in sandwiches or on pizza.

Don't use dark brown sugar. Its color will darken the onions and its molasses flavor is too assertive.

In a nonreactive 12-inch skillet, combine the oil, onions, sugar, vinegar and 1 teaspoon salt. Cook over medium-high, uncovered and stirring occasionally, until the pan is almost dry and the onions are slightly softened (they will retain some texture, not turn jammy and soft), about 15 minutes.

Transfer to a bowl or container and let cool. (In an airtight container in the refrigerator, the onions will keep for up to 1 week; bring to room temperature before serving.)

3 tablespoons extra-virgin olive oil

2 large red onions (about 1½ pounds), halved and sliced crosswise about ⅛ inch thick

½ cup packed light brown sugar

1 cup red wine vinegar

Kosher salt

ZUPPE

The real Italian wedding soup

Conventional wisdom holds that Italian wedding soup—or minestra maritata—is named not for when it is served, but rather for its perfect marriage of ingredients. Which is true. But that's not the whole truth.

Head to Campania—the southwestern chunk of Italy that is home to the Amalfi Coast—and you learn quickly that Italian wedding soup has nothing—and everything—to do with weddings. And that it is quite unlike the meatball-laden Italian American versions we know best in the United States.

All of this becomes evident when I visit the farm run by Antonietta di Gruttola and her husband, Rinaldo di Rubbo, in Ariano Irpino, about 100 kilometers inland from Naples. They grew up in the area and di Gruttola was taught by her mother to harvest the wild escarole, borage, chard, thistle and mustard greens that would go into our dinner that evening.

"My parents insisted I learn how to cook [minestra maritata] because it's such an important dish," she said. "It is eaten not just at weddings, but at any feast day. It has been an important dish in my life since my First Communion when I was 11. We ate it at my wedding. And at my daughter's wedding."

Despite that, the name nonetheless indeed refers to the marriage of ingredients—namely a mix of wild bittersweet greens and meaty broth. That meat—never meatballs—varies by occasion. For everyday serving, it's often chicken. For weddings and other special events, beef and pork—including bits of prosciutto and pancetta—are preferred. Either way, the finished dish is more about the vegetables and broth; the meat is treated more as a seasoning than main event.

"It is eaten not just at weddings, but at any feast day."

That evening, di Gruttola prepared the chicken version, first by building a broth from chicken, celery, tomatoes and garlic. In another pot, layers of wild greens and pecorino Romano. When the broth was ready, she strained it and poured it over the greens and cheese, then simmered it slowly until tender. The chicken was returned just at the end.

The result was, indeed, a lovely marriage, the broth savory and rich, the greens tender, shredded chicken punctuating it all. It was splendid, even if di Gruttola's medley of wild greens plucked from the orchard outside put her version a bit beyond what most home cooks in the U.S. could manage.

For that, I turned to the five sisters who run La Tavernetta Vittozzi in Naples, an off-the-track eatery where we've found recipe ease and inspiration many times before. They happily demonstrated their own take on this classic, preferring the richness of pork and beef, and accessible greens—escarole, broccoli leaves and savoy cabbage.

The dish began as cucina povera, they explain, using mostly scraps of meat to flavor ample—and inexpensive—greens. In time, special versions using better cuts for celebratory meals caught on. Theirs is a favorite at Christmas, as well as weddings.

Topped with croutons and a sprinkle of Parmesan cheese, the result is meaty, yet light and fresh, with flavors and textures that complement, not compete. Truly, a winning marriage.

—J.M. Hirsch

Minestra Maritata
Italian Wedding Soup

Start to finish: 2¾ hours (45 minutes active) Servings: 6

At the family-owned restaurant La Tavernetta Vittozzi in Naples, we were taught how to make the Campanian version of the classic dish, and we used the lessons learned for our own adaptation. The name of the dish on which this recipe is based is minestra maritata, which translates from the Italian as "married soup." It is not the Italian wedding soup of meatballs, greens and pasta that's popular in the U.S., though the two do share similarities. As in Naples, the meats in our recipe are bone-in cuts of beef and pork that give the broth richness and body. But for easier eating, after cooking we shred the meat and discard the bones. Pancetta also simmers in the mix along with a piece of Parmesan rind, each lending even more savoriness to the broth. La Tavernetta Vittozzi uses three varieties of wintry greens in their minestra maritata—cabbage, broccoli rabe and escarole, the latter two blanched separately before they are added to the soup. (This "marriage" of cooked greens and broth is part of what gives the dish its name.) To streamline, we opt for rabe or escarole (or a combination, if it suits you) and we simmer the vegetable directly in the broth. Rabe offers an assertive bitterness that nicely balances the richness of the soup; escarole is milder and cooks down to a silky, supple texture. Warm, crusty bread is the perfect accompaniment.

Don't bother with precision when prepping the onion, carrots and celery. The aromatics are simmered in the broth for flavor, but later are scooped out and discarded. If using escarole, be sure to wash it thoroughly as the frilly leaves tend to trap a good amount of grit.

In a large Dutch oven, combine the pancetta and oil. Cook over medium-low, stirring occasionally, until the pancetta begins to brown, about 10 minutes. Increase to medium, stir in the onion, carrots and celery, then cook, stirring occasionally, until the vegetables begin to soften, about 10 minutes.

Add the garlic, tomato paste, pepper flakes and 1 teaspoon salt; cook, stirring, until the tomato paste begins to stick to the pot and brown, 1 to 2 minutes. Add 10 cups water and the bay, then bring to a boil over medium-high, scraping up any browned bits. Add the ribs, beef shank and Parmesan rind. Return to a simmer, then cover, reduce to medium-low and cook, stirring occasionally, until a skewer inserted between the pork ribs and into the meat on the shank meets no resistance, about 2 hours. Remove from the heat.

Using tongs, transfer the ribs and shank to a large bowl; set aside to cool. Meanwhile, using a slotted spoon, remove and discard the solids from the broth. Tilt the pan to pool the liquid to one side, then use a wide spoon to remove and discard as much fat as possible from the surface of the liquid.

8 ounces pancetta, chopped

2 tablespoons extra-virgin olive oil

1 large yellow onion, roughly chopped

2 medium carrots, peeled and roughly chopped

1 medium celery stalk, roughly chopped

4 medium garlic cloves, smashed and peeled

3 tablespoons tomato paste

½ to ¾ teaspoon red pepper flakes

Kosher salt and ground black pepper

4 bay leaves

2½-pound rack pork baby back ribs, cut into 3 sections between the ribs

1-pound bone-in beef shank (1 to 1½ inches thick)

2-inch piece Parmesan cheese rind, plus finely grated Parmesan, to serve

1 bunch broccoli rabe, trimmed and roughly chopped, or 1 large head escarole, chopped, or a combination

½ cup lightly packed fresh basil, chopped

When the meats are cool enough to handle, shred the beef into bite-size pieces, discarding the fat, bone and gristle. Using a paring knife, cut the pork ribs between the bones to separate into individual ribs. Remove the meat from the bones and shred into bite-size pieces; discard the fat, bones and gristle. Set both meats aside.

Bring the broth to a simmer over medium-high. Add the rabe to the pot and cook, stirring often, until tender, 5 to 7 minutes. Stir in the shredded meats and cook, stirring, until heated through, about 2 minutes. Off heat, stir in the basil, then taste and season with salt and black pepper. Serve with grated Parmesan on the side.

Pasta e Patate

Pasta and Potatoes

Start to finish: 40 minutes   Servings: 6

Pasta e patate is classic Italian comfort food, a stewy combo of tender potatoes that have been simmered until they begin to break down, creating a velvety sauce for the pasta that cooks right in the mix. We learned several versions on a visit to southern Italy; our recipe combines the qualities we liked in those, and includes beans (canned, for convenience). Roman beans, which are firm yet creamy, also are known as borlotti or cranberry beans; if not available, look instead for pink beans. If you have a piece of Parmesan rind, toss it into the pot; it will infuse the stew with umami and an extra layer of flavor. Italians typically cook a mix of dried pasta shapes into this dish—it's a way to use up odds and ends in the pantry—so feel free to add whatever you like, though short, smallish shapes are best.

Don't use Yukon Gold or waxy potatoes for this. High-starch russets are best because they break down more readily. When stirring, don't fret if the potatoes begin to break apart. This helps the consistency of the stew.

In a large Dutch oven over medium, heat the oil until shimmering. Add the onion, carrot, and celery; cook, stirring occasionally, until lightly browned, 4 to 6 minutes. Add the garlic and red pepper flakes; cook, stirring, until fragrant, 30 seconds. Stir in the wine and cook until the liquid has evaporated, about 2 minutes.

Stir in the potatoes, beans, tomato, rosemary, Parmesan rind (if using), 1 teaspoon each salt and pepper and 4 cups water. Bring to boil over medium-high, then reduce to low, cover and simmer, stirring often, until the potatoes are just shy of tender, 6 to 8 minutes.

Stir in the pasta. Cook, uncovered and stirring occasionally, until the pasta is al dente and some of the potatoes have broken down to thicken the stew.

Off heat, remove and discard the rosemary and Parmesan rind (if used). Stir in the grated Parmesan and half of the basil. If the stew is too thick, thin with hot water to the desired consistency. Taste and season with salt and pepper. Serve drizzled with additional oil, sprinkled with the remaining basil and with additional grated cheese on the side.

3 tablespoons extra-virgin olive oil, plus more to serve

1 small yellow onion, finely chopped

1 medium carrot, peeled and finely chopped

1 medium celery stalk, finely chopped

2 medium garlic cloves, minced

¼ to ½ teaspoon red pepper flakes

⅓ cup dry white wine

1 pound russet potatoes, peeled and cut into ½-inch cubes

15½-ounce can Roman beans (see headnote), rinsed and drained

1 medium tomato, cored and chopped

6-inch rosemary sprig

1-inch piece Parmesan rind (optional), plus ½ ounce Parmesan cheese, finely grated (¼ cup), plus more to serve

Kosher salt and ground black pepper

8 ounces short pasta shapes, such as shells, elbows or gemelli

½ cup lightly packed fresh basil, chopped

Ciambotta

Italian Summer Vegetable Stew

Start to finish: 50 minutes   Servings: 6

The southern Italian vegetable stew known as ciambotta or cianfotta often is likened to Provençal ratatouille, but it sometimes contains potatoes, which give the dish a little more heft. We use a 12-inch skillet to make the stew; its wide surface area means that cooking happens more quickly than if the vegetables were piled on top of each other in a pot, resulting in fresher, brighter flavors, textures and colors. Serve warm or at room temperature as a side to grilled or roasted chicken, lamb, beef or fish. Or offer it finished with pecorino or Parmesan as a light vegetarian main with crusty bread alongside.

Don't worry about the vegetable mixture appearing dry when the ingredients are first added to the sautéed aromatics. Covered cooking will get them to soften and release their juices, which form a light, flavorful sauce.

In a 12-inch skillet over medium, heat the oil until shimmering. Add the onion, celery and garlic; cook, stirring occasionally, until the vegetables begin to soften, 3 to 4 minutes.

Add the tomatoes, eggplant, zucchini, potatoes, 1 teaspoon salt, ½ teaspoon black pepper and the pepper flakes. Stir to combine, then cover, reduce to medium-low and cook, stirring occasionally, until lightly saucy and a skewer inserted into the potatoes meets no resistance, 30 to 35 minutes.

Off heat, stir in the basil, then taste and season with salt and pepper. Serve drizzled with additional oil.

2 tablespoons extra-virgin olive oil, plus more to serve

1 medium yellow onion, chopped

2 medium celery stalks, sliced

3 medium garlic cloves, minced

3 ripe plum tomatoes (about 12 ounces), cored and chopped

1 small Italian eggplant (about 8 ounces), trimmed and cut into ½-inch cubes

1 medium zucchini (about 8 ounces), trimmed and cut into ½-inch cubes

8 ounces Yukon Gold potatoes, unpeeled, cut into ½-inch cubes

Kosher salt and ground black pepper

¼ to ½ teaspoon red pepper flakes

1 cup lightly packed fresh basil, shredded

In Sardinia, bold soups are built from herbs, not meat

Chef Luigi Crisponi is adamant. There really is nothing he can teach me about s'erbuzzu, a simple, brothy yet still thick soup of greens, beans and tiny, chewy nuggets of pasta. "There is no recipe," he says. "There's just herbs."

As many as 13 or even 14 herbs, in fact. None of which, without a recipe, is particularly helpful. I'd come to Gavoi—a tiny hillside town toward the northern end of Sardinia—to learn the local, rustic cuisine, a way of cooking drawn not from the sea around the Italian island, but from the land at the center of it.

Crisponi's restaurant—Santa Rughe, all stone walls and arched ceilings, massive windows overlooking rolling green—specializes in the traditional cooking that evolved as Sardinians embraced produce, grains and a bit of meat and dairy. S'erbuzzu seemed a prime example. Beans, broth, a little fat and tons of herbs. Mostly bitter and foraged.

"Beans, broth, a little fat and tons of herbs."

As I taste his version, I insist he try to teach me. The flavor is bold, yet fresh, herbal and light. The beans are meaty and tender. The bitterness of the greens—and there are so many it is impossible to know one from another—is balanced, pleasant against a rich ricotta salata cheese stirred in just before serving.

Crisponi relents and walks me through it. White beans soak overnight, then slowly simmer with a bit of browned pancetta.

Then the greens. He begins the list, only some of which I recognize. Finely chopped, they simmer until the beans are ready. Just before serving, the cheese and a bit of fregola—the small, pellet-like pasta Sardinia is known for—are stirred in. Just enough to thicken the broth. I continue to eat as Crisponi talks. I can taste the green of the hills I see outside.

Back at Milk Street, we loved the idea of a robust soup built not from meat, but fresh herbs. We did make a few changes for ease, including streamlining the list of greens to just parsley, arugula and tarragon, plus some fennel seeds to add complexity and mimic the wild fennel popular in Sardinia. We also opted for the speed of canned beans. The result may be a bit less foraged than the original, but it certainly is a recipe. An excellent one.

—J.M. Hirsch

S'erbuzzu

Sardinian Herb Soup with Fregola and White Beans

Start to finish: 45 minutes Servings: 4

We learned this hearty, herbal Sardinian soup from chef Luigi Crisponi at Santa Rughe restaurant in Gavoi. The soup can sometimes have more than a dozen varieties of wild herbs and greens and with both fregola (a pea-shaped Sardinian pasta) and white beans in the mix, the soup is as hearty and starchy as it is herbal. For our version, we narrowed the list of herbs and greens to those we felt had the most impact: parsley for grassiness, tarragon for sweet anise notes and arugula for pepperiness. We also used pancetta to build a savory backbone and ricotta salata cheese, as Sardinians do, for complexity. If you can't find fregola, substitute an equal amount of pearl couscous, but cook it for only five minutes before adding the beans, parsley and garlic. And if ricotta salata is not available, finely grated pecorino Romano is a reasonable swap, but halve the amount.

Don't forget to reserve the minced parsley stems separately from the chopped leaves. The stems go into the pot early on so they soften and infuse the broth with their herbal, minerally flavor; the leaves are added near the end so they retain their freshness and color.

In a large pot over medium, heat the oil and pancetta. Cook, stirring occasionally, until the pancetta is browned, 6 to 8 minutes. Stir in the parsley stems and fennel seeds, then add the wine and 1 teaspoon pepper, scraping up any browned bits. Bring to a simmer over medium-high and cook, stirring, until most of the moisture has evaporated, 2 to 3 minutes.

Add the broth and bring to a boil over high. Stir in the fregola and cook, stirring occasionally and adjusting the heat to maintain a simmer, until the fregola is just shy of tender, about 10 minutes. Add the beans, garlic, parsley leaves and half of the ricotta salata, then continue to cook, stirring occasionally and adjusting the heat to maintain a bare simmer, until the fregola is fully tender, about another 10 minutes.

Off heat, stir in the arugula and tarragon, then taste and season with salt and pepper. Serve sprinkled with the remaining ricotta salata and drizzled with additional oil.

2 tablespoons extra-virgin olive oil, plus more to serve

3 to 4 ounces pancetta, chopped

1 bunch flat-leaf parsley, stems minced, leaves roughly chopped, reserved separately

1½ teaspoons fennel seeds

½ cup dry white wine

Kosher salt and ground black pepper

2 quarts low-sodium chicken broth

¾ cup fregola (see headnote)

15½-ounce can large white beans, such as butter beans, rinsed and drained

3 medium garlic cloves, minced

4 ounces ricotta salata cheese (see headnote), crumbled (¾ cup)

4 ounces baby arugula (about 6 cups lightly packed), roughly chopped

½ cup lightly packed fresh tarragon, chopped

Emilia-Romagna's Sunday soup

Sunday lunch at Trattoria dai Mugnai in Monteveglio, a village outside of Bologna in the Valsamoggia region, is an intoxicating blend of history, pleasure, home-style food, family and hospitality. This is the essence of Emilia-Romagna—nobody ever asks about the "next big thing" in food, and why should they?

What they have already is deeply satisfying. As with many menus in the region, it is replete with tortellini, tagliatelle, farfalle, gramigna (a squiggly, candy cane-shaped pasta), bigoli (a thick spaghetti), cotoletta (a thin meat cutlet usually wrapped in prosciutto and napped with a Parmesan cream sauce), and various soups, pot roasts, vegetable plates and other dishes.

Stefano Parmeggiani and his wife, Serena, are consummate hosts, which you can tell just from their faces—smiles framed by round, ample cheeks and an effervescence in the eyes reminiscent of the local sparkling wine, pignoletto, which is quaffed even before lunch along with a strong caffè.

Stefano opened the restaurant in 2001 in a grain mill, which was owned by his father, Luigi, and was formerly outfitted as an oil mill and a cheese cave. The original building dates back to 1500; it was modified over the years, but by 1790, it was in its current form.

On this visit, it is the soup that caught my attention. Short, wide ribbons of fresh pasta floated like dumplings in a creamy bean puree subtly flavored with garlic and fresh herbs. It's not a looker—it is the essence of

"This version seemed just right not only in texture but in flavor."

rustic—and the marriage of beans and pasta is nothing new; I've even had this combination in northern Israel at a Palestinian table.

But this version seemed just right not only in texture but in flavor. It's simple, but it's not; it surprises with every spoonful. Borlotti beans (also known as Roman beans or cranberry beans) are the most likely choice in Italy; we opted for canned beans to make this dish weeknight-friendly. If you have a rind of Parmesan, throw it into the soup during cooking for added depth; just don't forget to remove it before puréeing in a blender.

– Christopher Kimball

Zuppa di Fagioli con Pasta
Italian Bean Soup with Fresh Pasta

Start to finish: 40 minutes Servings: 4

This is not your typical Italian bean and pasta soup. It's a simplified version of a hearty, rustic zuppa we tasted at Trattoria dai Mugnai in Monteveglio, a village outside Bologna. Short, wide ribbons of fresh pasta float dumpling-like in a creamy bean puree subtly flavored with garlic and fresh herbs. If you have a piece of Parmesan rind, simmer it with the beans; it releases savory flavors into the broth. For weeknight ease, we use canned Roman beans (also known as borlotti beans or cranberry beans). If you cannot find canned Roman beans, pintos, which have a similar color and texture, are a fine substitute. If you own an immersion blender, you can use it to puree the beans directly in the saucepan without first cooling the mixture for 10 minutes. Whichever type of blender you use, if you added a piece of Parmesan rind to the pot, remember to remove it before pureeing.

Don't use dried pasta for this soup, as it will not cook properly. Fresh pasta is key. Look for wide, ribbon-like fresh noodles such as pappardelle, tagliatelle or fettuccine and cut them into 2-inch lengths before use. If you can find sheets of fresh pasta, they work nicely, too—simply cut them into rough 2-inch squares. Don't puree the beans until completely smooth; leave them with some texture.

2 tablespoons extra-virgin olive oil, plus more to serve

1 medium yellow onion, chopped

Kosher salt and ground black pepper

2 tablespoons tomato paste

2 medium garlic cloves, smashed and peeled

Two 15½-ounce cans Roman beans (see headnote), rinsed and drained

2 teaspoons chopped fresh rosemary or sage

1 piece Parmesan rind (optional), plus finely grated Parmesan, to serve

8- to 9-ounce package fresh pappardelle, tagliatelle or fettuccine (see headnote), cut into 2-inch lengths

In a large saucepan over medium, heat the oil until shimmering. Add the onion and ¼ teaspoon salt, then cook, stirring occasionally, until translucent, about 4 minutes. Add the tomato paste and garlic. Cook, stirring often, until the tomato paste darkens slightly and begins to stick to the pan, about 3 minutes.

Add the beans, rosemary, Parmesan rind (if using), 5 cups water, ¾ teaspoon salt and ½ teaspoon pepper. Bring to a simmer over medium-high, then reduce to medium-low and cook, uncovered and stirring occasionally, until the beans are soft enough to be easily mashed with a fork, about 10 minutes.

Off heat, remove and discard the Parmesan rind (if used); let cool for about 10 minutes. Using a blender and working in 2 batches to avoid overfilling the jar, pulse the bean mixture until creamy but not completely smooth. Return the puree to the pot and bring to a simmer over medium.

Add the pasta and cook uncovered, stirring occasionally, until the pasta is al dente (refer to the package for cooking times, but begin checking for doneness a minute or two sooner than the directions indicate). Taste and season with salt and pepper. Ladle the soup into bowls, drizzle with oil and top with grated Parmesan.

In Umbria, flavor comes from the earth

A basket hanging from the crook of one arm, Silvia Buitoni stoops into the overgrowth, running her free hand through vivid patches of green that blanket the banks along this babbling, shallow stretch of Italy's Tiber River. She is foraging for wild edible herbs—chicory, radicchio, dandelion, arugula—as she was taught by her mother and grandmother.

Many before them did the same. Though mossy, quiet and shaded, this elbow of riverside also is a historic thoroughfare, a tiny part of the Via Francigena, a path that meanders from the cathedral in Canterbury, England, across Europe to the heart of Rome. Pilgrims have trod its 1,700 kilometers—and feasted on its greenery—since at least the 8th century.

"We have a park in the center of town and it's very beautiful, but it is different. This is natural. Earthy," Buitoni says. It's a term she'd use repeatedly to describe Umbria, its land, its culture, its people. Most importantly, its food.

It's why I'd come to this central region of Italy just south of Tuscany, where meals are built around robust brown Castelluccio lentils; the sorts of bitter, wild greens that now overflowed in Buitoni's basket; and peppery olive oil that we'd soon douse them all with. Rustic, visceral cooking that makes the most of whatever is on hand.

Back at Buitoni's sunlit apartment in Perugia, the hilltop heart of the region, windows on one side overlook an olive grove and fog-filled valleys that stretch to Assisi on the other. She'd offered to teach me two dishes that typify everything Umbrian: zuppa de lenticchie, a simple lentil soup, and torta al testo, a quick flatbread stuffed with sausage and wild greens.

As she begins cooking, the conversation moves quickly to aroma. Buitoni—and yes, she is of that Buitoni family, which sold the pasta company decades ago—is fascinated by the power of food aromas and memory. So much so, she wrote a book about it. And as her kitchen fills with sweet richness from vegetables, savory sausage and warm bread, it's easy to understand why. It is comfort and caring. It is social and jovial. It is everything we love about Italian food.

She starts with the soup, first making a soffritto of wild scallion, spring garlic, leggy celery as much about the leaves as the stalks, a carrot and ample olive oil. It is, as she said, earthy, sweet and rich. Then the lentils, eaten always, but celebrated particularly on New Year's Day as a symbol of luck because they resemble coins.

The mixture cooks with little liquid for a while, then tomato paste and just enough water are added to create a rich, robust broth. Soon a hearty, yet surprisingly light soup is ready. The lentils, similar in texture to France's green lentils du Puy, hold their shape, balancing a delicately sweet soup with nutty-savory flavor and toothsome texture.

"Rustic, visceral cooking that makes the most of whatever is on hand."

It's a lesson in maximizing simple, flavorful ingredients. Also in balancing earthy and sweet. I love it.

We then prepare the torta al testo, a reminder yet again that cultures around the world long ago sussed out how to get fresh bread on the table any day of the week. To wit, we spend more time on the fillings than on the bread itself. And neither side of the equation requires nearly as much effort as the splendidly delicious results suggest.

"Every family has their recipe for this. I grew up eating this," Buitoni says. "Some people put olive oil or Parmesan in the dough and it becomes richer. But I don't. The herbs are very potent. I like that."

The dough comes together in minutes, a mixture of flour, water and baking powder. It rests briefly, then is formed into rounds and cooked over low heat in a skillet (in lieu of the more traditional stone). Meanwhile, those wild herbs are wilted with olive oil, garlic and savory anchovies.

Garlicky sausages, split open, brown in a skillet nearby.

When the flatbreads are done— barely crispy outside, doughy and tender inside—Buitoni splits them like a pita pocket, stuffing them with the greens and sausages. The result is, simply, the ideal sausage sandwich. Warm bread wrapped around seared meat, the richness of it cut by the sweet bitterness of the wild herbs.

As Buitoni said, earthy. All of it. Deliciously so.

—J.M. Hirsch

Zuppa di Lenticchie
Umbrian Lentil Soup

Start to finish: 1 hour Servings: 4 to 6

In her kitchen in Perugia, home cook Silvia Buitoni taught us how to make brothy but hearty Umbrian lentil soup, or zuppa di lenticchie, a regional classic and a fine example of rustic Italian cooking. Of utmost importance, of course, are the lentils. Golden in tone with a pale green cast, Castelluccio lentils, which are grown in the Umbrian village of the same name, are the backbone of this simple but satisfying dish. Their flavor is nutty, earthy and subtly sweet, and though they become tender and plump with cooking, they still retain their shape beautifully and don't break down as they cook. Castelluccio lentils are worth seeking out in Italian markets or online—but if you can't find them, opt instead for French lentils du Puy, which are green-gray in color and have similar texture and flavor characteristics. Puy lentils may take a little longer to cook, so be sure to taste them for doneness.

Don't cook the lentils covered for the entire time. When they're just shy of tender, uncover the pot, turn up the burner half a notch and cook for a few more minutes. This allows some of the liquid to evaporate so the broth becomes thicker and richer.

In a Dutch oven over medium-high, heat the oil until shimmering. Add the onion, celery, carrots and ½ teaspoon salt; cook, stirring occasionally, until the vegetables are lightly browned, about 5 minutes. Add the garlic and cook, stirring, until fragrant, about 30 seconds. Add the tomato paste and cook, stirring often, until the paste begins to brown and stick to the bottom of the pot, about 2 minutes.

Add 6 cups water and scrape up any browned bits. Stir in the lentils, rosemary and pepper flakes. Bring to a simmer, stirring often, then cover and reduce to medium-low and simmer, stirring occasionally, until the lentils are just shy of tender, about 40 minutes.

Uncover, increase the heat to medium and cook, stirring occasionally, until the lentils are fully tender and the soup has thickened slightly, 8 to 10 minutes. Taste and season with salt and black pepper. Serve drizzled with additional oil and sprinkled with Parmesan.

3 tablespoons extra-virgin olive oil, plus more to serve

1 medium yellow onion, chopped

2 medium celery stalks, halved lengthwise and chopped

2 medium carrots, peeled, halved lengthwise and cut into ¼-inch pieces

Kosher salt and ground black pepper

2 medium garlic cloves, finely grated

3 tablespoons tomato paste

1¼ cups Castelluccio lentils (see headnote) or lentils du Puy, rinsed and drained

1 tablespoon minced fresh rosemary

¼ to ½ teaspoon red pepper flakes

Finely grated Parmesan cheese, to serve

Torta al Testo
Umbrian Flatbreads with Sausage and Broccoli Rabe

Start to finish: 50 minutes, plus resting time for the dough   Servings: 4

Torta al testo is a simple Umbrian flatbread that can be an accompaniment to soups or stews, or, as Perugia home cook Silvia Buitoni showed us, the bread can be split and filled to make fantastic sandwiches. Though some versions are leavened with yeast, Buitoni used baking powder for a quick-and-easy dough that can be shaped and skillet-cooked after just a brief rest. We added a small measure of olive oil to her formula to give the bread a little suppleness and richness. The filling for our torta al testo is based on Buitoni's, but instead of the foraged herbs and greens that she steamed then sautéed, we opted for broccoli rabe. To be efficient, prep the filling ingredients while the dough is resting. This recipe calls for a 12-inch cast-iron skillet (the steady heat of cast iron excels at even browning and cooking the flatbreads), but you will need a lid when sautéing the rabe. If your skillet lacks one, use a lid from a similarly sized pot or simply set a baking sheet on top.

Don't knead this dough as you would a yeasted bread dough or the flatbreads will be tough. Knead it just enough to bring it together into a smooth, cohesive mass; this should take less than a minute. Also, don't leave the broccoli rabe in the skillet while you assemble the sandwiches; be sure to transfer it to a plate. If left in the pan, the rabe may overcook because of the heat-retention properties of cast iron.

For the dough, in a large bowl, whisk together the flour, baking powder and salt. In a 2-cup liquid measuring cup, combine the oil and ½ cup water. While stirring, slowly pour the oil-water mixture into the dry ingredients. Stir until a shaggy dough forms, adding 1 to 3 tablespoons more water as needed if the mixture is too dry. Dust the counter with flour, then turn the dough out onto it. Knead until the dough is smooth and cohesive, about 30 seconds. Divide it in half, shape each piece into a smooth ball and set on a lightly floured surface. Cover with a kitchen towel and let rest for at least 15 minutes or up to 1 hour.

Using your hands, press each dough ball into a 5½-inch round.

Heat a 12-inch cast-iron skillet over medium-low until water flicked onto the surface immediately sizzles. Add 1 round to the skillet and cook until well browned in spots, about 4 minutes. Using a wide metal spatula, flip the round and cook until the second side is spotty brown, another 4 minutes. Transfer to a wire rack. Cook the second round in the same way. Let the flatbreads cool while you make the filling.

To make the filling, in the same skillet over medium-high, heat 2 tablespoons of the oil until barely smoking. Add the sausages, cover and cook, turning occasionally with tongs, until the centers reach 160°F, about 10 minutes. Transfer to a plate; reserve the skillet.

FOR THE DOUGH:

260 grams (2 cups) all-purpose flour, plus more for dusting

2 teaspoons baking powder

1 teaspoon table salt

¼ cup extra-virgin olive oil

FOR THE FILLING:

3 tablespoons extra-virgin olive oil, divided, plus more for drizzling

1 pound hot or sweet Italian sausages

1 bunch broccoli rabe, trimmed and halved crosswise

Kosher salt and ground black pepper

2 oil-packed anchovy fillets

2 medium garlic cloves, finely grated

¼ to ½ teaspoon red pepper flakes

To the skillet still over medium-high, add the broccoli rabe and ¼ teaspoon salt; stir to coat with the fat in the pan. Cover and cook, stirring, until just shy of tender, 4 to 6 minutes. Push the rabe to one side, then add the remaining 1 tablespoon oil, anchovies, garlic and pepper flakes to the clearing. Cook, stirring and mashing the mixture, until fragrant and the anchovies have broken down, about 1 minute. Stir the mixture into the rabe, then remove from the heat. Taste and season with salt and black pepper; scrape onto another plate.

To assemble, cut each sausage lengthwise into 4 planks of even thickness. Cut each flatbread in half to create 4 half moons. Using a serrated knife, split each piece horizontally. Drizzle the cut sides with oil, then lay the sausage on 4 of the pieces, dividing it evenly. Top the sausage with the rabe. Cover with the untopped sides of the bread and press firmly.

Tuscany's "cooked water" shows how deliciously simple ingredients can be transformed

If we're being honest, "cooked water" probably is the least alluring way to sell a recipe. But as so often is the case with the cucina povera of Italy, neither the name nor the simple ingredients do justice to what ends up on your plate.

"Tuscan cooking has a lot of respect for leftovers," Giulia Scarpaleggia explained as she glugged a generous pour of extra-virgin olive oil into a pot. We were enjoying some wine in the sunny kitchen of her home in Colle val D'Elsa. The same home her father and grandmother were born in and still share with her, her husband and their daughter.

She'd offered to teach me acquacotta, a classic Tuscan soup that somehow extracts richness from spare this-and-thats hanging about the kitchen. The name translates quite simply as cooked water. For good measure, they add stale bread.

Still not sold? Stay with me.

"Acquacotta comes from Maremma, a poor land that was marshlands. It really represents how poor the land was," Scarpaleggia, a cookbook author, explained. I know... Still not selling it. At all.

Into the pot, she added diced celery and onion. Most Italian soups start with those plus carrot, but carrots were too rich for Maremma, a coastal area of Tuscany. Red pepper flakes, garlic and salt went next.

This mix cooked down, sweetening as it softened, for about 15 minutes. As it sizzled, Scarpaleggia explained she'd learned the recipe by simply

> "It was intense, actually, thanks to being reduced, all those simple flavors concentrated."

knocking on a farmhouse door at the direction of a local vegetable seller. "We knocked on the door and she welcomed us into her house and she gave us four or five recipes," she said.

Somehow, the randomness suits this recipe.

Next, tomatoes. It's always refreshing to see that even in Italy canned tomatoes often are the first choice. They defy the seasonality that leaves most supermarket toma-

toes lacking. Using her hands, she crushed two cans of plum tomatoes into the pot, then let everything simmer down until thick and reduced by half. A hunk of Parmesan rind went in, too, for richness.

When the mixture had reduced by half, she used a spoon to create divots in it, then cracked one egg into each. It was starting to resemble shakshuka, minus the peppers and spice.

Spooned over toasted stale bread, the whole affair is...

beautiful! A chunky, boldly red sauce slowly softening crispy-toasty bread, the runny egg yolk breaking and sliding over it all. Scarpaleggia shaved pecorino over it all. It was robust and somehow fresh. It was intense, actually, thanks to being reduced, all those simple flavors concentrated.

Simple ingredients. Simply prepared. As ever, they amount to so much more.

—J.M. Hirsch

Acquacotta

Bread and Tomato Soup with Poached Eggs

Start to finish: 1½ hours (45 minutes active)   Servings: 4

In Colle di Val d'Elsa, cookbook author Giulia Scarpaleggia prepared this classic Tuscan soup for us. It is called acquacotta, or "cooked water," because the thrifty dish originally was made with nothing more than day-old bread, vegetables and hot water, with eggs poached directly in the mix. Scarpaleggia's soup was rustic and comforting, yet fresh and light. In our adaptation, we rub the warm toasted bread with a garlic clove before tearing the slices into pieces and placing them in each serving bowl. While we like runny yolks, feel free to let the eggs cook for eight to 10 minutes for a firmer set.

Don't allow the soup to boil when poaching the eggs. Maintaining a gentle simmer prevents the eggs from overcooking and ensures that the whites don't separate from the yolks.

¼ cup extra-virgin olive oil, plus more for brushing and to serve

1 medium red onion, finely chopped

1 large celery stalk, finely chopped

¼ teaspoon red pepper flakes

Kosher salt and ground black pepper

28-ounce can whole-peeled tomatoes, crushed by hand

2-inch piece Parmesan rind (optional), plus finely grated Parmesan, to serve

Four ¾-inch-thick slices country-style bread

1 medium garlic clove, smashed and peeled

4 large eggs

½ cup lightly packed fresh basil, torn

In a large saucepan over medium, heat the oil until shimmering. Add the onion, celery, pepper flakes and ½ teaspoon salt. Cook, stirring, until the vegetables are softened and lightly browned, 6 to 7 minutes. Stir in the tomatoes with juices, 4 cups water, the Parmesan rind (if using), 1 teaspoon salt and ½ teaspoon black pepper. Bring to a simmer over medium-high, then reduce to medium-low and cook, uncovered and stirring occasionally, until darkened and slightly thickened, about 1 hour.

Meanwhile, heat the broiler with a rack about 6 inches from the element. Generously brush both sides of each bread slice with oil and place in a single layer on a broiler-safe rimmed baking sheet. Broil until golden brown on both sides, 2 to 3 minutes, flipping halfway through and rotating the baking sheet as needed. Remove from the oven and lightly rub the garlic clove over both sides of each toast.

Tear the toasts into 1-inch pieces and divide evenly among 4 serving bowls; set aside.

When the soup is done, remove and discard the Parmesan rind (if using). Taste and season with salt and black pepper. With the soup simmering over medium, break 1 egg into a small bowl, ramekin or teacup. Add the egg to the soup by holding the bowl just above the surface, tilting it and letting the egg slide in. Working quickly, repeat with the remaining eggs, spacing them evenly and noting the order added. Simmer gently, covered and without stirring, until the whites are set but the yolks are still soft, about 6 minutes; do not boil.

Using a slotted spoon, remove the eggs in the order they were added, allowing excess liquid to drain off; place one in each serving bowl. Ladle the soup around the eggs. Drizzle with additional oil and sprinkle with basil and Parmesan.

It gets better the next day,
but you won't want to wait

To the English-speaking mind, Italian is such a lyrical language, it can be comedic how matter-of-fact Italians are when it comes to naming their foods. Tuscans seem particularly adept at this. Biscotti, for example. A delicious example of tender-meets-crispy that begs to be dunked in coffee or—more wonderfully—sweet vin santo wine. The translation? Twice-baked.

Likewise, acquacotta, a rich and hearty soup of tomatoes, bread and herbs topped with runny poached eggs that spill into and enrich the broth. The meaning? Cooked water.

And don't even get me started on panzanella, that marvelous marriage of tomatoes and bread and herbs and olive oil that pretty much screams summer. In English? Soaked bread. Doesn't that just set your heart pitter-pattering?

The romance somehow seems to get lost in translation. Which remains true for the ribollita that cookbook author Giulia Scarpaleggia was teaching me the day I pondered this in her sunny Tuscan kitchen, which opened to the courtyard of the idyllic stone home her father and grandmother were born in and still live in with her today. Talk about romance.

The dish is a hearty soup of white beans—some pureed, some left whole—with leeks, carrots, celery, cabbage, kale and garlic, all partnered with toasted bread and thickened in part by some of the starchy liquid in which the beans were cooked. It is at once rich and robust and light and vegetal. Care to guess the translation?

Re-boiled.

Sarcasm aside, there is a glorious utility to the language that in each case reflects not just the simplicity of the cooking, but also of the ingredients themselves, even the cuisine writ large. As the names suggest, here nothing is wasted and everything is repurposed.

That ribollita is no exception. The name references the tradition of cooking the dish one day, but not eating it until the next, at which point it is effectively re-boiled, becoming thicker and heartier. A nod to that seemingly universal understanding that soups and stews so often are so much better the next day.

Across Tuscany, traditions for making this classic vary, sometimes dramatically. In some parts, the thicker the ribollita, the better. "In fact, in Florence they spread it over a baking sheet and bake it until you can almost cut it," Scarpaleggia says.

"Soaked bread. Doesn't that just set your heart pitter-pattering?"

Her own version—which includes the Florentine use of thyme to season it—skews lighter and more tender, but still delivers big flavor. Her use of a little pancetta helps on that front. Same for the garlic, tomato paste and—of course, because this is Tuscany, after all—a finishing drizzle of peppery extra-virgin olive oil. The result is so much more flavorful than the simple ingredients suggest.

The second day is when the bread is added, stirred in until it breaks down, almost emulsifying the broth. In that way, it's similar to Tunisian lablabi, another bean and vegetable soup into which bread is stirred until it softens.

But as with lablabi, we preferred the bread on the crispier side, so in our version we resist the urge to stir it in. The crispy-chewy texture is the perfect contrast to the tender beans and greens.

We also found it flavorful enough to skip the 24-hour wait. Then again, there's nothing wrong with making a double batch just to ensure you can enjoy it reboiled tomorrow.

—J.M. Hirsch

Ribollita

White Bean and Vegetable Soup

Start to finish: 1½ hours (1 hour active) Servings: 6 to 8

We learned ribollita, a rustic Tuscan specialty that combines vegetables with white beans in a bread-thickened broth, from home cook and cookbook author Giulia Scarpaleggia. Ribollita, which means "re-boiled," gets its name from the dish's make-ahead tradition—it is not consumed the day it is made. Rather, the soup is reheated and eaten a day or so after. Our interpretation of ribollita is lighter than most because we left out potatoes, and instead of using bread as a thickener, we crisp bite-size pieces of a country loaf in the oven and either place them in the bottom of individual bowls before ladling in the soup or float them on top as a garnish. Two kinds of greens plus cannellini beans, along with the meatiness of pancetta, make the soup plenty satisfying, and Scarpaleggia's technique of pureeing a small portion of the beans gives the broth just the right creaminess. For best flavor, use dried beans that you've cooked yourself, but if you're pressed for time, two 15½-ounce cans of cannellini beans will do just fine.

Don't forget to rinse and drain the leek after slicing it. Leeks' layers trap lots of sand and grit, so it needs a good rinse before use.

In a blender, combine 1 cup beans and their liquid. Puree until smooth, about 30 seconds. Set aside. In a large Dutch oven over medium, combine 1 tablespoon oil and the pancetta. Cook, stirring, until browned, 3 to 4 minutes. Add the leek, carrots, celery and garlic; cook, stirring, until the vegetables are softened but not browned, about 5 minutes. Add the tomato paste, thyme and ½ teaspoon each salt and pepper; cook, stirring, until the paste sticks to the bottom of the pot, 2 to 3 minutes.

Add 8 cups water and the bean puree; scrape up any browned bits. Stir in the cabbage and kale, then bring to a simmer over medium-high. Cover, reduce to low and cook, stirring occasionally, until the greens are tender, 40 to 45 minutes.

Meanwhile, heat the oven to 375°F with a rack in the middle position. Arrange the bread on a rimmed baking sheet. Drizzle with the remaining 2 tablespoons oil and sprinkle with ½ teaspoon each salt and pepper. Toss until the bread is evenly coated, then bake until browned and crisp, about 10 minutes, stirring once about halfway through. Remove from the oven.

When the greens are fully tender, stir in the remaining beans. Cook, uncovered and stirring occasionally, for 10 to 15 minutes. Remove and discard the thyme, then taste and season with salt and pepper. Divide the bread among individual bowls, then ladle in the soup. Alternatively, ladle the soup into bowls, then garnish with the bread. Drizzle with additional oil.

3 cups cooked cannellini beans (p. 87), plus ¾ cup cooking liquid, or two 15½-ounce cans cannellini beans, ¾ cup liquid reserved, then drained

3 tablespoons extra-virgin olive oil, divided, plus more to serve

4 ounces pancetta, chopped

1 large leek, white and light green parts halved lengthwise, then sliced crosswise, rinsed and drained well

2 medium carrots, peeled and chopped into ¼-inch pieces

1 medium celery stalk, chopped into ¼-inch pieces

2 medium garlic cloves, minced

¼ cup tomato paste

Two 4-inch thyme sprigs

Kosher salt and ground black pepper

1 pound savoy or green cabbage, cored and sliced about ¼ inch thick

1 medium bunch (about 8 ounces) lacinato kale, stemmed, leaves sliced about ¼ inch thick

4 ounces country-style bread, cut or torn into bite-size pieces (about 3 cups)

The bready meatballs
that saved a city

The truth of the story almost doesn't matter. The romance of it is enough to charm you, especially in Gianni Tomasi's telling, the way he becomes animated, a little passionate even, foisting shots of the local grappa on you as he recounts the origins of canederli, northern Italy's go-to bready meatballs studded with bits of cured pork and cheese.

As he tells it, sometime not long before World War I, German soldiers tromped down from the Alps into his hometown of Trento, now a university city tucked into the valleys of the Trentino–Alto Adige region near the border with Liechtenstein. They approached the nearest farm and told the elderly woman there to feed them or they'd destroy her village.

The woman, of course, wasn't prepared to feed an invading army. But what she lacked in mise en place she made up for in ingenuity. She apparently had ample stale bread, some eggs, bits of speck—the local cured pork—and plenty of cheese. She mixed all of this together, formed it into meatball-like orbs, then simmered and served them in a meaty broth she also apparently had in abundance. The soldiers were so satisfied and impressed they spared the community.

As I said, who cares if it's true? Especially when Tomasi's subterranean restaurant—Antica Trattoria al Volt, so named for its vaulted stone ceilings that arch upward to the street level—serves some of the best, most tender, most incredibly savory canederli I encountered during a visit to the region. It's the sort of place where gossipy elderly men sit elbow-to-elbow with lunching students, where carafes of house wine flow freely and the cooking is done by Tomasi's wife and daughter.

Tomasi is the fourth owner of the trattoria, which dates to 1894, though he has had it for just 28 of those years. As he shuffles between tables, occasionally scolding customers who try to sit before he has finished setting the silverware, it's hard to judge his age. He might be weathered for 70 or rather sprightly for 100. Again, the truth really doesn't matter.

But that origin story? Seems a stretch. Versions of canederli are served across northern Italy and southern Germany and Austria (where they are known as Semmelknödel). I suppose the soldiers might have brought home with them the elderly woman's village-saving recipe, and if that telling works for you, no one is worse for it.

When Tomasi's canederli arrived at my table, it was two bready balls visibly studded with bits of meat and herbs—possibly some onion, too—resting in a shallow bowl of steaming broth. Maybe that sexes them up too much, because honestly they aren't much to look at. Kind of pale and lumpy looking. But break into one with a spoon and scoop up some of that broth?

They were just about everything you want on a cold, wet day. The steaming broth was rich and perfectly seasoned; it clearly had simmered

> **"They were just about everything you want on a cold, wet day."**

with plenty of bones for plenty of time. And the canederli themselves, though they looked heavy and dense, somehow remained light, softened with broth, but not sodden. They were savory and rich and a meal unto themselves.

You know where this is going, right? Tomasi and his wife wouldn't share the recipe. He grew up eating his grandfather's version and his recipe is based on that. But that's where it stops. Happily, Trento is a charming medieval town centered around winding cobblestone streets lined with seemingly endless shops that crank out amazing food. Pastificio Le Delizie is one of them and I was lucky enough to dart into it later that day to escape a miserably cold rain.

There, Mauro Pisoni and Pietro Gamboni stuff and fold by hand thousands of ravioli and tortelloni every day for local restaurants and shoppers. They also make canederli

that—I'd later learn—matched if not rivaled Tomasi's.

Pisoni and Gamboni also were generous with their recipe. They make thousands a day and offered to whip up a small batch for me. They started with the bread, a mix of finely ground white breadcrumbs, slightly larger almost panko-style bits, and large crouton-like hunks. That mix mattered, as in both Tomasi's and their canederli, the combination created texture.

To this, they added ample black pepper, some salt, chopped parsley and a pinch of nutmeg, an almost ubiquitous savory seasoning in these parts. A splash of milk moistened the whole affair before they mixed it gently by hand, being careful not to compress it. That light touch obviously was key to keeping the cooked canederli from becoming dense and heavy.

To this, they added ground speck and mortadella, a delicious mixture of cured meats, beaten eggs,

grated Parmesan cheese and a bit of flour, creating an almost paste-like dough. That was it. Using slightly wet hands, they formed them into balls, each slightly larger than a golf ball, which they dusted with fine breadcrumbs to prevent them from sticking together.

I took the raw canederli to my flat that night and whipped up a broth not nearly as good as I'd had at Antica Trattoria al Volt—even the best Airbnb isn't fit for that. It didn't matter. They were stunning. Light, savory and hearty without being heavy. I loved that they were more bread than meat—hence their lightness—yet held together for cooking like the sturdiest meatball.

Still, it doesn't take many to make a meal. The combination of meat, bread and cheese definitely leaves you satisfied, whether you're a German soldier making moves on a small Italian town or just a chilly, wet, hungry journalist.

—J.M. Hirsch

Canederli in Brodo
Bread Dumplings in Broth

Start to finish: 1¾ hours (30 minutes active)   Servings: 4

Stale country-style bread is the base for canederli, the rustic, generously sized dumplings that originate in the Alpine regions of northern Italy. Our version is based on the recipes we learned in the city of Trento from Gianni Tomasi, owner of Antica Trattoria al Volt, and from Mauro Pisoni and Pietro Gamboni of Pastificio Le Delizie pasta shop. Because we almost never have stale bread on hand, we put a baking sheet's worth of bread pieces in the oven to dry them and toast them only until crisp but not browned. We then grind the bread in a food processor, leaving some pea-size bits in with the finer crumbs to help give the dumplings a little airiness. Canederli are poached and served in broth. Homemade chicken broth, with its clean flavor and color makes for an especially satisfying soup, but store-bought works, too.

Don't be lax when mincing the mortadella. If the pieces are too large, the dumplings may not hold together. To mince, stack the slices, cut them into very thin ribbons, then cut the ribbons crosswise into small pieces. Finish by rocking the knife blade back and forth a few times over the pile to create even finer bits.

Heat the oven to 300°F with a rack in the middle position. Distribute the bread on a rimmed baking sheet. Toast in the oven, stirring occasionally, until dried and crisp but not browned, 25 to 30 minutes. Cool completely.

Meanwhile, in a large saucepan over medium, heat the oil until shimmering. Add the onion and ¼ teaspoon salt; cook, stirring occasionally, until translucent and softened, 4 to 6 minutes. Transfer to a large bowl; reserve the pot.

In a food processor, pulse the cooled toasted bread until mostly fine with a few pea-size pieces, 15 to 20 pulses; you should have about 1½ cups. Add the breadcrumbs to the onion in the bowl, followed by the milk, eggs, nutmeg, ¼ teaspoon salt and ½ teaspoon pepper; let stand for about 5 minutes to hydrate.

To the mixture, add the mortadella, Parmesan and parsley. Using a silicone spatula, mix until homogeneous, soft and sticky. Let rest at room temperature for 15 minutes. Meanwhile, in the saucepan, bring the broth to a simmer over medium; reduce to low and cover to keep warm. Place the flour in a wide, shallow bowl or a pie plate.

After the dumpling mixture has rested, uncover the broth and return to a simmer over medium. Divide the dumpling mixture into 8 portions, each about ⅓ cup, rolling each portion into a ball between the palms of your hands (it's fine if they do not form perfect spheres); place them on a plate. If the mixture is sticky, lightly moisten your hands with water to prevent sticking.

8 ounces country-style white bread, cut or torn into 1-inch pieces (about 6 cups)

2 tablespoons extra-virgin olive oil

½ medium yellow onion, finely chopped

Kosher salt and ground black pepper

¾ cup plus 2 tablespoons whole milk

2 large eggs, beaten

½ teaspoon ground nutmeg

4 ounces mortadella, minced into bits no larger than ¼ inch

1 ounce Parmesan cheese, finely grated (½ cup), plus more to serve

2 tablespoons finely chopped fresh flat-leaf parsley, plus more to serve

2 quarts homemade chicken broth (p. 257) or low-sodium chicken broth

¼ cup all-purpose flour

One at a time, coat the balls on all sides with the flour, shake off excess and lower into the broth. Once all the dumplings are in the pan, return the broth to a simmer and cook, uncovered and occasionally stirring and turning the dumplings, until the dumplings float to the surface, about 10 minutes.

Taste and season the broth with salt and pepper. Ladle the broth and dumplings into individual bowls, then sprinkle with additional parsley and Parmesan.

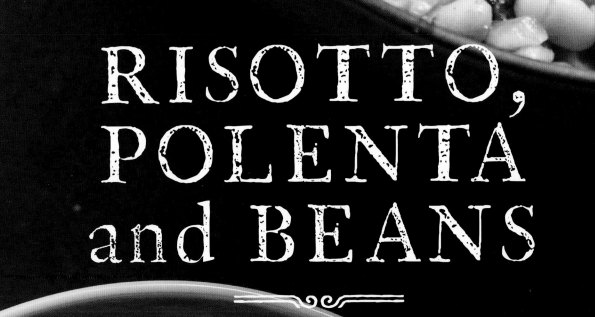

RISOTTO, POLENTA and BEANS

The secret ingredient to
Risotto alla Milanese? Speed

An empty restaurant is a bad sign. So when I walked into Trattoria Masuelli San Marco on a deserted drag through Milan, the urge to spin and walk was strong. But I'd traversed 28 hours and three countries to try their risotto. I was committed.

The glow of rainbow glassed mid-century modern chandeliers. The glint of a giant golden brass espresso maker perched on the steel and wood bar. None of it warmed the eerie silence of being alone in a restaurant that looked a bit too much like your great aunt's parlor crossed with a Chianti bottle.

My worry was wasted. All the warmth needed to melt the solitude arrived on a single white plate. A brilliant marigold pool of toothy-tender rice, the creamy liquid flecked with bold streaks of red. It was—simply—the taste of sunshine in my mouth. It was creamy without feeling heavy. The grains of rice were distinct, not gummy. It was looser, saucier than I'm used to. Wonderfully so. And those red filaments—the saffron—an aroma as much as a flavor.

By the end of the meal, my error was obvious. Risotto alla Milanese—the saffron-tinged dish of creamy rice flavored floral and dyed golden by the thread-like stigmas and styles of crocus flowers—is a centuries old tradition in Milan. And the staff had stayed open long beyond their normal shifts merely so I could try it.

Like all risotto, Milan's golden rendition is notoriously fussy to make, often delivering uninspired results. Heat the broth. Chop the onion. Toast the rice. Soften the onion. Cook off the wine. Slowly stir. Stir. Stir. Keep going. You'll get there. Finish with Parmesan. Only to end up with overly starchy, gluey rice simultaneously—puzzlingly—both over- and under-cooked.

My suspicion that there had to be a better way is what brought me to Milan, Italy's northern epicenter of fashion, design and risotto. I didn't expect to find it on my first night.

But the risotto at Trattoria Masuelli San Marco was one of those meals that lingers in your taste memory, so much so it drew me back the following night, at the expense of another reservation elsewhere. Father and son—chef and front-of-the-house—Max and Andrea Masuelli welcomed me into the kitchen at the height of a bustling dinner rush.

Lesson No. 1: Discard everything you think you know about risotto making. When the senior Masuelli took to the stove, risotto was made with blistering speed. Twenty minutes, give or take. This was no slow simmer with tiresome stirring, gently and slowly ladling in broth and waiting for it to be absorbed. This was dump-and-go risotto cooked at a rollicking boil.

Lesson No. 2: Ingredients I considered essential to risotto—chicken broth and onion—were nowhere to be seen. Translating for his father, Andrea explained that they preferred a simple vegetable broth (and much

> "Discard everything you think you know about risotto making."

more of it than I expected) made on the spot—onions, carrots, celery and water—for its cleaner, simpler flavor that didn't compete with the rice and saffron. Ditto for the onion. Its flavor detracts from the simplicity of the other ingredients, so they leave it out.

As a result, the cooking was fast and simple. Max began by steeping a generous pinch—more than a teaspoon—of saffron in ¼ cup of warm broth, the liquid quickly bleeding red. Meanwhile, he briefly toasted a large handful of carnaroli rice—the preferred short-grained white risotto rice in Milan; elsewhere in Italy, it's Arborio—in a bit of fat, then added ½ cup of room-temperature white wine—the source of the acidity that balances the richness of the rice starch and cheese—and brought it to a simmer. In a minute or so, the alcohol had cooked off and he ladled in the broth. All of it. All at once.

Back to a strong simmer, and it was mostly hands off. A bit of stirring and dramatic flipping every few minutes, but none of the constant motion or gentle heat I've always been told is essential for extracting the starch that produces risotto's classic creamy texture. When the rice was nearly al dente—"White at the center, transparent at the edges," Max explained—he added the saffron-infused broth, then stirred vigorously for several minutes, the rice darkening in stages from pale yellow to light orange to deep golden.

Off the heat, the finishing flourishes were added. Room-temperature butter and grated Parmesan—as with the wine, cold ingredients cool the rice too quickly—were stirred in, giving the risotto richness as it flowed loosely, cleanly onto a plate. In a move I learned is classic Milanese, Max then held the edge of the plate with his left hand, then smacked the bottom of it repeatedly and firmly with his right palm, leveling the risotto into a even, glistening pool.

Several nights later, my education in shortcut—yet stellar—risotto again continued unexpectedly. I wheedled my way into the kitchen at Trippa, where the heavily tattooed Diego Rossi—known for maximizing flavor with minimal ingredients, as well as for a gorgeously crisp fried tripe—agreed to show me his take on risotto alla Milanese.

Lesson No. 1. The Masuellis were on to something. Rossi shared their preference for vegetable broth and disdain for onion. In fact, much of the way he cooked risotto mirrored their own—the saffron added at the end, the speed of the cooking, the infrequent stirring, the loose sauciness from extra broth, the gorgeous brightness and lightness of the color and flavors.

But something was different. Everything was... heightened somehow. The flavors more crisp, the sauce somehow more luxurious with the butter and Parmesan almost popping.

Lesson No. 2. We weren't done paring away classic ingredients. Along with the onion and chicken broth, Rossi also leaves out the wine. All we want is its acidity, but to get that you need to cook off the alcohol. Even then, the wine too often leaves behind a booziness that muddles the other flavors. So Rossi cuts out the middle, brightening his risotto not with wine, but with a finishing splash of white sherry vinegar. He had me try it before and after adding it; the difference was astounding.

At Milk Street, we found the science supported these quick-cook methods. Because much of the starch is on the exterior of the rice, most of it is released at the start of cooking regardless of whether the liquid is added all at once or gradually during cooking. The key is the initial vigorous stirring, which helps that release. After that, frequent—but not constant—stirring is all that's needed to prevent the rice from sticking. And because there is no need to slowly extract the starch, the rice can be cooked at a higher temperature, resulting in a speedier risotto.

Encouraged by this, we adopted Rossi's use of vinegar over wine and made only minor modifications to the rest of their approach—bolstering their basic vegetable broth by adding just a bit of garlic and chopped plum tomato, as well as using about 1 cup more of it in the risotto than is conventional; easing up just a bit on the amount of saffron used (which some people can find overwhelmingly floral at higher amounts).

The result was a seven-ingredient risotto that was light, bright, on the table in just 25 minutes, and well worth dining alone for.

—J.M. Hirsch

Risotto alla Milanese

Start to finish: 40 minutes Servings: 4

In Milan we discovered that Italian chefs break all the rules we thought were sacrosanct for the richest, creamiest risotto—no onions, no chicken broth, and no endless stirring. Risotto alla Milanese gets its warm golden color and opulent flavor from saffron. The dish, a specialty of Milan, is the classic accompaniment to osso buco, or braised veal shanks, which also is a signature dish from the Lombardy region of northern Italy. Our iteration is based on risotto lessons learned at Trattoria Masuelli San Marco, where Max Masuelli and his son, Andrea, are at the helm, and at Trattoria Trippa, where Diego Rossi is chef. Medium-grain Italian rice is essential for achieving risotto with a rich, creamy consistency, as it has the ideal starch content. Arborio rice is the most common choice in the U.S., but in Milan—as well as at Milk Street—carnaroli is the preferred variety. We found that the grains better retained their structure and resisted overcooking. With careful cooking, however, Arborio will yield delicious results. A quick five-ingredient homemade vegetable broth (recipe facing page) is the best cooking liquid for this risotto; its fresh, clean flavor won't compete with the other ingredients. Serve in warmed, shallow bowls to prevent the rice from cooling too quickly.

Don't add the saffron to the saucepan of broth. Instead, remove ½ cup of the hot broth and steep the threads in that measured amount while you start the risotto. This way, all the saffron will make it into the rice even if you wind up with extra unused broth.

6 cups easy vegetable broth (recipe facing page)

1 teaspoon saffron threads

6 tablespoons salted butter, cut into 1-tablespoon pieces, divided

1 cup carnaroli or Arborio rice

1 ounce Parmesan cheese, finely grated (½ cup)

Kosher salt

4 teaspoons white balsamic vinegar

In a medium saucepan over medium, bring the broth, covered, to a simmer. Reduce to low to keep warm. In a small bowl or measuring cup, combine ½ cup of the hot broth and the saffron; set aside.

In a large saucepan over medium-high, melt 2 tablespoons butter. Add the rice and cook, stirring, until translucent at the edges, 1 to 2 minutes. Add 2 cups of the hot broth and bring to a boil, then reduce to medium and cook, stirring often and briskly, until most of the liquid is absorbed, 8 to 10 minutes; adjust the heat as needed to maintain a vigorous simmer. Add another 1½ cups hot broth and cook until most of the liquid is absorbed, 6 to 9 minutes.

Add the saffron broth and cook, stirring often and briskly, until the rice is just shy of al dente but still soupy, 3 to 5 minutes. If the rice is thick and dry or the grains are still too firm, add the remaining hot broth in ¼-cup increments and cook, stirring, until the rice is loose but not soupy and the grains are tender, with just a little firmness at the center.

Off heat, quickly stir in the Parmesan, the remaining 4 tablespoons butter and ¼ teaspoon salt; it's fine if the butter and cheese do not fully melt. Cover and let stand for 10 minutes.

(Reserve the remaining hot broth in the saucepan for adjusting the consistency of the risotto at the end, if needed.)

Stir to fully incorporate the butter and cheese, then stir in the vinegar. If the risotto is stiff and dry, stir in additional broth, a couple tablespoons at a time, until the risotto is "loose" but not soupy. Taste and season with salt. Serve immediately.

Easy Vegetable Broth

Start to finish: 30 minutes   Makes about 1½ quarts

In a large saucepan, combine **2 medium carrots** (peeled and chopped), **2 large celery stalks** (chopped), **1 large yellow onion** (chopped), **1 medium tomato** (roughly chopped) and **2 large garlic cloves** (smashed and peeled). Add **5½ cups water** and bring to a boil over high. Partially cover, then reduce to medium and cook for 20 minutes, adjusting the heat to maintain a lively simmer. Pour the broth through a fine-mesh strainer into a large bowl; discard the solids. Use immediately or cool to room temperature, cover and refrigerate for up to 5 days.

Risotto alle Tre Erbe

Three-Herb Risotto

Start to finish: 40 minutes Servings: 4

We learned the principles of cooking risotto in Milan, inspiring this take on the classic that's bright with fresh herbs and tangy lemon. At Trattoria Masuelli San Marco, Max Masuelli and his son, Andrea, use neither chicken broth nor onion, and at Trattoria Trippa, Diego Rossi showed us that skipping the traditional wine and adding a splash of vinegar at the end produces bright flavor. These unconventional approaches yield a risotto with an especially light, clean flavor. Here, we use a simple five-ingredient homemade vegetable broth as the cooking liquid. We also add a trio of fresh herbs and a touch of lemon zest, ingredients that nicely complement the Parmesan and butter.

Don't add the herbs to the risotto until the very end, just before serving, so they retain their bright color and fresh flavor. In fact, the risotto's 10-minute off-heat rest is an ideal time to prep the herbs.

6 cups easy vegetable broth (p. 77)

6 tablespoons salted butter, cut into 1-tablespoon pieces, divided

1 cup carnaroli or Arborio rice

1 ounce Parmesan cheese, finely grated (½ cup)

Kosher salt

¼ cup finely chopped fresh flat-leaf parsley

2 scallions, thinly sliced

2 teaspoons minced fresh thyme

½ teaspoon grated lemon zest

4 teaspoons white balsamic vinegar

In a medium saucepan over medium, bring the broth, covered, to a simmer. Reduce to low to keep warm. In a large saucepan over medium-high, melt 2 tablespoons butter. Add the rice and cook, stirring, until translucent at the edges, 1 to 2 minutes. Add 2 cups of the hot broth and bring to a boil, then reduce to medium and cook, stirring often and briskly, until most of the liquid is absorbed, 8 to 10 minutes; adjust the heat as needed to maintain a vigorous simmer. Add another 1½ cups hot broth and cook until most of the liquid is absorbed, 6 to 9 minutes.

Add another ½ cup hot broth and cook, stirring often and briskly, until the rice is just shy of al dente but still soupy, 3 to 5 minutes. If the rice is thick and dry or the grains are still too firm, add the remaining hot broth in ¼-cup increments and cook, stirring, until the rice is loose but not soupy and the grains are tender, with just a little firmness at the center.

Off heat, quickly stir in the Parmesan, the remaining 4 tablespoons butter and ¼ teaspoon salt; it's fine if the butter and cheese do not fully melt. Cover and let stand for 10 minutes. (Reserve any remaining hot broth in the saucepan for adjusting the consistency of the risotto at the end, if needed.)

Stir to fully incorporate the butter and cheese, then stir in the parsley, scallions, thyme, lemon zest and vinegar. If the risotto is stiff and dry, stir in additional broth, a couple tablespoons at a time, until the risotto is "loose" but not soupy. Taste and season with salt. Serve immediately.

Stop stirring your polenta!

The polenta I know—a cornmeal porridge too often too rich and dense with a heft of cheese, yet somehow simultaneously tasteless—is a tedium of attention and constant whisking over heat, low and slow. It's hard to imagine how Maria Teresa Marino has time for this.

Her family and its centuries-old grain mill buzz as she hoists a giant pot of polenta—golden, steaming and smooth—from the stove to a kitchen table scattered with bread and wine. Her husband, sons and their wives are a flurry, talking business, babies and the bubbles of their local asti spumante, mostly all at once.

But as the polenta is ladled into bowls—topped with a thin red sauce alluringly named bagna d'inferno, or hell's bath—the swirl ceases and spoons are lifted. In that rare quiet, it becomes obvious: This most definitely is not the polenta I know.

It is light and almost airy, with a sweet aroma, like freshly husked corn. The taste is creamy, not cloying or heavy. Most surprisingly, the flavor of the corn is bright, clean, singular and strong. This was the polenta I'd come to Italy to learn. Done well, it is a comforting foil for rich meats and sauces. Done badly—and it so often is—polenta is larded with cheese and fat that mask the simplicity of the corn.

Marino shrugs me off. The polenta cooks itself, she explains. Surely a humble exaggeration, but an explanation would need to wait. The family first wanted me to visit their mill across the courtyard to see the ancient process that made this meal possible.

Polenta has been a staple of northern Italian cuisine for several hundred years. Most recipes are intimidatingly overwrought, demanding precise temperatures of water and constant whisking for 30, 40, even 60 minutes. Then there is the copious cheese and butter, which can turn an already-heavy dish leaden.

The family's Mulino Marino (Marinos' Mill) is hidden in Cossano Belbo, a hilltop village of 1,000 people about two hours south of Milan. It is reached by terrifying single-lane gravel switchbacks through terraced vineyards. For centuries, the mill has been using 1.2-ton stone disks to grind a wide variety of grains into flours. The Marinos have been its custodians since the 1950s.

When I arrive at the mill—a yellow villa with soaring arched ceilings once part of the village castle, most of which was destroyed in a battle around the year 1200—I first notice the air, sweet and dry with the smell of corn. Inside, 25-kilogram sacks of flour are stacked in towers. Ten massive mills are designated for a specific grain—spelt, rye, wheat, barley and on. On this day, the corn hoppers are full.

Each mill uses two stones—6-foot rounds cut from the rock of the Pyrenees—that every few months must be freshly etched by hand using a

"The flavor of the corn is bright, clean, singular and strong."

pick and hammer, the pattern different for each grain. Though most commercial grain mills use steel blades, stones move more slowly and generate less heat, which can damage—and therefore diminish—both nutrients and flavor compounds. As the mills spin, grain spills into a hole cut into the center of the top stone and is crushed as the stones rotate, pushing the flour to the edge, where it pours out in a stream.

Though some of the equipment has been modernized—the stones now churn in stainless-steel cylinders—the mechanics of the process are mostly unchanged. The mills reserved for corn are still housed in massive wooden barrel-like containers, the gears and levers also wood. One worker dumps a sack of kernels into a hopper; a second monitors the cornmeal exiting below, adjusting the speed and fineness of the grind with an iron wheel. The cornmeal emerges warm, gritty and smelling strongly of oil and fresh sweetness.

In the midst of it, elderly women from the village totter in, and the Marino brothers stop grinding to sell them cornmeal. A cool rain is forecast—polenta weather. Compared to commercial operations, these mills work slowly, grinding just 250 kilograms of flour an hour. But this allows for more control over the quality, and to grind faster would risk burning the grains.

The medieval simplicity of the process—not to mention the impossible freshness of the product—seduced and worried me. Maria Teresa's polenta was so much better and so different than any I'd had. If the difference was due to the product rather than the cooking

method, our chances of replicating it at Milk Street were doomed.

Back in Maria Teresa's modern but simple kitchen—with windows that look down onto the stone courtyard outside the mill—I began to understand what sets her polenta apart. It isn't what she puts into the cornmeal or what she does to it. Rather, it is what she leaves out and what she doesn't do to it.

To start, there is no cheese. Nor butter. And, best yet, there is little stirring. All of it heresy to conventional polenta wisdom. Yet evidence that her approach works—brilliantly so, in fact—sits deliciously on my plate. Though only for moments: I eat it that quickly.

Maria Teresa walks me through the recipe, which involves little more than boiling salted water (far more than expected), then sprinkling in coarse cornmeal, returning it to a boil and stirring vigorously for 10 minutes. Cover, lower the heat and walk away. After an hour (the Marinos like to let it go longer, but admit it's usually done after about an hour), Maria Teresa uncovers the pot and vigorously stirs the polenta again for a few minutes. It's done.

No wonder the flavor of the corn is so pronounced, so naturally sweet, so simple. Sure, the cornmeal starts out more flavorful. But it isn't hidden by cheese and butter. Though it needs nothing—I could eat it plain by the bowl—the bagna dell'inferno is the polenta's perfect savory counterpunch.

–J.M. Hirsch

Polenta Classica
Soft Polenta

Start to finish: 1 hour 45 minutes (10 minutes active) Servings: 6

In a hilltop town in northern Italy, Maria Teresa Marino taught us the simple secrets to the lightest, most flavorful—and easiest!—polenta. No dairy, plenty of water and just a few short bursts of strategic stirring. Polenta, a savory cornmeal porridge, can be a disappointment in the U.S., tasting mostly of the cheese and fat that weigh it down. But Marino, whose family's grain mill in Cossano Belbo is centuries old, showed us a simpler way. We followed that lead, using more water than called for in conventional recipes—11 cups—and finished cooking the polenta in the oven rather than the stovetop, for more consistent, gentle heat. For the best flavor and texture, use coarse stone-ground cornmeal; fine cornmeal produced pasty, gluey polenta, while steel-ground cornmeal has less flavor. The finished polenta should be pourable; if it's too thick, thin with water as needed. This polenta is not enriched with butter or cheese, which allows the sweetness of the corn to be front and center. It's a perfect side to most braises and also can be paired with a flavorful sauce, such as spicy tomato sauce with garlic and anchovies (recipe facing page). Polenta also is great chilled, cut into squares and fried up tender and crisp; see instructions p. 85.

Don't use white cornmeal. Its flavor is milder than yellow cornmeal. (In Italy, it is used mostly for sweet preparations.) And don't skip the whisk for stirring the polenta as it cooks; its wires are more effective than a wooden spoon for breaking up lumps.

2 cups coarse stone-ground yellow cornmeal (see headnote)

Kosher salt and ground black pepper

Heat the oven to 375°F with a rack in the lower-middle position. In a large Dutch oven, whisk together the cornmeal, 1½ teaspoons salt and 11 cups water. Bring to a gentle simmer over medium-high, stirring frequently to prevent clumping. Transfer the pot, uncovered, to the oven and bake for 1 hour.

Remove the pot from the oven. Carefully whisk until smooth, then use a wooden spoon to scrape along the bottom and into the corners of the pot to loosen any stuck bits. Return the pot, uncovered, to the oven and cook until the cornmeal is thick and creamy and the granules are tender, another 10 to 30 minutes, depending on the cornmeal used.

Remove the pot from the oven. Vigorously whisk the polenta until smooth and use the wooden spoon to scrape the bottom, sides and corners. Let stand for 5 minutes. The polenta should thicken just enough for a spoon to leave a brief trail when dragged through; whisk in additional water, if needed, to thin the consistency. Taste and season with salt and pepper. Serve immediately.

Bagna dell'Inferno
Spicy Tomato Sauce with Garlic and Anchovies

Start to finish: 20 minutes Makes 2 cups

In a 12-inch nonstick skillet, combine **2 tablespoons extra-virgin olive oil, 5 oil-packed anchovies** and **5 medium garlic cloves** (minced). Cook, stirring occasionally and breaking up the anchovies, until the garlic is light golden brown, 2 to 3 minutes. Stir in ½ **teaspoon red pepper flakes** and **2 pints grape tomatoes** (1 pint halved, 1 pint left whole), then cover and cook, stirring occasionally, until most of the whole tomatoes have burst, 5 to 7 minutes. Using a fork or potato masher, gently mash the tomatoes. Off heat, stir in **3 tablespoons red wine vinegar** and **2 tablespoons extra-virgin olive oil.** Taste and season with salt and ground black pepper, then stir in ¼ **cup chopped fresh basil**.

Polenta Fritta
Fried Polenta

Start to finish: 25 minutes   Servings: 4

Soft polenta firms up as it cools, so Italians transform leftovers by cutting it into squares and frying until crisp outside and tender inside. If you plan to serve soft polenta one night and fry the extra in the next few days, scale up the polenta recipe so you have enough for both occasions. Increase the cornmeal to 2½ cups, the water to 13¾ cups and the salt to 5 teaspoons. While the polenta cooks, coat an 8-inch-square baking dish with 1 tablespoon extra-virgin olive oil. When the soft polenta has finished cooking, ladle 4 cups into the prepared baking dish and smooth it into an even layer. Cool to room temperature, cover with plastic wrap and refrigerate until firm, or up to two days. Fried polenta is a great accompaniment to stews, or it can be topped with cheese or sauce and served as an appetizer or light main course. In Italy, it's often served with chunks of Gorgonzola and a drizzle of honey.

Don't use polenta that has not been chilled until very firm. It's best to give the polenta at least a full day in the refrigerator before cutting and frying.

8-inch-square firm, chilled soft polenta (see headnote)

⅓ cup all-purpose flour

Kosher salt and ground black pepper

6 tablespoons extra-virgin olive oil, divided

Remove the polenta from the baking dish by inverting it onto a cutting board. Cut the polenta into 9 squares. In a shallow dish, whisk the flour, ¼ teaspoon salt and ½ teaspoon pepper, then lightly coat all sides of each square, shaking off any excess.

In a 12-inch nonstick skillet over medium-high, heat 3 tablespoons of the oil until barely smoking. Add 4 or 5 of the coated polenta squares and cook until lightly browned, about 4 minutes. Carefully flip each square and cook until lightly browned on the other side, another 3 to 4 minutes. Transfer the squares to a large plate, then wipe out the skillet. Repeat with the remaining oil and polenta squares.

Fagioli all'Uccelletto

White Beans with Sage, Garlic and Fennel

Start to finish: 45 minutes Servings: 4

Tuscan cooks add big flavor to beans by getting the most out of just a few ingredients. We take note, using sage three ways—finely chopped leaves, sage-infused oil and crumbled fried leaves—to intensify its deeply savory impact in this simplified version of the regional dish fagioli all'uccelletto. Any variety of canned white beans will work, though great northern and navy beans held their shape better than cannellini. To use dry beans, see our cooking instructions facing page. This dish is hearty enough to serve as a main—it's excellent with grilled rustic bread—but is also a good accompaniment to roasted chicken or pork.

Don't drain both cans of beans. The liquid from one of the cans creates a sauce-like consistency that keeps the beans succulent.

In a large Dutch oven over medium, heat 3 tablespoons of the oil until shimmering. Add the fennel, onion, garlic, chopped sage, red pepper flakes and ½ teaspoon salt. Cover and cook, stirring occasionally, until the vegetables have softened, about 15 minutes.

Stir in the tomatoes and the beans. Cook, uncovered, stirring occasionally and adjusting the heat as needed to maintain a gentle simmer, for 10 minutes. Taste and season with salt and pepper.

Meanwhile, line a plate with paper towels. In a 12-inch skillet over medium-high, heat the remaining 3 tablespoons oil until shimmering. Add the sage leaves and cook, flipping the leaves once, until the edges begin to curl, about 1 minute. Transfer to the prepared plate; reserve the oil.

Transfer the beans to a serving bowl, then drizzle with the sage oil. Coarsely crumble the sage leaves over the beans. Top with Parmesan.

6 tablespoons extra-virgin olive oil, divided

1 large fennel bulb, trimmed and finely chopped

1 medium yellow onion, finely chopped

4 large garlic cloves, finely chopped

3 tablespoons finely chopped fresh sage, plus 20 whole leaves

¼ teaspoon red pepper flakes

Kosher salt and ground black pepper

14½-ounce can diced tomatoes

Two 15½-ounce cans white beans (see headnote), 1 can rinsed and drained

Shaved or grated Parmesan cheese, to serve

How to Cook Dried Beans

Dried beans cooked on the stovetop can be frustratingly inconsistent. After much testing, we learned the most reliable and easiest method is to instead cook them in the oven. We start with an overnight soak in salted water. The salt is key; it softens the bean skins, allowing water to better penetrate, producing tender beans. Drained and combined with fresh water and a bit more salt, the beans are brought to a boil on the stovetop, then transferred to the oven for low-and-slow cooking that yields the perfect texture. And once the beans are in the oven, the cooking is hands off.

As we tested this approach, we learned that some varieties of beans can be trickier to cook than others. Their calcium content is a major factor. The higher the calcium, the better they hold their shape. Conversely, lower-calcium beans are more likely to blow out during cooking. And calcium content varies not only by type of bean, but also by where they are grown. Finally, the age of any dried beans also influences how quickly they tenderize (older beans take longer), so begin checking for doneness on the low end of the time range, but don't be surprised if they require even longer than suggested. After cooking, store the beans in their cooking liquid to maintain their plumpness.

Beans	Oven Temperature	Cook Time (in minutes)	Yield (in cups)
Cannellini	275°F	50–60	6
Chickpeas	275°F	45–70	7
Great Northern	275°F	35–45	6
Navy	275°F	45–60	6
Roman (Borlotti)	250°F	45–50	6

1 pound (2 to 2½ cups) dried beans (see chart)

Kosher salt

In a large bowl, stir together 2 quarts water, the beans and 1 tablespoon salt. Soak at room temperature for at least 12 hours or up to 24 hours.

Heat the oven to the desired temperature with a rack in the lower-middle position. Drain the beans and put them in a Dutch oven. Add 6 cups water and 1½ teaspoons salt. Bring to a rolling boil over medium-high; as the mixture heats, use a wide, flat spoon to skim off and discard the scum that rises to the surface. Once boiling, stir, then cover and transfer to the oven. Cook until the beans are tender but still retain their shape.

Remove the pot from the oven. Cool the beans in the liquid in the pot. If using right away, drain, reserving the liquid if needed. If storing, transfer the beans and liquid to a container, cover and refrigerate for up to 5 days.

In this simple pasta dish,
texture is the secret ingredient

It was a friend-of-a-friend-of-a-friend sort of suggestion. Go to Le Zie Trattoria in Lecce, an understated eatery where the menu of cucina povera offers an intimate introduction to the simple foods of Puglia, the slender heel of Italy's boot. Of course, understated is an understatement. I'd walked past it several times before realizing I'd been in front of it all along.

I ring the doorbell—for the door is locked—and chef-owner Anna Carmela Perrone greets me and leads me through the rooms of the home-turned-restaurant—walls papered with maps, garage sale paintings, photos of celebrity guests and business cards. As I sit with the menu, Perrone returns to the tiny galley kitchen, really just a hallway off the dining room.

Her story is a bit muddled, tantalizingly so. The home once was a wine shop, and either before or after it was a restaurant owned by three sisters, two of whom were "spinsters" known about town as "Auntie." "Let's go to the Aunties' restaurant" apparently was a common saying in the day. About 20 years ago, Perrone inherited it from a distant relative of somebody.

Whatever its lineage, Le Zie's food lives up to the billing: a delicious tour through a sun- and olive oil–drenched region. Ciambotta, a summer vegetable stew as much about the oil as the produce. Parmigiana alle melanzane, a glistening stack of eggplant planks. Orecchiette dressed with tomatoes and olive oil. Creamy fava bean puree with tender, bitter chicory.

But the standout was the ciceri e tria, a simple tangle of broad strips of pasta paired with chickpeas. Except it wasn't so simple. Half the pasta was the tender noodle we know. The other half was crisp, tan and crunchy, almost wonton-esque. The result was rich, creamy and unexpectedly textured—soft and crackling. The flavor of olive oil strong, but not heavy.

In the kitchen, the explanation became clear. Perrone cooks the pasta two ways—half of it in salted water, half fried in olive oil until crisp. Both then are tossed in a skillet with chickpeas and a bit of the starchy pasta cooking water, all of it simmering down to create a rich and textured—yet somehow weightless—sauce.

At Milk Street, this was a simple adaptation, mostly a matter of reducing the volume of oil needed to crisp the pasta and streamlining the method to make it a one-pot meal. Happily, we found the technique works as well with dried pasta as fresh. And we added lemon zest and juice, as well as a bit of parsley, to lighten and brighten the finished dish. A result as deliciously textured as Le Zie's history.

—J.M. Hirsch

"The result was rich, creamy and unexpectedly textured—soft and crackling."

Ciceri e Tria

Crispy Pasta with Chickpeas, Lemon and Parsley

Start to finish: 35 minutes Servings: 4

At her home-turned-restaurant in Lecce, Anna Carmela Perrone showed us a new take on texture by frying pasta to a lightly browned crisp and pairing it with al dente noodles and tender chickpeas. We use a 9-ounce package of fresh fettuccine and cut the noodles into 2-inch lengths; half is toasted in olive oil and the other half is simmered directly in the sauce. If you have trouble finding fresh pasta, use an 8.8-ounce package of dried pappardelle made with egg; the noodles are packaged in nests that are easy to break into pieces. Keep in mind, however, that dried pappardelle toasts more quickly than fresh pasta—in about 8 minutes. Lemon zest and juice and chopped fresh parsley add brightness to balance the starches. This dish is best served right away when the sauce is creamy.

Don't forget to reserve the chickpea liquid; you will need ¾ cup of it for making the sauce. And don't bother rinsing the chickpeas after draining off their packing liquid.

¼ cup extra-virgin olive oil

9 ounces fresh fettuccine, cut into rough 2-inch lengths, divided

15½-ounce can chickpeas, drained, liquid reserved

2 bay leaves

Kosher salt and ground black pepper

2 teaspoons grated lemon zest, plus 1 teaspoon lemon juice

½ cup lightly packed fresh flat-leaf parsley, chopped

In a large pot over medium, combine the oil and half of the pasta. Cook, stirring occasionally, until the pasta is crisp and deeply browned, 12 to 14 minutes. Using a slotted spoon, transfer to a medium bowl and set aside.

To the oil remaining in the pot, add the chickpeas and bay. Cook, stirring occasionally, until the chickpeas darken slightly and the bay is toasted, 2 to 4 minutes. Stir in the remaining pasta, ¾ cup of chickpea liquid (supplement with water if needed), 2¼ cups water, 1 teaspoon salt and ¾ teaspoon pepper. Bring to a simmer over medium-high and cook, stirring occasionally, until the pasta is heated through and slightly softened, about 2 minutes.

Add the toasted pasta and cook, stirring often and adjusting the heat as needed to maintain a gentle simmer, until the untoasted pasta is al dente and the sauce lightly clings, about 4 minutes. Remove the pot from the heat, then remove and discard the bay. Stir in the lemon zest and juice and parsley. Taste and season with salt and pepper.

In Amalfi, risotto involves a sizzle, a pop and three layers of lemon

For Giovanna Aceto, risotto begins and ends with lemon. And in the middle is sound.

So let's start in the middle. She'd already lightly browned an onion in olive oil, then added the rice, giving it all a vigorous stir. That's when she did something unexpected. She bent her head toward the skillet and paused, tilting her ear toward it.

She was listening. The rice was ready for the next step only once it started to pop. Sizzling is not enough, she said. It must pop. And when it did, Aceto knew it was ready for a splash of white wine, which she added without measuring.

"Quanto bastò," she said, waving at me. When it's enough. And with a splash and sizzle, it was.

Now back to the beginning. And end. We were in Amalfi on the lemon farm she oversees with her husband, Salvatore. They hang from trees everywhere, massive, bulbous, brilliant yellow. And they command an influence on the regional cooking that is just as bold and outsized.

She started her risotto by making a "broth," little more than lightly salted water simmered with ample thick strips of bright yellow lemon zest. It would be one of many ways she'd infuse her risotto with the region's signature flavor.

When the sizzling subsides, Giovanna ladles in the golden broth, turning the starches creamy. Once again, her next step throws me. I expect cheese, unctuously savory and classic to risotto. Instead, she stirs together an egg yolk, a couple tablespoons heavy cream, some parsley and the zest of yet another oversized Amalfi lemon.

After stirring the mixture into the risotto, now intensely yellow, she adds the juice of the lemon. The result is three layers of lemon flavor—the infused broth, the zest and the juice.

Of course, she isn't done yet. To serve it, Giovanna spoons the mixture into the skins of lemons hollowed to form cups. As she does so, she tells me about an alternative version she enjoys, adding plump shrimp just at the end of cooking and using their shells to further infuse the lemony broth. The finished risotto is creamy and rich, but without cheese and thanks to the lemon, it remains light, fresh and sweet.

—J.M. Hirsch

"The result is three layers of lemon flavor—the infused broth, the zest and the juice."

Risotto al Limone e Gamberetti con Basilico

Lemon and Shrimp Risotto with Basil

Start to finish: 45 minutes Servings: 4

On the Amalfi Coast, Giovanna Aceto showed us how to infuse a simple risotto with sharp citrus flavor, and finish it off with a creamy touch of egg and cream. To create a flavorful broth for simmering the risotto, we steep the shrimp shells and strips of lemon zest in water, and for citrus notes that register at every level, we stir in bright, puckery lemon juice and floral, fragrant grated zest just before serving. If you purchase shrimp that are already shelled, bottled clam juice is a fine substitute. Bring two 8-ounce bottles clam juice, 3 cups water, ½ teaspoon salt and the zest strips to a simmer in the saucepan and cook, covered, for 10 minutes to infuse, then strain as directed.

Don't uncover the pot for at least five minutes after adding the shrimp. Lifting the lid releases some of the residual heat that's needed to cook the shrimp.

Using a vegetable peeler (preferably a Y-style peeler), remove the zest from 1 of the lemons in long, wide strips; try to remove only the colored portion of the peel, not the bitter white pith just underneath. Using a rasp-style grater, grate the zest from the remaining lemon; set aside separately. Halve the lemons and squeeze ¼ cup juice; set the juice aside.

In a medium saucepan over medium, heat 2 teaspoons oil until shimmering. Add the shrimp shells and cook, stirring constantly, until pink, 1 to 2 minutes. Add 5 cups water, the zest strips and ½ teaspoon salt, then bring to a simmer. Cover, reduce to low and cook for 10 minutes. Pour the broth through a strainer set over a medium bowl; rinse out the pan. Press on the solids to extract as much liquid as possible, then discard. Return the broth to the pan, cover and set over low to keep warm.

In a large Dutch oven over medium-high, heat 1 tablespoon of oil until shimmering. Add the onion and ¼ teaspoon salt, then cook, stirring occasionally, until softened, 6 to 7 minutes. Add the rice and cook, stirring, until the grains are translucent at the edges, 1 to 2 minutes. Add the wine and cook, stirring occasionally, until the pan is almost dry, about 3 minutes. Add 3 cups of the hot broth and cook, stirring often and briskly, until a spoon drawn through the mixture leaves a trail, 10 to 12 minutes.

Add the remaining broth and cook, stirring, until the rice is tender, 8 to 10 minutes. Remove the pot from the heat; and stir in the shrimp. Cover and let stand until the shrimp are opaque throughout, 5 to 7 minutes.

Stir in the remaining 1 tablespoon oil, the lemon juice, egg yolk, cream, basil, and the grated zest. The risotto should be loose but not soupy; if needed, stir in water 1 tablespoon at a time to achieve the proper consistency. Taste and season with salt. Serve drizzled with additional oil.

2 lemons

2 teaspoons plus 2 tablespoons extra-virgin olive oil, divided, plus more to serve

12 ounces extra-large (21/25 per pound) shrimp, peeled (shells reserved), deveined and patted dry

Kosher salt

1 small yellow onion, finely chopped

1 cup carnaroli or Arborio rice

½ cup dry white wine

1 large egg yolk

2 tablespoons heavy cream

½ cup loosely packed fresh basil, roughly chopped

From Sicily, the real
pasta con fagioli

In Sicily, the cliché seems to stand—the Mafia is everywhere. Or rather, was. Even here at Cantina della Val di Suro, a sunbaked and sprawling winery perched on a hill nestled in a valley wedged between the Tyrrhenian Sea and the Madonie Mountains.

Accessed only via up-down-side-to-side-over-and-again gut-wrenching roads, the business until recently was owned by the Mafia, the vintages named for the family's children. Because of course. Yet neither the drive nor the lineage seems to bother the winery's cook, Piera Ferruzza, who'd agreed to teach me rustic Sicilian cooking.

At the moment, she's more focused on her beans—plump, brown borlotti that have simmered for an hour with chopped yellow onions and rosemary, the first and richly aromatic stage of pasta con fagioli, which she is preparing for me and Salvatore Messineo, the retired stolen art investigator to whom the Italian government entrusted the winery when it was taken from the Mafia. Because of course.

The winery's history is complex; Ferruzza's cooking is not. In a white plaster-and-terra cotta kitchen with soaring ceilings and views of rolling hills that stretch down to the sea, she prepares sausages so tender they bleed juices onto the roasted potatoes they accompany. Ditalini pasta is tossed creamy with ricotta and olive oil.

> "Such a simple marriage of ingredients, yet so satisfying."

on her outdoor patio kitchen over-looking a similarly evocative and equally rolling Sicilian countryside.

Of course, same is relative. In Sicily—as with much of Italy—"same" changes region to region, town to town, parent to child. Arena favors red over yellow onions, adds diced carrots and grape tomatoes; the former to sweeten the dish, the latter to add gentle acidity. She also adds wild fennel fronds that grow weed-like in her yard, adding a lightly peppery note. And she leaves off the cheese, allowing the starch of the pasta and beans to give the dish all the creamy body it needs.

Back at Milk Street, we created a streamlined hybrid of the two dishes. We liked Arena's addition of tomatoes, which helped lighten and brighten the heavier ingredients. But much as we loved her use of wild fennel—her husband tried to send me home with armfuls of it—it's not common here. Instead, we got the same anise flavor by combining fennel bulb and fennel seeds.

Though we liked the dish topped with ricotta salata, we liked it even better with the more assertively flavored pecorino Romano, a cousin cheese (ricotta salata is often made from the whey left in the making of pecorino Romano). The result was deli-cious, but still felt a bit flat. Our out-of-season tomatoes weren't adding the same sweetness or acidity as Arena's Sicilian variet-ies. So to brighten the dish a bit, we added lemon zest and juice.

The result was robust, yet light and herbal. A pasta even a Mafia don could love.

—J.M. Hirsch

And the pasta con fagioli—pasta with beans—a recipe that, if we are being honest, sounds better suited to college-dorm cooking. Yet in Ferruzza's hands, it is sub-stantial, rustic, clean and herbal. No. It is wonderful. Her method is simple: Those beans, thickly saucy and richly infused with rosemary and garlic, are tossed with more ditalini and a splash of the starchy cooking water. Grated ricotta salata cheese adds creamy-salty notes that balance the meaty yet tender beans. A whole greater than the sum.

Such a simple marriage of ingredients, yet so satisfying. But I wondered whether it was the wine talking—for it flowed liberally that lunch. Until later that day, when I made my way an hour inland to Castelbuono, a 14th-century hilltop town and home to Maria Enza Arena, a shopkeeper who'd agreed to teach me the same dish, cooking

Pasta con Fagioli
Pasta with Beans

Start to finish: 35 minutes Servings: 6

Sicilian cooks showed us how rosemary, lemon and tomatoes keep a rustic pasta and bean dish light and fresh. We were taught how to make pasta con fagioli by Piera Ferruzza, winery cook at Cantina della Val di Suro, and Maria Enza Arena, shopkeeper in the hilltop town of Castelbuono. In Italy, dried borlotti beans (often called cranberry beans in the U.S.) are used. For weeknight ease, we opted for canned beans. Some producers label canned borlotti beans as "Roman beans." If you cannot find them, use pink or kidney beans, which have a similar creaminess and mildly sweet flavor. Don't use cannellini beans, which are too tender. The pasta is boiled only until very slightly softened, then drained and rinsed to stop the cooking. It finishes cooking when combined with the beans and vegetables.

Don't rinse the canned beans after draining them; the starchy liquid clinging to them adds body to the sauce.

In a large Dutch oven over medium-high, bring 2 quarts water to a boil. Add the pasta and 1½ teaspoons salt. Cook, stirring occasionally, until just shy of al dente. Reserve 2 cups of cooking water, then drain and rinse with cold water until cool; set aside.

In the same pot, over medium-high, heat 3 tablespoons of oil until barely smoking. Add the tomatoes, then cover, reduce to medium and cook, stirring occasionally, until lightly charred, about 5 minutes. Add the onion, sliced fennel and ¼ teaspoon salt, then cook on medium-high, stirring occasionally, until the vegetables begin to soften, about 5 minutes.

Add the garlic, rosemary, fennel seeds and pepper flakes, then cook, stirring, until fragrant, about 30 seconds. Stir in the beans, broth and ⅛ cup of the reserved cooking water. Bring to a simmer over medium-high. Cover, reduce to medium and cook, stirring once or twice, until the vegetables are tender, about 10 minutes.

Add the pasta and cook, stirring frequently, until the pasta is al dente and the sauce is creamy, 3 to 5 minutes. If needed, add the remaining reserved cooking water 1 tablespoon at a time to reach the proper consistency. Off heat, stir in the lemon zest and juice and the remaining 2 tablespoons oil. Taste and season with salt and pepper. Serve with the cheese and additional oil for drizzling.

8 ounces campanelle or other short pasta

Kosher salt and ground black pepper

5 tablespoons extra-virgin olive oil, divided, plus more to serve

2 pints grape or cherry tomatoes

1 large red onion, chopped

1 large fennel bulb, halved, cored and thinly sliced

4 medium garlic cloves, minced

1 tablespoon minced fresh rosemary

1 teaspoon fennel seeds

¾ teaspoon red pepper flakes

Two 15½-ounce cans Roman beans (see headnote), drained but not rinsed

2 cups low-sodium chicken broth

2 teaspoons grated lemon zest, plus 2 tablespoons lemon juice

2 ounces pecorino Romano cheese, grated (1 cup)

In Veneto, cucina povera
tastes rich and full

Michela Tasca's calm poise belies an apparent love of the unexpected. Her vegetable stock, for example. An all-in affair that verges more on bisque than broth. Her career, too, from fashion designer to farmer. Even the farm itself is a model in the art of transformational pivots.

She stands in her mother-in-law's kitchen, one of several at the farm in Piombino Dese, a village 45 minutes northwest of Venice, and casually assembles samples of the region's rustic cooking. Pumpkin punctuated with onions, pine nuts and raisins. Bigoli pasta tossed with briny sardines and jammy onions. A simple rice and peas. Creamy polenta and shrimp.

And through each bite, her story—one of a farm and its family— unfolds. She met her husband, Ottorino Scquizzato, here in 1978. His sister was Tasca's friend and she wanted the two to meet. He didn't. "No, your friends are awful," he said. Or maybe not all of them. Their first date they ate rabbit stew and danced to Lucio Battisti in a room just off this same kitchen.

The farm has been in Scquizzato's family for nearly 100 years, a rambling assemblage of barns and bedrooms, stone paths that crunch under foot, mounds of pumpkins and winter squash that loiter in corners, and fowl. So many varieties of fowl. Except, it wasn't always a farm. And Scquizzato and the generations before him weren't always farmers.

Brooms, he says matter-of-factly while sitting—bundled against the chilly, rainy day—in what the family calls the Summer Room, a large hall with walls of black-and-white photos of relatives past. Until WWII, the tidy 4-hectare farm was home to the family's broom-making business. Old school straw brooms.

Then came the war. And with it, plastic. Natural brooms fell from favor, so his family did the first of several pivots. With 100 cows—a considerable number for the period—broom making gave way to dairy farming. But in time, the growth of industrial-scale agriculture forced yet another reckoning.

Tasca, meanwhile, worked with her father and siblings in fashion. But as the farm struggled, she decided it was time for a new challenge. The cows were replaced by heritage poultry and heirloom produce. Spare bedrooms were opened to paying guests, a nod to the many strangers who invited themselves over the years after mistaking the family's rollicking and sprawling dinners for a restaurant. And Tasca returned to school, earning a graduate degree in food culture.

As she stands in the kitchen this day, calmly stirring rice and peas—risi e bisi—you'd think it all was planned. Of course, that's the lesson. Tasca and Scquizzato reflect perfectly the food around them. Cucina povera, as the cooking of Veneto is, too often is translated too literally. Poor kitchen.

"Simple, beautiful, delicious and adaptive."

But that's not a reflection of the food or the people who prepare it.

There is nothing poor about this food. Rather, it is about making delicious whatever you happen to have around you. Just as Tasca and Scquizzato built a delicious life out of brooms. And cows. And produce. And fashion. And poultry.

And today, they build it for me from peas and rice.

The risi e bisi consists of tender, plump grains of starchy white rice cooked with peas. There is no dairy, but the rice nonetheless makes it creamy. "Risi e bisi is neither a risotto nor a soup. It is half and half," she explains. "It has too much broth to be a risotto. But it's too thick to be a soup." Except Tasca's take is different from any I've seen. Of course.

She begins by making a vegetable broth, but not like any I've had. Carrot, onion, celery and parsley simmer in water. This I expect. Some peas go in, too. But when most cooks would strain out and discard the vegetables, Tasca grabs an immersion blender and purees the mixture until smooth and minty green.

The rest is conventional. The results are anything but. Rice is cooked with pancetta and onion, with the rich broth slowly ladled in, plumping the rice. More peas—and I love that even here in Italy, when peas are out of season, frozen are just fine—are stirred in at the end, preserving their color and flavor. Grated Parmesan adds savory depth. The finished dish is equally fresh and rich, so much more than simple rice and peas. The secret, of course, is the broth, adding flavor and body.

More than anything, we loved Tasca's approach to food. Simple, beautiful, delicious and adaptive. Like her life. Like her farm.

—J.M. Hirsch

Risi e Bisi

Venetian Rice and Peas

Start to finish: 1¼ hours Servings: 4 to 6

At her B&B outside Venice, designer-turned-farmer Michela Tasca showed us how a pea puree gives traditional rice and peas a stylish and flavorful upgrade. Risi e bisi is a classic Venetian dish, traditionally eaten on April 25, St. Mark's Day. Much like risotto, the rice is rich and creamy because of the starchiness of the grains and how they are cooked. But risi e bisi typically is a bit soupier. Sweet peas stud the dish, and in the version taught to us by Tasca, owner of Ca' de Memi farm and bed and breakfast in Piombino Dese outside of Venice, the al dente grains were bathed in beautiful pale green broth, a result of peas pureed into the cooking liquid. For our version, we puree peas plus fresh parsley with a small amount of a broth infused with aromatics. To keep the flavors and color vibrant, we hold off on adding the puree, along with additional whole peas, until the rice has finished cooking. Pancetta provides salty, meaty backbone and fennel seeds, with their notes of licorice, complement the grassy, sweetness of the peas. Vialone nano is the preferred variety of Italian medium-grain rice for risi e bisi, but easier-to-find Arborio works just as well.

Don't thaw all of the peas. The 1 cup of peas that's blended with hot broth and parsley should be kept frozen so that the puree remains a brilliant green; the 1 cup stirred in at the end should be fully thawed and at room temperature so the peas don't cool the rice.

In a large pot, combine the carrot, the sliced onion, celery, fennel seeds, broth and 2 cups water. Bring to a boil over medium-high, then cover, reduce to medium-low and simmer until the vegetables have softened, 10 to 12 minutes.

Remove the pot from the heat and, using a slotted spoon, transfer the solids to a blender, draining off as much liquid as possible. Add 1 cup of the broth to the blender along with the still-frozen peas and the parsley; leave the remaining broth in the pot so it remains warm. Blend until the mixture is smooth, 1½ to 2 minutes; you should have about 3 cups puree. Set aside in the blender jar.

In a large saucepan over medium, combine the chopped onion, pancetta and 2 tablespoons butter. Cook, stirring occasionally, until the onion is lightly browned and the pancetta is rendered and lightly browned, 6 to 8 minutes. Add the rice and stir until the grains are coated with fat, then stir in 1 cup of the broth. Cook, stirring, until the liquid is mostly absorbed, about 5 minutes. Ladle in additional broth to barely cover the rice and simmer, stirring often, until the broth is mostly absorbed. Repeat the addition of broth and

---

1 medium carrot, peeled and thinly sliced

1 large white onion, half thinly sliced, half finely chopped

1 medium celery stalk, thinly sliced

2 teaspoons fennel seeds

1 quart low-sodium chicken broth, divided

2 cups frozen peas, divided (1 cup still frozen, 1 cup thawed and at room temperature)

2 cups lightly packed fresh flat-leaf parsley

3 to 4 ounces pancetta, finely chopped

4 tablespoons salted butter, cut into 1-tablespoon pieces, divided

1 cup vialone nano or Arborio rice

2 ounces Parmesan cheese, finely grated (1 cup), plus more to serve

Kosher salt and ground black pepper

simmering until mostly absorbed 4 or 5 times, until the rice is al dente and most of the broth has been used; this process should take 25 to 30 minutes.

Remove the pan from the heat and let stand uncovered for 5 minutes. Add the thawed peas and the puree, then stir until heated through, about 1 minute. Add the remaining 2 tablespoons butter and stir until melted. Stir in the Parmesan, then taste and season with salt and pepper. Serve sprinkled with additional Parmesan.

In a town better known for its music, we learned a new way with an old classic

Cremona is known for one thing, and it isn't risotto. Maybe it should be.

Tucked along the Po River in northern Italy, Cremona has been an epicenter of music since the 12th century, and has been home to some of the world's most renowned string instrument makers since the 16th century.

I went there on a lark, told it was a beautiful town for an afternoon stroll. Probably true, when it isn't a frigid downpour. Which is why instead of appreciating the town and its music scene, I dashed into Osteria Pane e Salame.

The Bread and Salami Restaurant.

Small, but airy with vaulted stone ceilings, the space began as a bar more than 60 years ago, eventually becoming a restaurant. Antonio Statella has owned the place for about 12 years. He doesn't know how it got its name.

But he does know that same name gave rise to what has become the restaurant's signature dish—Risotto Pane e Salame. I probably don't need to translate, right?

I was intrigued. Meat in risotto, while not common, I could wrap my head around. But bread? Worth a try. When it arrived at the table, there was no mystery to it. A creamy risotto studded with bits of meat, all of it topped with crunchy breadcrumbs and a dusting of Parmesan cheese.

It was impressively good. Creamy, rich, crunchy, meaty and savory all at once. The meat was tiny chunks of salamelle di Mantova, a local sweet and garlicky sausage. The breadcrumbs were irregular, some fine and melting into the rice, others big and chunky, all of it toasted in peppery olive oil and mixed with tons of rosemary.

Despite my apprehension of carb-on-carb, the combination was delicious. As chef Lexie Garcia walked me through the recipe, she explained that a former chef gets the credit for creating it. Apparently, he was inspired to combine dishes and ingredients from around the region—risotto from Milan, Parmesan from Parma, that wonderful sausage.

The bread? Just from the restaurant's name, Garcia said. In a town otherwise built on violins... Why not?

—J.M. Hirsch

"Creamy, rich, crunchy, meaty and savory all at once."

Risotto Pane e Salame
Risotto with Sausage and Herbed Breadcrumbs

Start to finish: 1 hour Servings: 4 to 6

In Cremona, chef Lexie Garcia taught us this unusual dish that pairs creamy rice with crisp breadcrumbs. Risotto pane e salame, or risotto with bread and sausage, is the signature dish of Osteria Pane e Salame. We developed a recipe based on the method taught to us by Garcia, chef at the osteria. In place of salamella di mantova, a local Lombardian sausage with mild garlic flavor, we use sweet or hot Italian sausage, and only enough to lend the rice meaty, porky flavor without weighing it down. Dry white wine supplies a touch of acidity, but as the cooking liquid, we use water, not broth, which allows the flavor of the rice, sausage, herbs and toasted bread to come through more clearly. We stir in a couple tablespoons of butter and Parmesan cheese at the end—an Italian technique called mantecatura, or blending—that helps develop additional creaminess in the risotto.

Don't discard the hot water in the saucepan until the risotto is completely finished. As the rice rests off heat in the saucepan for 10 minutes, its consistency will thicken, so you may need a little more hot water to thin it before serving.

3 tablespoons salted butter, cut into 3 pieces, divided

3 ounces country-style bread, torn into ½-inch pieces (about 2 cups)

1 teaspoon fresh rosemary, finely chopped

¼ cup lightly packed fresh flat-leaf parsley, finely chopped

8 ounces sweet or hot Italian sausage, casings removed

1 small yellow onion, finely chopped

Kosher salt and ground black pepper

1 cup carnaroli rice or Arborio rice

½ cup dry white wine

1 ounce Parmesan cheese, finely grated (½ cup), plus more to serve

In a medium saucepan over medium, bring 6 cups water, covered, to a simmer. Reduce to low to keep warm. In a large saucepan over medium, melt 1 tablespoon butter; add the bread and cook, stirring, until browned and crisp, 6 to 8 minutes. Add the rosemary and cook, stirring, until fragrant, about 30 seconds. Transfer to a bowl and stir in the parsley; set aside. Wipe out the saucepan.

In the same saucepan over medium, melt 1 tablespoon of the remaining butter. Add the sausage and cook, breaking it into small pieces, until no longer pink and beginning to brown, 5 to 6 minutes. Using a slotted spoon, transfer to a small bowl; set aside. To the fat remaining in the pan, add the onion and ¼ teaspoon each salt and pepper. Cook over medium, stirring occasionally, until softened, about 3 minutes.

Add the rice and cook, stirring, until the grains are translucent at the edges, 1 to 2 minutes. Add the wine and cook, stirring, until most of the liquid is absorbed, 1 to 2 minutes. Add 2 cups of the hot water and bring to a boil over medium-high. Reduce to medium and simmer, stirring often and briskly, until most of the liquid is absorbed, 8 to 10 minutes. Add another 2 cups hot water and cook until most of the liquid is absorbed and the rice is tender, with just a little firmness at the center of the grains, 6 to 9 minutes.

Off heat, quickly stir in the sausage and any accumulated juices, the remaining 1 tablespoon butter and the Parmesan; it's fine if the butter and cheese do not

fully melt. Cover and let stand 10 minutes. (Reserve the remaining hot water in the saucepan for adjusting the consistency of the risotto at the end, if needed.)

Stir to fully incorporate the butter and cheese. If the risotto is stiff and dry, stir in additional water, a couple tablespoons at a time, until the risotto is "loose" but not soupy. Taste and season with salt and pepper. Serve immediately, sprinkled with the breadcrumbs and additional Parmesan.

A soup that's a love affair
with simplicity

The menu at Trattoria Bel Mi' Colle reads a bit like a lyrical shopping list, each dish sprawling across multiple lines, offering ingredient combinations sometimes curious, but always alluring.

Il Tortino di Pecorino al Latte Crudo Saba con Formaggio dal Cuore Cremoso e Pera al Vin Santo for example. A creamy pecorino cheese pie with pears cooked in vin santo wine. Or Gli Gnocchi di Patata con lo Zafferano in Pistilli dell'Orto, Mandorle e Cipolla di Certaldo Caramallata. Gnocchi with saffron from the garden, almonds and caramelized onions.

Even the restaurant's name leans poetic, roughly translating as My Beautiful Hill Restaurant. It fits. Chef-owner Gabriele Borgianni's restaurant is nestled in the cozy valley below Colle Val d'Elsa, a Tuscan town perched almost cinematically atop a hill reachable only by narrow winding roads designed for carts, not cars.

In fact, from the start these sorts of romantic nods were baked into Trattoria Bel Mi' Colle, which occupies a building that dates to the 9th century and is home to the city's first commercial oven from the same period.

"My family was peasant. We had good, genuine proper food on the table when I was growing up," said Borgianni, who opened the restaurant in 2012 largely as a way to spend more time with his work and life partner; she handles the dining room while he manages the kitchen. "I've tried to

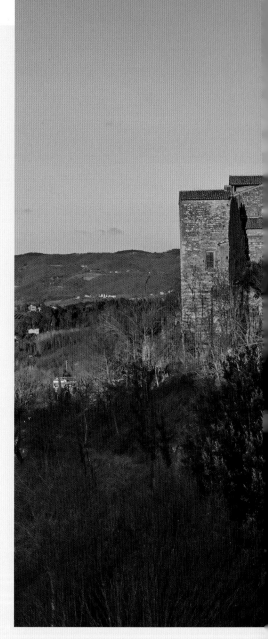

"A dish truly worth climbing up and down any beautiful hill for."

stay true to that in my cooking, respecting the ingredients."

Hence, the menu. If the business is a testament of his love for his girlfriend, the menu is for the bursting fresh ingredients he sources from nearby farms. And it shows. That pie actually was a puff of egg pastry filled with pecorino cream and candied fruit. The gnocchi were a wild blend of floral saffron, sweet onions and crunchy almonds, all bathing pillowy pasta.

And there was beef—Lo Stracotto di Guancia di Manzo con Cipolla di Certaldo e Chianti Classico—so tender you needed a spoon to eat it. Despite the mouthful of a name, it was little more than beef cheeks braised near forever in Chianti.

Simple dishes like that are where Borgianni's cooking—and this region's foods—truly shined. Easily the best dish he made was la striscia coi ceci, a humble chickpea and pasta soup. It's a classic, but he elevated it.

Garlic, rosemary, prosciutto and onion, all pureed, then added to chickpeas and tomatoes. When the beans are tender, most cooks would add pasta and call it good. Borgianni instead purees again, creating a rich liquid jammed with herbal-meaty flavor. Only then is the pasta added.

A dish truly worth climbing up and down any beautiful hill for.

—J.M. Hirsch

Striscia coi Ceci

Tuscan Chickpea and Pasta Soup

Start to finish: 50 minutes Servings: 4 to 6

Gabriele Borgianni, chef-owner at Trattoria Bel Mi' Colle in Colle di Val d'Elsa, showed us how to add texture and flavor to an everyday soup by pureeing some ingredients and toasting pasta to bring out its nutty flavors. Cooking in a centuries-old building in the Tuscan hills, Borgianni showed us how to cook striscia coi ceci, which translates as "strips with chickpeas." He pureed some of the ingredients for a soup that was especially rich and creamy and a perfect contrast to linguine-like pasta that was broken into pieces, toasted and cooked directly in the soup. We loved the flavors but wanted to lighten the dish, so we opted for more delicate capellini. Toasting the pasta prior to simmering it directly in the soup brings out nutty, wheaty notes. If you have spaghetti, it will work, but skip larger pasta shapes, such as shells or thick strands like fettuccine, as they will make the soup too heavy and starchy.

Don't blend the chickpea mixture without first letting it cool for about 15 minutes, and be sure to blend in batches, starting on the lowest speed and gradually increasing it. This helps ensure hot liquid won't spout out the top of the blender jar when the motor is turned on. Holding the lid securely in place with a kitchen towel or potholder also is a good idea.

2 tablespoons extra-virgin olive oil, divided, plus more to serve

4 ounces capellini, broken into ½-inch to 1-inch pieces

4 ounces pancetta, chopped

1 small yellow onion, chopped

2 medium garlic cloves, smashed and peeled

1 tablespoon fresh rosemary

Kosher salt and ground black pepper

3 tablespoons tomato paste

Two 15½-ounce cans chickpeas, rinsed and drained

2 tablespoons lemon juice, plus lemon wedges to serve

¼ cup lightly packed flat-leaf parsley, chopped

Finely grated Parmesan cheese, to serve

In a large saucepan over medium, combine 1 tablespoon oil and the pasta. Cook, stirring, until toasted and browned, 2 to 3 minutes. Using a slotted spoon, transfer to a small bowl; set aside. To the fat remaining in the pan, add the remaining 1 tablespoon oil and the pancetta. Cook over medium, stirring occasionally, until browned and crisped, 5 to 7 minutes. Using the slotted spoon, transfer to a paper towel–lined plate; set aside.

Return the pan to medium and add the onion, garlic, rosemary, 1 teaspoon salt and ½ teaspoon pepper. Cook, stirring occasionally, until the onion has softened, about 3 minutes. Add the tomato paste and cook, stirring, until the paste darkens and sticks to the pan, about 2 minutes. Add the chickpeas and 4 cups water; bring to a boil over medium-high, scraping up any browned bits. Reduce to medium-low and simmer, uncovered and stirring occasionally, until the chickpeas have softened and some have broken apart, 15 to 20 minutes. Remove from the heat and cool for 15 minutes.

Using a blender and working in 2 batches to avoid overfilling the jar, process the chickpea mixture until smooth, 1 to 2 minutes, scraping the blender jar as needed. Return the puree to the saucepan. Add 2 cups water and ½ teaspoon salt, then bring to a simmer over medium. Add the pasta and cook, stirring often and scraping along

the bottom of the pan to prevent sticking, until al dente, about 8 minutes. The soup should have a consistency similar to heavy cream; if needed, stir in water to thin.

Off heat, stir in the lemon juice. Taste and season with salt and pepper. Ladle into bowls, drizzle with additional oil and sprinkle with the parsley and reserved pancetta. Serve with lemon wedges and Parmesan on the side.

Bitter, sweet and crunchy, radicchio transforms risotto

Lino Tenimenti was tender, almost reverential as he picked through neatly stacked boxes of scarlet-streaked radicchio. Some resembled finger-like tendrils. Others were tightly bunched, many-layered oblongs. Finally, he settled on one that resembled a large, rose-tinted head of lettuce, sprawling with creased, crisp leaves.

"This isn't radicchio," he told me, splaying its leaves. "It's a work of art."

And a delicious one, at that. I love radicchio in all its many varieties, but until visiting Tenimenti's farm—where his family has grown radicchio for nearly 50 years—I had no idea how truly varied it can be. Nor how much work it takes to produce it.

Treviso, a centuries old city in northern Italy cut through by numerous canals, is known for three things—prosecco, tiramisù and radicchio. It's a trio that belongs together, because after enough sparkling wine and creamy, coffee-sodden dessert, the crisp, gently bitter-fresh crunch of radicchio brings welcome balance.

Lino explained that how bitter, how beautiful, how crisp, even how a radicchio is shaped all depend as much on location as variety. Radicchio is a chameleon, he explained, adapting well to most any weather and climate by changing its shape, color and taste. So the plants grown at his farm can be wildly different than those produced even at a neighboring farm.

And getting it from farm to table is an ordeal. The plants spend several months in the earth, where they look entirely inedible—overgrown, wilted weeds seemingly better suited for a witch's brew. Pulled from the dirt, they are trimmed and floated in massive tanks of circulating spring water for another month, a process that crisps and plumps them.

"This isn't radicchio. It's a work of art."

Only at this stage do they begin to resemble the vegetable we know. Prepping them for the produce aisle is a three-person job. The first further trims away the outer leaves, finally revealing the beautiful interior. A second deftly slices off the roots, then dunks the head in a tub of water to clean it. A final person again trims away exterior leaves.

Italians eat the resulting heads—now less than a quarter of the starting size—numerous ways, including mixed with ricotta and stuffed into pasta shells, as well as paired with sweet scamorza cheese and heaped onto crispy crostini.

But my favorite involved roughly chopping the radicchio and stirring it into another northern Italian specialty: risotto.

As I ate my way around the city, I noticed that successfully marrying crunchy radicchio with creamy rice is all a matter of timing. By far, the best version I ate was at Trattoria Toni de Spin—a restaurant that dates to the 1800s—where chef Guido Severin is careful to add only some of the radicchio at the start of the cooking.

It mattered. That early addition cooked down with the rice and onion, its bitterness mellowing and its crunch giving way to a

sweet creaminess that complemented the starchy rice. But the bulk of the radicchio was added only during the final minutes of cooking, allowing it to keep its assertive flavor and crunch, becoming the perfect counterpoint to the risotto.

Other versions I ate built on this, adding pork—sometimes as sausage, sometimes as pancetta or guanciale—the richness of which balanced the vegetable. Also copious red wine, staining the dish until the entire thing looked rather radicchio-like.

Indeed, a work of art.

—J.M. Hirsch

Risotto al Radicchio con Vino Rosso e Pancetta

Radicchio–Red Wine Risotto with Pancetta

Start to finish: 50 minutes Servings: 4 to 6

In Treviso, famous for its radicchio, local cooks showed us how to balance the crisp bitterness of the rosy-hued vegetable with creamy rice, red wine and the richness of butter. Radicchio, a purple-hued member of the chicory family, contains anthocyanins, or red pigments, that give the dish its characteristic mauve hue. In Treviso, we tried versions made by home cook Alessandra Bianchi and chef Guido Severin of Trattoria Toni de Spin. To balance radicchio's bitterness, pork often joins the mix. We use pancetta for its salty complexity. Butter also is an important ingredient in radicchio risotto. It lends a sweet, dairy richness that beautifully rounds out the flavors. In lieu of vegetable or chicken broth, we use a combination of red wine and water. Red wine is a key ingredient, so be sure to choose one you would drink, preferably an Italian variety. We like a fruity, light-bodied red wine, such as barbera or Valpolicella.

Don't add all the radicchio at once. Half the head gets cooked down with the rice, allowing it to melt and sweeten. The second half is added toward the end of cooking. This keeps it crisp, creating contrast with the creamy grains.

4 ounces pancetta, chopped

3 tablespoons salted butter, cut into 1-tablespoon pieces, divided

1 small red onion, finely chopped

1 cup carnaroli or Arborio rice

1 cup dry red wine (see headnote)

8-ounce head radicchio, bruised outer leaves removed, halved, cored and chopped into ½-inch pieces (about 3 cups)

1 ounce Parmesan cheese, finely grated (½ cup), plus more to serve

Kosher salt and ground black pepper

1 tablespoon finely chopped fresh chives

In a medium saucepan over medium, bring 6 cups water, covered, to a simmer. Reduce to low to keep warm. In a large saucepan over medium-high, combine the pancetta and 1 tablespoon butter. Cook, stirring, until the pancetta has rendered its fat and begins to brown, 4 to 5 minutes. Using a slotted spoon, transfer half of the pancetta to a small bowl; set aside.

Return the pan to medium-high and add the onion. Cook, stirring, until softened, 3 to 4 minutes. Add the rice and cook, stirring often, until the grains are translucent at the edges, 1 to 2 minutes. Add the wine and cook, stirring and scraping up any browned bits, until mostly evaporated, 3 to 4 minutes.

Stir in half of the radicchio followed by 2 cups of the hot water.

Bring to a boil, then reduce to medium and simmer, stirring often and briskly, until most of the liquid is absorbed, 8 to 10 minutes. Add another 2 cups hot water and cook until most of the liquid is absorbed, 6 to 9 minutes.

Add the remaining radicchio and another ½ cup hot water. Cook, stirring, until the rice is loose but not soupy, and is tender, with just a little firmness at the center, about 3 minutes. Off heat, stir in the remaining 2 tablespoons butter and the Parmesan. If the risotto is stiff and dry, stir in additional hot water, 1 tablespoon at a time, to achieve the proper consistency; you may not need all of the water. Taste and season with salt and pepper. Serve immediately, sprinkled with the reserved pancetta, chives, additional Parmesan and ground black pepper.

Fagioli in Salsa

White Beans and Tomatoes with Anchovies and Vinegar

Start to finish: 25 minutes Servings: 4

This simple and remarkably flavorful bean dish was inspired by a classic from Italy's Veneto region, fagioli in salsa (or fasoi in salsa). It usually is made with borlotti beans, extra-virgin olive oil, anchovies and garlic. We use canned cannellini beans and include a generous amount of vinegar, as is traditional, to lend a pleasant sharpness. Cherry or grape tomatoes add juiciness, sweetness and color, and lots of chopped parsley lends fresh, grassy notes. Depending on what you have in your refrigerator, feel free to swap in another herb, such as basil, or a big handful of peppery arugula.

Don't bother chopping the anchovy fillets. They will break down during cooking as they are stirred into the carrot-garlic mixture.

In a 12-inch skillet, combine the oil and garlic. Cook over medium, stirring occasionally, until the garlic starts to brown, 1 to 2 minutes. Add the carrot and anchovies; cook, stirring, until the anchovies are completely broken down, 1 to 2 minutes.

Add the vinegar, reduce to medium-low and cook, stirring, until the vinegar is reduced by about half, about 5 minutes. Add the beans and tomatoes; cook, stirring, until the tomatoes are slightly softened, 5 to 8 minutes.

Off heat, stir in the parsley. Taste and season with salt and pepper. Serve drizzled with additional oil.

¼ cup extra-virgin olive oil, plus more to serve

3 medium garlic cloves, thinly sliced

1 large carrot, peeled and finely chopped

4 to 6 oil-packed anchovy fillets

½ cup white or red wine vinegar

Two 15½-ounce cans cannellini beans, rinsed and drained

1 pint cherry or grape tomatoes, halved

1 cup finely chopped fresh flat-leaf parsley

Kosher salt and ground black pepper

Ceci e Acciughe con Pasta

Chickpeas and Pasta with Herbs and Anchovies

Start to finish: 35 minutes Servings: 6 to 8

In the tranquil historic center of Prato in northeastern Tuscany, chef Vladimiro Gori taught us to tuck pasta into well-seasoned chickpeas for a deliciously saucy meal. Gori, chef and owner at Osteria Su Santa Trinità, taught us to make ceci e acciughe, or chickpeas with anchovies. Traditionally, it is a side dish of chickpeas cooked in olive oil infused with sage, rosemary and anchovies, with a bit of the bean cooking liquid creating a delicious sauce. But Gori sometimes tosses the mixture with short pasta, which we liked. We love curly or hollow pasta shapes that are close in size to the chickpeas and that have grooves and nooks to collect the silky sauce. If you'd prefer to use dried chickpeas, see p. 87 for cooking instructions. You will need 3 cups cooked and drained chickpeas, plus ½ cup cooking liquid.

Don't throw out the liquid left behind after draining the chickpeas. Called aquafaba, it has a silky texture and subtly sweet, nutty flavor. We use ½ cup of the liquid as part of the sauce and to add complexity to the dish.

In a large pot, bring 4 quarts water to a boil. Add the pasta and 1 tablespoon salt and cook, stirring occasionally, until just shy of al dente. Reserve ¾ cup of the cooking water, then drain. Return the pasta to the pot; set aside off heat.

In a 12-inch skillet over medium-high, combine the oil, anchovies, garlic, sage and rosemary. Cook, stirring, until fragrant and the garlic is golden, 1½ to 2 minutes. Add the chickpeas and pepper flakes. Cook, stirring and swirling the skillet, until the chickpeas are sizzling and golden, 3 to 4 minutes. Stir in the reserved chickpea liquid and lemon zest.

Scrape the chickpea mixture into the pot with the pasta and set over medium. Add ½ cup of the reserved pasta water and ¼ teaspoon each salt and black pepper. Cook, stirring, until the pasta is al dente, 2 to 3 minutes; add more pasta water as needed until the sauce clings. Off heat, stir in the lemon juice. Taste and season with salt. Serve drizzled with additional oil and sprinkled with black pepper.

1 pound cavatelli, orecchiette or ditalini

Kosher salt and ground black pepper

¼ cup extra-virgin olive oil, plus more to serve

8 to 10 oil-packed anchovy fillets, roughly chopped

4 medium garlic cloves, thinly sliced

2 tablespoons chopped fresh sage

2 tablespoons minced fresh rosemary

Two 15½-ounce cans chickpeas, drained, ½ cup liquid reserved (see headnote)

¼ to ½ teaspoon red pepper flakes

2 teaspoons grated lemon zest, plus 2 tablespoons lemon juice, divided

PASTA

In Amalfi, we learned new respect for the simple lemon

There was a time in Amalfi when only the women carried the lemons, hoisting onto their heads 140-pound crates jammed and glowing with softball-sized citrus. Trudging 1,500 steeply terraced steps blanketed green and dotted yellow downward to the Gulf of Salerno, to the markets, to the port, to the limoncello factories, wading through jasmine scented breezes.

Today, they get help. From the men. From a shaky, 52-year-old cable car. Yet much is unchanged. The lemons—sfusato Amalfitano, special to the hills of this valley-locked city along Italy's western coast—still underpin nearly everything here, infusing the economy, the cuisine, the culture, even the wine, produced from vines that share the lemon tree soil.

For six generations, Salvatore Aceto's family has grown lemons on these hills, his family arriving from Sicily around 1700. As he leads a strenuous tour of his farm, which steps its way up the hill to overlook the town, he plucks a lemon tenderly from branches supported by a lattice of dried willow branches overhead, the fruit's skin a gnarl of golden lumps.

"We don't have blood in the veins," says Aceto, who gave up a career in business to return to run the farm. "We have lemon juice. Lemons are everything for us."

In the U.S., lemons too often play too simple a role in our cooking, relegated to sweets or used as a simple acid that brightens, but rarely brings full force of flavor. I'd reached out to Aceto because in Amalfi cooks understand the transformative power of this simple fruit. I had no idea how deeply that conviction ran.

Of the lemon, nothing is wasted. The juice, of course, flavors everything, from chicken and octopus to pasta and cakes. Also the fragrant zest. But even the leaves are in play. Older leaves are smoldered to smoke cheese. Tender, young leaves are battered and fried in olive oil, says Aceto, whose nearly 3,000 lemon trees can produce 70 tons of lemons a season.

And these lemons—brought to the region centuries ago from the Middle East—are of another order, and not simply by size. The hills protect the trees from cold northern winds, allowing them to bask in a blend of cool sea breeze and strong coastal sun, a microclimate responsible for the fruit's delicate sweetness and low acidity.

Aceto's farm remains a family affair. His brother, Marco, transforms a third of each harvest into 80,000 liters of the local sweet-tart limoncello liqueur. His 86-year-old father, Luigi, still helps with the harvest, hauling 55-pound tubs down those many, many steps. And his wife—he and Giovanna met as teenagers in the lemon grove, of course—offers cooking lessons.

That day, she greets me from an open-air stone patio kitchen perched at the top of the hillside, lemon trees on all sides. She'd offered to teach

"The result is amazing, creamy, light, fresh. The taste of sunshine."

me three simple dishes that use lemons to deliver strikingly bright, citrusy flavor to everyday ingredients with weeknight-friendly time and effort. It was an easy sell.

She begins with spaghetti tossed with lemon pesto, a dish inspired by the classic basil-based pesto Genovese and one Giovanna feeds her family several times a month. But in this case, finely grated lemon zest—so much lemon zest!—stands in for the basil, creamy almonds take the place of pine nuts, and garlic—which might overwhelm the lemon—is simply left out.

The entire affair comes together in minutes, the pesto ingredients stirred together raw, waiting for the cooked pasta and a bit of its starchy water to be tossed and pull everything together. The result is phenomenal—al dente pasta with a sauce that hints at bright citrusy sweetness, yet remains decidedly

savory. The lemon accents without overwhelming.

For the next dish, she makes the pasta itself fresh, kneading into it more of that vibrant lemon zest. Sometimes she even adds the lemon zest to the cooking water, yet another effortless way to pull more of the flavor into the finished dish. But it's the simple sauce she makes next that I find so fascinating.

Working quickly with a knife, Giovanna trims away the white pith from the lemon she denuded of its zest until she is left with a juicy oblong of citrus flesh. She trims the segments away from the membranes, flicking out any seeds, then chops it and mounds the flesh in a skillet. To that, she adds chopped garlic, olive oil, salt and nothing else.

The pasta emerges tender and aromatic from boiling water in minutes, it and some of the water joining the ingredients in the pan.

A bare minute over low heat—"We want to keep the flavors fresh as much as possible"—then she finishes it with yet more zest and a sprinkle of parsley. The result is amazing, creamy, light, fresh. The taste of sunshine.

Salvatore wastes little time eating each dish as quickly as Giovanna serves it. He considers the lemons. That he eats. That hang above his head. That dictate his every day. Here, they are a part of everything in ways that cannot be teased apart.

"If we abandon (the farm), you don't just create problems for our family. You create a disaster for the community. Everything falls down. We have houses, a church and people. They all rely on lemons. I have to stay here. I don't have a choice," he says. And he seems pleased to do so.

—J.M. Hirsch

Fettuccine al Limone e Aglio

Lemon-Garlic Fettuccine

Start to finish: 40 minutes Servings: 4

In Amalfi, Giovanna Aceto showed us this delicious pasta dish of handmade lemon fettuccine tossed with a simple, quick sauté of garlic, olive oil and fresh lemon segments. To mimic the sweet, mild flavor of Amalfi lemons using the standard lemons available in U.S. supermarkets, we temper their tartness and acidity with a little sugar. Briefly cooking the lemon segments softens both their tang and texture so the pieces break down and disappear into the noodles. In place of freshly made lemon pasta, we opt for store-bought fresh fettuccine but boil it in water infused with strips of lemon zest; we later use some of the pasta water to build the sauce, and we chop the softened zest strips for tossing into the tangle of noodles.

Don't forget to remove the seeds from the lemon segments, as they have an unpleasant texture and flavor. Also, don't use more than 2 quarts water to boil the pasta. The goal is to create starchy, well-seasoned pasta water with which to make the sauce.

4 lemons

2 teaspoons white sugar, divided

Kosher salt and ground black pepper

3 tablespoons extra-virgin olive oil, divided, plus more to serve

9 ounces fresh fettuccine

2 medium garlic cloves, finely grated

½ teaspoon red pepper flakes

¼ cup finely chopped fresh flat-leaf parsley

Finely grated Parmesan cheese, to serve

Using a vegetable peeler (preferably a Y-style peeler), remove the zest from 2 lemons in long, wide strips; try to remove only the colored portion of the peel, not the bitter white pith beneath. Grate the zest from the remaining 2 lemons; reserve in a small bowl. Using a paring knife, cut about ½ inch off the top and bottom of one of the lemons and stand it on a cut end. Working from top to bottom, cut away the pith following the contours of the fruit, exposing the flesh. Now cut along both sides of the membranes separating the sections to free the segments. Remove and discard the seeds from the segments, then add the segments to a small bowl along with the juices. Repeat with a second lemon. Reserve the remaining 2 lemons for another use.

To the grated zest, add ½ teaspoon of the sugar and ½ teaspoon salt. Mix together with your fingers, then stir in 1 tablespoon of the oil; set aside. To the lemon segments and juice, add ½ teaspoon of the remaining sugar and ½ teaspoon salt; stir to combine and set aside.

In a large pot, combine 2 quarts water, 1½ teaspoons salt, the remaining 1 teaspoon sugar and the zest strips. Bring to a boil, cook for 2 minutes, then remove and reserve the zest. Add the pasta and cook until al dente, about 3 minutes. Reserve 1½ cups of the cooking water, then drain the pasta and return it to the pot. Finely chop the zest strips; set aside.

In a 12-inch skillet over medium, cook the remaining 2 tablespoons oil, garlic and pepper flakes, stirring, until the garlic is light golden, 1 to 2 minutes. Add the lemon segments with juices and cook, stirring, until fragrant and warmed through, about 30

seconds. Immediately add the mixture to the pasta in the pot along with ½ cup of the reserved pasta water, then toss to combine. Add the grated zest mixture, the parsley and the chopped zest, then toss again, adding more pasta water as needed so the pasta is silky and lightly sauced. Taste and season with salt and black pepper. Serve drizzled with additional oil and sprinkled with Parmesan.

Spaghetti al Pesto di Limone
Spaghetti with Lemon Pesto

Start to finish: 25 minutes Servings: 4

This pasta dish is modeled on the spaghetti al pesto di limone that Giovanna Aceto made for us on her family's farm in Amalfi. The lemons commonly available in the U.S. are more acidic than Amalfi's lemons, so to make a lemon pesto that approximates the original, we use a little sugar to temper the flavor. For extra citrus complexity, we add lemon zest to the pasta cooking water; the oils from the zest lightly perfume the spaghetti, reinforcing the lemony notes of the pesto.

Don't forget to remove the lemon zest from the boiling water before dropping in the pasta. If left in as the spaghetti cooks, the zest may turn the water bitter, and the strips are a nuisance to remove from the strands of cooked noodles.

Using a vegetable peeler (preferably a Y-style peeler), remove the zest from the lemons in long, wide strips; try to remove only the colored portion of the peel, not the bitter white pith just underneath. You should have about ⅓ cup zest strips.

In a large pot, combine 2 quarts water, 1½ teaspoons salt, 1 teaspoon of sugar and half of the zest strips. Bring to a boil and cook for 2 minutes, then remove and discard the zest. Add the spaghetti and cook until al dente. Reserve 1½ cups of the cooking water, then drain the pasta and return it to the pot.

Meanwhile, in a food processor, combine the remaining zest strips, the almonds, Parmesan, the remaining ½ teaspoon sugar and ¼ teaspoon each salt and pepper. Process until the mixture resembles coarse sand, 10 to 20 seconds. Add the oil and process just until the oil is incorporated (the mixture will not be smooth), about another 10 seconds; set aside until the pasta is ready.

To the spaghetti in the pot, add the pesto and ¾ cup of the reserved pasta water, then toss to combine; add more reserved pasta water as needed so the pesto coats the noodles. Toss in the chives. Taste and season with salt and pepper. Serve drizzled with additional oil and with additional grated Parmesan on the side.

4 lemons

Kosher salt and ground black pepper

1½ teaspoons white sugar, divided

1 pound spaghetti

½ cup slivered almonds

1 ounce (without rind) Parmesan cheese, cut into rough 1-inch pieces, plus finely grated Parmesan to serve

⅓ cup extra-virgin olive oil, plus more to serve

2 tablespoons finely chopped fresh chives

Fabio Berti and Alessandro Gozzi make fun out of pasta, Bologna style

The first thing that happens after we pull up in our white van outside of Trattoria Bertozzi, a short drive from central Bologna, is that our guide, Alessandro, is given a huge bear hug by the other Alessandro, co-owner of the trattoria. This is a far cry from the heyday of the hushed temples of gastronomy—Alain Ducasse or Joël Robuchon—where one came to pray to the culinary gods. The two owners, Fabio Berti and Alessandro Gozzi, live full-throttle, hugging every ounce of enjoyment from life, whether Gozzi is spitting a mouthful of water at Berti or each of them sporting a tortellino (the Italian singular for tortellini) stuck to their foreheads. Their menu starts out with the following: "You can make a call, send texts, take a selfie, play Candy Crush, take photos of dishes and tweet." But instead, they suggest that "you have some chit-chat, even if about nothing, but with the illusion in our hearts that we are not yet dead." A warning, of sorts, but done with great poetry. With that, I stepped into the kitchen to learn how to make gramigna Bertozzi, with guanciale, zucchine, zafferano e scaglie di Parmigiano: a curly, macaroni-style pasta with zucchini and a saffron cream sauce topped with shavings of Parmesan. I was also there to have a good time.

Bolognese cuisine is often called "Bologna la Grassa" ("Bologna the Fat"), since local ingredients both define the cooking and are inherently rich: Parmesan cheese, pork, veal, beef, butter, cream, truffles and cured meats such as prosciutto. Local menus are full of dishes such as cotoletta alla Bolognese (a thin slice of veal with prosciutto and cheese), ragù Bolognese (a pasta sauce and lasagna filling), brasato di manzo (braised beef) and large plates of salumi. Yet one also finds lighter, simpler dishes such as tagliatelle with onion ragout, tortellini in brodo, passatelli (a quick pasta

"In Bologna, zucchini is married to pasta with the addition of cream and cheese."

made from breadcrumbs, Parmesan and eggs) or a large plate of sautéed wild mushrooms.

Fresh vegetables, however, tend to become ingredients rather than stars of the show. Zucchini is stuffed. Spinach is served with butter and Parmesan. You can get a simple mixed salad, but we are talking iceberg here—not an Alice Waters foraged mélange. So when it comes to a pasta dish with zucchini, do not expect California cuisine; in Bologna, zucchini is married to pasta with the addition of cream and cheese. Yet the artistry of balancing fat with flavor to produce a dish that is more than the sum of its parts—neither heavy nor bland, but light on the palate and full-throttle like the

trattoria's owners—is a thing to behold.

For gramigna Bertozzi, the method was simple: Sauté guanciale; add half-rounds of zucchini and then some of the pasta water (the pasta had been cooked separately); simmer a few minutes; add a bit of cream, saffron and some almost-cooked gramigna pasta; then finish cooking in the skillet to marry the pasta and sauce. Top with shards of Parmesan.

Here at Milk Street we had to switch out a couple of ingredients—pancetta for the harder-to-find guanciale, and cavatappi, gemelli or a similar pasta for gramigna—but we took the rest of the recipe pretty much as gospel. We ended up with half-and-half instead of cream

(I am quite sure that neither Gozzi nor Berti would understand the culinary point of half-and-half) and ended up with a quick skillet pasta that transformed a pound of zucchini into a full-flavored dish that echoes the essential lessons of Bolognese cuisine—background notes of cured meat, a counterpoint of flavor (saffron), something fresh (zucchini) and a bit of dairy and pasta cooking water to pull it all together. Oh, and topping of Parmesan as a final flourish.

Perhaps this cuisine should be called "Cucina Divertimento" (fun)! And, while you are at it, stick a tortellino on your forehead, drink wine and laugh. That is the best recipe for a healthy heart.

—Christopher Kimball

Gramigna Bertozzi
Pasta with Zucchini, Pancetta and Saffron

Start to finish: 40 minutes   Servings: 4

This is our version of a fantastic pasta offering from Trattoria Bertozzi in Bologna. In lieu of guanciale (cured pork jowl), we opted for easier-to-find but equally meaty pancetta, and we lightened up the dish's richness by swapping half-and-half for the cream. The restaurant uses gramigna pasta, a tubular, curled shape from the Emilia-Romagna region. We found that more widely available cavatappi or gemelli works just as well combining with the zucchini and catching the lightly creamy sauce in its crevices.

Don't boil the pasta until al dente. Drain it when it has a little more bite than is desirable in the finished dish; the noodles will cook a bit more in the sauce. Also, don't forget to reserve 2 cups of the cooking water before draining the pasta.

Halve the zucchini lengthwise, then use a spoon to scrape out the seeds. Slice each half lengthwise about ¼ inch thick, then cut the strips crosswise into 1-inch sections. In a large pot, boil 4 quarts of water. Add the pasta and 1 tablespoon salt, then cook, stirring occasionally, until just shy of al dente. Reserve 2 cups of the cooking water, then drain. In a small bowl, combine 1½ cups of the reserved water and the saffron; set aside the remaining ½ cup water.

While the pasta cooks, in a 12-inch skillet over medium, cook the pancetta and garlic, stirring occasionally, until the pancetta has rendered some of its fat and begins to crisp, about 3 minutes. Remove and discard the garlic, then stir in the zucchini and ½ teaspoon pepper. Cook, stirring occasionally, until the pancetta is fully crisped and the zucchini is lightly browned, 4 to 6 minutes.

Add the pasta and the saffron water to the skillet. Bring to a simmer over medium-high and cook, stirring often, until the pasta is al dente, 4 to 5 minutes. Add the half-and-half and cook, stirring, until the sauce is lightly thickened and clings to the pasta, about 1 minute. Off heat, taste and season with salt and pepper. If needed, stir in additional reserved pasta water 1 tablespoon at a time to create a lightly creamy sauce. Transfer to a serving bowl and top with Parmesan.

1 pound zucchini

12 ounces short, curly pasta, such as cavatappi or gemelli

Kosher salt and ground black pepper

½ teaspoon saffron threads

3 ounces pancetta, finely chopped

1 medium garlic clove, smashed and peeled

½ cup half-and-half

1 ounce Parmesan cheese, shaved with a vegetable peeler

The creamiest pesto has no cheese, nuts or basil!

With a gentle scooping motion, Antonio Cioffi dredged a spoon over the surface of the... gelato? It curled up, brilliant green, smooth and so luxuriously chilly-creamy I couldn't help but wonder how heart-stoppingly delicious a spoonful would be. Was it pistachio? Mint? Maybe sweet green tea?

Not quite. Cioffi dropped the scoop into a skillet. As it melted, he added barely tender spaghetti. Flicking the pan back and forth with a practiced wrist, he quickly married the two into a brilliantly dressed pasta. It was not, in fact, gelato. Rather, it was a complete rethinking of pesto—vibrant emerald, deeply herbal and unlike any I'd ever tasted.

I'd come to Ravello—a hillside town on Italy's Amalfi Coast, where pine trees shaped like hot air balloons and scrubby rosemary bushes the size of cars dot terraces punctuated by churches with bells echoing down to the Tyrrhenian Sea—to learn Cioffi's modern takes on the region's classic cucina povera.

That day at his La Vecchia Cantina we dined on an ancient style of terrine his mother made, various bits of pig boiled until richly savory and sliceable like pie. And on pillowy-tender gnocchi, made with just flour and boiling water, a tradition that dates to a time when even potatoes were considered an extravagance.

But the star was his spaghetti al pesto di prezzemolo, or spaghetti with parsley pesto. Creamy, herbal and rich with hints of briny-savory, it was nothing like the classic pesto Genovese from 1,000 kilometers north, which gets its creamy richness and granular texture from pine nuts and Parmesan. This had neither.

The recipe was simple. Cioffi plunged a whole bunch of fresh parsley into boiling water for mere seconds, then pulled it out and plunged it into ice water. It's a process that preserves the intense green of the fresh herb. It also breaks down the plant's cell walls, allowing it to puree more smoothly. This explains the pesto's exceedingly creamy texture.

Pureed with olive oil, a hint of garlic, a drizzle of colatura di alici—a fermented condiment similar to Asian fish sauce—and a bit of lemon (it is the Amalfi Coast, after all), the result was fresh and grassy, savory and sweet. Tossed with al dente pasta, it tasted of summer in a bowl.

As for that gelato? A chef's trick that proved unnecessary at home. Cioffi goes through so much of this pesto at the restaurant that he prepares it in batches, which he freezes. Home cooks looking to preserve summer's herbs could, too, of course.

–J.M. Hirsch

"Creamy, herbal and rich with hints of briny-savory."

Spaghetti al Pesto di Prezzemolo
Spaghetti with Parsley Pesto

Start to finish: 25 minutes Servings: 4 to 6

On the Amalfi Coast, chef Antonio Cioffi taught us how to make a better pesto by blanching parsley before plunging it into ice-cold water and pureeing it for an exceedingly green and creamy texture. "Spaghetti with parsley pesto" is the literal translation, from the Italian, of spaghetti al pesto di prezzemolo, but it does not sufficiently convey the deliciousness of this dish. This recipe is our adaptation of the one taught to us by Cioffi at La Vecchia Cantina in Ravello. Cioffi uses neither nuts nor Parmesan in his incredibly savory parsley pesto. Rather, its umami richness and full, complex flavor came from colatura di alici, an Italian fermented anchovy condiment akin to Southeast Asian fish sauce. As we worked to re-create the dish, we learned that though the two fish-based ingredients share similarities, they were not interchangeable in this application. Colatura di alici is saltier, less pungent and smoother in taste than fish sauce. It does, however, require a trip to an Italian specialty store, so in its stead, we found just a single oil-packed anchovy fillet, rinsed and patted dry, to be a good substitute. If you wish to use a different pasta than spaghetti, twisty shapes such as fusilli and gemelli work nicely.

Don't skip the step of "shocking" the parsley in ice water after briefly blanching it. This immediately stops the cooking, keeping the color and flavor bright and fresh. Also, don't worry about wringing every last drop of water out of the parsley before pureeing. A little moisture is fine and helps with easy blending.

In a large pot, bring 4 quarts water to a boil. Fill a medium bowl with ice water and set it near the stovetop. To the boiling water, add 1 tablespoon salt and the parsley; cook, stirring, until just wilted, about 15 seconds. Using a slotted spoon or mesh sieve, immediately scoop out the parsley and transfer it to the ice bath. Let stand, stirring once or twice, until fully chilled, about 2 minutes. Reduce the heat under the pot to medium.

Remove the parsley from the ice bath and squeeze with your hands until mostly dry. Roughly chop the parsley, then add it to a blender along with the garlic, colatura de alici or anchovy and the oil. Puree on high, scraping the blender jar as needed, until the mixture is smooth and thick, 1 to 2 minutes. If the parsley doesn't fully break down, while the blender is running, drizzle in cold water 1 teaspoon at a time as needed until the pesto is smooth.

Return the water to a boil over medium-high. Add the pasta and cook, stirring occasionally, until al dente. Reserve about ¾ cup of the cooking water, then drain the pasta and return it to the pot. Add the pesto and ½ cup of the reserved pasta water; cook over

---

Kosher salt and ground black pepper

1 large bunch flat-leaf parsley (about 4 ounces), trimmed of bottom 1 inch

1 small garlic clove, smashed and peeled

2½ teaspoons colatura di alici (see headnote) or 1 oil-packed anchovy fillet, rinsed and patted dry

¾ cup extra-virgin olive oil, plus more to serve

1 pound spaghetti

4 teaspoons grated lemon zest, plus 4 teaspoons lemon juice, plus more grated zest to serve

medium, vigorously tossing and
stirring, until the pesto clings to
the spaghetti, about 2 minutes.
Stir in the lemon zest and juice and
toss in more reserved pasta water
1 tablespoon at a time as needed

so the spaghetti is well sauced.
Remove from the heat, then taste
and season with salt and pepper.
Serve drizzled with additional
oil and sprinkled with additional
lemon zest.

No guanciale? Try zucchini!

Claudia Rinaldi was adamant but unconvincing when she assured me it's possible to make a satisfying, still-rich and utterly comforting pasta carbonara in which the hallmark fatty guanciale is replaced by zucchini. Because... Seriously?

Still, I'll admit to being intrigued. When properly cooked, zucchini can straddle a wonderful line between meaty and rich, yet still light and fresh. A pasta carbonara—too often a larded, hefty dish—able to walk that same line was alluring.

Rinaldi—a cookbook author and blogger who lives on the outskirts of Rome—and I had started the day at her neighborhood pasta shop, the sort of place where if they don't have the fresh noodle you want, they'll make it for you on the spot.

Back at her apartment, Rinaldi—who learned to cook from her Sicilian grandmother and was the sort of child who asked for anchovies for her 8th birthday—assured me that while it may sound like misguided vegetarianism, zucchini carbonara is a real dish with deep roots in Italy's tradition of cucina povera, or making do (and dinner) with whatever is available.

Crisped guanciale—cured pork cheeks—pecorino Romano cheese, eggs and ample black pepper are the classic combination that, when tossed with pasta and a bit of its starchy cooking water, transforms into carbonara.

When meat wasn't an option, people substituted whatever was abundant and inexpensive, in this case zucchini. The trick, Rinaldi explained, is getting a rich sear on the zucchini before adding any other ingredients. This is what produces the savory richness we want in the finished dish.

Rinaldi's cooking was simple and speedy. She browned her zucchini—which she'd cut into thin rounds—in garlic-infused olive oil. While unlikely to be mistaken for pork, that combination of searing zucchini, sizzling oil and garlic certainly evoked the meaty aromas we were hoping for.

Combined with egg, cheese, pepper and pasta, the zucchini indeed delivered as promised. Browned but not mushy, the vegetable had a toothsome quality that kept it satisfying. Another lesson that making do never has to disappoint.

—J.M. Hirsch

"Combined with egg, cheese, pepper and pasta, the zucchini indeed delivered as promised."

Carbonara Vegetariana alle Zucchine

Zucchini Carbonara

Start to finish: 40 minutes   Servings: 4 to 6

We learned this fantastic vegetarian riff on pasta carbonara from Roman home cook Claudia Rinaldi. The guanciale or pancetta traditionally used is replaced by garlicky, golden-brown zucchini that itself brings a meatiness to the dish. The squash is sautéed and the pasta boiled, then the two are tossed with a mixture of umami-packed Parmesan, tangy pecorino Romano, rich eggs and starchy pasta cooking water. The resulting sauce is silky-smooth and creamy, yet light. We added lemon zest to the mix, which brings fresh, zingy notes, as well as red pepper flakes for subtle heat.

Don't add the egg-cheese mixture until the pot is off the heat. This will prevent the eggs from overcooking and ensure that the sauce's texture is velvety smooth.

In a small bowl, whisk together the whole egg plus yolk, both cheeses, the lemon zest and ½ teaspoon black pepper; set aside. In a 12-inch nonstick skillet over medium, combine 1½ tablespoons of the oil and the garlic. Cook, stirring occasionally, until the garlic is lightly browned, 2 to 3 minutes. Remove and discard the garlic, then add half the zucchini in an even layer and sprinkle lightly with salt. Cook, without stirring, until golden brown on the bottoms, 3 to 4 minutes.

Stir the zucchini, flipping the slices, then redistribute in an even layer. Cook until golden brown on the second sides, another 3 to 4 minutes. Transfer to a plate. Add the remaining 1½ tablespoons oil to the skillet, then cook the remaining zucchini in the same way. Off heat, add the first batch of zucchini to the second in the skillet. Stir in the pepper flakes and set aside.

In a large pot, bring 4 quarts water to a boil. Stir in the pasta and 1 tablespoon salt, then cook, stirring occasionally, until al dente. Reserve about 1 cup of the cooking water, then drain. Return the pasta to the pot, then add ½ cup of the reserved pasta water and the zucchini. Cook over medium-high, stirring, until heated through, about 1 minute.

Off heat, add the egg mixture; stir until the sauce thickens slightly and clings to the pasta and zucchini, 2 to 3 minutes. If needed, add reserved pasta water 1 tablespoon at a time to adjust the consistency. Taste and season with salt and black pepper. Serve sprinkled with additional black pepper and cheeses.

1 large egg plus 1 large egg yolk

1 ounce pecorino Romano cheese, finely grated (½ cup), plus more to serve

1 ounce Parmesan cheese, finely grated (½ cup), plus more to serve

1 tablespoon grated lemon zest

Kosher salt and ground black pepper

3 tablespoons extra-virgin olive oil, divided

2 large garlic cloves, smashed and peeled

1½ pounds small to medium zucchini, trimmed and sliced into ¼-inch rounds

¼ to ½ teaspoon red pepper flakes

1 pound rigatoni, mezzi rigatoni or ziti

Pasta con Melanzane, Pomodorini e Gorgonzola

Spaghetti with Eggplant, Tomatoes and Gorgonzola

Start to finish: 40 minutes   Servings: 6

This hearty, rustic pasta was inspired by a dish that we tasted at Antica Osteria Pisano in Naples. Chunks of eggplant are lightly browned in olive oil, then simmered with cherry (or grape) tomatoes along with some of the starchy pasta-cooking water, forming a simple sauce. But what really pulls the dish together, both in flavor and consistency, is the creamy, savory Gorgonzola cheese tossed in at the end. To be efficient, prep the basil during the five-minute standing time after sprinkling the cheese onto the pasta.

Don't discard the remaining pasta water after adding 1½ cups to the eggplant-tomato mixture. You will need some of it to adjust the consistency of the pasta after the cheese is mixed in.

In a large pot, bring 2 quarts water to a boil over medium high. Stir in the pasta and 1 tablespoon salt, then cook, stirring occasionally, until just shy of al dente. Reserve about 2 cups of the cooking water, then drain; set aside.

In a 12-inch skillet, heat the oil over medium-high until barely smoking. Add the eggplant and ½ teaspoon salt. Cook, stirring occasionally, until golden brown and starting to soften, 5 to 6 minutes. Add the tomatoes and cook, stirring occasionally, until the tomatoes begin to break down, 3 to 4 minutes.

Add the garlic and pepper flakes; cook, stirring, until fragrant, about 30 seconds. Add 1½ cups of the reserved pasta water and bring to a simmer. Add the spaghetti and cook, stirring occasionally, until the pasta is al dente, about 2 minutes.

Remove the pan from the heat. Scatter the Gorgonzola over the pasta mixture, cover and let stand for 5 minutes to soften the cheese. Toss, adding more reserved water as needed so the noodles are lightly sauced. Add the basil and toss again, then taste and season with salt and black pepper.

1 pound spaghetti

Kosher salt and ground black pepper

¼ cup extra-virgin olive oil

1-pound eggplant, cut into 1-inch chunks

1 pint cherry or grape tomatoes, halved

2 medium garlic cloves, minced

½ teaspoon red pepper flakes

4 ounces Gorgonzola cheese, crumbled (1 cup)

1 cup lightly packed fresh basil, chopped

Pasta Fresca con Carciofi e Pecorino

Rigatoni with Artichokes, Basil and Pecorino

Start to finish: 30 minutes Servings: 4 to 6

This recipe is our weeknight adaptation of the pasta fresca con carciofi e pecorino that we ate at Antica Osteria Delle Travi in Bari. The flavors are bright and fresh, and the prep is a breeze (chopping the basil is as arduous as it gets here). Be sure to purchase jarred marinated artichoke hearts—they offer much more flavor than canned or frozen. You will need three 12-ounce jars to get the 3 cups drained artichokes called for. The hearts usually are halved or quartered; there's no need to chop them after draining, as they will break apart during cooking.

Don't forget to save 2 cups of the cooking water before draining the rigatoni. You will need the starchy seasoned water to create a sauce that lightly coats and marries the artichokes and pasta.

In a large Dutch oven, bring 4 quarts water to a boil. Stir in the pasta and 1 tablespoon salt, then cook, stirring occasionally, until just shy of al dente. Reserve about 2 cups of the cooking water, then drain the pasta.

Wipe out the pot, add the oil and heat over medium-high until shimmering. Add the artichokes and cook, stirring, until well browned, 5 to 7 minutes. Add the garlic and pepper flakes, then cook, stirring, until fragrant, about 30 seconds. Return the pasta to the pot, along with 1½ cups of the reserved pasta water. Cook, uncovered and stirring often, until the pasta is al dente and little liquid remains, 3 to 5 minutes.

Remove from the heat. Add the pecorino, lemon zest and juice, basil and butter, then stir until the butter is melted. Stir in additional pasta water 1 tablespoon at a time until slightly saucy. Taste and season with salt and pepper.

1 pound rigatoni

Kosher salt and ground black pepper

¼ cup extra-virgin olive oil

3 cups drained oil-marinated artichoke hearts (see headnote), patted dry

4 medium garlic cloves, finely grated

½ teaspoon red pepper flakes

2 ounces pecorino Romano cheese, finely grated (1 cup)

1 tablespoon grated lemon zest, plus 2 tablespoons lemon juice

1 cup lightly packed fresh basil, chopped

3 tablespoons salted butter, cut into 3 pieces

Rome's best no-cook pasta sauce

Cacio e pepe and a foul temper. When you ask about Felice Trivelloni, you never hear about just one; they are inseparably synonymous with the Roman restaurateur. His take on this classic pasta was as epic as his tendency to gruffness.

It's something his grandson, Franco Ines, chuckles about. Felice, after all, translates as "happy." Now, Ines runs the family restaurant, Felice a Testaccio, a boisterously popular eatery tucked on a corner of Rome's once rough-and-tumble Testaccio neighborhood.

Which might explain Trivelloni's surly side; he often sent away would-be diners, even regulars and those with reservations. As family lore tells it, Trivelloni had a soft spot for his hardscrabble neighbors and kept seats open at the restaurant just in case they needed a meal.

Today, the vibe—in and outside the eatery—is a bit more refined. Trivelloni, who started the restaurant in 1936 after selling wine from a cart as a teenager, worked both the kitchen and dining room for 73 years.

Luckily, his recipes remain. Today, they are prepared by chef Emiliana Rossetti, who learned them from Trivelloni. The menu is an ode to Roman classics, including saltimbocca alla Romana. But really the focus is the pastas. As it should be.

There is carbonara, of course. And its cousins, gricia and all'Amatriciana. The rightful star is the cacio e pepe, a famously rich swirl of tonnarelli pasta coated with both pecorino Romano and Parmesan cheeses, as well as ample black pepper.

It deserves its reputation, striking a beautiful balance of creamy and rich with peppery and bright. But that fame risks overshadowing an equally delicious offering, a not-quite-natively Roman creation by Trivelloni himself.

The simply named spaghetti alla Felice marries perfectly al dente pasta to an entirely uncooked sauce of ricotta cheese, tomatoes and tons of herbs. The result is fresh and creamy with just hints of sweetness and acidity from the tomatoes.

And the process could not be simpler. Rossetti began by lightly crushing cherry tomatoes, then combining them with a riot of chopped herbs—basil, mint, oregano, thyme and marjoram—a bit of ricotta cheese and a sprinkle of salt.

When the pasta was ready, she tossed it repeatedly with the sauce, the heat of the spaghetti lightly warming it, drawing the flavors together. That was the extent of the cooking.

The taste was simple and summery. And it made me glad I didn't need to joust with Trivelloni's sour side to get a taste.

—J.M. Hirsch

> "The taste was simple and summery."

Spaghetti alla Felice
Pasta with Ricotta, Tomatoes and Herbs

Start to finish: 45 minutes Servings: 4

A family-owned restaurant that opened in 1936, Felice a Testaccio in Rome is known for serving up traditional fare, including tonnarelli cacio e pepe. But it was the spaghetti alla Felice that caught our attention during a recent visit. Piping-hot, just-drained al dente pasta was tossed with grape tomatoes, olive oil, a mixture of fresh herbs and ricotta cheese. The dish was creamy but not at all heavy, and the bright, fresh flavors and textures were simple and elegant. Adapting the recipe, we learned that good-quality whole-milk ricotta is key. Look for a brand made without gums or stabilizers; it will taste purer and sweeter and have a superior texture. As for the herbs, use a mix of a few types listed in the recipe to achieve a wide spectrum of flavors, from anise sweetness to menthol freshness, hints of citrus to earthy, woodsy notes. If you choose to add marjoram and/or oregano, do so sparingly, as they are very assertive herbs.

Don't use more than 7 cups of water to boil the pasta. It's a scant amount, but intentionally so. The pasta cooking water is added to the sauce and noodles as they're tossed; its starchiness loosens the sauce and helps it cling to the linguine.

In a large bowl, combine the tomatoes, sugar, ¼ cup of the oil, 1 teaspoon salt and ½ teaspoon pepper. Toss, then, using a potato masher, gently crush the tomatoes until they release some juice. Let stand at room temperature for at least 15 minutes or up to 1 hour, stirring occasionally.

To the tomato mixture, add the herbs and fold until incorporated. Stir in 1 cup of the ricotta; set aside. In a small bowl, stir together the remaining ricotta, the remaining 2 tablespoons oil, ½ teaspoon salt and ¼ teaspoon pepper; set aside.

In a large pot, bring 7 cups water to a boil. Stir in the pasta and 1 teaspoon salt, then cook, stirring often, until the pasta is al dente. Drain the pasta in a colander set in a large heatproof bowl. Shake the colander to remove as much water as possible, then add the pasta to the tomato-ricotta mixture; reserve the cooking water. Using tongs, toss to combine, adding reserved pasta water 1 tablespoon at a time until the sauce clings to the noodles.

Divide the pasta among individual bowls, drizzle with additional oil and serve, offering the seasoned ricotta and Parmesan cheese on the side.

2 pints grape or cherry tomatoes, halved

¼ teaspoon white sugar

¼ cup plus 2 tablespoons extra-virgin olive oil, divided, plus more to serve

Kosher salt and ground black pepper

1½ cups finely chopped mixed fresh herbs, such as mint, basil, thyme, oregano and/or marjoram (see headnote)

15- or 16-ounce container whole-milk ricotta cheese

1 pound spaghetti or linguine

Finely grated Parmesan cheese, to serve

Pasta e Piselli

Orecchiette with Tomatoes, Peas and Pancetta

Start to finish: 45 minutes Servings: 4 to 6

Home cook and Pompeii resident Antonella Scala taught us her recipe for pasta e piselli, a slightly brothy yet chunky dish that lands somewhere between soup and generously sauced pasta. We adapted the recipe for an ultra-easy one-pot affair. To form the flavor base, we use the rendered fat from pancetta crisped in olive oil to sweat a chopped onion until softened and sweet. Chopped plum tomatoes followed by a couple tablespoons of tomato paste cook down in the pot, supplying depth of flavor and umami. We cook the pasta directly in the mix, not separately, which lends the sauce starchiness and body, then peas, parsley and pecorino are stirred in at the finish. Scala used a mix of small pasta shapes, but we chose orecchiette and cavatelli, cup-like shapes that capture peas and boast a hearty, almost dumpling-like texture. At the end of cooking, be sure to wait about five minutes before serving. This allows the consistency to thicken slightly.

Don't bother defrosting the peas. There is enough heat in the pot to thaw the frozen peas, and adding them while cold prevents overcooking so they retain their texture and color. However, if your peas are caked in ice, before use, simply rinse them under running cold water so they break apart.

In a large Dutch oven over medium, combine the oil and pancetta; cook, stirring, until browned and crisped, 5 to 7 minutes. Using a slotted spoon, transfer the pancetta to a paper towel–lined plate. To the fat remaining in the pot, add the onion. Cook, stirring, until softened but not browned, about 3 minutes.

Add the tomatoes and cook, stirring often while gently pressing on them to encourage them to soften, until they have broken down to a pulpy consistency, about 5 minutes. Add the tomato paste; cook, stirring, until the paste darkens and begins to stick to the pot, about 2 minutes.

Add 2 quarts water and bring to a boil over high. Add the pasta and cook, uncovered and stirring occasionally, until al dente, about 10 minutes. Off heat, add the pancetta, peas, parsley and pecorino; stir until the cheese has melted and the peas have thawed, about 1 minute. Let stand, uncovered, for 5 minutes to thicken slightly. Taste and season with salt and pepper. Serve drizzled with additional oil and sprinkled with additional pecorino.

2 tablespoons extra-virgin olive oil, plus more to serve

4 ounces pancetta, chopped

1 medium yellow onion, finely chopped

12 ounces plum tomatoes, cored and chopped

2 tablespoons tomato paste

1 pound orecchiette or cavatelli (see headnote)

2 cups frozen peas

1 cup lightly packed fresh flat-leaf parsley, roughly chopped

2 ounces pecorino Romano cheese, finely grated (1 cup), plus more to serve

Kosher salt and ground black pepper

In Venice, Parmesan, radicchio and walnuts marry to create the perfect pasta

Morning sun splashing off the rippling canals turns the wine and Aperol spritzes into gems, the clustered glasses glowing golden and ruby. Venice, after all, is a drinking town. And by 10 a.m. the crowds gathered at bistro tables along Rio Della Misericordia—or River of Mercy—may well already be onto their second or third pour.

It's part of Venetians' deliciously peculiar relationship with bars, which open early and from which emerge dozens of cicchetti, small bites of savory nibbles nestled onto crostini or polenta. Baccalà mantecato, a pâté made from dried salt cod, is classic. But there also are tiny potatoes fried with rosemary. Hard-cooked eggs with anchovies. Dozens of cheeses. Mushrooms bathed in herbs and oil. Bitter greens sautéed with garlic and chili.

Custom calls for meandering the canals with friends, stopping at one bar after another, chasing each bite with an ombra de vin, tiny glasses that translate as a shadow of wine. Some people walk. True Venetians boat, plying the waterways with flat-bottomed gondolas that can stretch 32 feet, navigating from standing perches at the back with a long wooden paddle.

This is how I meet—and drink with—Francesco Bernardi, a university librarian and talented home cook who offered to introduce me to cicchetti culture as well as some of Venice's classic pastas and risottos. All of it by traversing the canals in a bright blue gondola he uses as part of one of the city's many boating cooperatives that make ownership accessible.

In time, we wind our way, water lapping as we duck our heads to clear low-lying pedestrian bridges overhead, to Rialto Mercato, an open-air market beneath a stone pavilion at the edge of the Grand Canal. Boisterous fishmongers taunt one another, shouting joking insults back and forth amid cascades of laughter. That seafood dominates the city's cuisine is obvious, if only by the richness of the lagoon on which it sits and the antics of the many men and women selling it.

Less obvious is the love of radicchio. That is, until you see the heaps of the crispy, bittersweet and brashly purple vegetable piled high at one stall after another. It makes its way into numerous cicchetti, sometimes raw and cupping other nibbles, sometimes tender and sautéed to sweetness. We buy a bagful from which Bernardi promises a simple, rich pasta.

Back at his loft apartment—a crisscross of ancient wooden beams overhead, windows with views of piazzas, shelves with jars of capers, spices, wine corks and olive branch sprigs—Bernardi tosses a pile of penne to boil in a bare amount of water. It's a technique we see over and again across Italy, cooking pasta in far less water than expected. It's a simple trick for creating a particularly starchy water, which itself becomes a key ingredient.

> "Chopped walnuts, parsley, black pepper and ample olive oil follow and coalesce."

While the pasta cooks, Bernardi combines olive oil and lightly crushed garlic in a skillet, cooking them just enough to flavor the oil before discarding the cloves. It's yet another subtlety sometimes missing from Italian-American cooking, which tends to add garlic by heaps and mounds. In Italy, garlic isn't brash; it's a nuance. Use it to flavor the oil, but no more.

Bernardi—who learned to cook from his mother, as well as from the sort of fascination with cookbooks one expects from a librarian—then tosses in sliced radicchio, which wilts for less than a minute, long enough to retain a slight crunch, yet also sweeten with the heat. It is followed by the now just-tender pasta as well as the super starchy cooking water clinging to it.

You can see the sauce come together almost immediately, the water thickening and pulling the ingredients together. Chopped walnuts, parsley, black pepper and ample olive oil follow and coalesce. Then, a handful of grated and gloriously briny cheese made by his cousin from three or four cows in the nearby mountains. It melts and—again thanks to all that starchy water—emulsifies into a smooth sauce.

The finishing flourish, a drizzle of brightness—lemon juice that so perfectly balances the rich cheese and nuts. The result is an amazing blend of salty-savory-sweet-bitter, the walnuts adding both crunch and creaminess. Good enough, in fact, to make me forget I've been drinking since 8 a.m.

—J.M. Hirsch

Pasta con Radicchio, Noci e Pepe Nero

Pasta with Radicchio, Walnuts and Black Pepper

Start to finish: 40 minutes Servings: 4

In Venice, where radicchio is much loved, home cook Francesco Bernardi taught us his recipe for this simple yet delicious and elegant dish. Chopped radicchio is browned in garlic-infused olive oil, its flavor becoming rich and complex and its texture softening slightly. The layers of pleasantly bitter notes—from the radicchio and the toasted walnuts—are perfectly balanced by the nuttiness and umami of Parmesan, the bright tang of lemon juice and the pungency of black pepper.

Don't begin cooking the radicchio until after the pasta has been drained because the radicchio takes only a couple of minutes in the skillet. If it waits in the pan for the pasta to finish, the radicchio will lose its texture. Also, don't stir the radicchio too often during browning so it caramelizes nicely, creating compounds that build depth of flavor.

In a 12-inch skillet over medium, toast the walnuts, stirring often, until fragrant and lightly browned, about 3 minutes. Transfer to a cutting board; reserve the skillet. Let the nuts cool slightly, then finely chop; set aside.

In a large saucepan, bring 2 quarts water to a boil. Add the pasta and 1 tablespoon salt, then cook, stirring occasionally, until al dente. Reserve ½ cup of the pasta cooking water, then drain.

In the same skillet over medium-high, combine the oil and garlic; cook, occasionally turning the cloves, until golden brown, 2 to 3 minutes. Remove and discard the garlic, then add the radicchio, ½ teaspoon salt and ¼ teaspoon pepper; stir to coat. Distribute the radicchio in an even layer and cook, stirring only once or twice, until well browned and tender-crisp, 2 to 4 minutes.

Add the pasta to the skillet and stir. Add half of the Parmesan, half of the walnuts and ¼ cup of the reserved pasta water. Reduce to medium and cook, stirring constantly and vigorously, until the pasta is lightly sauced, 1 to 3 minutes; add additional pasta water as needed if the mixture looks dry.

Off heat, stir in the remaining Parmesan, half of the parsley and the lemon juice. Taste and season with salt and pepper. Serve drizzled with additional oil and sprinkled with the remaining walnuts, the remaining parsley, generous grindings of black pepper and additional Parmesan.

⅓ cup walnuts

12 ounces penne rigate

Kosher salt and ground black pepper

2 tablespoons extra-virgin olive oil, plus more to serve

2 medium garlic cloves, smashed and peeled

8-ounce head radicchio, bruised outer leaves removed, halved, cored and chopped into ½-inch pieces (about 3 cups)

1 ounce Parmesan cheese, finely grated (½ cup), plus more to serve

2 tablespoons chopped fresh flat-leaf parsley

2 teaspoons lemon juice

From humble ingredients,
creamy richness

Several times a year, a miracle is said to occur inside Cattedrale di San Gennaro, an imposing gray duomo at the heart of Naples. Deep inside—in a lavish and gilded chapel—a vial of dried blood from the city's patron saint, Januarius, liquefies. If it doesn't, legend predicts tragedy will strike the city.

With rumbling Mount Vesuvius and the ruins of Pompeii just in the distance, it's perhaps a warning worth heeding. But truthfully, I'm more interested in a slightly less macabre liquid—the water at a rollicking boil on the stovetop of Antonella Scala's rooftop kitchen. She'd invited me to her home at the foothills of the volcano to teach me a seemingly banal pasta: noodles, cauliflower and cheese.

Turns out, I underestimated how Scala—a talented home cook and host of pop-up dinners—could transform those humble ingredients, even the water itself, into creamy richness.

Scala's process was simple. She blanched a cauliflower whole, then cut it into tender florets, which browned quickly in a skillet of garlic-infused oil. But the water in which the cauliflower cooked wasn't done yet. She next cooked the pasta in it, letting the sweet flavor of the vegetable seep in. The pasta then joined the cauliflower in the skillet. Finally, she used the cooking water again, this time to marry pecorino Romano and aged provolone cheese to the rest, creating a creamy sauce.

Back at Milk Street, the recipe adapted easily. For speed, we cut the cauliflower in half before blanching. Like Scala, we discarded the garlic just after it infused the oil, while a sprinkling of red pepper flakes brightened the dish. A deliciously simple pasta; banality—and tragedy—averted.

—J.M. Hirsch

> ## "She'd invited me to her home at the foothills of the volcano to teach me a seemingly banal pasta: noodles, cauliflower and cheese."

Pasta ai Due Formaggi e Cavolfiore

Two-Cheese Pasta with Cauliflower

Start to finish: 40 minutes Servings: 4

We learned this recipe that transforms cauliflower, cheese and water into a rich and creamy dish from home cook Antonella Scala in Pompeii. We loved how it uses the same water to both parcook the cauliflower and to cook the pasta. Parcooking means the cauliflower browns quickly when it is later added to the skillet. It also enriches the water, infusing the pasta with some of the vegetable's flavor. To contrast the cauliflower's subtle sweetness, we like equal amounts of salty, savory pecorino Romano cheese and aged provolone (also called provolone piccante, or sharp provolone). If you can't find aged provolone, regular provolone is an acceptable, though milder, substitute. Short, twisty pasta shapes such as campanelle and cavatappi combine perfectly with the cauliflower florets. We boil the pasta for only 5 minutes (it will be well shy of al dente), then finish cooking it directly in the skillet with the cauliflower.

Don't forget to reserve 2½ cups of the cooking water before you drain the pasta. You'll need it for simmering the cauliflower and for creating the sauce. Also, don't add the grated cheeses all at once. Sprinkling each one over the surface of the pasta and stirring before sprinkling on more prevents the cheese from clumping.

Kosher salt and ground black pepper

2-pound head cauliflower, halved and trimmed of leaves

3 tablespoons extra-virgin olive oil, plus more to serve

1 medium garlic clove, smashed and peeled

½ teaspoon red pepper flakes, plus more to serve

8 ounces short, curly pasta, such as campanelle, cavatappi or fusilli

1½ ounces pecorino Romano cheese, finely grated (¾ cup), plus more to serve

1½ ounces aged provolone cheese (see headnote), finely grated (¾ cup), plus more to serve

In a large pot, bring 4 quarts water to a boil. Add 1 tablespoon salt and the cauliflower halves, then cook for 5 minutes; begin timing from the moment the cauliflower is added to the pot. Using tongs, transfer the cauliflower to a cutting board; reserve the pot and the water. When the cauliflower is cool enough to handle, chop the florets and stems into pieces slightly smaller than the pasta, discarding the thick, tough core. You should have about 4 cups. Return the water to a boil.

In a nonstick 12-inch skillet over medium, cook the oil and garlic, stirring often, until the garlic is golden brown, 2 to 3 minutes. Remove and discard the garlic, then add the cauliflower, pepper flakes and ¼ teaspoon salt. Increase the heat to medium-high and cook, stirring occasionally, until the cauliflower is well browned, 7 to 9 minutes.

Meanwhile, add the pasta to the boiling water and cook, stirring occasionally, for 5 minutes. Reserve about 2½ cups cooking water, then drain. Add the pasta and ¼ teaspoon black pepper to the skillet with the cauliflower, then stir in 1 cup of the reserved cooking water. Cook over medium-high, stirring often, until the pasta is al dente, 3 to 5 minutes. If the pan becomes dry before the pasta is done, add another ¼ cup cooking water and continue to cook.

When the pasta is al dente, with the skillet still over medium-high, stir in another ¼ cup cooking water. Sprinkle on the pecorino, then stir until the cheese is evenly distributed and melted.

Sprinkle on the provolone, then stir until the pasta is glossy and lightly coated with melted cheese. Remove the pan from the heat. If the mixture looks sticky and dry, stir in additional cooking water a few tablespoons at a time until the proper consistency is reached. Taste and season with salt and black pepper. Serve drizzled with additional oil and sprinkled with additional cheese and pepper flakes.

Pasta con Pomodorini, Salsiccia e Melanzane

Pasta with Italian Sausage, Tomatoes and Eggplant

Start to finish: 35 minutes Servings: 4 to 6

This pasta dish, loosely based on a sausage and eggplant ragù taught to us by Maria Enza Arena in Castelbuono, Sicily, is ideal for summer. It uses in-season tomatoes and eggplant, and because the pasta is cooked directly in the sauce, there's no need to heat up the kitchen with a large pot of boiling water. Hot Italian sausage adds a little spiciness, but use sweet sausage if that's your preference.

Don't stir the tomatoes more than just once or twice after adding them to the pot. Uncovering to stir releases heat and slows the rate at which the tomatoes burst and release their juices. However, do make sure to stir regularly after the pasta is added to prevent the starchy noodles from sticking to the pot.

In a large pot over medium-high, combine the oil, tomatoes, onion and ¾ teaspoon salt. Cover and cook, stirring only once or twice, until the tomatoes begin to burst, 5 to 7 minutes. Add the sausage and cook, uncovered and using a wooden spoon to break up the meat and tomatoes, until the sausage is no longer pink, 2 to 3 minutes.

Stir in the eggplant. Add 1 quart water and bring to a boil. Stir in the pasta, nutmeg and ½ teaspoon pepper. Cover, reduce to medium and cook, stirring occasionally and maintaining a vigorous simmer, until the pasta is al dente, 10 to 12 minutes.

Taste and season with salt and pepper, then stir in the basil. Serve drizzled with additional oil and sprinkled with cheese.

3 tablespoons extra-virgin olive oil, plus more to serve

2 pints cherry or grape tomatoes

1 small red onion, finely chopped

Kosher salt and ground black pepper

8 ounces hot Italian sausage, casing removed

1 pound eggplant, peeled and cut into ¾-inch cubes

1 pound campanelle, gemelli or cavatappi pasta

¾ teaspoon grated nutmeg

1 cup lightly packed fresh basil, torn if large

Finely grated Parmesan or pecorino Romano, to serve

Orecchiette con Pomodorini e Coriandolo

Orecchiette with Coriander and Cherry Tomatoes

Start to finish: 25 minutes Serves: 4 to 6

This recipe, inspired by an unusual pasta dish we tasted during a dinner hosted in a grove of 1,000-year-old olive trees in Puglia, uses few ingredients but is packed with flavor. We layer in the warm, slightly citrusy flavor of coriander by blooming the spice in oil; most of it is simmered into the sauce and a couple teaspoons of the infused oil are drizzled on the finished dish. The cherry tomatoes, gently mashed after a few minutes of cooking, break down into a silky sauce that pairs perfectly with coin-sized, cup-shaped orecchiette pasta. Ricotta salata cheese is a milky, salty, crumbly cheese; grate it on the large holes of a box grater. If you can't find it, use an equal amount of queso fresco.

Don't forget to reserve 1 cup of the pasta cooking water before draining the orecchiette, as you'll need the starchy liquid to make the sauce. Also, don't forget to reserve 2 teaspoons of the coriander-infused oil for drizzling over the finished dish.

In a large pot, bring 4 quarts water to a boil. Add the pasta and 1 tablespoon salt, then cook, stirring occasionally, until just shy of al dente. Reserve 1 cup of the cooking water, then drain the pasta; set aside.

Wipe dry the same pot, then set over medium, add the coriander and toast until fragrant, about 1 minute. Add the oil and cook until infused, about 2 minutes. Measure 2 teaspoons of the oil into a small bowl and set aside. Add the tomatoes and garlic to the pot, cover and cook, stirring once or twice, until softened and the oil has taken on a reddish hue, 4 to 6 minutes. Add ½ teaspoon salt and gently crush the tomatoes with a potato masher to release some of their liquid. Continue to cook, stirring to combine with the oil, for about 1 minute. Add the reserved cooking water, bring to a simmer over medium-high and cook, stirring occasionally, until the liquid is slightly reduced and the tomatoes are completely softened, about 3 minutes.

Add the pasta and cook, stirring often, until the pasta is al dente and has absorbed some of the liquid, 2 to 4 minutes. Stir in the lemon zest, then taste and season with salt and pepper. Transfer to a serving bowl, drizzle with the reserved oil and top with the cheese and basil.

1 pound orecchiette pasta

Kosher salt and ground black pepper

2 tablespoons ground coriander

¼ cup extra-virgin olive oil

2 pints cherry or grape tomatoes

6 medium garlic cloves, thinly sliced

1 teaspoon grated lemon zest

1 ounce ricotta salata cheese, grated (¼ cup)

¼ cup lightly packed fresh basil, torn

Finding Italy's forgotten pastas

In his tiny restaurant kitchen 30 minutes north of Rome, surrounded by the fantastically rustic fresh pasta he rolls and cuts by hand, Filippo Guarera uses the same word over and again to describe the cooking he and his wife do—sacred.

Probably fitting given the eatery's name—Osteria del Cardinale. Or, The Cardinal's Tavern. Of course, Guarera has no idea how the place got its name. He and Paola Saviotti have been its stewards for just the last 17 years of its long life. "Probably because some cardinal passed by," he says with a shrug. The couple's spirituality really is directed more at the food anyway.

The couple keep their restaurant casual—its hodgepodge of glassware is stacked randomly in a grandmother's hutch and lunching firemen linger around mismatched tables—and their intentionally affordable menu is built largely from recipes even many Italians have forgotten, yet somehow simultaneously feels comfortable and familiar.

"It's important to go in search of recipes that go back 100 years or more," he says. "I regard these recipes as sacred to the land and feel people should not lose hold of them."

Which is what brought me there. I'd heard rumors of a deliciously simple pasta dish from Puglia in southern Italy that Guarera had re-created. The name really said it all—fettuccine alla cipolla. Onion fettuccine.

The recipe name sums up much of the ingredient list. To it, Guarera adds copious wild oregano he grabs from outside, a generous hand of pecorino Romano cheese, a bit of salt and pepper, and not a lot else. "It's a harmony, the oregano and sweet onions," he says.

It truly was. A sweet and savory tangle of onions wound around those robustly tender-chewy noodles. But, as often is the case, trying to re-create it at home proved a challenge. Relying on such a simple array of ingredients, means they must be truly excellent to shine. And the options we often have in U.S. supermarkets just don't deliver.

Luckily, the solutions were as simple as the original recipe itself. A bit of red pepper flakes and lemon zest helped compensate for the more flavorful and sweet onions Guarera used. And even the best dried pastas we tried couldn't compete with his homemade fettuccine. We found whole-wheat pasta actually was a better substitute.

The result was subtle, yet richly flavored and sacrificed none of its wonderful simplicity. I might even describe it as sacred.

—J.M. Hirsch

> "It's a harmony, the oregano and sweet onions."

Penne alla Cipolla

Pasta with Pecorino and White Wine–Onion Sauce

Start to finish: 40 minutes Servings: 4 to 6

This simple pasta starring barely caramelized onions simmered in white wine, tangy pecorino Romano, black pepper and dried oregano for earthy, herbal contrast is inspired by a Pugliese classic made for us by chef Filippo Guarera. The dish traditionally is made with sweet Italian Tropea onions and Gaurera prepared a version of it for us at his restaurant Osteria del Cardinale in Campagnano di Roma, about 30 minutes north of Rome. Cooking the onions until tender and just beginning to brown boosts their sweetness, providing a perfect counterpoint to sharp, salty cheese. We added lemon zest to bring citrusy brightness to the sauce. After trying the dish with a handful of pasta types, we found that hearty whole-wheat noodles were our favorite; their nuttiness complements the onions, cheese and oregano. We preferred the short, chunky shape of penne, which gave the dish some heft; fusilli works, too, though we found that the spirals sometimes broke apart as they cooked in the sauce.

Don't hold back when vigorously stirring and tossing the pasta after adding the cheese. This ensures the cheese melts quickly and evenly to create a silky, clingy sauce.

1/3 cup extra-virgin olive oil

1 pound yellow or white onions, halved and sliced about 1/8 inch thick

Kosher salt and ground black pepper

1/4 cup dry white wine

1/2 teaspoon dried oregano

1/4 to 1/2 teaspoon red pepper flakes

1 pound whole-wheat penne

2 ounces pecorino Romano cheese, finely grated (1 cup), plus more to serve

1 tablespoon grated lemon zest

2 tablespoons finely chopped fresh flat-leaf parsley

In a 12-inch skillet over medium, combine the oil, onions and 1/4 teaspoon salt. Cook, stirring occasionally, until the onions soften and begin to brown, 15 to 18 minutes. Add the wine and cook, stirring, until reduced by about half, about 1 minute. Stir in 1/2 teaspoon black pepper, the oregano and pepper flakes. Set aside off the heat.

While the onions cook, in a large pot, bring 4 quarts water to a boil. Add the pasta and 1 tablespoon salt, then cook until just shy of al dente. Reserve 1 cup of the cooking water, then drain and return the pasta to the pot. Stir in the onion mixture and 1/2 cup of the reserved pasta water.

Add the cheese and cook over medium, vigorously stirring and tossing, until the sauce clings to the pasta, 1 to 2 minutes. If needed, toss in additional pasta water 1 tablespoon at a time to adjust the consistency. Stir in the lemon zest and parsley, then taste and season with salt and black pepper. Serve sprinkled with additional cheese.

Bologna's ridiculously simple pasta

Bologna is a mystery. Originally Etruscan, then Roman, now home to the oldest university in the world, it is a destination that, up until 10 years ago, was mostly overlooked by travelers. It wears its medieval clothing well, with stunning marble-faced arcades, leaning towers, cobblestone streets, fountains and narrow alleys filled with vegetable stands, fish markets and salumi vendors.

Underneath this showy exterior is the love of simplicity that underlies all Italian cooking. Yes, there are restaurants such as Massimiliano Poggi outside Bologna that remind one of the heady days of nouvelle cuisine. But for the most part, the cooks in Bologna stick to basics: fettuccine alla Bolognese, tortellini in brodo, passatelli, cotoletta, crespelle, ragùs, and the simplest of pastas, such as tagliatelle with butter and prosciutto.

Any good traveler is always on the lookout for that one dish, the game-changer, and the Emilia-Romagna region makes the perfect hunting ground. In my case, it was a Parmesan cream sauce I had with gramigna pasta at Trattoria Bertozzi in Bologna. It is so ridiculously simple—cream, grated Parmesan and lemon juice—that it barely qualifies as a recipe, yet it solves the problem of Alfredo, carbonara, cacio e pepe and other creamy pasta sauces that easily end up gluey, stringy or congealed.

Back at Milk Street, we made only two small changes: We added Parmesan rind to the cream along with two bay leaves to boost flavor. Once the cream had reduced at a low simmer, about 10 minutes, we whisked in the lemon juice—which helped thicken the cream—and then the cheese until the Parmesan melted into a fluid, creamy sauce. Nothing could be simpler, which for any Italian cook is the highest compliment.

–Christopher Kimball

"Any good traveler is always on the lookout for that one dish, the game-changer."

Pasta con Crema di Parmigiano
Pasta with Parmesan Cream

Start to finish: 25 minutes   Servings: 4 to 6

The key to this simple, ultra-rich sauce, our adaptation of the Parmesan cream perfection we discovered at Trattoria Bertozzi in Bologna, is using good-quality true Parmesan cheese (Parmigiano-Reggiano). We simmer a piece of Parmesan rind into the cream for added flavor and umami; some supermarkets and cheese shops sell just rinds, or you can simply cut the rind off your chunk of Parmesan.

Don't use domestic Parmesan or even true Parmesan that's pre-grated. Neither will yield the correct flavor and consistency.

In a medium saucepan over medium, combine the cream, Parmesan rind and bay. Bring to a simmer and cook, stirring occasionally and adjusting the heat as needed, until slightly thickened and reduced to 2 cups, 10 to 15 minutes.

Remove the pan from the heat, then remove and discard the cheese rind and bay. Whisk in the lemon juice; the mixture will thicken slightly. Whisk in the cheese a handful at a time, then continue to whisk until completely smooth.

Taste and season with pepper, then set aside uncovered.

In a large pot, bring 4 quarts water to a boil. Add 1 tablespoon salt and the pasta, then cook, stirring occasionally, until al dente. Reserve ½ cup of the cooking water, then drain. Return the pasta to the pot.

Pour the sauce over the pasta and toss until well coated, stirring in additional pasta water as needed to thin. Taste and season with salt and pepper. Serve sprinkled with additional black pepper.

2½ cups heavy cream

2-inch Parmesan rind, plus 6 ounces Parmesan cheese, finely grated (3 cups)

2 bay leaves

2 tablespoons lemon juice

Kosher salt and ground black pepper

1 pound linguine or spaghetti

On an Italian island, a simple pasta is transformed by land and sea

Chiesa del Santo Sepolcro is a church divided. Wedged into one of Cagliari's many steep and sweeping hills that tug the Sardinian capital toward the Tyrrhenian Sea, the weathered stone exterior betrays little of the give-and-take that plays out inside. Only a waft of freshly baked bread, a hint of garlic and fresh herbs, suggest something unusual.

Beyond the entry, two-in-one churches blur and break. To the right, pews and an altar for Roman Catholics, the medieval building's first inhabitants. Directly ahead, bold and gilded with icons, space for Eastern Orthodox congregants. A divided solution to a shared problem—keeping a church alive in an era of dwindling attendance.

Today, the entire space is given to a parastas, a food-fueled and melodic memorial service for a member of the Romanian immigrant community. For me, it's an unintended pit stop, a fortuitous escape from a downpour en route to the home of a man who has offered to teach me about fregola, the Italian island's signature nugget-like pasta.

As the priest conducts the Orthodox liturgy for several dozen people, a lone woman at the back fusses over card tables tucked around the pews. A friend died two weeks ago; she has assembled the traditional feast. Rice and beans with mushrooms. Diamond-shaped flaky pastries. Rice pudding adorned with brightly colored gumdrops in the form of a cross. A thick bread braided as a crucifix. Plump stuffed cabbage leaves glistening with oil. Each dish with a thin, lit candle plunged into the center. Bottles of wine and grape and orange Fanta soda to the side.

As the service ends, the priest moves toward the tables. The congregants approach him, each holding a platter of food with extended arms. With incense and bells swinging, he blesses each in turn. The meal begins as the priest recedes to the vestibule, attendees building precarious plates they perch on their laps in the pews.

Invited to join them, I sample everything, but am most taken by the stuffed cabbage. Some are filled with an aromatic mix of rice and herbs. But the ones that most hold my attention contain the very ingredient I'd come to Sardinia for—fregola, a tiny pasta that resembles pearl couscous but cooks up chewy-tender.

The cabbage with rice is fine, but those with fregola are fantastic. Treated like rice, the fregola produces a cabbage filling at once meaty, light, savory and satisfying. Encouraged, I leave to meet Vincenzo Aresu, a former pharmaceutical executive who has dedicated his retirement to cooking. He has offered to teach me the simple, four-herb fregola he perfected over years of entertaining medical clients.

Aresu's 17th-century home inspires awe. Rescued from abandon, it boasts vaulted stone ceilings, walls of frescoes, catwalk lofts and an atri-

"It is rich, but not heavy. Briny, but not fishy."

um-style kitchen that opens to a church-like dining room dominated by a massive wooden table. He shrugs when asked how he learned to cook. His mother was awful in the kitchen. He watched her, then taught himself.

Sardinian cuisine evolved despite rather than because of the sea, he explains. Buffeting centuries of invaders meant moving inland and avoiding the coast. That shaped Sardinian cooking, historically drawn mostly from vegetables, grains, dairy and lamb. Only in recent decades has the abundance of seafood been tapped.

Like the pastas of southern Italy, fregola is made from nothing but semolina flour and water. Formed into thick pellets, it is dried, similar to couscous. But then it is toasted until lightly browned. This explains why it retains more chew than couscous after cooking. And like many pastas, it often is best when cooked in the sauce, allowing it to better absorb the flavors of the other ingredients while releasing starch that thickens the dish.

Aresu's sauce begins with meaty chunks of guanciale crisped in olive oil. The fregola is added, toasting in the savory fat. Meanwhile, handfuls of fresh herbs — basil, parsley, mint and wild fennel — are pureed with a bit of ricotta salata cheese and a mix of pine nuts, walnuts and almonds. The result is pleasantly granular, savory and boldly herbal.

After adding water to plump the fregola, Aresu stirs in the herb puree. He warms it, though not so long as to dull the freshness of the herbs. He then adds a final flourish of olive oil and grated cheese — Parmesan and the local aged pecorino Sardo. The result is richly meaty — though little meat is used in the recipe — and explosively herbal, a vibrant greenness balanced by cheese and starchy, chewy pasta. And it occurs to me: The fregola once again was treated like rice. Deliciously so. The entire process reminded me of the risottos of Milan.

Aresu rounds out the meal with chunks of a friend's local sausage, another friend's olive oil-packed marinated artichoke hearts and pickled porcini mushrooms. But I keep going back for the fregola. As I reach for another helping, he tells me that though it's less traditional, I also must try a seafood fregola. And he knows the perfect place.

For nearly 60 years, Aresu has eaten weekly at Trattoria Lillicu. Sometimes he brings his own homemade wine and olive oil, sharing with diners at nearby tables. "If you eat alone, you are an unhappy person." We meet there a few hours after our lesson. He is greeted warmly, offered chunks of pecorino as he gives nodding approval to a long table of prepped antipasti.

Longevity here is the norm; the same family has run the restaurant since it opened in the 1930s. Most waiters have worked here for 20 or 30 years. Our chef, Francesco Pinna, has been at the stove for 22 years. His father worked here for 40. The long dining room — pink plaster walls, stone mosaic floors, white marble tables, red granite counters — fills quickly to capacity, some 100 boisterous locals.

Waiters whip in and out with carafes of wine. Our dinner comes in waves. Burrida, a vinegary cold seafood soup. Artichokes awash in olive oil. Tiny fried fish, crisp and lemony, that Aresu eats by the handful. A seafood platter with bright red shrimp, calamari, red snapper. Two giant fish covered in cherry tomatoes, surrounded by hunks of bread fried crisp and soaking up the juices.

My favorite, predictably, is the seafood fregola, a brothy bowl of tiny irregular pasta nuggets bathed in tomato sauce and heaped with mussels, shrimp and calamari. It is rich, but not heavy. Briny, but not fishy. All balanced by the acidity of a brightly flavored sauce spiked with garlic and red pepper flakes. And again, fascinatingly similar to risotto, yet with more robust chew.

The next day, I return so Pinna can teach me the seafood dish I'd eaten the night before. It begins in the skillet, with olive oil, red pepper flakes, garlic, parsley and cherry tomatoes all simmered until saucy. Then the seafood. Then broth and fregola. In short order, it is done — tender, chewy and brightly flavored.

Back at Milk Street, we followed the leads of Pinna and Aresu — treating the fregola similar to rice. Adapting the recipes was mostly about streamlining and substituting for hard-to-find ingredients. The biggest adaptation was the fregola itself. We loved it, but wanted an option for people who couldn't find it. The solution was pearl couscous, which essentially is untoasted fregola. Toasting it in a large, dry pot for 5 minutes worked wonderfully. A simple solution for a fantastic pasta, treated like rice whether by land or by sea.

—J.M. Hirsch

Fregola alle Erbe e Pecorino
Fregola with Herbs and Pecorino

Star to finish: 1 hour   Servings: 4

On the island of Sardinia, Vincenzo Aresu showed us how to bring out the tender, chewy goodness of Sardinia's nugget-like pasta by treating it like rice. Adding liquid in multiple additions gives the grain-like pasta a thick, creamy consistency. Fregola likely requires a trip to the Italian grocery or specialty store. If you have trouble finding it, an equal amount of toasted pearl couscous is a good stand-in; see sidebar for toasting instructions. Also reduce the amount of chicken broth to 4 cups, adding it in two additions of 2 cups each. After cooking for eight to 10 minutes following the second addition of broth, cooking is done; remove the pot from the heat and let stand, uncovered, for four minutes.

Don't use regular chicken broth or the dish may be too salty; low-sodium is best. Also, make sure to let the fregola stand for about 4 minutes before serving; the pasta absorbs additional liquid and sets up slightly.

½ cup sliced almonds

2 tablespoons extra-virgin olive oil, plus more to serve

2 ounces thinly sliced pancetta, finely chopped

1 small yellow onion, finely chopped

4 medium garlic cloves, finely grated

1 tablespoon fennel seeds, ground

¼ teaspoon red pepper flakes

2 cups fregola (see headnote)

½ cup dry white wine

5 cups low-sodium chicken broth, divided

2 ounces pecorino Romano cheese, finely grated (1 cup)

¼ cup chopped fresh flat-leaf parsley

¼ cup chopped fresh basil

¼ cup chopped fresh mint

1 tablespoon lemon juice

Ground black pepper

In a large pot over medium-low, toast the almonds, stirring often, until golden brown, about 5 minutes. Transfer to a small plate, let cool, then roughly chop; set aside.

In the same pot, increase heat to medium and combine the oil and pancetta, then cook, stirring occasionally, until crisp, 2 to 3 minutes. Add the onion and cook, stirring occasionally, until softened, about 5 minutes. Stir in the garlic, fennel seeds, pepper flakes and fregola, then cook, stirring, until the garlic is fragrant, about 30 seconds. Add the wine and cook, stirring occasionally, until reduced to a syrup, 2 to 4 minutes.

Stir in 2 cups of broth. Bring to a simmer over medium-high and cook, uncovered and stirring occasionally, until most of the liquid has been absorbed, 8 to 10 minutes. Stir in another 2 cups broth and cook, stirring, until most of the liquid has been absorbed, 8 to 10 minutes. Stir in the remaining 1 cup broth and cook, stirring constantly, until the fregola is tender and the mixture is creamy but not soupy, another 6 to 8 minutes. Remove from the heat and let stand uncovered until slightly thickened, about 4 minutes.

Stir in half the pecorino, all but a couple tablespoons of each herb, the lemon juice and 1 teaspoon black pepper. Divide among serving bowls, then sprinkle with the almonds, remaining herbs and additional oil.

Faux Fregola

Pearl couscous, sometimes called Israeli couscous, makes an acceptable substitute for Sardinian fregola, but it must be toasted. To toast, put the couscous in a dry, large pot (the same one you'll later use to cook the dish). Cook over medium, stirring often, until golden brown, about 5 minutes. Even after toasting, the couscous will absorb liquid differently than fregola, so be sure to adjust the broth as directed in the recipe headnote.

Fregola con Gamberi e Pomodorini

Fregola with Shrimp and Tomatoes

Start to finish: 1 hour 10 minutes Servings: 4

This is our simplified version of the fregola with seafood and tomato sauce taught to us by chef Francesco Pinna at Trattoria Lillicu in Sardinia. Cooking the pasta in chicken broth and bottled clam juice that were first simmered with shrimp shells adds deep complexity without calling for a lengthy ingredient list. If your shrimp already are shelled, remove the tails and use those to infuse the liquid. And if you have trouble finding fregola, an equal amount of toasted pearl couscous is a good stand-in; p. 159. You'll also need to reduce the chicken broth to only 2 cups. After cooking the fregola for 8 to 10 minutes following the second addition of shrimp-infused broth, remove the pot from the heat before adding the shrimp.

Don't fully cook the shrimp when browning them. They'll be only parcooked when they come out of the pot, but will finish in the residual heat of the fregola. After adding the shrimp to the fregola, don't forget to cover the pot, as this traps heat for cooking the shrimp.

In a medium microwave-safe bowl, combine the shrimp shells, clam juice, chicken broth, bay, thyme and peppercorns. Microwave on high until the shrimp tails are pink and the mixture is hot, 4 to 5 minutes. Pour through a fine-mesh strainer set over another medium bowl; discard the solids in the strainer.

Season the shrimp with salt and pepper. In a large pot over medium-high, heat 1 tablespoon of oil until barely smoking. Add half the shrimp and cook without stirring until well browned on one side, 2 to 3 minutes. Transfer to a large plate. Repeat with another 1 tablespoon oil and the remaining shrimp.

Return the pot to medium-high. Add 1 tablespoon of the remaining oil. Add the tomatoes, onion, carrot and ¼ teaspoon salt, then cook, stirring, until the tomatoes are spotty brown and the onion has softened, 3 to 5 minutes.

Add the garlic and fregola, then cook, stirring, until the garlic is fragrant, about 30 seconds. Stir in 2 cups of the shrimp broth, then bring to a simmer. Reduce to medium and cook, stirring occasionally, until most of the liquid is absorbed, 8 to 10 minutes. Stir in another 2 cups broth, return to a simmer and cook, stirring, until most of the liquid is absorbed, 8 to 10 minutes. Stir in the remaining 1 cup broth and cook, stirring constantly, until the fregola is tender and the mixture is creamy but not soupy, 6 to 8 minutes.

Off heat, stir in the shrimp and accumulated juices, remaining 1 tablespoon oil, lemon juice and parsley. Cover and let stand until the shrimp are opaque throughout, 5 to 7 minutes. Taste and season with salt and pepper.

1½ pounds extra-large (21/25 per pound) shrimp, peeled (shells reserved), deveined and patted dry

Two 8-ounce bottles clam juice

3 cups low-sodium chicken broth

4 bay leaves

1 sprig fresh thyme

1 tablespoon black peppercorns

Kosher salt and ground black pepper

4 tablespoons extra-virgin olive oil, divided

1 pint cherry or grape tomatoes, halved

1 medium yellow onion, finely chopped

1 medium carrot, peeled, halved lengthwise and thinly sliced

2 medium garlic cloves, finely grated

1 cup fregola (see headnote)

2 tablespoons lemon juice

½ cup finely chopped fresh flat-leaf parsley

The pope's pasta carbonara

It supposedly was the signature pasta of Pope Pius XII, but had he tasted some of the versions of it I was served, I suspect history might have let this dish fade from memory. Mushy noodles coated in sticky-dry over-scrambled eggs, all punctuated by limp peas, flaccid strips of deli ham and either not nearly enough cheese or so much it obliterated all other flavors.

Which is a hard sell for what ultimately would be one of the best, most indulgent pastas I've ever eaten.

Let me rewind. We're talking about pasta alla papalina, which roughly translates as pasta for the pope. Now almost 100 years old, it has become a classic—if little known—Roman pasta. As the story goes, during the early 1930s then Cardinal Eugenio Pacelli asked Ceseretto Simmi, a restaurateur with several eateries near the Vatican, if he could prepare a lighter, more sophisticated version of the traditional Roman carbonara.

Carbonara—rich with guanciale and sharp pecorino Romano cheese—was considered a brash dish. "So my grandfather went to my grandmother and said, 'Make carbonara, but use prosciutto instead of guanciale and Parmesan instead of pecorino,'" said Simmi's granddaughter, Elizabetta Simmi, who now has her own restaurant near the Vatican.

"Truly, a pasta fit for a pope."

And yes, pasta alla papalina is on the menu. "The cardinal suggested it and my grandfather created it, a softer carbonara."

It worked because both the cheese and meat were lighter, more nuanced options, which toned down the intensity of the carbonara. The cardinal supposedly was pleased, dining at the elder Simmi's restaurant often. A few years later, he went on to become pope and "his" pasta gained fame, becoming a mainstay of Roman restaurants.

But history wasn't kind to this dish (nor to the pope, whose legacy has been dogged by accusations of aiding the Nazis during World War II). At some point, many chefs replaced the prosciutto with deli ham and—good lord, why?—added canned peas. They also lost the knack for only adding the eggs off heat, allowing them to warm slowly and emulsify into a creamy sauce, rather than curdle into an oddly scrambled mess. Hence the state of the dish when I ate my way through Rome.

It seemed a recipe not worth reviving. That is, until I ate at restaurant Mamma Angelina in the north of Rome. There, chef Andrea Dell'Omo was willing to go off menu for me, researching the history of the dish and creating a version that took it back to Simmi's. Prosciutto. Parmesan. Gently whipped egg yolks. All gently tangled together.

It took Dell'Omo all of about 30 minutes to make and when he mounded it on my plate, creamy and golden, it was... stunning. All the rich comfort of carbonara, but Elizabetta Simmi was right. It was softer. Truly, a pasta fit for a pope.

—J.M. Hirsch

Pasta alla Papalina

Spaghetti witih Prosciutto, Parmesan and Peas

Start to finish: 40 minutes Servings: 4 to 6

In Rome, we learned to make pasta alla papalina—a lighter, brighter riff on classic carbonara. The dish has been popular since the 1920s, when, as the story goes, Cardinal Pacelli, who later became Pope Pius XII, asked chef Ceseretto Simmi to create a more elegant take on the Italian staple. Simmi swapped the traditional pairing of guanciale and pecorino Romano for prosciutto and Parmesan: a slightly less robust yet equally delicious combination. Our version was inspired by chef Andrea Dell'Omo of restaurant Mamma Angelina, who prepared for us a breathtakingly good rendition. We've incorporated frozen peas as well, which have become a common addition; they add freshness as well as attractive pops of green.

Don't worry about thawing the peas. They will "cook" quickly when tossed with the hot pasta, retaining their bright green color and fresh flavor. Also, be sure to remove the pot from the burner before adding the egg-cheese mixture. Residual heat will gently cook the yolks, ensuring they don't curdle but instead create a richness that coats the pasta.

5 large egg yolks

¼ cup heavy cream

2 ounces Parmesan cheese, finely grated (1 cup), plus more to serve

Kosher salt and ground black pepper

1 pound spaghetti or linguine

3 tablespoons salted butter, cut into 2 or 3 pieces

1 small red onion, finely chopped

4 ounces sliced prosciutto, cut into ¼-inch ribbons

1 cup frozen peas

In a medium bowl, whisk together the egg yolks, cream, Parmesan and 2 teaspoons pepper; set aside. In a large pot, bring 4 quarts water to a boil. Add the spaghetti and 1 tablespoon salt, then cook, stirring occasionally, until al dente. Reserve about 1 cup of the cooking water, then drain and return the pasta to the pot; set aside.

In a 12-inch skillet over medium, melt the butter. Add the onion and cook, stirring occasionally, until beginning to soften, 2 to 3 minutes. Add the prosciutto and cook, stirring occasionally, until slightly crisped, 4 to 5 minutes. Remove the pan from the heat, transfer about one-quarter of the prosciutto-onion mixture to a small plate and reserve for garnish.

Scrape the remaining prosciutto-onion mixture into the pasta in the pot, then add the peas and ¼ cup reserved pasta water. Cook over medium-high, stirring, until warmed through, 1 to 2 minutes. Off heat, add the egg-cheese mixture; stir until the sauce thickens slightly and clings to the pasta, 2 to 3 minutes. If needed, toss in reserved water 1 tablespoon at a time to adjust the consistency. Taste and season with salt and pepper. Serve topped with the reserved prosciutto-onion mixture and additional Parmesan.

Sicily's simple pastas

Glistening and splayed on the road, the 280-kilogram tuna lay amid the evening scrum—a dusky piazza tumbling with chattering nonnas, couples on promenade and children punting soccer balls. It was dinner time in Borgo Vecchio, Palermo's oldest quarter. I'd come for Sicily's simple, on-the-table-in-minutes pastas, but first the tuna had a lesson to teach.

At the center of the square, a young cook stood sentry over a long grill of coals he fanned with a wooden pizza peel. Over the embers, rough-cut tuna steaks, sizzling and billowing as he sloshed them with olive oil and lemon juice, the piazza filling with savory and smoke.

It was unregulated, unauthorized and almost certainly unsanitary. I was all in. For €9 (about $10), the fishmonger hacked me two robust steaks from the tuna, directing me to carry them to the cook. Another few euros earned my steaks a spot on the grill, along with generous splashes of vinaigrette. For bread, I was sent to Santarita Panificio, the bakery across the street. For wine, the supermercato next to it. For plastic cups and the loan of a corkscrew, the bar opposite the square (a bargain at €1).

The meal merged on a shaky plastic table under a darkening sky, laundry flapping from clothes lines above. The tuna—utter simplicity, utterly delicious. The barest of ingredients, flavors heightened but unmasked. It was rich and meaty, balanced by sweet, clear lemon, a lesson that trailed me across a weeklong circumnavigation of the island.

In Sicily, the nuts and sweets of North Africa long ago married the richness of classic Italian cooking, producing a cuisine where ingredients are combined sparingly to create brightness, ever blending sweet and savory. I'd come to find two easy pasta dishes I'd heard brokered that balance. I didn't realize a third would find me.

My exploration of Sicilian pastas began in Castelbuono, a hilltop town in northern Sicily. Vincenzo Ippolito and his wife, Maria Enza Arena, welcomed me to a dayslong feast fueled by homemade wine decanted from an ancient barrel in a shed. It began in their outdoor kitchen overlooking fog-filled valleys—a local shepherd kicked it off with 40 liters of raw goat milk he transformed into three varieties of fresh ricotta over a bonfire in an old washing machine tub—and ended with a pasta-making lesson in the summer home of a friend down the mountain.

That friend, Benedetto Giacalone, a military police officer, used oxen hands to mash semolina flour, water and salt into a supple dough that the rest of us rolled, stretched and pressed into a pea pod-shaped pasta called gnocchi cavati. Indentations made by our fingertips formed tiny basins to capture pesto Trapanese, a raw tomato sauce from Trapani, Giacalone's seaport hometown in northwestern Sicily.

"Beyond sheer simplicity, the trio of pastas had a common thread: nuts."

Like the tuna, the pesto—once reserved for Sunday dinner—was a study in simplicity. Giacalone finely grated a handful of garlic cloves into a large wooden mortar, then used a pestle to mash them with coarse salt to form a smooth, wet paste. A handful of chopped grape tomatoes and more mashing. This pulpy-garlicky mix was then stirred into a large bowl of chopped tomatoes and torn fresh basil. Olive oil for peppery bite and richness, and the sauce was done.

Separately, coarse breadcrumbs were lightly toasted with olive oil, then set aside. The final ingredient, a flourish I would see over and again in Sicily: nuts, toasted and crushed. We used almonds that day, though the pistachios for which Sicily is known are also common. When the pasta was cooked, it was added to the tomatoes, steam lifting aromas of garlic, basil and

sweetness as it was spooned into bowls. Breadcrumbs and almonds were sprinkled over each serving, creating a dish at once raw, rich and sweet, tender and crunchy, an almost instant sauce that was bold, fresh and bright.

While all this was happening, Giacalone's wife, Lea Venturella, focused on sarde a becca-fico, a side dish I was certain never would make the pages of Milk Street. Working at the other end of the long table— closer to where a television shared space with a pizza oven—she made a mash of chopped raisins, pine nuts, garlic, parsley, breadcrumbs and olive oil, which she stuffed into fileted sardines, rolling them into tight bundles and snugging them into a pan. After baking, they were delicious—that same Sicilian sweet-savory-tender-crunchy—but also daunting. Raisin-stuffed sardines? That's a hard sell.

Not knowing that dish would dog me, I headed three hours southeast—wending past smoking Mount Etna—to Sicilia in Tavola, a stone arched trattoria in Siracusa. Owner Doriana Gesualdi offered to teach me a similarly simple and bold—but this time warm—sauce of pistachios, tomatoes and little else. "We don't use garlic because we want you to taste the pure pistachios," she explained.

In minutes—less time than the pasta cooked—chopped grape tomatoes were reduced to a sauce in a skillet of sizzling olive oil. A splash of starchy pasta cooking water first loosened, then thickened them. Coarsely ground pistachios mixed with olive oil went in next, simmering and reducing. Next, the pasta—plump ricotta-stuffed ravioli. Onto the plate and topped with more crushed pistachios, all in under 10 minutes. There it was again—a

simple, sparing mix that nonetheless produced pronounced flavors and textures. Sweet tomatoes and rich, savory nuts created an almost creamy sauce, the latter also offering crunch to offset the tender pasta.

Gesualdi also wanted to show me something unhelpfully named pasta Siracusa. Turned out to be the local version of a dish known as pasta con le sarde, or pasta with sardines. While much of Sicily dines eagerly, frequently on sardines, in Siracusa they favor the poor person's alternative—briny-savory anchovies. And so, garlic and anchovies browned and melted in sizzling olive oil before being tossed with pasta, breadcrumbs and parsley. Deliciously crunchy and rich, yet light. Again, on the table in minutes.

There was something familiar about this, but understanding it took another 500 kilometers around and up the southwestern side of Sicily, returning to Palermo. There on the fringes of Vucciria Market—a neighborhood still pockmarked by WWII wounds and rough enough to be skipped by tourists—I was pulled into the kitchen of Vecchia Trattoria da Totò. Husband and wife Giuseppe and Piera di Noto offered a signature dish: pasta Palermitana.

Piera deftly and speedily combined garlic, anchovies, pine nuts and raisins in a skillet of hot olive oil, cooking them until the fruit plumped and the anchovies melted. Pasta was added and tossed until richly coated, then dusted with coarse breadcrumbs. Another 10-minute dish that tasted of hours. The tender raisins added pops of sweetness against the salty anchovies and pungent garlic. And again

with the nuts and breadcrumbs for texture. That's when it struck me. This was a more elaborate version of Gesualdi's pasta Siracusa. Strike that. Both of them were Venturella's stuffed sardines recast as an easy pasta dish.

Beyond sheer simplicity, the trio of pastas had a common thread: nuts. Sicilians use them liberally for texture and richness to balance sweet ingredients like tomatoes and raisins.

Adapting them at Milk Street was easy.

We loved the contrasting textures of crushed and chunked tomatoes in Giacalone's pesto Trapanese, but streamlined using a food processor, adding some tomatoes first, the rest later. We also liked the richness of adding some of the almonds to the processor with the garlic and salt.

Gesualdi's pasta with pistachio-tomato pesto was equally simple. We followed her recipe with few exceptions, adding fresh mint and lemon zest for their bright, fresh flavors. We also added a savory sprinkling of grated Parmesan or pecorino Romano cheese.

Likewise, the pasta Palermitano (or Siracusa, as you like). We mostly stuck with Piera's recipe, though we liked more anchovies. We balanced the salty richness with white wine vinegar, a combination in keeping with Sicily's love of agrodolce, a sweet-and-sour vegetable sauce.

Deliciously simple, though perhaps lacking the romance of tuna grilled in the street. Then again, I later heard that a similar feast the same night a few piazzas away left several people hospitalized. So maybe pasta is the better choice.

—J.M. Hirsch

Pasta Con Pistacchi, Pomodorini e Menta
Pasta with Pistachios, Tomatoes and Mint

Start to finish: 20 minutes   Servings: 4

This recipe is our take on a pistachio- and tomato-dressed pasta taught to us by Doriana Gesualdi, owner of Sicilia in Tavola, in Siracusa. Sicily is known for its pistachios, so it's no surprise that the colorful, subtly sweet nuts feature heavily in the region's cuisine. With lemon zest and mint as accent ingredients, the flavors are fresh and bright. Just about any variety of pasta worked well, but we particularly liked long strands, such as linguine and spaghetti.

Don't use raw pistachios; opt for roasted, as they don't require toasting before chopping. Either salted or unsalted worked well.

In a large pot, bring 4 quarts water to a boil. Add the pasta and 1 tablespoon salt, then cook, stirring occasionally, until just shy of al dente. Reserve about 2 cups of the cooking water, then drain the pasta.

In a 12-inch skillet over medium, combine the oil and tomatoes. Cook, stirring only once or twice, until the tomatoes have softened and the oil has taken on a reddish hue, 4 to 6 minutes. Stir in half the pistachios, 1½ cups of the reserved cooking water and ¼ teaspoon each salt and pepper. Bring to a simmer and cook, stirring occasionally, until the mixture is slightly reduced and the tomatoes are completely softened, about 2 minutes.

Add the pasta and lemon zest, then cook, stirring frequently, until the pasta is al dente and has absorbed most of the liquid but is still quite saucy, 2 to 4 minutes. Off heat, stir in the mint, then taste and season with salt and pepper. If the pasta is dry, add more cooking water, 1 tablespoon at a time. Transfer to a serving bowl, then sprinkle with the remaining pistachios and drizzle with additional oil. Serve with cheese.

12 ounces pasta (see headnote)

Kosher salt and ground black pepper

¼ cup extra-virgin olive oil, plus more to serve

1 pint grape or cherry tomatoes, halved

½ cup shelled roasted pistachios, finely chopped, divided

1 tablespoon grated lemon zest

2 tablespoons roughly chopped fresh mint

Grated Parmesan or pecorino Romano cheese, to serve

Gemelli alla Pesto Trapanese
Gemelli with Tomato-Almond Pesto and Croutons

Start to finish: 30 minutes Servings: 4

A food processor brings weeknight ease to pesto Trapanese, Sicily's fresh and flavorful no-cook tomato sauce. When we sampled this sauce in Sicily, it was made the traditional way, with a large mortar and pestle. A food processor gets it done faster and more easily. Topped with crisp, olive oil–infused croutons and toasted almonds, the dish is served warm or at room temperature after the pasta has had a few minutes to soak in the flavorful sauce. Instead of blanched, slivered almonds, you also could use sliced or whole almonds that have been roughly chopped.

Don't overprocess the second addition of tomatoes. The first half is pulsed to create a juicy sauce, but the rest are pulsed only until roughly chopped so that tomato chunks add bursts of bright color and texture.

¾ cup slivered almonds

12 ounces gemelli or other short pasta

Kosher salt and ground black pepper

4 medium garlic cloves, smashed and peeled

½ cup lightly packed fresh basil, torn if large

2 pints cherry tomatoes, divided

6 tablespoons extra-virgin olive oil, divided, plus more to serve

3 ounces crusty white bread, torn into rough ½-inch pieces (about 1¾ cups)

In a 10-inch skillet over medium-high, toast the almonds, stirring frequently, until golden brown and fragrant, 3 to 5 minutes. Transfer to a small bowl and set aside; reserve the skillet.

In a large pot, bring 4 quarts water to a boil. Add the pasta and 1 tablespoon salt, then cook, stirring occasionally, until al dente. Reserve about ½ cup of the cooking water, then drain the pasta.

Meanwhile, in a food processor, process ½ cup of the almonds, the garlic and 1 teaspoon salt until finely chopped, about 30 seconds. Add the basil and half of the tomatoes, then pulse until chopped and well combined, 4 to 6 pulses. Add the remaining tomatoes and 2 tablespoons of oil, then pulse just until the whole tomatoes are broken up, about 3 pulses. Transfer to a serving bowl, add the pasta and ¼ cup of the reserved cooking water, then toss. Let stand, tossing once or twice, for 10 to 15 minutes to allow the pasta to absorb some of the sauce.

While the pasta stands, in the same skillet used to toast the almonds, toss the bread, remaining 4 tablespoons oil and ¼ teaspoon each salt and pepper. Cook over medium, stirring frequently, until the bread is crisp and golden brown, 5 to 7 minutes.

Scatter the toasted bread and the remaining ¼ cup almonds over the pasta. Drizzle with additional oil and sprinkle with pepper.

Spaghetti Siracusa

Spaghetti with Anchovies, Pine nuts and Raisins

Start to finish: 30 minutes   Servings: 4

This pasta dish features the classic Sicilian flavor combination of savory, sweet and sour and was inspired by a recipe from Vecchia Trattoria da Totò run by Guiseppe and Piera di Noto in Palermo. Toasted breadcrumbs, sprinkled on just before serving, provide pleasant crispness. We preferred fluffy panko breadcrumbs over regular powder-fine breadcrumbs, but crushing or chopping the panko before toasting ensured better blending with the pasta. Crush the panko in a zip-close plastic bag with a meat pounder or rolling pin, or simply chop it with a chef's knife on a cutting board.

Don't overcook the pasta after adding it to the sauce. The noodles should be al dente and slippery. If needed, loosen them by tossing with additional reserved pasta water.

In a large pot, bring 4 quarts water to a boil. Add the spaghetti and 1 tablespoon salt, then cook, stirring occasionally, until just shy of al dente. Reserve about 1½ cups of the cooking water, then drain the pasta.

While the pasta cooks, in a 12-inch skillet over medium, combine 2 tablespoons oil and the panko. Cook, stirring often, until golden brown, 3 to 5 minutes. Transfer to a small bowl and set aside; wipe out the skillet.

Set the skillet over medium-high and add the remaining 4 tablespoons oil, the pine nuts, raisins, anchovies and garlic. Cook, stirring, until the anchovies have broken up and the garlic is golden brown, about 2 minutes. Stir in the vinegar and cook until syrupy, 30 to 60 seconds. Add 1 cup of the reserved pasta water and ¼ teaspoon each salt and pepper and bring to a simmer.

Add the pasta, reduce to medium, and cook, occasionally tossing to combine, until the pasta is al dente and has absorbed most of the moisture but is still a little saucy, about 2 minutes. Remove from the heat. If the pasta is dry, add more cooking water, 1 tablespoon at a time. Stir in the parsley, then taste and season with salt and pepper. Transfer to a serving bowl. Sprinkle with the panko and top with additional oil and pepper.

12 ounces spaghetti

Kosher salt and ground black pepper

6 tablespoons extra-virgin olive oil, divided, plus more to serve

⅓ cup panko breadcrumbs, finely crushed or chopped (see headnote)

¼ cup pine nuts, finely chopped

3 tablespoons golden raisins, finely chopped

10 oil-packed anchovy fillets, patted dry

8 medium garlic cloves, finely chopped

2 tablespoons white wine vinegar

½ cup lightly packed fresh flat-leaf parsley, chopped

Claudio Furlanis deliciously upends a classic Italian pasta

Claudio Furlanis has a way of upending classic Italian cooking. He also is a master at honoring it, keeping flavors clean and—importantly—familiar. It's a dichotomy delicious to explore at Osteria ai Promessi Sposi, his back alley eatery seductively hidden from the tourists who swamp the canal-side lanes of Venice.

His pasta all'amatriciana, for example. The classic savory-spicy sauce is made from guanciale, tomatoes, chili flakes, and not a lot else. This being a seafood city, in Furlanis' kitchen the cured pork is replaced by shrimp and scallops that he soaks in whiskey, sugar and salt, then smokes over smoldering oak chips.

The result, tossed with a tangle of barely tender pasta that finishes cooking in the sauce, is sweet, savory and every bit as meaty as—and yet, somehow lighter than—the traditional recipe. Familiar, delicious, different.

The feeling is similar with his bigoli with tomatoes and anchovies. A classic combination in which fresh tomatoes and anchovy fillets melt and meld in a skillet, forming a salty-savory-sweet sauce that comes together in minutes and clings to the noodles. Cucina povera happily meets Tuesday night cooking.

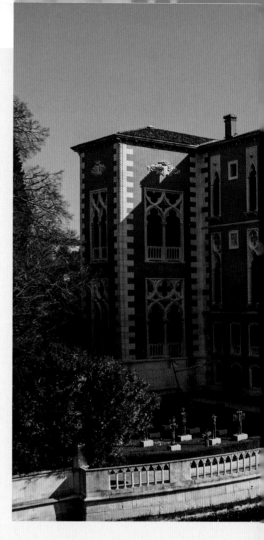

"Familiar, delicious, different."

But Furlanis, who has run the restaurant since 2008 and been cooking professionally since he was 15, has easy upgrades even to this simple dish. First, the tomatoes—cherries, for their reliable sweetness. Rather than use them raw, he roasts them first, thickening and concentrating their sugary-savory side. Only then do they go in the skillet.

His second tweak is a large onion. Sliced and oiled, it caramelizes slowly over low heat in that same skillet. Not browned, but definitely jammy. The perfect foil to the briny-rich anchovies and now super-sweetened tomatoes.

A little different. A lot familiar. Every bit delicious.

—J.M. Hirsch

Rigatoni con Pomodorini e Acciughe
Rigatoni with Cherry Tomatoes and Anchovies

Start to finish: 30 minutes Servings: 4 to 6

At Osteria ai Promessi Sposi in Venice, chef Claudio Furlanis taught us how to make a dish of his own creation—pasta tossed with cherry tomatoes, sautéed onion and anchovies. Furlanis briefly roasted the tomatoes to render them soft and juicy and to concentrate their flavor before introducing them to the other ingredients. The umami quotient was deliciously high from the tomatoes and anchovies, and with the sauce cooked into the pasta until the noodles were perfectly al dente, each bite was extraordinarily satisfying and flavor-filled. This recipe is our adaptation of his dish. We swapped rigatoni or ziti for the very large, short, tube-shaped noodles we had in Venice and added some garlic and pepper flakes for a little pungency. We also like to finish the pasta with grated Parmesan.

Don't use more than 6 cups of water to boil the pasta. The amount is scant, but intentionally so in order to create a starchy liquid to use later, when saucing the noodles. Also, be sure to drain the pasta when it's shy of al dente. It will finish cooking directly in the sauce, where it absorbs lots of flavor.

2 pints cherry or grape tomatoes

6 tablespoons extra-virgin olive oil, divided

Kosher salt and ground black pepper

2 medium garlic cloves, smashed and peeled

1 large yellow onion, finely chopped

5 oil-packed anchovy fillets

½ teaspoon red pepper flakes

1 pound rigatoni, ziti or mezze rigati pasta

Finely grated Parmesan cheese, to serve

Heat the oven to broil with a rack about 6 inches from the element. Line a broiler-safe rimmed baking sheet with foil. In a large bowl, toss together the tomatoes, 2 tablespoons of the oil and ½ teaspoon each salt and pepper. Transfer the mixture, including the oil, to the prepared baking sheet and broil until the tomatoes are blistered and most have burst, 8 to 10 minutes; set aside.

In a 12-inch skillet over medium-high, combine the remaining 4 tablespoons oil and the garlic; cook, stirring, until the garlic is lightly browned, about 2 minutes. Remove and discard the garlic, then stir in the onion and ½ teaspoon salt. Reduce to medium, cover and cook, stirring occasionally, until the onion is fully softened but not browned, about 10 minutes. Add the anchovies and pepper flakes; cook, stirring, until the anchovies have broken down, about 5 minutes.

Stir in the tomatoes with juices. Bring to a simmer over medium-high and cook, stirring often and pressing on the tomatoes that did not burst during broiling, until the tomatoes have broken down and a spatula drawn through the sauce leaves a trail, 3 to 5 minutes. Remove the pan from the heat.

In a large pot, bring 6 cups water to a boil. Add the pasta and 1 teaspoon salt, then cook, stirring occasionally, until the noodles are tender on the exterior but still quite firm at the center. Drain the pasta in a colander set in a large bowl; reserve the cooking water. Return the pasta to the pot and stir in the tomato mixture followed by 2 cups of the reserved pasta water. Cover and cook over medium, stirring

occasionally, until the pasta is al dente, 5 to 7 minutes, adding more reserved water as needed so the sauce clings to the noodles. Taste and season with salt and pepper. Serve sprinkled with Parmesan.

In Rome, broccoli is a sauce, not a side

A broccoli sauce is a hard sell anywhere in the world, but particularly in Rome, the city of—let's be honest— more alluringly simple pastas like cacio e pepe and carbonara.

So I expected little from the primo at Pipero Roma—Allesandro Pipero's posh restaurant not far from the Pantheon—rigatoni dressed sparingly with a thin, bright green sauce I initially mistook for pesto.

One bite dismissed that notion but also didn't provide clarity. The pasta, of course, was perfectly al dente. The sauce, which most definitely was not pesto, was light, tasting as bright as its hue—thin, clean and herbal, but still rich.

In fact, it tasted little of broccoli. Not sulfurous or harsh. Nor raw or fibrous. Just simple, smooth freshness with rich, savory flavor that lingered behind it.

It was good enough to draw me into the kitchen, where sous chef David Puleio explained how they extract such delicate flavor from so robust a vegetable. The answer was entirely unexpected: broccoli leaves.

In fact, the dish is one of a family of Italian recipes in which a boldly flavored green vegetable—asparagus is another common choice—is blanched until tender, then pureed with simple seasonings and a bit of starchy pasta cooking water.

The result is a light, bright sauce that belies its starting point. The result—and intent—is to enhance rather than cloak the pasta.

Pipero Roma's version was a simple emulsion of blanched broccoli leaves pureed with butter—an unusual choice in olive oil country—garlic, red chili and a splash of water. It came together in minutes, the finishing flourish a bit of the city's go-to pecorino Romano cheese.

Simple though it was, bringing this back to Milk Street presented challenges. Broccoli leaves are few on the crowns sold at U.S. supermarkets. An alternative was clearly needed.

We considered an entirely new green—spinach—but that was too grassy. Instead, we worked with what was available and abundant: the broccoli

"Just simple, smooth freshness with rich, savory flavor that lingered behind it."

stalks. Peeled of their tough skins, they pureed wonderfully after a brief boil, developing the same silky, smooth texture I'd had in Rome.

We kept the garlic and butter, which gave the sauce a creamier note than olive oil, but favored the ease and convenience of red pepper flakes over a fresh chili. But while the flavor was good, the color was wan, nothing like the vibrant green sauce I'd loved in Rome.

The solution brought us back to spinach. Just a bit of baby spinach added to the broccoli brightened the dish, keeping both the flavor and color bright. We also found the sauce benefited from stirring a bit of the cheese into it, giving it a richer body and deeper savory flavor.

–J.M. Hirsch

Rigatoni con Salsa di Broccoli

Rigatoni with Roman Broccoli Sauce

Start to finish: 35 minutes Servings: 4

This is an adaptation of a pasta we had in Rome where cooks use the leaves that grow around heads of broccoli to make a flavorful sauce for pasta. In the U.S., most of the leaves are stripped off before broccoli is sold. Our recipe instead uses the stems, which are equally flavorful and produce a silky sauce. Baby spinach retains the color of the original recipe.

Don't undercook the broccoli stems. We're accustomed to cooking vegetables until crisp-tender, but the stems here should be cooked until fully tender.

In a large pot, bring 4 quarts water and 1 tablespoon salt to a boil. Peel the broccoli stems, reserving any leaves, and cut crosswise into ½-inch rounds. Add the stems and leaves to the boiling water and cook until fully tender, about 10 minutes. Stir in the spinach and cook until wilted, about 20 seconds. Using a slotted spoon, transfer the vegetables to a blender; reserve ½ cup of the cooking water. Keep the water at a boil.

Cut the broccoli florets into 1- to 1½-inch pieces. Add the florets to the boiling water and cook until crisp-tender, about 3 minutes. Using the slotted spoon, transfer to a colander and rinse under cold water until cooled. Again keep the water at a boil.

To the blender, add the garlic, butter, capers, pepper flakes, ¼ teaspoon salt, 1 tablespoon of the lemon zest and the reserved broccoli cooking water. Puree until smooth and bright green, about 30 seconds. Taste and season with salt and pepper.

Stir the rigatoni into the boiling water and cook until al dente. Reserve ½ cup of the cooking water, then drain. Return the pasta to the pot and add the broccoli florets, the broccoli puree, ¼ cup of the reserved cooking water, the remaining 1 tablespoon lemon zest and the cheese.

Cook over medium, stirring constantly, until the sauce thickens slightly and the pasta is well coated, 1 to 2 minutes. Remove from the heat. Taste and season with salt and pepper.

1 pound broccoli, stems and florets separated

Kosher salt and ground black pepper

1½ cups packed baby spinach

2 medium garlic cloves, chopped

4 tablespoons salted butter, cut into 4 pieces

1 tablespoon drained capers

½ teaspoon red pepper flakes

2 tablespoons finely grated lemon zest, divided

12 ounces rigatoni pasta

1 ounce pecorino Romano or Parmesan cheese, finely grated (½ cup), plus more to serve

Pasta alla Pecorara
Shepherd's-Style Pasta

Start to finish: 1 hour Servings: 6 to 8

Known as "shepherd's-style pasta," pasta alla pecorara gets its name from its use of sheep's milk cheese and local vegetables. We were inspired by Abruzzese home cook Luisa Carinci, who enhanced her version with pancetta. Carinci seasoned her sauce with marjoram, which grows abundantly in the region and tastes like a sweeter, more delicate oregano. If you can't find it, fresh oregano works fine. The sauce traditionally is paired with a handmade ring-shaped pasta called anellini. In its place, we call on store-bought orecchiette, which does an excellent job of catching chunks of the rustic sauce.

Don't rush the cooking of the pancetta and aromatics. Keeping the pot covered and the heat on medium-low will give the pancetta time to render its fat and for the aromatics to relinquish their flavor and become meltingly soft.

In a Dutch oven over medium, heat ¼ cup oil until shimmering. Add the zucchini, eggplant, bell pepper, 1 teaspoon salt and ½ teaspoon pepper. Cook, stirring, until the vegetables are tender but still hold their shape, 10 to 12 minutes. Transfer to a plate and set aside.

To the fat remaining in the pot, add the pancetta, onion, carrots

and celery. Cover and cook over medium-low, stirring occasionally, until the pancetta is beginning to brown and the vegetables are softened, 18 to 20 minutes.

Meanwhile, in a large pot, boil 4 quarts water. Add the pasta and 1 tablespoon salt, then cook, stirring occasionally, until al dente. Reserve 1 cup of the cooking water, then drain. Drizzle the pasta with the remaining 1 tablespoon oil and toss.

To the mixture in the Dutch oven, add the tomatoes, marjoram and ½ cup pasta water. Bring to a simmer over medium and cook, uncovered and stirring, until a wooden spoon drawn through leaves a trail, 5 to 6 minutes. Add the pasta and vegetables; cook, stirring, until heated through, 2 to 3 minutes. Stir in the basil and Parmesan; add additional cooking water as needed if the mixture looks dry. Taste and season with salt and pepper. Serve topped with ricotta, additional oil and additional Parmesan.

¼ cup plus 1 tablespoon extra-virgin olive oil, plus more to serve

1 large zucchini (about 12 ounces), cut into ½-inch cubes

1 small Italian eggplant (about 8 ounces), cut into ½-inch cubes

1 medium red bell pepper, stemmed, seeded and cut into ½-inch pieces

Kosher salt and ground black pepper

4 ounces pancetta, chopped

1 small yellow onion, finely chopped

2 medium carrots, peeled and finely chopped

1 medium celery stalk, finely chopped

1 pound orecchiette

14½-ounce can crushed tomatoes

1 tablespoon finely chopped fresh marjoram or oregano

1 cup lightly packed fresh basil, chopped

½ ounce Parmesan cheese, finely grated (¼ cup), plus more to serve

Whole-milk ricotta or crumbled ricotta salata cheese, to serve

Pasta con Asparagi e Pancetta
Fettuccine with Asparagus and Pancetta

Start to finish: 45 minutes Servings: 4 to 6

In Mompeo, home cook Alfonsina Cortegiani showed us how she makes pasta con asparagi e pancetta, an elegant dish featuring wispy wild asparagus and fresh egg noodles. For our adaptation, look for slender asparagus—about the size of a pencil—and cut the spears on the diagonal into 2-inch lengths. If only thick spears are available, slice them about ½ inch thick on a very sharp bias and sauté them for an extra minute or so to ensure the asparagus is properly cooked through. The asparagus is done when the pieces are tender-crisp—they should be supple enough to bend with the noodles but have a little crispness at the core. To contrast the sweet, grassy notes of the asparagus but to pair with the porky notes of the pancetta, we prefer the pecorino Romano cheese over Parmesan.

Don't add the pasta to the boiling water until the asparagus has had a chance to sauté for a few minutes. Fresh pasta cooks in just a couple of minutes, so once it's added to the pot, the dish comes together very quickly.

In a large pot, bring 4 quarts water to a boil. Meanwhile, in a 12-inch skillet over medium-high, combine the oil and pancetta. Cook, stirring occasionally, until the pancetta has rendered its fat and is golden brown, 4 to 6 minutes. Remove from the heat and, using a slotted spoon, transfer the pancetta to a small bowl; set aside.

To the boiling water, add the pasta and 1 tablespoon salt, then cook, stirring often, until the pasta is just shy of al dente. Reserve 1½ cups of the cooking water, then drain. Rinse the noodles under cold running water, tossing constantly, until completely cool to the touch. Set aside; reserve the pot.

Return the skillet to medium and add the garlic and pepper flakes (if using). Cook, stirring often, until the garlic is lightly browned, about 1 minute. Stir in the asparagus, ½ cup reserved pasta water and ¼ teaspoon each salt and black pepper. Bring to a simmer over medium-high and cook, uncovered and stirring occasionally, until tender-crisp, about 3 minutes.

Transfer the asparagus to the now-empty pot. Add the pasta, another ½ cup reserved pasta water and the pecorino. Cook over medium-high, tossing, until the cheese is melted and the pasta is well coated, 2 to 3 minutes; add more reserved water as needed so the pasta is lightly sauced. Off heat, toss in the pancetta and lemon juice. Taste and season with salt and black pepper.

2 tablespoons extra-virgin olive oil

4 ounces pancetta, chopped

Two 9-ounce packages fresh fettuccine

Kosher salt and ground black pepper

4 medium garlic cloves, minced

¼ teaspoon red pepper flakes (optional)

12 to 16 ounces slender asparagus (see headnote), ends trimmed, cut into 2-inch lengths on a sharp diagonal

2 ounces pecorino Romano cheese, finely grated (1 cup)

2 tablespoons lemon juice

Pasta Cremosa di Patate e Carciofi

Creamy Potato and Artichoke Pasta

Start to finish: 40 minutes Servings: 4 to 6

In Veneto, chef Matteo Albani prepared a contradiction of a pasta dish. It was lush and creamy, yet entirely free of dairy. His secret, we learned, was the humble potato. He boiled it, then pureed it and its starchy cooking water before using it to enrich his sauce. We found that simply mashing the potato had a similar effect, while negating the need to haul out a blender. We experimented with Yukon Golds, but ultimately, a high-starch russet yielded the creamiest sauce. As for artichoke hearts, we tried all the usual prepared suspects: jarred, canned and frozen. When sautéed with cherry tomatoes, garlic and herbs, canned and frozen artichoke hearts became mushy. Jarred won out because they held their shape.

Don't use grilled or marinated artichokes. The smokiness from the grill and garlickiness of the seasoned oil muddy the dish's otherwise bright, clean flavors.

In a large pot, combine the potato and 4 quarts water. Bring to a boil over high and cook until a skewer inserted into the potato meets no resistance, about 8 minutes. Using a slotted spoon, transfer the potato to a small bowl. Add ¼ teaspoon salt and ¼ cup of the cooking water, then mash with a fork until smooth. If needed, add more cooking water 1 tablespoon at a time until the potato is completely smooth and has the consistency of pourable yogurt; set aside. Return the water to a boil.

In a 12-inch skillet over medium, heat the oil until shimmering. Add the artichoke hearts, shallot, rosemary sprig and ½ teaspoon each salt and pepper. Cook, stirring, until the shallot has softened and the artichoke hearts are just beginning to brown, about 3 minutes. Add the garlic and cook until fragrant, about 30 seconds.

Stir in the tomatoes and cook, stirring, until they begin to break down, about 3 minutes. Add the wine and cook, stirring and scraping up any browned bits, until reduced by half, about 3 minutes. Remove and discard the rosemary, then stir in the potato mixture. Remove the skillet from the heat.

Meanwhile, to the boiling water, add the pasta and 1 tablespoon salt. Cook, stirring occasionally, until just shy of al dente. Reserve 1 cup of the cooking water, then drain. Return the pasta to the pot.

Add the sauce to the pasta and cook over medium-high, tossing, until the pasta is al dente, 3 to 5 minutes. Add reserved cooking water as needed so the sauce clings to the noodles. Taste and season with salt and pepper. Serve drizzled with additional oil and sprinkled with parsley and Parmesan.

1 medium russet potato (about 8 ounces), peeled and cut into 1-inch chunks

Kosher salt and ground black pepper

¼ cup extra-virgin olive oil, plus more to serve

12-ounce jar artichoke hearts, drained, patted dry and chopped (about 1½ cups)

1 medium shallot, finely chopped

5-inch rosemary sprig

2 medium garlic cloves, finely chopped

1 pint cherry or grape tomatoes, halved

½ cup dry white wine

1 pound campanelle or fusilli

Chopped fresh flat-leaf parsley, to serve

Finely grated Parmesan cheese, to serve

Italy's best pasta sauce has a secret ingredient

The wine spigots at the cash register—men popping in to fill tiny glasses with the house white, then ambling on. The construction workers making a quick lunch of exquisitely crisp-plump fried anchovies. The bickering between mother (in the kitchen) and son (at the counter) during the rush to serve regulars beneath the white stone arches of their 10-table trattoria.

It's all a bit much, really. A Central Casting cliché that feels unreal. But La Cantinetta is real. And lunch at this convenience store/enoteca/eatery—where cat food and wine and potato chips and packages of pasta share shelves—has changed little since Maria Notaro took over more than 60 years ago. It also happens to serve some of the best food in Naples.

Not that you'd easily find it. It's hidden on the city outskirts on a residential street on the wrong side of the tracks of Stazione di Napoli Centrale. I almost walked past, wine and water bottles stacked unceremoniously outside its double-wide doors, but for its sidewalk menu board. Scrawled casually were the words I'd spent more than a week searching for.

Zuppa forte.

I've eaten my way across Italy dozens of times, but never had I encountered a mystery the likes of zuppa forte, literally "strong soup." A translation that does poor justice to this pasta sauce-bruschetta topping-soup mashup that everyone I encountered knew and loved yet somehow knew little about. How is it made? What are the ingredients?

Non lo so. Chiedi al macellaio. I don't know. Ask the butcher. I heard it over and again.

I learned bits and pieces along the way, but nothing that completed the picture about a dish best described as a highly concentrated, intensely flavored, gently spicy and deeply meaty tomato "sauce" that verges on paste and also happened to be one of the best things I'd ever tasted in Italy. Hence, my mission to master its secrets.

Stumbling upon Notaro's shop, which she runs with her son, Luigi Tufano, on my last day in the city felt like a windfall. The octogenarian welcomed me into her kitchen, where she quickly boiled spaghetti until al dente, then combined it, some of its cooking water and a generous scoop of zuppa forte, tossing it all until perfectly wedded.

It was a rich, savory, spicy, meaty, sweet explosion. This is the Italian meat sauce we never knew how deeply we longed for. Importantly, there was a depth to it, something I couldn't quite identify and had never tasted in an Italian pasta sauce. There was a complexity that I didn't quite understand but that insisted I keep eating.

Before meeting Notaro, I'd spent a week scouring the city to learn the origins of zuppa forte, also called zuppa di soffritto. The tomato paste–looking sauce—deeply red, incredibly thick and speckled with

> "It was a rich, savory, spicy, meaty, sweet explosion."

small hunks of meat—shows up on almost no menus, but can be found at nearly every butcher, big bowlfuls sitting in the deli case, sold by the scoop.

But have you tried interviewing Neapolitan butchers? From most, I got at best partial answers about offal, tomato paste and lung meat. Some said it was cooked for days, some for hours. Ingredient list? What's that? Most directed me to random restaurants "down the street," where I reliably encountered answers equally sparing.

My first real clues came from Salvatore Giugliano, chef at Mimì alla Ferrovia, a restaurant his grandfather opened in 1944. He modernizes classic Neapolitan recipes, and though zuppa forte isn't on his menu, he'll make it for diners who ask for it. "The generation of my father, it's part of their story," he says. And he enjoys reviving it. "There's a new generation of guys who are interested in recipes like this, the return to the old dishes."

Zuppa forte, it turns out, dates to at least the 1800s and is a classic example of the region's cucina povera, cooking that made the best of whatever was on hand. The poor worked the land, and the noblemen fed them the offal and other less desirable bits of meat. Combine that with tomatoes—this is pomodoro country, after all—and you've got a great sauce.

Though times have changed, traditionally it was a long-simmered sauce, as most in this region were. Men and women worked the fields, meaning dinner needed to simmer low and slow all day. Thus "strong soup," a highly concentrated sauce that packs intense flavor and is just as good spread on toasted bread as diluted and tossed with pasta.

All of which made sense. But it didn't explain that... something deeper I could taste but not identify. Giugliano shrugged. Salsa al peperoncino, of course. Of course...

Fermented chili paste, the key ingredient in zuppa forte. A thick paste of cooked and pureed sweet

and hot chilies that is then fermented. A classic, if often overlooked, ingredient of the cooking of Campania. It adds that funky, savory-sweet depth to everything it touches. Much like Japanese miso and Korean gochujang.

In fact, when I finally tracked down salsa al peperoncino— apparently it is sold, even to butchers, only from shops that sell cod... because, why not?—and tasted it on its own, I found it almost identical (though a bit less complex) to gochujang.

Thankfully, Notaro was happy to walk me through her recipe. It indeed involved lots of tomato paste and salsa al peperoncino and offal. Also ample bay leaves, garlic and rosemary. And plenty of simmering. All fine, except the offal. Americans' appetite for offal, and its accessibility, is limited.

When I voiced this concern to Tufano, he shook his head dismissively. He loves his mother's zuppa forte, still made with all those spare bits and pieces. But times are changing. People today want different cuts. Do you think people in the 1800s would have used offal if they could have used pancetta or other premium cuts? No! The spirit of this recipe, he said, is to use what you have. So use what you have!

So Tufano set our course for recreating this Neapolitan classic. Offal was out, but deeply flavorful pancetta was in. Salsa al peperoncino can be challenging to find in the U.S., but gochujang has become widely available. Now add tomato paste, bay leaves, rosemary and garlic, and you have a very respectable version of simply the best pasta sauce I've ever eaten.

—J.M. Hirsch

Pasta alla Zuppa Forte
Pasta with Spicy Tomato and Pancetta Sauce

Start to finish: 30 minutes Servings: 4 to 6

This take on zuppa forte is based on the wonderfully balanced, intensely flavorful version we tasted at La Cantinetta, a tiny eatery/grocery/store/wine shop in Naples where octogenarian Maria Notaro did the cooking. Zuppa forte, also known as zuppa di soffritto, is an old-school Neapolitan dish made by slow-cooking meats with garlic and other aromatics, along with tomatoes and preserved chilies, until reduced and concentrated. The rich, thick, spicy paste-like mixture can be spread on crusty bread, though it's more commonly diluted and used as soup base or pasta sauce. Zuppa forte traditionally was made with odds and ends of meats, including offal, but the Neapolitan cooks we consulted said pancetta would be a reasonable stand-in. (For best flavor, it's important to purchase pancetta that contains a decent amount of fat. In our experience, the type sold pre-diced is too lean and cooks up with a tough, leathery texture.) We then determined a combination of tomato paste, browned to develop flavor, and canned whole tomatoes, blended until smooth, yielded the best taste and consistency, and that simmering the sauce in a skillet was a quick way to concentrate it. The preserved chilies were the most difficult ingredient to approximate. We landed on Korean gochujang, which may seem out of place, but the thick, fermented paste delivers a similar complex spiciness along with welcome notes of umami. If you can source Calabrian chili paste, which is spicy, tangy and salty, it, too, is great. Salvatore Giugliano at Ristorante Mimì alla Ferrovia serves his zuppa forte–dressed pasta with fresh basil and ricotta, garnishes that complement the richness and intensity of the sauce.

Don't use canned tomato puree or canned crushed tomatoes, which have slightly tinny, metallic flavors that only become more pronounced in the finished sauce. The flavor of whole tomatoes, blended until smooth, is fresher and cleaner.

14½-ounce can whole peeled tomatoes

2 tablespoons gochujang (see headnote) or 1 tablespoon Calabrian chili paste

¼ cup extra-virgin olive oil

4 ounces pancetta (see headnote), chopped

4 medium garlic cloves, minced

4 bay leaves

2 tablespoons tomato paste

1 sprig rosemary

Kosher salt and ground black pepper

1 pound penne, ziti or rigatoni pasta

½ cup lightly packed fresh basil, torn

Whole-milk ricotta cheese, to serve

In a large pot, bring 4 quarts water to a boil. In a blender, puree the tomatoes with juices and gochujang until smooth, 30 to 60 seconds; set aside.

While the water heats, in a 12-inch skillet, combine the oil, pancetta, garlic, bay, tomato paste, rosemary and ½ teaspoon pepper. Cook over medium, stirring often, until the pancetta has rendered some of its fat and the tomato paste darkens and begins to stick to the pan, 6 to 8 minutes. Add the pureed tomato mixture and bring to a simmer, scraping up any browned bits. Simmer, uncovered and stirring often, until very thick and the fat separates, about 10 minutes.

Meanwhile, when the water reaches a boil, add 1 tablespoon salt and the pasta; cook, stirring occasionally, until just shy of al dente. Reserve about 1½ cups of the

cooking water, then drain the pasta and return it to the pot. (If the sauce is done ahead of the pasta, remove the skillet from the heat.)

Scrape the sauce into the pot with the pasta and add ¾ cup of the reserved cooking water. Cook over medium, stirring and tossing often, until the sauce clings and the pasta is al dente, 2 to 4 minutes; add more reserved pasta water as needed to loosen the noodles if the mixture is very dry and sticky.

Off heat, remove and discard the bay and rosemary. Taste and season with salt and pepper, then stir in the basil. Serve topped with dollops of ricotta.

Pestosino Calabrese

Pasta with Sun-Dried Tomato and Red Pepper Pesto

Start to finish: 40 minutes Servings: 4 to 6

The sauce here is our version of the oil-based pestosino calabrese, also known as salsa piccante, which we learned in Italy from "Papa" Mario Conforti. It is not classic Calabrian pesto, which is creamy and typically includes ricotta and fresh produce. We found that the closest approximation of the fruity, sweet, mildly spicy dried Calabrian chilies he used in abundance is a combination of dried New Mexico chilies, jarred roasted peppers and red pepper flakes. The pesto is not spicy, but it is intense; tossing it with pasta and finishing the dish with ricotta cheese brings balance. If you can, make it a few days ahead, refrigerate it in an airtight container and bring to room temperature before use. The flavors bloom and deepen on standing.

Don't skip the step of soaking the toasted chilies and tomatoes in boiling water. After plumping, they break down more easily in the food processor for a better-textured sauce.

In an 8-inch skillet over medium, toast the chilies, turning with tongs, until fragrant, 2 to 3 minutes. Transfer to a medium bowl along with the sun-dried tomatoes. Add boiling water to cover. If needed to keep the ingredients submerged, place a small plate or saucer on top. Let stand until the tomatoes are plump and the chilies are softened, 10 to 15 minutes.

Drain the tomato-chili mixture and add to a food processor along with the roasted peppers, capers and brine, garlic and oregano. Process until mostly smooth, scraping the bowl as needed, about 30 seconds. With the machine running, drizzle in the oil. Transfer to a small bowl and stir in the pepper flakes, ¾ teaspoon salt and ¼ teaspoon black pepper. Set aside, or, if making ahead, cover and refrigerate for up to 5 days (bring to room temperature before use).

In a large pot, boil 4 quarts water. Add the pasta and 1 tablespoon salt, then cook, stirring occasionally, until al dente. Reserve ¾ cup of the cooking water, then drain and return the pasta to the pot. Add the pesto and ½ cup reserved water; cook over low, stirring, until well coated, about 3 minutes; add additional cooking water if needed so the pasta is evenly sauced. Off heat, taste and season with salt and black pepper. Serve with dollops of ricotta cheese.

3 New Mexico chilies (½ ounce), stemmed and seeded (see headnote)

1 cup drained oil-packed sun-dried tomatoes, rinsed

Boiling water, as needed

⅓ cup drained roasted red peppers, patted dry

2 tablespoons drained capers, plus 2 teaspoons caper brine

1 medium garlic clove, roughly chopped

½ teaspoon dried oregano

½ cup extra-virgin olive oil

¼ teaspoon red pepper flakes

Kosher salt and ground black pepper

1 pound short pasta, such as penne rigate, mezzi rigatoni or gemelli

Whole-milk ricotta cheese, to serve

Pasta con Pangrattato Aglio e Noci

Spaghetti with Garlic and Walnut Breadcrumbs

Start to finish: 45 minutes   Servings: 4 to 6

This pasta dish was one of the best things we ate during our trip to Southern Italy. It was prepared for us by Giancarlo Suriano, whose condiment company specializes in preserving regional ingredients, such as Calabrian chilies and Tropea onions. He added chopped walnuts, chilies and oregano to simple toasted breadcrumbs, amping up the flavor and texture of the pantry-friendly dish. To mimic the fruitiness of Calabrian chilies, we opted for Fresnos, which are easier to come by in the U.S. They're spicier than Calabrian chilies, though, so we seed them to temper the heat. If you prefer a kick, leave the seeds in one or both of them. Red pepper flakes also work well; just add half to the breadcrumb mixture and half with the anchovies, as you would the fresh chilies.

Don't hesitate to add more pasta cooking water if the spaghetti is dry. (During testing, we often wound up using all of the reserved liquid.) It's fine if the pasta has some extra sauciness before you top it with the breadcrumbs; the noodles eventually will absorb the moisture.

In a 12-inch skillet over medium, toast the bread, stirring, until lightly golden and dry, about 10 minutes. Transfer to a plate and cool; reserve the skillet. In a food processor, process the walnuts until chopped, about 10 pulses; transfer to the skillet. Add the bread to the processor and process to rough crumbs, about 1 minute. Add 3 tablespoons oil, half the parsley, half of the chilies, the oregano and ¼ teaspoon each salt and pepper. Process until incorporated, about 10 seconds.

Transfer the breadcrumb mixture to the skillet. Cook over medium, stirring, until crisp and golden, 5 to 7 minutes. Transfer to a plate and cool; wipe out and reserve the skillet.

Meanwhile, in a large pot over medium-high, boil 4 quarts water. Add the spaghetti and 1 tablespoon salt. Cook, stirring occasionally, until the spaghetti is just shy of al dente. Reserve 1½ cups of the cooking water, then drain.

In the skillet, combine the remaining 3 tablespoons oil, the remaining parsley, the remaining chilies, the garlic and the anchovies. Cook over medium, stirring, until the anchovies have dissolved and the garlic is fragrant and golden, about 3 minutes. Add the spaghetti and 1 cup of the reserved pasta water, then cook, tossing, until al dente and the sauce clings to the noodles, 2 to 3 minutes. Add more reserved pasta water as needed to loosen the noodles if they are dry and sticky; it's fine if some sauce pools in the skillet. Taste and season with salt and pepper. Transfer to a serving bowl and top with the breadcrumb mixture and drizzle with additional oil.

1 ounce country-style bread, cut or torn into rough ½-inch pieces (about 1 cup)

¾ cup walnuts

6 tablespoons extra-virgin olive oil, divided, plus more to serve

½ cup lightly packed fresh parsley, chopped, divided

2 Fresno chilies, stemmed, seeded and minced (see headnote) or ¼ teaspoon red pepper flakes, divided

¼ teaspoon dried oregano

Kosher salt and ground black pepper

1 pound spaghetti

4 medium garlic cloves, minced

3 to 5 oil-packed anchovy fillets, patted dry and roughly chopped

Maccheroni con Aglio e Maggiorana
Pasta with Lemon-Marjoram Sauce

Start to finish: 35 minutes Servings: 4 to 6

In Mompeo, a village about 30 miles northeast of Rome, home cook Alfonsina Cortegiani taught us how she makes maccheroni con aglio e maggiorana, a simple, delicious pairing of pasta with fresh marjoram, garlic and olive oil, finished with cheese. The no-cook, pesto-adjacent sauce came together so easily and quickly it hardly constituted a recipe. Cortegiani mixed crushed herbs and garlic with oil in a large bowl, then tossed in just-drained, steaming-hot pasta. The noodles' heat coaxed out bold flavors and aromas. In our adaptation, we also throw in some parsley. If you cannot find marjoram, oregano is a good substitute, though its flavor is slightly more savory and assertive. A 0.5- to 0.75-ounce "clamshell" container should contain enough herb to yield ⅓ cup chopped.

Don't wait to mix the sauce ingredients. Combine them as soon as you start heating the pasta water. This gives the garlic time to steep in the lemon juice, which helps tame its fieriness. Also, when combining the drained pasta with the sauce, be sure to add only ¼ cup reserved cooking water. As you toss with tongs, if more water is needed so the noodles are silky and well coated, add only 1 tablespoon at a time, but use restraint so the pasta isn't watered down.

In a large pot, boil 4 quarts water. Meanwhile, in a large bowl, stir together the Parmesan, parsley, marjoram, oil, lemon zest and juice, garlic, pepper flakes and ½ teaspoon each salt and pepper.

To the boiling water, add the pasta and 1 tablespoon salt, then cook, stirring occasionally, until al dente. Reserve ½ cup of the cooking water, then drain.

To the bowl, add the pasta and ¼ cup of the reserved pasta water. Toss, adding more pasta water 1 tablespoon at a time if needed so the noodles are lightly sauced; there should not be any liquid pooled in the bowl. Taste and season with salt and black pepper. Serve sprinkled with additional Parmesan.

1 ounce Parmesan cheese, finely grated (½ cup), plus more to serve

⅓ cup finely chopped fresh flat-leaf parsley

⅓ cup finely chopped fresh marjoram or oregano

¼ cup extra-virgin olive oil

1 tablespoon grated lemon zest, plus 3 tablespoons lemon juice

3 medium garlic cloves, minced

¼ teaspoon red pepper flakes

Kosher salt and ground black pepper

1 pound bucatini or spaghetti

PASTA
CLASSICA

Solving the problem of
cacio e pepe

I arrived in Rome early one Wednesday last July and soon encountered the biggest culinary mystery of my career, cacio e pepe.

My first take was that a simple three-ingredient pasta dish is no mystery. But after consuming a half-dozen variations, it became clear that the simplest recipes are often the most difficult. The cheese needs to be melted fully, without bumpy nibs like flotsam. Second, the sauce should neither be dense like Alfredo nor should it be a mere whitewash of pecorino. Third, it should not inspire a race to shove it down the gullet before it congeals and turns gluey as it cools. Finally, the pasta, the cheese and the pepper need to forge a culinary harmony that, when perfected, makes this one of Italy's greatest dishes.

Yotvata

After checking in to the Hotel Mozart off of Via Corso (the bathroom was so small I could barely open the shower door without stepping onto the toilet seat), I grabbed an Uber to Yotvata in the old Jewish neighborhood, based on a recommendation from Leah Koenig, author of "Portico." They specialize in carciofi alla giudia (Jewish-style fried artichokes), which were the best in Rome—light as a feather, suggesting the world's thinnest potato chips. I then ordered the cacio e pepe.

The sauce was rich—perhaps a bit too rich and abundant. The waiter, Michael Melek, was kind enough to share the recipe: Cook the pasta, add it wet to a skillet with butter, and then add the pecorino Romano to the pan with the pepper. No extra pasta cooking water was used. The result was on the heavy side, although delicious, but the use of butter was an outlier.

Flavio al Velavevodetto

Next up was a restaurant, Flavio al Velavevodetto, where I enjoyed a private cooking lesson with Flavio de Maio, the chef/founder. He used an immersion blender to make a thick paste of pecorino, pepper and water—much like Play-Doh—which was used to turn out endless portions of cacio e pepe with little last-minute effort. (He keeps a large batch of the paste on hand.) He cooked the pasta, added it wet to a bowl along with a couple of spoonfuls of the cheese paste, tossed the pasta, and then added a bit of hot pasta water at the end in small increments to get just the right texture. This produced a very good result, less rich than Yotvata, but his method is best suited to a working restaurant, not a home kitchen.

Colline Emiliane

At Colline Emiliane, Massimo Scortichini cooks food from Emilia-Romagna, including fresh pasta made daily. The restaurant is famous for hosting

> **"You want some sauce with the pasta, but not too much— this is not Alfredo or carbonara."**

Federico Fellini and Michelangelo Antonioni back in the day and for framed illustrations drawn by Fellini, the most famous being a frenetic naked woman running amok with a butterfly net. His cacio e pepe was high-end: He uses three types of peppercorns—black, red and pink—and also three different types of pecorino, some young and some well aged. (At Rome's Trionfale market, I discovered pecorino is not one thing but many, depending on aging and terroir—nobody in Rome buys "pecorino" per se; instead, they ask for a specific type.) Scortichini also did something unusual: He

cooked a small amount of garlic in a skillet with EVOO. In a large bowl, he whisked together a sauce with the cheese and pepper using hot pasta cooking water as a base. Then he tossed in the wet cooked pasta and finished the dish in the skillet with the oil-garlic mixture. Delicious.

Antico Falcone

The next day for lunch, I went to Antico Falcone, where the food is spectacular (I had enjoyed a bang-up lunch there years before). The Egyptian chef, Mimmo Galal, has his own cacio e pepe method, which includes two parts

Parmesan to one part pecorino. Using hot pasta water, he whisks the sauce in a bowl with the pepper and then adds the wet cooked pasta, tossing vigorously and then adding additional water or cheese as needed.

The good news is that I get paid sufficiently to subject myself to plate after plate of cacio e pepe; the bad news is that I was no closer to a final recipe. But I did come away with two thoughts. First, the pasta cooking water was the key fourth ingredient in this recipe, helping to create a smooth sauce, binding it to the pasta. Second, I was concerned that local Roman ingredients might be critical to great cacio e pepe.

Back at Milk Street, we tried the recipes from Rome with mixed success. Since we knew that the starch content of the pasta cooking water was key, we kept reducing the amount, finally settling on just 4½ cups. This did provide starchy cooking water (although some additional water is added during cooking). Next, we decided to use a skillet, not a stockpot. With so little water, the pasta and the sauce could be made together, plus the skillet offers more control and access than a deeper saucepan or pot. (A nonstick skillet is preferable, since cheese will not stick to the surface, although a regular stainless steel pan delivers good results.) So far, so good.

But we hit a snag when we tried different brands of pasta; some produced a creamy, starchy sauce and others did not. Was it possible that the brand of pasta makes a big difference, that some brands release more starch than others? Pasta is made up of starch and protein; the former gelatinizes, and the latter forms an insoluble rigid structure during cooking. Higher-protein pastas (the more expensive brands) do a better job of forming a compact, netlike structure, which better traps starch, resulting in less starch leached into the cooking water.

The problem was that our tests determined that the more expensive pastas released more starch than cheaper supermarket brands. To confirm our suspicions about starch release, we tested a high-quality pasta brand, DeCecco, against a cheaper brand, Barilla. They were cooked in the same amount of water, and then we used a dilution of iodine to measure starch content in the resulting cooking water. The iodine turns the water blue in the presence of starch. And indeed, DeCecco showed a deeper blue color than Barilla. That confirmed that better pastas leach out more starch, contrary to what the science says.

One detail we noticed in our experiments is that expensive pastas have a rougher outer surface than the cheaper brands, which is often attributed to the type of die used in extruding the pasta dough: a bronze die creates a rougher surface than a Teflon die. (The latter extrudes pasta more quickly, hence it is used by lower-quality brands. The reason that bronze dies produce rougher pasta is not due to the hardness of bronze; it is due to the "slip stick" effect. When the pasta dough moves through a bronze die, a series of small stops and starts occurs, which produce a rougher exterior.) Food scientists will tell you that a rough surface has more surface area, and therefore it will release more starch. OK, one point in our favor.

The real "aha" moment came when we spoke with Rolando Ruiz Beramendi, who makes pasta under the high-end Rustichella d'Abruzzo brand. He explained that lower-quality pastas are dried quickly after being extruded—the temperature is fixed at just under 200°F, and the pasta dries in under 5 hours, whereas Rustichella is dried at 120°F for over 50 hours. Combined with Teflon dies, the cheaper brands produce pasta that is "caramelized." That is, the sugars that result from the breakdown of

starch by heat and moisture react with proteins, which turns the pasta yellow. Further, the surface of cheaper pastas are, in effect, annealed—a polymer-like coating hardens the surface and prevents the starch from leaching out into the cooking water. (Pick up an inexpensive brand of spaghetti and you can feel the hard, almost plastic exterior coating.)

Finally, bronze dies leave some flour on the surface of the dried pasta, which also helps make the cooking water starchier. (When speaking with my local Rome guide, Arianna Pasquini, she pointed out that although Italians may not have invented pasta per se, the genius of Italian pasta is about perfecting the drying process, which results in the best pastas with the best texture.) So now we had science on our side; better pastas release more starch.

In prior versions of this recipe, we were concerned that the quality and age of the cheese—pecorino and Parmesan—might affect the creaminess and stability of the sauce. The good news is that our low-water skillet method, plus high-quality pasta, solved this problem. Even with run-of-the-mill cheese, the sauce was smooth and luscious. However, the fineness of the grate was important—you want the finest possible texture to expedite melting. The big surprise was that pre-grated supermarket cheese worked just fine. (Be sure to get a high-quality brand.) We also mixed Parmesan and pecorino for optimal flavor, as many chefs did in Rome.

As for the peppercorns, this is one area where many recipes come up short. (And it's important—after all, pepper is in the title.) We toasted 1 tablespoon of whole peppercorns and then ground them in either a small coffee grinder or a mortar and pestle. We added ½ teaspoon each salt and pepper at the outset of cooking, along with 2 tablespoons of the cheese mixture, which helped flavor the pasta and provided a nice base of cheesy water for the finished dish.

So, the final recipe begins with 12 ounces of pasta placed into a large nonstick skillet with 4½ cups of water, 2 tablespoons of cheese and ½ teaspoon of the toasted, ground peppercorns. Cook over medium-high, tossing occasionally, until the pasta is just shy of al dente and most of the water has been absorbed—you should have no more than 1 cup of liquid. Now add the cheese mixture in three batches, tossing the pasta constantly. Add more water if necessary to finish cooking the pasta and melting the cheese. You want some sauce with the pasta, but not too much—this is not Alfredo or carbonara. Off heat, add 1 teaspoon of the remaining pepper and let sit for 2 minutes so that the sauce "tightens" a bit more. The good news is that this cacio e pepe will not turn gluey quickly, as is the case with many other recipes.

One last thought about cacio e pepe. Beramendi pointed out that Italians care more about the pasta than the sauce. They love pasta that tastes like a good artisanal bread. That is why they want a pasta that remains a tad chewy after cooking and has good flavor, and it's why they want the pasta to stand up to the sauce, not be drowned in it. A good cacio e pepe has just enough sauce to coat the pasta but not so much that the taste of the pasta itself gets lost.

So, in the end, we had learned a lot about Italian pasta. Brand matters, not just for taste and chew, but for the starchiness of the water. Second, never over-sauce your pasta—Italians say that pasta dishes are first and foremost about pasta. And, finally, using a smaller amount of cooking water is a good kitchen hack when you want to create a smooth, creamy sauce that will cling to the pasta, and by all means, feel free to cook the pasta in a skillet.

As Fellini said, "Life is a combination of magic and pasta." We agree.

—Christopher Kimball

Cacio e Pepe

Start to finish: 35 minutes Servings: 4

We visited restaurant and home kitchens across Rome to find out how the science of pasta, cheese and water can create a reliable skillet cacio e pepe. Six chefs and cooks each taught us their method for making the pasta classic, and once back in the Milk Street kitchen, we got to work devising our own formula. We quickly learned that the variety of pasta—as well as how you harness its starch—are key to achieving the subtly creamy sauce that's really more a cheesy, clingy coating. Bronze-cut spaghetti is essential. This type of pasta is extruded through a bronze die that leaves the noodles with a rough, floury appearance instead of the smooth, sleek sheen of less expensive pastas extruded through nonstick die. (Widely available DeCecco is "bronze drawn" and works in this recipe, as do premium brands such as Rustichella d'Abruzzo.) By using an unconventional method of starting bronze-cut pasta in a minimal amount of room-temperature water in a skillet, then using that starchy water as the basis for the "sauce," we were able to attain the perfect consistency. (Bonus: this technique requires only one pan.) As for the cheeses—we landed on equal parts nutty Parmesan and sharp, funky pecorino. The cheeses must be finely grated so they readily melt; use the fine holes of a box grater or a wand-style grater, or cut the cheese into chunks and grind them together in a food processor. Lastly, toasting the pepper before coarsely grinding it enhances its flavor and aroma. Adding some of the pepper along with a couple tablespoons of grated cheese to the pasta water deeply seasons the noodles. This also results in a more velvety finish. Once made, cacio e pepe doesn't hold well, so make sure serving bowls and forks are at hand. If you can, warm the bowls in advance so the pasta better retains its creaminess once plated.

Don't try to cook a full pound of pasta; it won't fit comfortably in the skillet and will throw off the flavor, texture and timing. Twelve ounces is the ideal amount. Some brands of pasta take longer to cook than others and absorb more moisture; if the amount of water in the pan looks too scant to cook the spaghetti until just shy of al dente, add another ½ cup water. On the other hand, if there is still a generous amount of liquid in the pan when the pasta is just shy of al dente, go ahead with the addition of cheese. Cooking for a minute or two after all the cheese has been melted in will "tighten up" the consistency.

1 tablespoon whole black peppercorns

2 ounces pecorino Romano, finely grated (1 cup)

2 ounces Parmesan cheese, finely grated (1 cup)

12 ounces bronze-cut spaghetti (see headnote)

Kosher salt

In a 12-inch skillet over medium, toast the peppercorns, shaking the pan often, until fragrant, 2 to 3 minutes. Transfer to a spice grinder and let cool, then pulse until coarsely ground, 8 to 10 pulses. (Alternatively, transfer the peppercorns to a mortar, let cool and crush with a pestle until coarsely ground.) In a small bowl, toss together both cheeses.

To the same skillet, add the spaghetti, placing the noodles parallel to each other in the center

of the pan, then add 2 tablespoons of the cheese mixture and ½ teaspoon each salt and pepper. Add 4½ cups water. Bring to a boil over medium-high and cook, uncovered and frequently moving the pasta about with tongs but keeping it submerged as much as possible, until just shy of al dente; when done, the pasta will no longer be fully submerged and there should be a fair amount of starchy liquid (at least 1 cup) in the pan. If the pasta is very underdone and the water is already quite reduced, add another ½ cup water and cook, stirring often, until just shy of al dente.

With the pan still on medium-high, add about half of the remaining cheese mixture and toss until fully melted. Add the remaining cheese mixture in 2 more additions, tossing until melted after each. The liquid will have formed a thin sauce that pools in the pan. With the skillet still on medium-high, continue tossing the spaghetti until al dente and lightly sauced, with a small amount of creamy sauce (about ¼ cup) pooled in the skillet; the timing will vary based on how much liquid was in the pan before the first addition of cheese. But at this point, cooking should take a couple of minutes at the most.

Off heat, toss in 1 teaspoon of the remaining pepper, then let stand for 1 to 2 minutes; during this time, the sauce will "tighten" a bit more. Toss again. Taste and season with additional salt, if needed. Offer the remaining pepper on the side.

Spaghetti alla Carbonara

Start to finish: 40 minutes   Servings: 4

Despite its short ingredient list and reputation as dead-easy to make, pasta alla carbonara rarely is great. The eggs go from raw to scrambled in an instant; the window for achieving the perfect luxurious consistency is woefully narrow. Our skillet-only recipe (no need to boil a pot of water!) harnesses the thickening effect of the starch released by the pasta as it cooks in just 4½ cups water to create a sauce with the ideal richness, silkiness and clingability. We add the yolks, tempered with a little of the pasta-cooking liquid, at the end, and the residual heat of the pasta and pan heat them to just the right degree without risk of curdling. If you can find guanciale, or cured pig jowl, use it for the deepest, porkiest flavor, otherwise pancetta works. Bronze-cut spaghetti is essential here. This type of pasta is extruded through a bronze die that leaves the noodles with a rough, floury appearance. It not only releases more starch during cooking, its surface texture better grips the sauce. Widely available DeCecco is "bronze drawn" and works, as do premium brands such as Rustichella d'Abruzzo.

Don't use all the rendered fat from the guanciale; measure out only 1 tablespoon for combining with the yolks. Too much pork fat can make the dish cloying. If you use pancetta, however, it may not render a tablespoon. In that case, supplement with extra-virgin olive oil.

2 ounces pecorino Romano (without rind), finely grated (1 cup)

2 ounces Parmesan cheese (without rind), finely grated (1 cup)

2 ounces guanciale or pancetta, chopped

Extra-virgin olive oil, if needed

4 large egg yolks

12 ounces bronze-cut spaghetti (see headnote)

Kosher salt and ground black pepper

In a small bowl, toss together both cheeses. In a 12-inch skillet over medium, cook the guanciale, stirring occasionally, until browned and crisp, 4 to 6 minutes. Using a slotted spoon, transfer to a small bowl; set aside. Measure 1 tablespoon of the rendered fat into another small bowl; if you used pancetta and do not have 1 tablespoon rendered fat, make up the difference with olive oil. Pour off and discard any remaining fat in the skillet and reserve the skillet.

To the rendered fat, whisk in 2 tablespoons of the cheese mixture, the egg yolks and 1½ teaspoons pepper; set aside. To the skillet, add the spaghetti, placing the noodles parallel to each other in the center of the pan, then add 2 tablespoons of the pecorino-Parmesan mixture and ½ teaspoon each salt and pepper. Add 4½ cups water. Bring to a boil over medium-high and cook, uncovered and frequently moving the pasta about with tongs but keeping it submerged as much as possible, until just shy of al dente; when done, the pasta will no longer be fully submerged and there should be a fair amount of starchy liquid (at least 1 cup) in the pan. If the pasta is very underdone and the water already is quite reduced, add another ½ cup water and cook, stirring often, until just shy of al dente.

With the skillet still on medium-high, add about half of the remaining pecorino-Parmesan mixture and toss until fully melted. Add the remaining cheese mixture in 2 more additions, tossing until melted after each. The liquid will have formed a thin sauce that pools in the pan. Continue tossing the spaghetti until al dente and lightly sauced, with a small amount of creamy sauce (about ¼ cup) pooled in the skillet; the timing will vary based on how much liquid was in the pan before the first addition of cheese. But at this point, cooking should take a couple of minutes at most.

Remove the pan from the heat. Add 1 tablespoon of the sauce in the skillet to the yolk mixture and whisk to combine. Now add the yolk mixture to the pasta; toss until evenly distributed and the sauce clings to the noodles. Toss in the guanciale. Taste and season with salt. Serve sprinkled with additional pepper, if desired.

Pasta alla Gricia

Spaghetti with Guanciale and Pecorino

Start to finish: 40 minutes Servings: 4

To make this minimalist pasta dish, we employ the same unconventional technique we use to make cacio e pepe (p. 198), another Roman classic. Our pasta alla gricia is a one-pan affair that utilizes the starch released by the pasta as it cooks to create a lightly thickened sauce that clings to the noodles. Because the starch is a key ingredient, it's important to seek out bronze-cut spaghetti. This variety has been extruded through a bronze die that leaves the strands with a rough, floury surface instead of the smooth sheen of inexpensive pasta. (Widely available DeCecco is "bronze drawn" and works in this recipe, as do premium brands such as Rustichella d'Abruzzo.) Guanciale is cured pork cheek. It's meatier and saltier than pancetta, and purists would not make pasta alla gricia without it. Look for guanciale in Italian markets, but if pancetta is the only option, it still will yield delicious results.

Don't forget to add 1 tablespoon olive oil to the skillet if using pancetta, which is leaner than guanciale, to help with browning. Then make sure to pour off the rendered pork fat from the skillet before adding the pasta. If left in, it will make the dish greasy. Also, don't try to cook a full pound of pasta; it won't fit in the skillet and will throw off flavor, texture and timing.

2 ounces pecorino Romano cheese, finely grated (1 cup)

2 ounces Parmesan cheese, finely grated (1 cup)

4 ounces guanciale or pancetta, chopped

1 tablespoon extra-virgin olive oil, if using pancetta

12 ounces bronze-cut spaghetti (see headnote)

Kosher salt and ground black pepper

In a small bowl, toss both cheeses. In a 12-inch skillet over medium, cook the guanciale or the pancetta and oil, stirring occasionally, until browned and crisp, 4 to 6 minutes. Using a slotted spoon, transfer the meat to a small bowl; set aside. Pour off and discard the fat or reserve for another use.

To the same skillet, add the spaghetti, placing the noodles parallel to each other at the center, then add 2 tablespoons of the cheese mixture and ½ teaspoon pepper. Add 4½ cups water. Bring to a boil over medium-high and cook, uncovered and frequently moving the pasta with tongs but keeping it submerged, until just shy of al dente. When done, the pasta no longer will be fully submerged and there should be a fair amount of starchy liquid (at least

1 cup) in the pan. If the pasta is very underdone and the water is already quite reduced, add another ½ cup water and cook, stirring, until just shy of al dente.

With the pan still on medium-high, add about half of the remaining cheese mixture and toss until fully melted. Add the remaining cheese mixture in 2 more additions, tossing until melted after each. The liquid will form a thin sauce that pools in the pan. With the skillet still on medium-high, toss the spaghetti until al dente and lightly sauced, with a small amount of creamy sauce (about ¼ cup) pooled in the skillet; the timing will vary by how much liquid was in the pan before the first addition of cheese. But at this point, cooking should take a couple of minutes at most.

Off heat, toss in the guanciale and ½ teaspoon pepper, then let stand for 1 to 2 minutes; during this time, the sauce will "tighten" a bit more. Toss again. Taste and season with salt and pepper.

For the best pesto,
let the basil shine

If it isn't made with basil, pine nuts, cheese, garlic, salt and olive oil—and nothing more—it isn't pesto. If it isn't pounded chunky-smooth loudly and rhythmically with a mortar and pestle, it isn't pesto. And if the pine nuts aren't raw or if the cheese isn't a blend of Parmesan and pecorino Sardo... Well, you get the idea...

Of all these things, Roberto Panizza—Italy's leader in a movement to preserve and celebrate traditional pesto making—is adamant and clear. And that left me convinced we had a dim chance of replicating his recipe back home.

I'd come to Genoa—birthplace of the classic mash of basil, pine nuts, garlic and cheese—to learn what differentiated the pesto of the old world from the too often potently garlicky, blandly oily and wanly herbal sauces we make—or buy—back home.

My first taste was during an early morning stroll through Mercato Orientale—a boisterous food market under the arched cloister of a former convent, an eruption of zucchini blossoms, crumbly pecorinos and luminescent tomatoes. I'd happened upon La Forneria 2, a bakery stall plying thick, doughy focaccia, tiny dimpled bacio di dama (ladies' kisses) cookies, and a pot of deeply thick pesto.

With a "Mi amore!" and a puckered air kiss, shopkeeper Manuela Bettinelli handed me a thick slab of focaccia slathered thicker with a deep green and wildly aromatic schmear of pesto Genovese.

One bite was all it took. Even cold, it was astounding. Herbal and peppery, but not pungent. The taste of sun and grass in marriage. It was rich, fresh and robust in flavor and texture, flecked with basil leaf and granules of Parmesan.

To discern the alchemy of great pesto, I needed to head across the street and into Piazza Colombo, a congested square that's home to Il Genovese, a 100-year-old trattoria run by Panizza. True to Italian cliché, he learned to make it from his mother.

"Pesto is not the name of a family of sauces," he admonished. "It is the name of this sauce. Only this sauce. Those with other ingredients are different sauces."

He pulled from the trunk of his car a 300-year-old 45-kilogram white marble bucket-like mortar and a baseball bat-size wooden pestle once used in a monastery. A modern version of the earliest cooking tool—a rock with which to bash food. An action, of course, from which the sauce takes its name—pestare, to crush, grind or tread on.

As Panizza worked, it was evident that pesto Genovese is a sauce of a different order. And the difference traces to its roots. Pesto began simply—a paste of salt and garlic. A lot of garlic. Genoa's sailors used it to make their spoiled foods palatable. Over time, basil and olive oil were added, later pine

> "If it is possible to smell the color green, this was it."

peppery-herbal aroma. He ground and ground, breaking down the leaves, mixing them. And as they mixed, blending with the garlic-pine nut paste, the color muted from bright to creamy green.

A bit of coarse salt. A bit of ground Parmesan. A bit of extra-virgin olive oil. All far less than I would have thought. In fact, everything but the basil was used in seemingly miniscule volumes. Which suddenly made sense. This is a basil sauce. The point is to highlight, not mask, the herb. Panizza's final flourish—shavings of pecorino Sardo, a smoked pecorino closer in taste to aged gouda than to its better known cousin, pecorino Romano.

As Panizza finished, the pesto clung thick to the pestle. If it is possible to smell the color green, this was it. The taste richly herbal without overpowering. The garlic a high note, not a domineering force. Again, a revelation. Relegated to the background, garlic plays the role of an acid, gently nudging all the other flavors forward without demanding the spotlight itself. As for the texture? Coarse, grainy and too thick.

And then it occurred to me. Of course it's too thick. It wasn't finished. A true pesto Genovese isn't complete until it is wedded to pasta—and thinned by the water that cooked it. We thin our pesto with too much oil, and the result is a fatty, unctuous mess with dull flavor. Panizza tossed heaps of his pesto with freshly boiled gnocchi and their starchy cooking water, the sauce immediately melting into and coating the tender knobs of pasta.

As we ate, Panizza offered additional lessons. Never toss the

pasta and pesto over heat; this is a raw sauce and direct heat muddies its flavor. Always use the youngest, most tender basil; it has the freshest, brightest flavor and breaks down easily. And never, ever use a food processor, a tool increasingly popular even in Genoa. The flavor, the texture will be wrong, closer to mayonnaise.

But Panizza wouldn't let me take his word for any of this. He insisted I drive an hour south following the Ligurian Sea, then take a sharp left inward and upward into the tiny mountaintop town Campo de Ne. There, beyond a church tower and a parade of devotees reenacting the procession of the cross—up the mountain bearing full-sized crucifixes—I would find La Brinca, a farm-fed family-run trattoria. And there, I would find more excellent pesto.

And so I did. As I ate four pesto-drenched dishes—chestnut flour gnocchetti, potato gnocchetti, a local pancake-like flatbread called testaieu, and a ribbon-ish pasta called taglierini—overlooking terraced vineyards as green as the sauce, chef-son Simone Circella offered an additional lesson: Order matters. Much.

We tend to dump all the ingredients at once into the processer, then hit the button. Trouble is, that treats all of the ingredients the same. But great pesto isn't merely a paste of a few ingredients. Nor just the ratios that balance them. The order in which they are combined determines how thoroughly they are crushed, an equation that changes the flavor and texture of the finished pesto.

The pine nuts and garlic should be creamy and smooth. The basil

nuts and cheese. The garlic receded to a background flavor. But if the biting, garlicky sauces we eat in the U.S. are any indication, it seems we never got the memo.

Panizza dropped two small garlic cloves into the mortar, then pounded them to a smooth paste. Then he added pine nuts. Again, he bashed. Over and again, until the mixture resembled creamy peanut butter. Only then did he add the basil, giant bunches of young, tender leaves, so much it seemed he was preparing salad for 12, not sauce for four. As he mashed and ground, there was an explosion of

does taste better. A processor purees, releasing more water from the basil, thinning the flavor, and creating a uniformity of texture. But when the herb is crushed with a mortar and pestle, less water is released and the leaves are reduced to tiny flavor- and aroma-rich shreds that taste and feel better in our mouths.

And there was another problem. The basil used in Genoa is smaller and more tender, making it easy to crush. The basil in most American grocery stores is more mature and tougher, with leaves four or five times the size. When we followed Panizza's recipe using American basil in a mortar and pestle, we developed sore arms and never got the proper texture.

Our solution required we ignore his advice (no food processor) and adhere strictly to Circella's (order above all). With a bit of trial and error, we found the processor did an excellent job of reducing the garlic and pine nuts to a smooth paste and—with careful pulsing—it didn't over-process the cheeses.

We then added the basil, but putting the leaves in whole didn't work; reducing them to fine shreds required too much processing. But using a knife to coarsely chop the basil before adding it—and then pulsing just a few times—we were able to get the perfect shreds we wanted without risk of pureeing.

Panizza might not approve of our method—and we admit we miss the romance of using the mortar and pestle—but we were thrilled that our food processor version nearly matched the flavor and texture of his pesto.

—J.M. Hirsch

should be pulverized, not pureed, retaining distinct flecks of leaf. The cheese should be granular. None of those distinctions is possible if all of the ingredients are mashed—or processed—at once.

Tackling this recipe back at Milk Street posed challenges. Changing our ratios of ingredients—more basil, less garlic and oil—was easy. Changing the order we add the ingredients to ensure each is treated properly was easy. Overcoming the fact that most Americans don't have giant marble mortars? Not so easy.

Complicating matters, pesto made with a mortar and pestle

Pesto alla Genovese

Start to finish: 30 minutes   Makes about 1 cup

We traveled from a bustling town square in Genoa to a tiny hilltop town on the Ligurian coast to learn the basics of classic pesto alla Genovese: Use good cheese, keep the pine nuts raw, don't stint on the basil, and don't dump everything in at once. In Genoa, chef Roberto Panizza showed us the pesto, traditionally made in a mortar and pestle, is nothing more than basil, pine nuts, cheese, garlic, salt and olive oil, emphasis on the basil. We use a food processor for convenience but follow the tradition of processing ingredients separately to ensure we preserve the appropriate texture of each. Good quality cheese is essential for a rich, full-flavored pesto. Seek out true Italian Parmesan cheese, as well as pecorino Sardo, a sheep's milk cheese from Sardinia. If you can't find pecorino Sardo, don't use pecorino Romano, which is too strong. The best substitute is manchego, a Spanish sheep's milk cheese. To store pesto, press a piece of plastic wrap against its surface and refrigerate for up to three days.

Don't toast the pine nuts. In Italy, the pine nuts for pesto are used raw. Don't be tempted to add all the ingredients at once to the food processor. Adding them in stages ensures the pesto has the correct consistency and texture, and that it won't end up thin and watery, the result of overprocessing.

1¾ ounces Parmesan cheese (without rind), chopped into rough 1-inch pieces

1 ounce pecorino Sardo cheese (without rind), chopped into rough 1-inch pieces

¼ cup pine nuts

2 medium garlic cloves, smashed and peeled

Kosher salt

⅓ cup extra-virgin olive oil, divided

2½ ounces fresh basil (about 5 cups lightly packed)

12 ounces dried pasta

In a food processor, process both cheeses until broken into rough marble-sized pieces, about 10 seconds, then pulse until they have the texture of coarse sand, 5 to 10 pulses, scraping the bowl as needed. Transfer to a small bowl.

In the food processor, combine the pine nuts, garlic and ¼ teaspoon salt. Process until a smooth, peanut butter–like paste forms, about 1 minute, scraping the bowl as needed. Add the cheeses and about ½ of the oil and process until mostly smooth, 10 to 20 seconds, scraping the bowl as needed; the mixture should hold together when pressed against the bowl with a silicone spatula.

Using a chef's knife, roughly chop the basil, then add to the food processor. Pulse about 10 times,

scraping the bowl several times, until the basil is finely chopped and well combined with the cheese mixture. Add the remaining oil and pulse just until incorporated, about 2 pulses. The pesto should be thick, creamy and spreadable.

In a large pot, bring 4 quarts water to a boil. Add the pasta and 1 tablespoon salt, then cook, stirring occasionally, until just shy of al dente. Reserve about ½ cup of the cooking water, then drain the pasta. Transfer the pasta to a large warmed bowl and top with the pesto. Pour in ⅓ cup of the reserved cooking water for long pasta shapes (such as spaghetti and linguine) or ¼ cup cooking water for short pasta shapes (such as penne and fusilli). Toss to combine.

A speedier puttanesca

On the outskirts of modern Pompeii, I meet Antonella Scala, a petite whirlwind of laughter and glittering blue eyeshadow who hosts pop-up dinners in her rooftop kitchen.

With the volcano as our imposing backdrop, Scala offers to teach puttanesca, a tawdry-storied sauce I thought I knew. I was wrong.

There are many supposed explanations of puttanesca, the least bawdy of which is that it was intended to be quick and dirty. The dirty part I get. Built on the boldness of anchovies, copious garlic, brash olives and capers, fresh herbs and tons of tomatoes, it's a sauce that plays to our base desires.

But quick? At least not in American-Italian cooking. Simmered, rich and sloppy, sure. The prototypical bubbling stovetop pot. Weeknight friendly? Not so much.

Scala turns it all on its head. First, there is no bubbling pot; puttanesca is a speedy skillet sauce. Second, the term "sauce" comes with a caveat. Scala's sauce coats the pasta so thickly it borders on paste. Finally, that ingredient list. Items I thought sacrosanct are nowhere to be seen.

She starts by heating olive oil in a large skillet. As it warms, a head's worth of whole garlic cloves goes in. A pinch of red pepper flakes. Two minutes over high heat and I hear the sizzling, smell the spice. Next, olives green and black, whole and added by the handful. Then capers, at least ⅓ cup. We've nailed the dirty.

It simmers and crackles, but seems hardly a sauce. And where are the anchovies? The herbs? Turns out, there will be none. They aren't traditional. Instead, Scala removes and discards the garlic. All of it. The cloves have done their job, she explains; they flavored the oil. Leaving them in would overwhelm the other ingredients.

Then she cracks a can. A can? Here, in the land of perfect tomatoes, she opens a can of cherry tomatoes bathed in the barest of liquid. Spattering slightly, they join the bubbling in the skillet. Even in Italy, canned are more reliably sweet than fresh, Scala assures. By the time they have thickened and reduced, the boiling spaghetti is barely al dente. She drains it and adds it to the skillet, where it absorbs what little liquid there is—yet so much of its flavor. Minutes later, the pasta is perfectly cooked.

It is rich and thickly coated, exceedingly savory. The flavors are simple and distinct: bracing, briny olives; sweet chunks of tomatoes; herbal, salty capers; unifying it, a mellow wisp of garlic. Garnished with parsley and a sparing sprinkle of Parmesan, it's simply the best tomato sauce I've ever eaten. And it took all of about 20 minutes to get to the table.

It owes its delicious potency to maximizing flavor by minimizing liquid, creating a concentrated sauce that coats the pasta, rather than pooling in

"It is rich and thickly coated, exceedingly savory."

the bowl. It finishes cooking the pasta in the skillet with the sauce, letting it absorb flavor rather than just water. And it uses garlic in a way that is easier and better balanced, allowing it to infuse the dish without domineering.

Back at Milk Street, the recipe adapted easily. We stuck close to Scala's version, substituting canned whole tomatoes (that we lightly crushed) for the canned cherry variety that isn't common here. And though not traditional, we

liked the bright pepperiness we got by stirring in a bit of fresh basil at the end.

We'd braved Vesuvius, and in the process found a better way to sauce pasta.

– J.M. Hirsch

Spaghetti Puttanesca

Start to finish: 25 minutes   Servings: 4

In the shadow of Vesuvius, Antonella Scala taught us a better way to sauce pasta by using plenty of olives and going light on the garlic. We think of puttanesca as a saucy dish built on anchovies. But in Naples, where it originates, two varieties of briny olives and pungent capers, not anchovies, give the dish bold savoriness that balances the sweetness of the tomatoes. We call for a generous amount of capers, which often are sold in small bottles or jars. When shopping, you will need to buy two 4-ounce bottles to get the ½ cup drained capers needed for this recipe. So that the spaghetti is extra-flavorful and each noodle is seasoned throughout, we boil it in water for just five minutes—it will be underdone at the center—then finish cooking it directly in the sauce.

Don't use more than 2 quarts of water to boil the pasta; the idea is to concentrate the starches in the cooking water, which later is used to thicken the sauce.

In a large pot, bring 2 quarts water to a boil. Add 1½ teaspoons salt and the spaghetti, then cook, stirring occasionally, for 5 minutes. Reserve 2 cups of cooking water, then drain and set aside.

In a 12-inch skillet over medium, heat 1 tablespoon of oil and the garlic cloves, then cook, stirring often, until the garlic is light golden brown, about 1 minute. Off heat, remove and discard the garlic. Add the pepper flakes, both types of olives and the capers, then cook over medium-high, stirring, until the capers begin to brown, about 1 minute. Add the tomatoes and cook, stirring occasionally, until most of the liquid has evaporated, 5 to 7 minutes.

Add the reserved tomato juice and 1 cup of the reserved cooking water; bring to a simmer. Add the pasta and toss to coat. Cover and cook, tossing occasionally, until the pasta is al dente and the sauce clings lightly to the noodles; add more cooking water if needed.

Remove from the heat, cover and let stand for 3 minutes. Stir in the basil, cheese and remaining 1 tablespoon olive oil. Taste and season with salt and black pepper. Serve topped with additional cheese.

Kosher salt and ground black pepper

12 ounces spaghetti

2 tablespoons extra-virgin olive oil, divided

3 medium garlic cloves, smashed and peeled

1 teaspoon red pepper flakes

½ cup pitted Kalamata olives, roughly chopped

½ cup pitted green olives, roughly chopped

½ cup (two 4-ounce bottles) drained capers, rinsed, patted dry and chopped

28-ounce can whole peeled tomatoes, drained, 1 cup juices reserved, tomatoes crushed by hand into small pieces

½ cup lightly packed fresh basil, chopped

1 ounce Parmesan or pecorino Romano cheese, grated (½ cup), plus more to serve

Homemade Orecchiette

Start to finish: 2 hours, plus resting Makes about 1 pound uncooked pasta

Small and cup-shaped, orecchiette, meaning "little ears," come from southern Italy. The pasta traditionally is made using only semolina: a strong flour milled from durum wheat with a high gluten content. Our version calls for equal parts semolina and all-purpose flour: the latter keeps the dough soft for easy workability while the former provides the structure and elasticity required for shaping it, as well as nutty-sweet flavor. Using the instructions below, the same dough can be formed into cavatelli, a small shell pasta that resembles a tiny hot dog bun, and pici, a rustic hand-rolled spaghetti. When cooking fresh orecchiette, keep in mind it will take only about five minutes to reach al dente, which is considerably less time than store-bought dried orecchiette. The pasta is best cooked within a few hours of shaping.

Don't flour the surface on which you'll be forming each piece of dough. Flour will cause the dough to slip, but shaping is easier if it sticks slightly to the surface.

To make the dough in a food processor: In a food processor, combine both flours; pulse a few times to combine. With the machine running, slowly add ¾ cup water through the feed tube. Process until the dough forms pea-sized clumps, about 25 seconds. If the dough is too sandy and dry to form clumps, pulse in more water, a few drops at a time; if the dough feels sticky, add more all-purpose flour or semolina, a sprinkle at a time.

To make the dough by hand: In a large bowl, whisk together both flours. Make a well in the center, then add ¾ cup water. Using a fork, stir in a circular motion, starting in the center and gradually moving outward to incorporate the water and flour mixture, until a shaggy dough forms. Using your hands, bring the dough together and knead, swiping along the edges of the bowl to incorporate any dry bits. If the dough resists coming together, add more water, a few drops at a time; if the dough feels sticky, add more all-purpose flour or semolina, a sprinkle at a time. The dough should be moist enough to form a cohesive mass without sticking to the sides of the bowl; it's fine if it's a little crumbly. (See directions p. 214.)

Lightly dust the counter with semolina and turn the dough out onto it. Knead until soft, smooth and springy, about 10 minutes. Form into a ball, cover with plastic wrap and let rest at room temperature for at least 20 minutes or for up to 1 hour. Alternatively, wrap tightly in plastic wrap and refrigerate up to 2 days; if refrigerated, let the dough stand at room temperature for 1 hour before proceeding.

Lightly dust 2 rimmed baking sheets with semolina. Unwrap the

1¼ cups all-purpose flour, plus more as needed

1¼ cups semolina flour, plus more as needed and for dusting

Kosher salt, for cooking

Homemade Cavatelli

Follow the recipe to make the dough and portion the first piece into ¼-inch pieces. Dust a gnocchi board with semolina or have ready a dinner fork. Holding the board or fork, with the backside of the tines facing up, at an angle, press a piece of dough into the board or fork tines with the side of your thumb and swipe downward; the dough will curl, creating a U shape with ridges on the outer side. Transfer to a prepared baking sheet and repeat with remaining dough.

Pici *Hand-Rolled Thick Spaghetti*

Follow the recipe to make and rest the dough, then cut it in half. Flatten both pieces into disks; cover one lightly with plastic wrap. Dust the counter with semolina and set the second disk on top. Using a rolling pin dusted with semolina, roll the disk to an even ⅛-inch thickness. Using a chef's knife and a decisive cutting motion (do not use a sawing action), slice the dough into ¼-inch thick strips. Lightly dust the counter with semolina, then using your fingertips, gently roll the dough back and forth against the counter into long, thin noodles about ⅛ inch in thickness. Transfer to a prepared baking sheet, keeping the noodles separate to avoid sticking. Repeat with remaining dough.

dough and cut it into quarters. Set 3 pieces aside and cover lightly with plastic wrap. Using your palms, roll the remaining piece into a log. Lightly dust the counter with semolina, then roll the log to form a rope about ½ inch in diameter; if the rope's length becomes difficult to manage, cut it in half, then roll the pieces separately.

Cut the rope into ¼-inch pieces and lightly dust with semolina. On an unfloured area of the counter, set 1 piece cut side up. Press the flat of your thumb into the center of the piece and, while applying light pressure, smear or drag the dough against the counter with slight twisting action; the dough may curl a bit around your thumb. The finished shape should resemble a shallow cup that is thinner at the center and thicker at the perimeter. Set the orecchiette on a prepared baking sheet. Shape the remaining dough pieces in the same way; try to keep the orecchiette separated on the baking sheet to avoid sticking. Repeat with remaining dough. If not cooking right away, let stand uncovered at room temperature up to 4 hours.

To cook the orecchiette, follow the directions in the pasta recipe you are making, or in a large pot, bring 4 quarts water to a boil. Add 1 tablespoon salt and the orecchiette, then cook, stirring occasionally, until al dente. Reserve some of the cooking water if directed in your recipe, then drain the pasta.

How to make Homemade Orecchiette

1. To make the dough by hand, in a large bowl, whisk together the flours. Make a well in the center, then pour in ¾ cup water. Stir with a fork, starting in the center and gradually moving outward, until a shaggy dough forms.

2. Using your hands, knead the dough in the bowl, incorporating any dry bits. The dough should be moist enough to form a cohesive mass without sticking to the sides of the bowl; it's fine if it's a little crumbly.

3. Dust the counter with semolina and turn the dough out onto it. Knead until smooth and springy, about 10 minutes. Form into a ball, cover with plastic wrap and let rest at room temperature for at least 20 minutes or up to 1 hour.

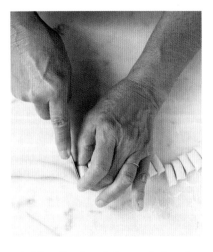

4. After the dough has rested and been divided, roll one piece into a log. Dust the counter with semolina, then roll the log into a rope about ½ inch in diameter. Cut the rope into ¼-inch pieces.

5. Dust the pieces with semolina. Take one piece and set it cut side up on an unfloured area of the counter.

6. Press the flat of your thumb into the center of the piece and, while applying light pressure, smear or drag the dough against the counter with slight twisting action; the dough may curl a bit around your thumb. Shape the remaining dough in the same way.

Pasta Fresca all'Uovo
Fresh Egg Pasta

Start to finish: 40 minutes, plus resting   Makes 1 pound pasta

Fresh egg pasta is rich in flavor and has a delicate yet satisfying texture that's both tender and sturdy. Unlike dried pasta, where the sauce is paramount, well-made fresh pasta shines alongside its pairing, as in our elegantly delicate fettuccine Alfredo (p. 222). To make these luxurious, golden-hued noodles, we use a fairly large number of egg yolks plus a whole egg, along with all-purpose flour and just a small amount of water. Determining the right amount of eggs is a balancing act—too many and the dough becomes difficult to roll out, as the fat in the yolks disrupts the formation of gluten. But too few and the dough will lack the desired richness. Given multiple passes through a pasta machine to produce long, thin sheets, the dough can be filled and made into ravioli, tortellini or other stuffed shapes, or it can be cut into fettuccine, tagliatelle or pappardelle as instructed in the directions. If you don't own a pasta machine but are skilled with a rolling pin, the dough can be rolled into sheets by hand.

Don't hold back when flouring the pasta dough to roll and cut into strands. A generous coating prevents the noodles from sticking and becoming a jumbled mess. Be sure to lift the pasta and shake off excess flour before cooking it. Too much starch in the cooking water can cause the pot to overflow.

1 large whole egg, plus 7 large egg yolks

260 grams (2 cups) all-purpose flour, plus more for dusting

Kosher salt, for cooking

In a 2-cup liquid measuring cup or small bowl, beat together the whole egg, egg yolks and 2 tablespoons water.

To make the dough in a food processor: Put the flour in a food processor. With the processor running, slowly stream in the egg mixture. Process until the dough leaves the sides of the bowl in large chunks, 1 to 2 minutes. If the dough feels dry and doesn't hold together when pinched, add water, 1 teaspoon at a time, as needed. If the dough feels sticky, you will have the chance to knead in more flour after turning the dough out onto the counter.

To make the dough by hand: Put the flour in a large bowl and make a well in the center. Add the egg mixture; using a fork, stir the flour into the eggs, working from the outside edges into the center, until all of the flour is incorporated. Form into a rough ball. If the dough feels dry and doesn't hold together when pinched, add water, 1 teaspoon at a time, as needed. If the dough feels sticky, you will have the chance to knead in more flour after turning the dough out onto the counter.

Continued p. 217

Lightly dust the counter with flour; if the dough feels wet and sticky, apply a heavier layer of flour to the work surface. Turn the dough out onto it and knead until smooth and shiny, 5 to 10 minutes. Press a finger into the surface of the dough; it should bounce back quickly, within 2 seconds. Cover the dough with a kitchen towel or plastic wrap and let rest at room temperature for 1 hour, or wrap tightly in plastic wrap and refrigerate up to 24 hours.

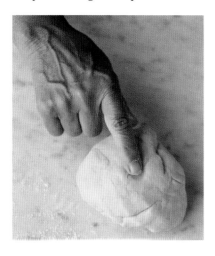

Line a rimmed baking sheet with a kitchen towel and lightly dust with flour. If the dough has been refrigerated, let it stand, still wrapped in plastic, at room temperature for about 15 minutes before proceeding.

Uncover or unwrap the dough and cut it into quarters. Set 3 pieces aside and cover with plastic wrap. Shape the remaining piece into a rough 4-by-6-inch rectangle. Using a pasta machine or a stand mixer fitted with a pasta attachment, roll the dough through several times, gradually reducing the thickness setting on the machine, until it forms a long sheet about 1/16 inch thick. It's important that the dough

be of an even thickness. If the pasta sheet is longer than 14 inches, cut in half for slightly shorter lengths.

Dust the surface of the dough with flour, then accordion-fold it into thirds; set it on a cutting board. Using a chef's knife and a decisive cutting motion (do not use a sawing action), cut the dough crosswise into 1/4-inch-wide strips for tagliatelle or fettuccine, up to 1/2 inch wide for pappardelle. Unfold the pasta and transfer to the prepared baking sheet, gently separating the strands, then toss to lightly coat with flour; keep uncovered. Roll and cut the remaining dough in the same way.

If not cooking right away, dust with additional flour and keep uncovered at room temperature for up to 1 hour, or cover with a kitchen towel and refrigerate for up to 12 hours.

To cook the noodles, follow the directions in the pasta recipe that you are making, or in a large pot, bring 4 quarts water to a boil. Add 1 tablespoon salt and the pasta, then cook, stirring occasionally, until al dente. Reserve some of the cooking water if directed in your recipe, then drain the pasta.

The search for the real fettuccine Alfredo

Disdain, disbelief, dismissal. Brace for them all. It's the cycle of responses that spill eagerly from Italians to questions about a dish Americans consider culinary canon. Fettuccine Alfredo? Tourist food. An American bastardization. Nobody eats it.

And they are right. The two Roman restaurants that tug-of-war over claims to serving the most authentic fettuccine Alfredo are hotspots for the bus tour masses, complete with walls plastered black-and-white with headshots of celebrities of yore.

A murky and romanticized origin story—at least in conventional telling—doesn't help. Worse yet, American fettuccine Alfredo bears so little resemblance to the recipe in that backstory it's almost unfair to call the dish Italian.

Except, they also are completely wrong.

Fettuccine Alfredo, it turns out, may well be one of the primordial Italian pastas. And it most certainly is eaten by everyday Italians. Here, there and everywhere. It's also nothing like you think. Most importantly, it's unbelievably delicious.

But learning this would require a 1,000-mile journey across Italy via planes, trains and Fiats, winding from Roman trattorias to the towering cheese caves of Parma, and ending in a medieval hilltop village seemingly lost to time.

Ristorante Alfredo alla Scrofa

Creamy and so rich, fettuccine Alfredo is ubiquitous to Italian-American menus. But something clearly was lost in translation. Larded with heavy cream, milk, garlic, flour and multiple varieties of cheese, most American Alfredo is a sodden, fatty mess. And don't even talk about adding chicken, shrimp or mushrooms to the equation.

So let's establish one thing at the outset. True fettuccine Alfredo contains just five ingredients: fresh egg fettuccine, butter, Parmigiano-Reggiano cheese, water and salt. Warmed by the just-cooked pasta, the butter and cheese should melt into a smooth, creamy marriage, a bond held tight by the starchy water in which the fettuccine was cooked.

Deceptively simple. So much so—as I would learn—it is shockingly easy to mess up.

Any exploration of fettuccine Alfredo must begin where its mythology was born. Ristorante Alfredo alla Scrofa sits a short walk from Rome's too-often-too-packed Piazza Navona, tucked onto a cobblestone side street—Via della Scrofa—the name of the signature dish spelled out in lit green letters that tower up the face of the building.

The story begins in 1908, not long after Alfredo di Lelio opened this restaurant. As lore tells it, his wife was weak from childbirth. To restore

"The trick is to use less butter and less cheese and more cooking water to get a creamy, but light sauce."

her strength, he reached for a recipe recorded as early as the 15th century, called simply "Roman macaroni." Pasta, butter, salt and cheese. Apparently it worked; his wife insisted di Lelio add the ancient recipe to his menu.

Nobody cared. That is, until 1920, when American actors Douglas Fairbanks and Mary Pickford dined with di Lelio and were smitten with the dish, tossed fresh and with such flair at the table with a fork and spoon. Word spread and soon everyone from Albert Einstein and Amelia Earhart to Sir Arthur Conan Doyle and—eventually—Jimi Hendrix crowded the dining room.

World War II forced a reset. A Jew, di Lelio left Rome in 1943, selling the restaurant to two of his staff, Peppino Mozzetti and Ubaldo Salvatori. They continued the tradition, and their grandchildren still run the restaurant today, selling more than 20 kilograms of fettuccine Alfredo a day, accounting for roughly three-quarters of their sales.

"It's a real gesture of love, moving the fettuccine with one fork and one spoon, making this normal pasta into this very special sauce," grandson Mario Mozzetti tells me the day I visit. "We are selling pasta in its simplest form."

Simple. And substantial. My lesson begins in Ristorante Alfredo alla Scrofa's kitchen, where tissue-thin fettuccine—"It absorbs more sauce," Mozzetti explains—is cooked in salted water for 25 seconds. With a fork, the strands are dredged from the water—much still clinging to it—onto a platter where copious softened butter has been mashed flat with fingers.

The chef hands the platter to a waiter, who carries it still steaming to a station just outside the kitchen. From a bucket, he spoons onto it tremendous heaps of 24-month-aged Parmigiano-Reggiano grated powder fine. Fork and spoon in hand, he takes it to the diner's table where, with intensity, he tosses. And tosses. And tosses. And tosses. And tosses.

The result—after many minutes—is a mound of pasta plumped with butter and slicked with a cheese sauce sordidly thick and rich. Undeniably delicious. Unbelievably heavy. And, oddly and somewhat disappointingly, not particularly cheesy.

Huh?

Il Vero Alfredo

But di Lelio's story wasn't finished. In 1950, the war safely behind him, he returned to Rome and opened a new restaurant, Il Vero Alfredo, or the True Alfredo, just a few minutes away from the original. More walls plastered with more headshots, now Ella Fitzgerald and Ernest Borgnine, Jean-Paul Sartre and Walt Disney.

Today, it is run by his granddaughter and great-granddaughter, Ines di Lelio and Chiara Cuomo. The recipe is almost identical, with interesting differences. The fettuccine isn't nearly so thin, giving

the finished dish a pleasant chew. The cheese is younger, aged just 16 months. And there is less of it. The butter, too.

Assembly is the same, tableside again, this time using a golden spoon and fork set gifted and engraved by Fairbanks and Pickford in 1927. Though the fettuccine itself is heavier, the finished dish is ever-so-slightly lighter than the version served on Via della Scrofa, a change that unexpectedly gives the savory-creamy cheese more—not less—presence.

And yet, it still is torridly heavy. Mind you, both versions are wonderful, sinfully so. But I start to understand why Italians dismiss the dish. Despite its simplicity, I'd never make this at home, an indelible, weighty tangle of fat and starch. But the recipe's ancient

lineage intrigues me. So I ask Ines and Chiara about that, and they mention names I've never heard.

Pasta in bianco. Burro e Parmigiano. Pasta pancia sconvolta.

Fettuccine Alfredo, it seems, has many names. And the last translation makes me laugh. White pasta. Butter and Parmesan. Upset belly pasta. That ancient Roman macaroni, it turns out, evolved into the chicken soup of Italy, into the dish Italians make—particularly for children—when they feel sick.

"When people used to come here, my grandfather was asked, 'What's your specialty?' He'd say, 'Fettuccine with Parmigiano and butter,'" Ines said. They always responded the same. "But we're not ill!"

Caseificio Ugolotti

Armed with this understanding—and confident no upset belly could handle a pasta pancia sconvolta as heavy as the Alfredos I'd tasted in Rome—I went in search of a lighter version. Il Vero Alfredo had demonstrated that with the cheese, less was more. I needed to understand this. So I headed north to Parma, home of Parmigiano-Reggiano.

Caseificio Ugolotti wasn't the idyllic dairy I was expecting. A modern warehouse wedged next to a McDonald's on a busy road on the outskirts of town, it nonetheless maintains the age-old Italian tradition that the master cheesemaker gets a house on-site as part of his compensation. For good reason. "They are like children," Attilio Buccella says of his cheese. "You care for them from the morning you make them until the day they are sold."

His lesson? With Parmigiano-Reggiano, a lot becomes a little, and a little goes a long way.

Parmigiano-Reggiano, which can be made only in Italy's Parma region, consists of just three ingredients: cow's milk, rennet and salt. A simplicity that belies the complex process during which 1,200 liters of fresh milk are reduced to two 50-kilogram wheels of fresh cheese. Brined and aged for many months, those wheels lose at least another 5 kilograms, a reductive process that creates a cheese of intense complexity.

Caseificio Ugolotti's seemingly unromantic locale transforms the instant I step into the warehouse, two stories tall and stacked with nearly 12,000 massive wheels of Parmigiano-Reggiano from floor to ceiling. The smell is sensual, a wave of umami that washes over you, never breaking. We taste the cheese fresh, and aged 12 months, 24 months and 36 months. Powerful doesn't capture it. This isn't Parmesan. This is Parmigiano-Reggiano. Potently so.

Shove too much in your mouth— and the temptation is high—and you lose it, an onslaught of flavor through which you can appreciate nothing. Let just a bit melt on your tongue, transform into the essence of savory in your mouth, now *that* you can appreciate. I was starting to understand why the Alfredos in Rome had left me wanting.

Castelnuovo di Porto

Just 30 minutes north of Rome, in a tiny hilltop village—Castelnuovo di Porto—the threads come together. Here, in a town of winding cobblestone roads and

homes that cling precariously to the walls of a medieval castle, I meet Francesca Guccione, a home cook who learned her recipes from her mother and grandmother.

She doesn't know fettuccine Alfredo, but she certainly knows pasta in bianco. And her recipe, masterfully, synthesizes everything I'd been trying to understand. Guccione has been cooking since she was 9, and her kitchen spills into the rest of the house, cutting boards and other kitchen tools stacked on white plaster windowsills above a terra-cotta floor.

She cooks by instinct, and her instincts are spot on as she walks me through her pasta in bianco. The pasta—thick, eggy fettuccine— is cooked in barely enough water, producing a super-starched, almost white cooking water that is as important an ingredient to the finished dish as are the cheese and butter. For it is that starch that will bind them smoothly.

The creaminess of the sauce, she explains, isn't from the cheese and butter. They are key, of course, but too often cooks lean too heavily on them. "The trick is to use less butter and less cheese

and more cooking water to get a creamy, but light sauce," she explains as she adds to a barely warm skillet just a tiny fraction of the butter I'd seen elsewhere.

When the pasta is not quite al dente, she forks it out into the skillet with the now softened, slightly melted butter. That starchy cooking water splashes along with the noodles into the pan. But that's not enough; she adds another two ladlefuls. And then she tosses. And tosses. And tosses. Minutes go by, those starches and butter and noodles bonding.

Only at this point, when the sauce already looks creamy, does she add sprinkles of Parmigiano-Reggiano, a bit at a time, punctuated with more tossing and more tossing and more tossing.

The result is magical and balanced. Creamy and coated and rich, but not thick or heavy. Luscious, not overwrought. I can taste every ingredient, the butter, the pasta, the cheese. It's a cooperative, not a domination.

"Che bello!" Guccione pronounces. I agree wholeheartedly.

—J.M. Hirsch

Fettuccine Alfredo

Start to finish: 30 minutes Servings: 4 to 6

Made the Italian way, fettuccine Alfredo bears little resemblance to the unctuous, cream-based pasta dish that's popular in the U.S. We scoured Italy for the best versions, and our favorite was prepared by Francesca Guccione in Castelnuovo di Porto, just outside Rome. Rich, luxurious and elegant but neither heavy nor cloying, Guccione's fettuccine Alfredo, like other Roman recipes for the dish, consists of only fresh pasta, Parmigiano-Reggiano cheese, butter and salt. The secret lies in using high-quality ingredients and combining them in just the right way, and in just the right volumes. We adapted her winning formula but incorporated a technique we saw employed at a couple restaurants of putting softened butter (rather than melted) into the bowl in which the hot pasta will be tossed. Of utmost importance is the cheese. Purchase a hefty chunk of true Parmigiano-Reggiano—not the pre-shredded stuff—trim off the rind (save it for simmering into soups and stews), cut 6 ounces into rough ½-inch pieces and whir them in a food processor until very finely ground. This helps ensure the cheese melts readily. High-fat butter also is key. In Europe, butter typically has a fat content of around 85 percent; standard American butter is only about 80 percent fat. That 5 percent difference has a big impact on the flavor and consistency of the finished dish. At the grocery store, some types of high-fat butter are labeled "European-style"; Plugrá and Kerrygold are two widely available brands. If the butter also happens to be cultured, all the better, but this is not essential. We learned from Guccione that patience also is an important ingredient. Tossing the pasta with the cheese in small additions and while gradually adding some starchy pasta-cooking water takes time but yields a sauce that is velvety-smooth. We highly recommend serving the pasta in individual bowls that have been gently warmed.

Don't use more than 2 quarts water to cook the pasta. It's a small amount by intention, as the starchy liquid is used as an ingredient in the sauce. Also, don't drain the pasta in a colander. Use tongs to lift the noodles out of the water and drop them, with ample water clinging to them, into the bowl lined with the butter slices. You may need some pasta cooking water to adjust the consistency of the sauce just before serving, so don't prematurely discard it.

8 tablespoons salted European-style butter (see headnote), sliced about ½ inch thick

6 ounces Parmigiano-Reggiano cheese (without rind), cut into rough ½-inch chunks

16 to 18 ounces fresh fettuccine, homemade (p. 215) or store-bought

Kosher salt

Line a large bowl with the butter slices, placing them in a single layer along the bottom and up the sides of the bowl; let stand at room temperature until the butter is softened.

Meanwhile, in a food processor, process the cheese until very finely ground, about 40 seconds; transfer to a medium bowl (you should have about 1½ cups).

In a large pot, bring 2 quarts water to a boil. Add the pasta and 1½ teaspoons salt, then cook, stirring often, until the pasta is al dente. Remove the pot from the heat. Using tongs, transfer the pasta from the pot, with ample water clinging to it, to the butter-lined bowl. Using the tongs, quickly stir and toss the pasta, incorporating the butter, until the butter is fully melted. Add ½ cup pasta water and toss until the water has been absorbed.

Add 1 cup of the cheese, tossing, ⅓ cup at a time, tossing and adding the next addition only after the previous one has been incorporated. Next, toss in ½ to 1 cup more pasta water, adding about ¼ cup at a time, until the sauce clings to the pasta and only a small amount pools at the bottom of the bowl.

Let stand for 2 minutes to allow the sauce to thicken slightly. If needed, toss in additional pasta water a little at a time until the sauce once again clings to the pasta and only a small amount pools at the bottom of the bowl. Taste and season with salt. Divide among warmed serving bowls and serve immediately with the remaining cheese on the side for sprinkling at the table.

Rich, savory and dairy-free:
Puglia's classic pasta dish

Sitting at a wobbling wooden table on the cobblestone street just outside her home, arms solid from 54 years of kneading pasta, Nunzia da Scalo effortlessly works a pile of semolina flour and a bit of water into a bowling ball–size mound of pale, skin-soft dough. It's a scene on repeat at tables stationed streetside outside kitchens across Bari.

Da Scalo rolls hunks of the dough into thin ropes, and cuts each into ½-inch chunks. Then—with a quick flip of a small knife—one at a time she drags each chunk across the table, transforming it into the tiny cup-like orecchiette pasta for which Puglia (the heel of the Italian boot) is known. They will dry on a screen in the sun for an hour before being bagged and sold to passersby and local chefs who whir past on scooters.

In the north of Italy, pasta is a flour-and-egg affair. In the south, where poverty shaped the cuisine, eggs were a luxury. Semolina flour and water, and nothing else. The result is tender and meaty. And when shaped as orecchiette— literally, little ears—it is exceptionally good at cupping bits of chunky sauce.

One such sauce is what brought me to da Scalo's home—orecchiette con cime di rapa, or pasta with bitter greens. A heap of orecchiette studded with bits of broccoli rabe, all assembled in a skillet and married with savory anchovies and pops of chili.

It seems too simple to be so good. But the starchy, chewy pasta balances the bittersweet broccoli rabe. The anchovies melt, bathing the other ingredients without dominating. Rather than add real heat, the chili flakes brighten and lighten.

As da Scalo leads me into her kitchen, where 25-kilogram sacks of semolina lean in a corner, I have one concern. I'd learned a version of this dish years ago outside Pisa, where the finished dish is doused with grated Parmesan. In Puglia, cheese also was a luxury. They prefer the poor man's alternative: breadcrumbs. I wonder whether this dish will be nearly as good.

Da Scalo's method is simple. As the pasta cooks, the broccoli rabe is blanched and anchovies are sautéed in copious olive oil, melting into a savory sauce. When ready, the orecchiette and greens are added, cooked for a moment, then finished with a flourish of chili flakes and breadcrumbs.

When I take a bite, I expect it to be flat without the cheese. Quite the opposite. Uncluttered by the heft of dairy, the bitter broccoli rabe, savory anchovies and punchy chili flakes shine brighter. The breadcrumbs add texture, a pleasant crunch that soaks up the flavorful sauce.

Back at Milk Street, we opted for broccolini over harder-to-find broccoli rabe. And we first toasted the breadcrumbs with olive oil and half the anchovies to ensure the breadcrumbs would be just as flavorful as the rest of the dish. The result was both savory and rich. No cheese needed.

—J.M. Hirsch

> "It seems too simple to be so good."

Orecchiette con Cime di Rapa

Orecchiette with Broccolini

Start to finish: 40 minutes   Servings: 4

In the port city of Bari, home cook Nunzia da Scalo taught us this classic southern Italian pairing of starchy, chewy pasta with pleasantly bittersweet greens. Orecchiette with broccoli rabe (orecchiette con cime di rapa) is a signature pasta dish from the Puglia region. The bitterness of rabe is challenging for some palates, so we use sweeter, milder Broccolini. However, if you like the assertiveness of rabe, it can easily be used in place of the Broccolini, though rabe will cook a little more quickly. We boil the pasta in a minimal amount of water, then the starchy liquid that remains becomes the base for the sauce that marries the orecchiette and Broccolini. A finishing sprinkle of toasted seasoned breadcrumbs adds a crisp texture.

Don't use fine dried breadcrumbs instead of panko breadcrumbs. Their sandy, powdery texture doesn't offer the light, delicate crispness of panko.

6 tablespoons extra-virgin olive oil, divided

8 medium garlic cloves, 4 minced, 4 thinly sliced

8 oil-packed anchovy fillets, minced

¾ cup panko breadcrumbs

1½ pounds Broccolini, trimmed and cut crosswise into ¼-inch pieces

½ to 1 teaspoon red pepper flakes

Kosher salt and ground black pepper

12 ounces orecchiette pasta

In a large Dutch oven over medium-high, heat 2 tablespoons of oil until shimmering. Add the minced garlic and half the anchovies, then cook, stirring, until fragrant, about 45 seconds. Add the panko and cook, stirring, until golden brown, about 3 minutes. Transfer to a bowl and set aside; wipe out the pot.

In the same pot over medium-high, heat 2 tablespoons of the remaining oil until shimmering. Add the Broccolini, pepper flakes, sliced garlic, ¾ teaspoon salt and ½ teaspoon black pepper. Cook, stirring occasionally, until the Broccolini is crisp-tender and the garlic is golden brown, 6 to 7 minutes. Add ½ cup water and continue to cook, stirring, until most of the moisture has evaporated and the Broccolini is fully tender, about 2 minutes. Transfer to a medium bowl and set aside.

In the same pot over medium-high, boil 5 cups water. Add 1 teaspoon salt and the pasta, then cook, stirring occasionally, until the pasta is al dente. Stir in the Broccolini mixture, the remaining 2 tablespoons oil and the remaining anchovies. Continue to cook over medium-high, stirring constantly, until the liquid has thickened enough to cling lightly to the pasta and Broccolini, about 1 minute. Remove from the heat, then taste and season with salt and pepper. Transfer to a serving bowl and sprinkle with the breadcrumbs.

Killer spaghetti.
Deliciously so

After teetering on the brink of ruin, a mound of twirled spaghetti streaked with black bits emerges from Celso Laforgia's kitchen. The pasta, spaghetti all'assassina, is beyond merely browned—it is charred, barely coated in tomato sauce and flecked with burnt pieces.

Just the way he likes it.

"It's quite dark, but the pasta has a good balance between bitter, crunchy, crispy and spicy," says Laforgia, chef of Urban l'Assassineria in Bari. "That's the best way."

Anyone who covets the chewy, overdone corner pieces of lasagna understands. But the scorching of this unique pasta dish—whose name means "killer's spaghetti" for its menacing amount of red chili spice—is not its only intriguing quality.

Besides a deliberate char that gives the noodles and sauce smoky, bitter notes, the pasta also is cooked "a risottatura" or like risotto, which creates a spectrum of textures from a single ingredient.

After sautéing garlic and fresh red chilies in olive oil, a small amount of tomato puree is cooked until it reduces slightly. Dry spaghetti then is placed in the sauce, where it remains untouched until it sizzles and browns on the bottom.

Then broth made from diluted tomato paste and more puree is poured over the noodles, gradually added ladle by ladle, as you would with rice for risotto. As the pasta absorbs liquid and flavor, the toasted spaghetti softens unevenly, and the sauce mellows the char's bitterness, bringing it into balance with the tomato's caramelized natural sugars.

Subtly smoky, spicy and deeply rich with flavor, the pasta is so beloved in Bari that devotees formed the Academy of Spaghetti all'Assassina. In restaurants, members insist that the pasta be cooked in iron or steel pans because they can handle higher heat, and they periodically check up on restaurants to review their cooking technique.

Thankfully, they permit nonstick skillets at home. All the better because with cast iron, we had trouble finding the balance between pleasantly charred and outright burnt. Using nonstick, we got better browning on the noodles by pressing them down with a spatula to increase contact with the skillet.

To make the recipe pantry friendly, we omitted the fresh chilies in favor of crushed red pepper. And though some recipes call for 2 tablespoons of chili flakes plus fresh red chilies, we toned it down to less than a teaspoon. Still spicy but more manageable, our assassina came out chewy, crispy and deeply flavored. Simply to die for.

– Albert Stumm

"It's quite dark, but the pasta has a good balance between bitter, crunchy, crispy and spicy."

Spaghetti all'Assassina
Charred Red Sauce Spaghetti

Start to finish: 30 minutes Servings: 4 to 6

Chef Celso Laforgia showed us how to get just the right balance of spice, crunch and char required for spaghetti all'assassina—or killer's spaghetti—a unique dish from Bari in which the pasta is cooked start to finish in a skillet. A warm tomato broth is added to the noodles a little at a time, much like the classic technique for risotto. We cook pasta, undisturbed, in an even layer so it chars and crisps, adding texture and flavor. The finished dish is dryish, but pleasantly so, and deliciously intense in flavor, with tasty, crunchy-chewy bits akin to the edges of a baked lasagna. A few things of note: Basic brands of spaghetti, such as Barilla, work best for this, not high-end pastas with a rough, floury appearance, as they tend to release a large amount of starch during cooking. Second, for controlled charring, make sure to use a heavyweight nonstick 12-inch skillet that conducts heat evenly. Lastly, the spaghetti strands must all be parallel when they go into the pan and they remain that way, more or less, throughout cooking.

Don't try to squeeze 1 pound of pasta into the skillet. It's too much for the amount of sauce and will crowd the pan. Also, don't stir the pasta as it simmers. Undisturbed cooking with only two flips allows the spaghetti to develop crispness and deep, flavorful charring.

14½-ounce can tomato puree (1½ cups)

3 cups boiling water

1 tablespoon tomato paste

1 teaspoon white sugar

Kosher salt and ground black pepper

¼ cup extra-virgin olive oil

3 medium garlic cloves, finely chopped

¾ teaspoon red pepper flakes

12 ounces spaghetti (see headnote)

Finely grated pecorino Romano or Parmesan cheese, to serve

In a medium bowl or 1-quart liquid measuring cup, combine the tomato puree, boiling water, tomato paste, sugar, 1 teaspoon salt and ½ teaspoon black pepper. Whisk until the tomato paste dissolves.

In a heavy-bottomed 12-inch nonstick skillet, combine the oil, garlic and pepper flakes. Set over medium-high and cook, stirring, until the garlic no longer smells raw, 1 to 2 minutes. Stir in ¾ cup of the tomato mixture. Place the spaghetti in the center of the pan with the noodles parallel to each other, distributing them in an even layer. Using a spatula, press down on the noodles. Cook without stirring and occasionally pressing down until the tomato mixture at the edges is reduced and deeply browned and the pasta is sizzling, about 5 minutes.

Slide a spatula under half of the spaghetti and flip the noodles, then do the same with the second half; the bottom of the noodles should be spottily charred. Once again, distribute the pasta as best you can in an even layer. Ladle on 1 cup of the tomato mixture, pouring it over and around the pasta. Cook without stirring but pressing down, until the liquid is reduced and once again browned at the edges of the pan and the pasta is sizzling, 3 to 4 minutes.

Flip the pasta in the same way and ladle on another 1 cup tomato mixture. Cook in this way until the pasta is al dente but crusty and spottily charred; this will require

another 2 or 3 additions of tomato broth; you may not use all the broth. Finish with a flip of the pasta (not with an addition of broth). Off heat, taste and season with salt and black pepper. Sprinkle with grated pecorino Romano or Parmesan.

Pasta alla Norma

Penne with Eggplant, Tomatoes and Ricotta Salata

Start to finish: 50 minutes Servings: 4

We roast eggplant for better flavor and texture for this take on classic Sicilian pasta alla Norma. The dish, eggplant and pasta in tomato sauce, is said to take its name from a 19th-century Bellini opera. The eggplant usually is fried before being added to the sauce, but we opted to roast it to concentrate its flavor and condense its porous texture. The eggplant is in the oven for about 30 minutes unattended; use that time to prep the other ingredients and simmer the tomatoes to make the sauce. Ricotta salata is a firm cheese with a milky, salty flavor. Do not substitute fresh ricotta; a mild feta is a more appropriate substitute.

Don't forget to reserve about ½ cup of the pasta cooking water before draining. You'll need the starchy, salted liquid to help bring together the eggplant, pasta and sauce during the final simmer.

Heat the oven to 475°F with a rack in the upper-middle position. Line a rimmed baking sheet with kitchen parchment. In a large bowl, toss the eggplant with 4 tablespoons oil and ¾ teaspoon salt. Distribute in an even layer on the prepared baking sheet and roast until browned and tender, 30 to 35 minutes, stirring once halfway through. Remove from the oven and set aside.

While the eggplant roasts, in a 12-inch skillet over medium-high, heat the remaining 2 tablespoons oil until shimmering. Add the garlic and pepper flakes and cook, stirring, until fragrant, about 30 seconds. Add the tomatoes and ¾ teaspoon salt, then cover and cook, occasionally shaking the pan, until the tomatoes begin to release their liquid, about 1 minute. Stir in the vinegar, then use the back of a large spoon to crush the tomatoes. Cover, reduce to medium and cook, stirring occasionally, until the mixture breaks down into a lightly thickened sauce, 8 to 9 minutes. Remove from the heat and cover to keep warm.

In a large pot, bring 4 quarts of water to a boil. Stir in the pasta and 1 tablespoon salt, then cook, stirring occasionally, until the pasta is just shy of al dente. Reserve about ½ cup of the cooking water, then drain and return the pasta to the pot.

Add the eggplant, tomato sauce and ¼ cup of the reserved pasta water to the pasta. Cook over medium, stirring, until the sauce begins to cling to the pasta, 2 to 3 minutes. Stir in half of the basil, then taste and season with salt and pepper. Serve sprinkled with the remaining basil and the ricotta salata.

1-pound eggplant, peeled and cut into ¾-inch cubes

6 tablespoons extra-virgin olive oil, divided

Kosher salt

8 medium garlic cloves, finely chopped

½ teaspoon red pepper flakes

2 pints cherry or grape tomatoes

2 tablespoons white balsamic vinegar

12 ounces penne or mezze rigatoni pasta

½ cup lightly packed fresh basil, roughly chopped

2 ounces ricotta salata cheese, shredded on the large holes of a box grater

Less sauce. More flavor

Mario Ive's pasta all'Amatriciana was unlike any Italian red sauce I'd ever tasted. Bright, bold and... barely there?

I'd come to Rome to learn one of the country's simplest tomato-based pastas. My teacher was Ive, a retired artillery colonel in the Italian army who decades ago wrote a Roman cookbook in France. Because why not?

As Ive's house white wine—bought from a fill-your-own-jug counter nearby—flowed freely into our tumblers, he prepared the minimalist equation of pasta, tomatoes, guanciale and pecorino Romano.

The dish is a member of the family of classic Roman pastas, all of which grew out of cacio e pepe. Add guanciale (cured pig jowls) to cacio e pepe and it becomes gricia. Add tomatoes to gricia and you have Amatriciana.

Done in the Italian-American red sauce tradition, Amatriciana is a soupy, wet affair. But as Ive worked in his tiny apartment kitchen in the Roman suburbs—where, clichéd as it sounds, aromas of garlic, tomatoes and roasted meat wafted through the marble courtyard—it was clear this would be something else entirely.

Ive's recipe was a striking and speedy contrast to the sauces I'm familiar with. A bit of olive oil. A few ounces of guanciale. Four tiny canned tomatoes. No more. And no juices.

Ive cooked it all down until there was barely any moisture in the skillet, just a thick, richly aromatic tomato-pork paste. Into this he stirred the pasta and just enough of its starchy cooking water to loosen the sauce to coat. The pasta finished cooking in the sauce, its flavor permeating the noodles. He finished with pecorino Romano and many generous grinds of black pepper. In about 15 minutes it was on the table.

Despite the sparing use of, well, everything except cheese and pepper, the flavor was intense. It got its punch from cooking down and concentrating small amounts of tomatoes and meat. The result was a sauce with less liquid but more flavor and coating power.

For Milk Street's version, we stuck with Ive's minimalism, right down to the pasta cooking water. While we typically cook pasta in 4 quarts of well-salted water ("It should taste like seawater," as Ive put it), for this dish we used half that. We also undercooked the pasta. This upped the flavor in two important ways.

First, it concentrated the starch from the noodles; following Ive's example, we used that cooking water to thicken and bind the tomatoes. Second, by only partially cooking the pasta in the water, we let it finish cooking in the sauce, thereby absorbing a more flavorful liquid.

Amatriciana is often topped with pecorino Romano cheese, but we wanted it to infuse the entire dish. The solution was to simmer a chunk

> "Despite the sparing use of, well, everything except cheese and pepper, the flavor was intense."

of the cheese with the pasta as it cooked. Though unconventional, it allowed the cheese to season the pasta throughout, resulting in a more fully flavored finished dish.

We found that one 14½-ounce can of whole tomatoes (even Italians favor canned varieties for their deeper flavor), drained and cooked down, was plenty to dress four servings. Likewise, just 3 ounces of pancetta—more widely available than guanciale—provided ample flavor.

—J.M. Hirsch

Spaghetti all'Amatriciana

Start to finish: 40 minutes Servings: 4 to 6

In his small apartment kitchen in the Roman suburbs, Mario Ive taught us how to make Italian-style pasta all'Amatriciana, lightly sauced but deeply flavored. A minimalist equation of pasta, tomatoes, guanciale and pecorino Romano cheese, Amatriciana is served in Rome with barely any sauce, as we learned from Ive, retired artillery colonel in the Italian army and cookbook author. We prefer the robustness of guanciale, but pancetta also works; if possible, look for fattier pieces. One small can of tomatoes is all that is needed for the perfect balance of fat and acid. We intentionally undercook the pasta; it finishes in the sauce.

Don't discard any of the rendered guanciale fat; it's essential for the dish's flavor. The fat adds richness while balancing the acidity from the tomatoes and the heat from the pepper flakes.

In a large pot, bring 4 quarts water to a boil. Meanwhile, in a 12-inch skillet over medium, heat the oil until shimmering. Add the guanciale and cook, stirring, until well browned and crisp, 5 to 7 minutes. Using a slotted spoon, transfer to a paper towel–lined plate and set aside.

Return the skillet to medium and add the garlic; cook, stirring, until light golden brown, 1 to 2 minutes. Add the pepper flakes and cook, stirring, until fragrant, about 30 seconds. Off heat, carefully add the wine. Return the pan to medium-high, and cook, scraping up any browned bits, until the liquid is reduced by half, about 5 minutes. Add the tomatoes with juices and ¼ teaspoon each salt and black pepper.

Cook, stirring occasionally, until the sauce is slightly thickened, 3 to 5 minutes; remove and discard the garlic. Set aside off heat until the pasta is ready.

While the sauce is cooking, add the pasta and 1 tablespoon salt to the boiling water. Cook, stirring occasionally, until the pasta is just shy of al dente. Reserve 1 cup of the cooking water, then drain. Return the pasta to the pot.

Add the sauce to the pasta and cook over medium-high, tossing to combine, until the pasta is al dente, 3 to 5 minutes; add reserved pasta water as needed so the sauce clings to the noodles. Off heat, toss in the guanciale. Taste and season with salt and black pepper. Serve sprinkled with pecorino.

2 tablespoons extra-virgin olive oil

4 ounces guanciale or pancetta, chopped

2 medium garlic cloves, smashed and peeled

¼ teaspoon red pepper flakes

½ cup dry white wine

14½-ounce can whole peeled tomatoes, crushed by hand

Kosher salt and ground black pepper

1 pound spaghetti

Pecorino Romano cheese, finely grated, to serve

SHAPED
and
BAKED
PASTA

In search of ragù Bolognese

Osteria dell'Orsa, Bologna

On my first night in one of Bologna's cheap osterias, I realized that ragù Bolognese is about meat, not dairy. My journey to uncover the authentic ragù Bolognese started at Osteria dell'Orsa in a narrow alley in Bologna. The small eatery had been recommended by Matt Goulding, my guide and author of "Pasta, Pane, Vino," as a cheap spot that does a respectable job with local classics.

Seated at a common wooden table in the front dining room off the kitchen, I ordered the tagliatelle with ragù Bolognese (the other mainstay is tortellini in brodo), greens that turned out to be a bowl of iceberg-like lettuce, and a quartino of potable house wine.

Through the serving window, I saw the 20-something chef standing in front of a huge ragù-streaked stockpot. He wore a sauce-spattered apron and eased a sizable slither of wet tagliatelle into a large skillet, ladling in sauce and wrist-flipping the ingredients until the pasta was modestly coated. All he lacked was a cigarette dangling precariously from the corner of his mouth as he shouted "Pronto!"

The first bite told the story. Ragù Bolognese is a silky, rich meat sauce, pure and simple. No herbs and no layers of competing flavors. I was to discover that, like everything in Bologna, this sauce, at its best, is redolent with local ingredients. In this case, meat. It was nothing like the dairy-infused American version I had taken to be gospel. To understand this sauce, however, I had to head to salumeria Bruno e Franco to better appreciate the key ingredients.

Bruno e Franco, Bologna

Standing beside a large leg of prosciutto, the proprietor explained the process of curing the meat—it is salt-cured for at least a year—and the local preference for a sub-cut, the culatello, which is a boneless portion of the leg with bigger flavor and softer texture.

Looking around the small shop, I noted that everyone was impeccably suited with red caps, pristine white smocks and, in some cases, bow ties, all giving the shop an air of professionalism—a laboratory of sorts—promoting the notion that there is a science to producing the perfect slice of prosciutto, mortadella, speck, pancetta or guanciale.

What also was clear is that Bolognese cuisine is not about variety, it's about local. There are few dishes that do not use what is produced in the region: salumi, truffles, Parmesan, porcini, the local sparkling wine pignoletto and balsamic vinegar from Modena, just an hour's drive to the northwest.

But "local" is controversial. Today, Italy imports much of its food— beef from Brazil, pork from Poland, tomatoes from China and olive oil

> "Ragù Bolognese is a silky, rich meat sauce, pure and simple."

from Morocco. This is referred to as 10,000-kilometer cuisine, sourcing ingredients worldwide. But many Italian chefs and salumi producers are pushing back, trying to return to 2 kilometers. And this international trend is nothing new. In the 1930s, under Mussolini, the "grain wars" initiated the importation of foreign ingredients to feed the population.

Amerigo, Savigno

To make a truly local ragù Bolognese, my next stop was Amerigo, a Michelin-starred establishment in Savigno, a short drive out of town. Founded in 1934 by chef Alberto Bettini's grandparents, the front room is a small retail store next to the dining room, where Roberta Galletti, an energetic and well-muscled pasta-maker, was rolling out huge sheets of dough on a large sunlit table using a yard-long rolling pin.

She transferred the sheets to a second table, where she cut squares with an ancient wheeled pasta cutter, topped them with dollops of Parmesan cream, then shaped them into tortellini with the help of the snowy-haired Giuliana Vespucci, the proprietor's mother.

I headed to the small kitchen for my ragù lesson from chef Giacomo Orlandi, one of the cooks. The prep had been done. The soffritto (onion, celery and carrot) had been cooked, the pancetta diced and the beef and pork ground. Also ready was a small carafe of white wine and a modest bowl of canned tomatoes.

Bettini explained in detail exactly where the beef and pork had been raised. All nearby—a clear indicator that the soul of ragù Bolognese is its local provenance. The fat content of the meat lends a lubricity and depth to the sauce without milk or cream. In fact, when I asked Orlandi about the lack of dairy, he looked puzzled. Cream in ragù Bolognese? No!

In time, I learned that Italians will sometimes add dairy, but only on the second or third day after the ragù is made. This is when the flavor begins to flatten, so cooks add other ingredients to touch it up. Lambrusco, for example. Parmigiano-Reggiano. Or, yes, milk or cream. Mystery solved.

As I watched Orlandi work, I dispensed with another American myth about dairy in Bolognese. I had been told that milk or cream helps soften the meat. However, Orlandi sautéed the beef and pork

did like boneless beef short ribs, however, and ground our own meat in a food processor since preground supermarket beef and pork produced a miserable ragù.

Now that we had mastered the sauce, lasagna alla Bolognese was the logical next step. On my last night in Bologna, I ordered the lasagna Bolognese at Osteria Broccaindosso, which turned out to be my favorite restaurant meal of the visit. We started with an enormous platter of sautéed porcini, another of assorted salumi, and an excellent bottle of barbera.

And then I tucked into the lasagna, which was a revelation. It was a saucy, tender marriage of ragù Bolognese, spinach noodles and creamy besciamella (the Italian version of French béchamel sauce) without the typical over-baked top layer or stomach-bomb of fistfuls of grated mozzarella. In fact, cheese was mostly absent here except, perhaps, as a modest sprinkling of Parmigiano-Reggiano between the layers.

For our version, we added just a bit of Parmigiano-Reggiano to the besciamella, and we used half-and-half instead of milk because it was more stable and less likely to break. No mozzarella. No chewy cheese topping.

Though many recipes are hard to translate to the American kitchen, both the ragù and the lasagna are very close to the original, even with American ingredients. Go to Bologna for the architecture, the colonnades and the nonne (grandmothers). But if you want an excellent ragù Bolognese, you can prepare it at home, no passport required.

—Christopher Kimball

for less than 30 seconds each. Not enough time to crisp up any bits and pieces. The meat starts out soft and stays that way throughout the 5-hour cooking time. (He admitted that he would cut the cooking time for smaller quantities; these were restaurant portions.)

Back at Milk Street, we had our work cut out for us since we did not have access to the same high-fat meat that Orlandi did. But we did follow the basic rules: no garlic, no milk or cream, and a long simmer, in our case with smaller amounts, two hours.

Tomato paste and beef broth helped increase the meatiness of our store-bought beef and pork. We tried a variety of pork cuts: prosciutto instead of pancetta (we went with the latter, the authentic choice) and pork ribs instead of pork shoulder. We preferred the shoulder; we

Lasagna alla Bolognese

Start to finish: 1 hour 20 minutes (30 minutes active), plus cooling Servings: 8 to 10

In Bologna, we learned that Italy's iconic lasagna starts with a ragù that is a silky, rich meat sauce, pure and simple, to serve over pasta or polenta. Paired with creamy besciamella (the Italian version of French béchamel sauce) and layered between sheets of flat noodles, it also makes lasagna Bolognese, an iconic dish of the Emilia-Romagna region, if not of Italian cuisine as a whole. Our take was inspired by a version we ate at Osteria Broccaindosso in Bologna. We liked Barilla oven-ready lasagna noodles for this recipe, preferring them even over fresh sheet pasta. Both the ragù and the besciamella should be warm for lasagna assembly; the ragù reheats well in a large saucepan over medium and the besciamella can be microwaved in a covered 1-quart liquid measuring cup or medium microwave-safe bowl. A serrated knife is best for cutting the lasagna for serving.

Don't use the noodles without first soaking them. Unsoaked noodles absorb moisture from both the ragù and besciamella, leaving the lasagna too dry. But don't soak them for longer than 10 minutes or in water hotter than 140°F, as the noodles may overhydrate, resulting in a soggy lasagna and too-soft, broken pasta.

12 no-boil 6½-by-3½-inch lasagna noodles (see headnote)

6 cups ragù Bolognese, warmed (p. 242)

3 cups Parmesan besciamella, warmed (p. 243)

4 ounces Parmesan cheese, finely grated (2 cups), plus more to serve

Heat the oven to 350°F with a rack in the middle position. Place the noodles in a 9-by-13-inch baking dish, then add hot tap water (about 120°F) to cover. Let stand for 10 minutes, moving the noodles around halfway through to ensure they do not stick together.

Remove the noodles from the water and arrange in a single layer on a kitchen towel; pat dry with paper towels. Pour off and discard the soaking water and wipe out the baking dish. Distribute 2 cups ragù evenly in the baking dish, then place 3 noodles in a single layer on top. Spread ½ cup of the besciamella evenly over the noodles, all the way to the edges. Sprinkle ½ cup Parmesan in an even layer. Pour 1 cup ragù on top and spread evenly. Repeat the layering 3 more times, using the remaining noodles, besciamella and ragù, then cover the baking dish tightly with foil.

Bake until the edges of the lasagna are bubbling, 30 to 35 minutes. Remove the foil and bake until the surface is lightly browned, 15 to 20 minutes. Cool on a wire rack for 30 minutes. Cut into pieces and serve sprinkled with additional Parmesan.

Ragù Bolognese

Start to finish: 4 hours (40 minutes active) Makes about 8 cups

We learned how to make ragù Bolognese at chef Alberto Bettini's Michelin-starred Amerigo restaurant outside Bologna. After several tests in the Milk Street kitchen, we determined beef and pork that we ground ourselves in a food processor yielded superlative flavor and texture; supermarket ground meats made insipid sauces. Also, try to purchase pancetta in a large chunk from the deli counter, and if it comes in casing-like plastic, make sure to remove and discard the wrap before use. The next best option is packaged already diced pancetta; if pre-sliced is the only option, it will work, but will cost a lot more. Since the ragù demands several hours of slow simmering, we depend on the oven to get the job done, as its even, steady heat means hands-off cooking. The amount of fat that rises to the surface of the finished sauce will vary, depending on the fattiness of the meats. When cooking is complete, skim off and discard as little or as much as you like, bearing in mind that at least some is desirable for silkiness and richness of flavor. The finished ragù can be cooled to room temperature and refrigerated for up to three days. This recipe makes enough sauce for lasagna Bolognese, with leftovers for another night's pasta dinner.

Don't trim the fat from the beef and pork. The fat makes the ragù rich and supple, and carries the flavors of the other ingredients. Also, don't process the beef and pork too finely; a coarse grind yields the best-textured sauce. Finally, don't forget to uncover the pot after the first hour of simmering to allow the liquid to reduce and the flavor and consistency to concentrate.

Heat the oven to 325°F with a rack in the lower-middle position. In a large Dutch oven over medium, combine the oil, onion, celery and carrot; cook, uncovered and stirring occasionally, until the vegetables are softened and jammy, about 20 minutes.

Meanwhile, in a food processor, puree the tomatoes with juices until smooth; transfer to a medium bowl. Add half of the beef to the food processor and pulse until coarsely ground, 7 to 10 pulses, then transfer to another medium bowl; repeat with the remaining beef. Repeat with the pork, in batches, adding it to the beef. Finally, process the pancetta to a coarse paste, about 30 seconds; add to the other meats.

When the vegetables are softened, add the tomato paste and cook, stirring, until the paste begins to stick to the pot and brown, about 5 minutes. Add the wine and cook, scraping up any browned bits, until the pot is almost dry, 2 to 3 minutes. Stir in the ground meats, followed by the broth, tomato puree and bay. Bring to a simmer over medium-high, breaking up any large clumps of meat, cover and transfer to the oven. Cook for 1 hour.

3 tablespoons extra-virgin olive oil

1 medium yellow onion, finely chopped

1 medium celery stalk, finely chopped

1 medium carrot, peeled and finely chopped

28-ounce can whole tomatoes

1½ pounds boneless beef short ribs, cut into rough 1-inch chunks

1 pound boneless pork shoulder, cut into rough 1-inch chunks

6-ounce piece pancetta, cut into rough ½-inch chunks (see headnote)

2 tablespoons tomato paste

½ cup dry white wine

1 quart low-sodium beef broth

2 bay leaves

Kosher salt and ground black pepper

Remove the pot from the oven. Stir, then return to the oven uncovered. Continue to cook until the meat is tender, the sauce is thick and the volume has reduced to about 8 cups, 2 to 2½ hours.

Remove the pot from the oven. If desired, use a wide, flat spoon to skim some or all of the fat from the surface. Taste and season with salt and pepper, then remove and discard the bay.

Parmesan Besciamella

Start to finish: 30 minutes Makes about 3 cups

In a large saucepan over medium, melt **4 tablespoons salted butter** (cut into 4 pieces). Whisk in ¼ **cup all-purpose flour**, then cook, whisking constantly, for 2 minutes. While whisking, gradually add **3 cups half-and-half** and bring to a simmer. Add **2 bay leaves**, ½ **teaspoon freshly grated nutmeg** and ¼ **teaspoon kosher salt**, then reduce to low. Cook, uncovered and whisking often, until the sauce thickens, reduces slightly and no longer tastes of raw starch, 8 to 10 minutes. Off heat, whisk in **2 ounces (1 cup) finely grated Parmesan cheese**. Cool for 5 minutes. Remove and discard the bay, then taste and season with salt and pepper.

Rolled lasagna? No! It's rotolo

It's a sight that would stop any lasagna-lover in their tracks. From a tiny corner of Rome's Trionfale Market—already splayed with an array of tempting food—beckons tray upon tray of smooth, spiraled discs made of pasta wrapped around a thick, creamy filling of ricotta and spinach. It's as though a classic lasagna had been rolled into a cheesy log, then cut into slabs.

It was Annamaria Moretti—owner of the tiny Pasta all'Uovo shop—who quickly disabused us of that notion. We learned that they are rotolo di ricotta e spinaci, or rolled pasta with ricotta and spinach. Tomato-tomahto? Certainly not in Rome, for rotolo is a classic Italian recipe unto itself.

This was Milk Street's first encounter with rotolo di ricotta e spinaci, but far from mine. Years ago, I met rotolo in Exile. That is, while working at Restaurant Exile, so named for its remote location in lower New York City, a rock's throw from the Hudson River. It was the mid-1980s, no internet, no cell phones. To find the restaurant, you needed hand-written directions and a dose of steady nerves to brave the rundown stretch of abandoned buildings.

Once inside, the restaurant was confident in its identity, aiming high with white tablecloths and Italian-Mediterranean classics done creatively well. There, I served rotolo as a waitress, not cook. But I soon found myself hounding the chef to allow me to work kitchen shifts (for free!) to learn how to make it. Astoundingly, he agreed, and my waitressing days were done. It turns out that rotolo, with its winding, spiraled beauty, lured me off one path and onto another. That of my future.

The traditional way of making rotolo begins with homemade pasta, rolled out by hand into a large, thin sheet. The filling is a mix of ricotta and spinach, with mozzarella and Parmesan adding creaminess and savory depth. Once the filling is spread over the pasta, the whole thing is rolled up tight and the ends are sealed.

The roll then is wrapped in cheesecloth or a kitchen towel and simmered in water until cooked. Once cool, the roll is sliced into rounds (revealing the spiral), then reheated in an oven or skillet and served with tomato sauce. And it tastes as good as it looks. The filling is light, creamy and rich. The pasta, sitting on its edge, is fork-tender with a delicate chew.

To compare notes, I called Exile's then sous-chef, Shelley Boris, now chef and co-owner of Fresh Company Catering and Dolly's Restaurant in Garrison, N.Y. Referring to Exile's executive chef, "Bruce would make the rotolo every day and it was finicky. The pasta could end up too thick or too thin, or the center would cook unevenly. But other times it came out great." She laughed, adding that the time spent on it far exceeded its profitability but that it was too popular to take off the menu.

> **"It tastes as good as it looks. The filling is light, creamy and rich."**

In Rome, Moretti sells her rounds by the kilo for easy, take-home cooking. Just arrange them in a pan with some tomato sauce, pop them in the oven for a bit, and dinner is served, an Italian version of take-out. Here at Milk Street, we set out to create a home cook-friendly version.

We started with the pasta. We love homemade—and it's not hard to make—but rolling out large sheets evenly enough for a dish like this? Not so easy. We tried using purchased fresh pasta sheets, but they can be difficult to find, and their size and thickness vary by brand. We next considered dried, no-boil lasagna noodles, but they seemed doomed because they're far smaller than what's needed for

rolling up. And would their texture hold up?

It did! The texture comes out perfectly fork-tender. And because the noodles are parcooked, the rolls don't need poaching—this was a game-changer. Their size turned out to be less of an issue than we expected. After a brief simmer in water to soften the noodles, we found their edges could be over-lapped to form longer sheets that were easy to roll around our filling.

The spinach and cheese filling remains simple, with an important caveat. During early trials, the filling would sink down while the slices baked, ruining their appearance. After a bit of research, we realized this was due to excess moisture, particularly in the ricotta.

Options available at most American supermarkets tend to be of lower quality compared to ricottas in Italy. Here, they tend to contain more water, which evaporates during cooking and contributes to the sinking problem.

The solution was easy. Place the ricotta in a mesh strainer and stir for a brief stint to rid it of excess water; this makes it denser and closer in texture to Italian-made ricottas. Also, because spinach tends to give off water as it cooks, we first wrap it in a kitchen towel and squeeze it dry. The result: no more sagging filling.

The result: a perfectly textured home-style rotolo. Just don't call it rolled lasagna.

– Bianca Borges

Rotolo di Ricotta e Spinaci
Pasta Rotolo with Spinach and Ricotta

Start to finish: 3½ hours (1½ hours active) Servings: 6 to 8

At her pasta shop in Rome, Annamaria Moretti showed us how to make rotolo, a rolled lasagna-like dish that combines fork-tender pasta with a light, creamy and rich filling. Typically rotolo di ricotta e spinaci—or ricotta and spinach roll—is prepared with homemade sheets of pasta, but after a bit of trial and error we found we could layer strips of store-bought oven-ready lasagna noodles (look for 7-by-3½-inch noodles; we like those made by Barilla and Ronzoni) to create sheets. Though intended to be used dry, we cook them briefly so they soften enough to roll around the cheese and spinach filling. For make-ahead convenience, the rolls can be frozen overnight, then thawed for 10 minutes until soft enough to slice and bake. (If freezing overnight, be sure to also refrigerate the reserved pasta water that's added to the tomatoes for making the sauce.)

Don't allow the water to return to a boil after adding the lasagna noodles or they may tear. Immediately turn the heat to low. And be sure to stir as they soften, which will prevent them from sticking together. An 8- or 9-ounce box will include more noodles than are needed for the recipe, so you will have a few extra noodles in case a few break or tear.

Wrap the spinach in a kitchen towel and squeeze to wring out as much moisture as possible. Put half of the spinach in a food processor; set the rest aside. Drain the ricotta in a large mesh strainer, stirring with a silicone spatula to remove as much liquid as possible.

To the processor, add the ricotta, fontina, half of the basil, the egg, nutmeg, 1 teaspoon salt and ½ teaspoon black pepper. Process until smooth, about 1 minute. Add the Parmesan and remaining spinach, then pulse until finely chopped, 8 to 10 pulses. Transfer to a medium bowl, cover and refrigerate. Clean the processor bowl and blade, then return them to the base.

Line a rimmed baking sheet with plastic wrap. In a large pot, boil 4 quarts water. Stir in 1 tablespoon salt, then add the lasagna noodles and immediately reduce to low. Cook, stirring occasionally, until just shy of al dente, 2½ to 3 minutes; do not simmer or boil. Reserve 1 cup of cooking water, then drain and rinse under cold water.

Place 1 lasagna noodle on the counter with a short end facing you. Layer a second noodle so its bottom short end overlaps the first noodle's top end by ½ inch (creating a single long sheet). Lightly press the overlap to seal. Place 1 cup filling in the center and spread it evenly, leaving a ½-inch border around all edges. Starting with the edge closest to you, roll into a tight cylinder, using a finger to wipe clean any excess filling at the far end as you finish rolling. Press the overlap to seal.

1-pound bag frozen chopped spinach, thawed, divided

Two 15- or 16-ounce containers whole-milk ricotta cheese

4 ounces fontina cheese, shredded (1 cup)

1 cup lightly packed fresh basil, chopped, divided

1 large egg

½ teaspoon freshly grated nutmeg

Kosher salt and ground black pepper

3 ounces Parmesan cheese, finely grated (1½ cups), plus more for serving

12 to 14 oven-ready lasagna noodles from one 8- or 9-ounce box (see headnote)

28-ounce can whole peeled tomatoes

2 tablespoons extra-virgin olive oil

2 medium garlic cloves, smashed and peeled

¼ teaspoon red pepper flakes

Holding the roll in one hand, use a butter knife to smooth any filling that is spilling out. Place the roll seam down on the prepared baking sheet. Repeat 4 times, making 5 rolls total. Cover with plastic wrap, then freeze until firm enough to hold their shape when cut, about 1½ hours.

To make the sauce, in the processor, puree the tomatoes with juices until mostly smooth, about 20 seconds. In a medium saucepan over medium, combine the oil and garlic. Cook, stirring, until starting to brown, 1 to 2 minutes. Discard the garlic, then add the tomatoes, pepper flakes, remaining basil, 1 teaspoon salt, ½ teaspoon black pepper and reserved pasta water. Simmer, uncovered and stirring, until slightly thickened, 6 to 8 minutes. Off heat, taste and season with salt and pepper.

About 20 minutes before ready to bake, heat the oven to 400°F with a rack in the middle position. Set aside 1½ cups sauce for serving; spread the remainder in a 9-by-13-inch baking dish. Using a chef's knife, cut each chilled pasta roll crosswise into 4 slices, each about 1 inch thick. Arrange the slices cut side up in a single layer over the sauce. Tightly cover the baking dish with foil and bake until the sauce is bubbling, 35 to 40 minutes.

Remove from the oven, uncover and let stand 10 minutes. In a small saucepan over medium, heat the reserved sauce. Spoon ¼ cup sauce onto serving plates, then use a spatula to set a few rolls on top of the sauce on each plate. Sprinkle with additional Parmesan.

For Better Ricotta, Break Out Your Strainer

When we try to re-create Italian recipes using supermarket-quality ricotta cheese, we always have the same problem—lackluster flavor and watery texture. That's because most U.S. ricottas have a higher moisture content than Italian versions.

Traditionally, ricotta is made from whey, rather than milk. The whey is heated until the proteins form curds. But commercial U.S. ricotta is made from milk and is coagulated with additives, creating a more watery cheese. While some higher end ricottas are strained, most supermarket versions aren't. But that gave us an idea for how to handle the problem.

First, read the label. You want one that contains just milk and/or whey, salt and an acid. Avoid any with additives, stabilizers or preservatives. Next, strain it. Straining supermarket ricotta in a mesh strainer for 30 minutes, stirring occasionally, produced a cheese almost as good and dry as better brands, and it worked well in lasagna, stuffed shells and our pasta rotolo.

As we tested this, we tasted many brands. Our favorite was an artisanal variety by Bellwether Farms made from cultured milk and salt; it shed the least liquid. Meanwhile, Frigo ranked at the bottom, tasting sour and pasty and featuring various stabilizers.

From cucina povera,
a no-potato gnocchi

Antonio Cioffi's hilltop restaurant—with its stunning views of the valleys and peaks of Italy's extravagant Amalfi Coast and an enviable perch at the gateway to Ravello, a town steeped in centuries of tourism—seems an unlikely place to preserve the cucina povera of Campania. Yet that's precisely Cioffi's mission, even if he nonetheless still sells plenty of pizzas to tourists.

As we enter his La Vecchia Cantina, we are ushered to a glass-walled room to appreciate those views. As well as a slice of his mother's specialty made just for us, an ages-old recipe at the edge of extinction—gelatina di maiale. For those unfamiliar, it's the odds and ends of a boiled pig's head with raisins and pine nuts, all set in gelatin in the form of a pie.

"Given 10 years, nobody is going to make this anymore," he says. "It will be forgotten."

Whatever your feelings about meat in gelatin, it's always sad when an ancient dish—and therefore the culture, history and even people around it—teeters on extinction. And actually, it was lovely. A reminder that plenty of people know plenty of things we do not, and that it would serve us well—sometimes deliciously so—to learn from them.

Luckily, Cioffi was happy to share other lessons, too. All grounded in the cooking of whatever is available. The dominant pasta variety, for example, is pasta mista. Consider that Italian for scraps, because it's a mix of whatever odds and ends shapes are left, dumped together and cooked as you like. That pretty much captures the region's culinary sensibility.

"It was perfect for people with no time to cook and cool potatoes."

It also explains Campania's take on gnocchi, the pillowy dumpling-like pasta made elsewhere in Italy from a combination of potatoes and flour. But Cioffi—who learned to cook watching his father work in restaurants, then set to kitchen jobs himself at age 10, when his father died—favors the southern Italian approach: flour, water and nothing else.

Historically, the people of Campania were farmers with little money and less time. Their cooking evolved to reflect it. "This gnocchi was simpler, easier and cheaper," Cioffi said. "It was perfect for people with no time to cook and cool potatoes."

The method was joyously simple. Water was heated, flour was stirred in, then cooked for a few minutes until a thick dough formed. After cooling, it was a basic gnocchi forming technique—roll into long snakes, cut into small chunks, then roll the chunks over the tines of a fork to create sauce-trapping crevices. Boil, sauce and done.

Though this method eliminated all of the worry of getting the potatoes just right for the proper texture, I expected the result to be denser and heavier than what I was used to. Quite the opposite. These were airy and light! Cioffi offered multiple sauce ideas, but our favorite was a simple blend of crisped pancetta, garlic, red pepper flakes and fresh herbs. It was all it took to elevate simple to sensational. Because, as he said, sometimes the simpler the food, the more delicious it is.

—J.M. Hirsch

Gnocchi di Farina with Pancetta and Garlic

Start to finish: 1 hour Servings: 4 to 6

In the coastal hilltop town of Ravello, Antonio Cioffi taught us the simple pleasures of "la cucina povera" with his no-fuss, two-ingredient gnocchi. Gnocchi made with mashed potatoes are undoubtedly the best-known variety of the pillowy Italian dumplings, but gnocchi di farina are simpler to prepare and, arguably, equally delicious. Farina is Italian for "flour," and these gnocchi di farina are made with nothing more than flour, water and salt. They exemplify the thriftiness and pragmatism of la cucina povera, or Italian peasant cooking, that transforms the most basic and economical ingredients into hearty, soulful, satisfying food. Our gnocchi di farina, finished simply with pancetta, garlic and Parmesan cheese, is our adaptation of the recipe we learned from Cioffi, chef at La Vecchia Cantina in Ravello. If you wish to make the gnocchi in advance, they can be simmered and drained as directed in the recipe, but let them cool to room temperature on the wire rack. Once cooled, transfer the gnocchi to a baking sheet that has been lined with kitchen parchment and misted with cooking spray; cover with plastic wrap and refrigerate for up to 24 hours. Remove the chilled gnocchi from the refrigerator about 1 hour before you're ready to finish and serve the dish.

Don't boil all of the gnocchi at once. This will overcrowd the pot and lower the temperature of the water, which will result in mushy, overdone exteriors. Also, don't forget to reserve about 1½ cups of the cooking water after the final batch of gnocchi has been simmered and removed. The starchy liquid is needed for making the sauce. If you're making the gnocchi in advance and are refrigerating them, the cooking liquid you reserve for finishing the dish also will need to be refrigerated.

Kosher salt and ground black pepper

2 cups (260 grams) all-purpose flour, plus more for dusting

4 ounces pancetta, finely chopped

3 tablespoons extra-virgin olive oil, divided

6 medium garlic cloves, thinly sliced

¼ to ½ teaspoon red pepper flakes

1 tablespoon lemon juice

2 tablespoons finely chopped fresh flat-leaf parsley or basil

1 ounce Parmesan cheese, finely grated (½ cup)

Line a rimmed baking sheet with kitchen parchment. Set a wire rack in a second rimmed baking sheet. In a large saucepan, bring 2 cups water to a boil over medium-high. Reduce to low and add 1 teaspoon salt. While stirring with a silicone spatula, gradually add the flour. After all the flour has been added, cook the mixture, stirring constantly, until it forms a smooth, stiff, evenly moistened dough, about 2 minutes. Remove the pan from the heat.

Lightly dust the counter with flour, set the dough on top and lightly flour the dough; the dough will be still hot to the touch. Using a rolling pin, roll the dough about ½ inch thick (exact dimensions do not matter), then use a bench scraper to fold the dough into thirds. Repeat the process 3 or 4 more times, or until the dough is still warm to the touch but workable; add more flour as needed to prevent sticking. Using your hands, knead the dough until smooth and elastic, about 3 minutes. Cover with a kitchen towel and let rest for 15 minutes.

Using the bench scraper, divide the dough into 9 equal pieces and re-cover with the towel. Using your hands, roll one piece of dough against the counter into a rope about 18 inches long and about ¾ inch in diameter. Cut the rope into ½-inch pieces and lightly dust the pieces with flour. Dip the back of the tines of a fork into flour, then gently press into each piece to create a ridged surface. Transfer the gnocchi to the parchment-lined baking sheet; try to not allow them to touch. Shape the remaining pieces of dough in the same way.

In a large pot, bring 4 quarts water to a boil. Add 1 tablespoon salt and about one-third of the gnocchi. Return to a boil, stirring once or twice, and cook for 2 minutes (the gnocchi will float to the surface even before they are cooked through).

Using a slotted spoon and allowing excess water to fall back into the pot, transfer the gnocchi in batches to the wire rack set over the baking sheet; spread them out so they don't touch. The gnocchi will be very soft at this point, but will firm up as they cool. Cook and drain the remaining gnocchi in the same way, in two more batches.

After the final batch of gnocchi has been transferred to the rack, reserve about 1½ cups of the cooking water; discard the remainder. Let the gnocchi cool for at least 10 minutes or up to 1 hour to allow them to firm up.

When you are ready to serve, in a 12-inch nonstick skillet over medium, cook the pancetta, stirring often, until browned and crisped, 5 to 7 minutes. Using a slotted spoon, transfer to a small bowl; set

aside. Pour off and discard all but 1 tablespoon of the fat, then add 1 tablespoon of the oil and the garlic to the pan. Cook over medium, stirring, until the garlic is light golden brown, about 2 minutes. Using the slotted spoon, transfer to the bowl with the pancetta. Return the pan to medium and add the gnocchi, pepper flakes and ½ cup of the reserved cooking water. Cook, stirring and tossing often, until the gnocchi are heated through, 3 to 5 minutes; add up to ½ cup more reserved cooking water as needed to form a silky sauce. Add the pancetta and garlic; cook, stirring, until heated through, about 1 minute.

Off heat, stir in the remaining 2 tablespoons oil, lemon juice and parsley. Taste and season with salt and black pepper. Serve sprinkled with the Parmesan.

Gnocchi alla Romana

Start to finish: 2¼ hours (30 minutes active) Servings: 4 to 6

These baked dumplings, a favorite in Rome, are a delicious contrast of crispy, cheesy exteriors and tender innards. They're quite different from the more widely known potato-based gnocchi. Instead, they're made from a stovetop semolina dough that's spread into a thinnish layer on a baking sheet and chilled until firm. The slab then is cut into rounds or squares, doused in butter and cheese and baked. As their name suggests, gnocchi alla romana are popular in Rome, though some believe the recipe was created a few hundred miles north, in Piedmont. This theory stems from the inclusion of butter and Parmesan—both ingredients common in northern Italy, but less frequently used in Roman fare. The dumplings' cheesy, delicately crisp exteriors and pillowy-soft insides make them deeply satisfying. Be sure to thoroughly chill the dough before slicing and shingling the gnocchi in the baking dish—they're far easier to handle when cold.

Don't dump the semolina into the hot milk all at once. Adding it gradually while whisking will result in a smooth, lump-free mixture.

6 tablespoons salted butter, cut into 1-tablespoon pieces, plus 2 tablespoons salted butter, melted

5 cups whole milk

1¾ cups semolina flour

3 ounces Parmesan cheese, finely grated (1½ cups), divided

¾ teaspoon grated nutmeg

Kosher salt and ground black pepper

2 large eggs, lightly beaten

Rub a 1-tablespoon piece of butter over a rimmed baking sheet (approximately 13-by-18 inches) and a 9-by-13 inch baking dish; set aside.

In a large saucepan over medium, heat the milk to just below a simmer. While whisking constantly, slowly stream in the semolina. Switch to a silicone spatula or wooden spoon and cook, stirring often, until the mixture is thick, slightly elastic and pulls away from the sides of the pan, 6 to 8 minutes.

Off heat, add the remaining 5 tablespoon-size pieces of butter, half of the Parmesan, the nutmeg and 1¼ teaspoons each salt and pepper; stir until the butter is melted and incorporated. Add the eggs, then stir vigorously until well combined.

Pour the mixture into the center of the prepared baking sheet and, using a spatula, spread into an even layer all the way to the edges.

Refrigerate, uncovered, until fully chilled, about 1 hour; for longer storage, once chilled, cover with plastic wrap and refrigerate up to 24 hours.

About 20 minutes before you plan to bake, heat the oven to 425°F with a rack in the upper-middle position.

Remove the baking sheet from the refrigerator. Using a dinner knife, cut the semolina slab into quarters lengthwise and sixths crosswise to make 24 rough squares. Remove the pieces from the baking sheet (a thin metal spatula works well) and arrange them in the prepared baking dish, shingling them to fit. Brush the melted butter onto the gnocchi, then sprinkle with remaining Parmesan.

Bake until the cheese is melted and the gnocchi are browned in spots, 30 to 35 minutes. Cool for about 10 minutes before serving.

Pasta 'Ncasciata

Baked Pasta with Eggplant, Sausage and Fontina

Start to finish: 1¼ hours (50 minutes active) Servings: 4 to 6

Roasted eggplant and a simple sauce bring everyday ease to this baked pasta inspired by the Sicilian dish known as pasta 'ncasciata, typically served for Sunday lunch and celebratory occasions. While recipes vary, most include short pasta noodles sauced with a meaty ragù and topped with fried eggplant and caciocavallo, a Southern Italian stretched-curd cheese made from cow's or sheep's milk. Often, cured meats, meatballs and even hard-cooked eggs are added to create a hearty, hefty dish. We throw together an easy ragù with Italian sausage—sweet or hot, it's up to you—and roast the eggplant instead of frying it. For the cheesy goodness, we layer on fontina and Parmesan, then bake the dish in the oven until the cheese is melted and nicely browned.

Don't forget to reserve 2 cups of the sauce before adding the drained pasta in the pot. You'll need the sauce for spreading on top of the second pasta layer.

Two 1-pound globe eggplants

6 tablespoons extra-virgin olive oil, divided

Kosher salt and ground black pepper

1 pound penne or gemelli pasta

1 pound sweet or hot Italian sausage, casing removed

28-ounce can whole peeled tomatoes, crushed by hand

3 medium garlic cloves, minced

¼ to ½ teaspoon red pepper flakes

1 cup lightly packed fresh basil, chopped

8 ounces fontina, provolone or whole-milk mozzarella cheese, shredded (2 cups)

2 ounces Parmesan or pecorino Romano cheese, finely grated (1 cup)

Heat the oven to 400°F with a rack in the middle position. Using a vegetable peeler on each eggplant, peel off strips of skin spaced about 1 inch apart. Cut the eggplants crosswise into slices ½ inch thick, then arrange in a single layer on a baking sheet. Brush on both sides with 3 tablespoons of the oil and season lightly with salt and black pepper. Roast until soft with some browned spots, 25 to 30 minutes, flipping halfway through.

Meanwhile, in a large pot, boil 4 quarts water. Add the pasta and 1 tablespoon salt, then cook, stirring occasionally, until al dente. Reserve 2 cups of the cooking water, then drain. Set aside.

In the same pot over medium, heat 2 tablespoons of the remaining oil until shimmering. Add the sausage and cook, breaking it into small pieces, until starting to brown, 5 to 6 minutes. Stir in the tomatoes with juices, garlic, pepper flakes and ½ teaspoon black pepper. Bring to

a simmer over medium-high, then reduce to medium-low and cook, uncovered and stirring until slightly reduced, 10 to 15 minutes. Stir in the basil and 1½ cups of the reserved cooking water. Remove from the heat and transfer 2 cups of the sauce to a small bowl. Stir the pasta into the sauce in the pot, then taste and season with salt and black pepper.

Brush a 9-by-13-inch baking dish with the remaining 1 tablespoon of the oil. Distribute half of the sauced pasta in an even layer in the prepared baking dish. Layer on the eggplant, overlapping as needed. Spread half of the reserved sauce over the eggplant, covering it completely, then sprinkle with half each of the fontina and Parmesan. Distribute the remaining pasta evenly on top, followed by the remaining reserved sauce, then sprinkle evenly with the remaining cheeses. Bake until the cheese is melted and browned in a few spots, 15 to 20 minutes. Cool for 10 minutes.

Cucina povera: A cooking lesson in Monteveglio

Monteveglio is a tiny village on top of a mountain roughly 12 miles west of Bologna, featuring stone houses and cobblestone streets closed to traffic. It could easily double as a Universal Studios set; the one that offers the "authentic" rural Italian experience. Remains of Roman villas date back to the first century A.D., though the area has been inhabited since the Neolithic period.

There are two main attractions: the pieve, or rural church that has a baptistery, and our main destination, a small restaurant/hotel called Trattoria del Borgo. The church sits at the top of the summit; a monk in classic garb (brown robe, rope belt) except for conspicuous earmuffs is mowing the lawn, all but oblivious to the village's comings and goings.

I walk the cobblestone streets, trying to see past the facades that obscure private, shaded back gardens but can catch only glimpses through half-open wooden gates, one or two ancient bicycles just beyond the entrance. The view of the valley is stunning and uniquely Italian. These lands have been cultivated for thousands of years, and nothing looks wild or out of place. The light is ebbing with a big-screen glow, and it is time for my cooking lesson.

Trattoria del Borgo's owner, Paolo Parmeggiani, is thoroughly modern in the Italian style: affable, charming and the consummate host. On his stone patio overlooking the valley, he explains some of the culinary history of the region. After the wheat was harvested, fields would be burned and any remaining wheat berries would be gathered by the poor, hence the term farina dei poveri. A related term—cucina povera—is an important concept in Italy. It combines a style of cooking that is authentic, local and from the land.

Other common culinary terms are cucina espressa and cucina immediata—which also describe passatelli, the quick homemade pasta dish we are about to make: a mixture of breadcrumbs, eggs and grated cheese, passed through a potato ricer-like passatelli maker into boiling water and served with chicken broth.

The entrance to Trattoria del Borgo is up a short flight of stone steps into a small wine bar, reminding me of an Austrian gasthaus—small, dark and intimate. Up a second flight of stairs, one reaches the kitchen; a small prep area leading into a tiny, modern workspace, plenty of room since the trattoria has just six tables. Parmeggiani's menu is a mix of simple classics (tagliatelle verdi con ragù al classico Bolognese) and more daring options such as the millefoglie di lingua di manzo (beef tongue with a salsa verde) or that evening's passatelli, served not with the traditional broth but with a white sauce made from rabbit, pheasant and guinea fowl. Hardly cucina povera! This ability to change gears from poor to rich, from old to new, is very much in evidence in the Bologna region. The town may be old, but the cooking isn't.

"It is one of the best dishes of my life and also the fastest."

Parmeggiani has three bowls prepared, one filled with breadcrumbs, one with eggs, and the other with finely grated Parmesan. (Parmigiano-Reggiano is made in Emilia-Romagna and finds its way into almost every dish.) I ask about the recipe and learn that one uses six handfuls each of breadcrumbs and cheese, plus eggs as binder.

He combines the mixture by hand, which takes no more than two minutes, until he has a soft dough, which he places into a metal passatelli maker. He extrudes the dough over boiling water, cutting it into short lengths with a knife, and cooks it for just a few minutes, similar to spaetzle.

The only other ingredient besides salt is nutmeg—which, oddly enough, makes all the difference, adding just enough interest to provide character. Passatelli is served in a bowl with chicken broth and, if you are in Emilia-Romagna in the fall, copious shavings of modestly priced white truffles (which, at the outset of the season, are a slightly disappointing mix of potato and truffle). It is one of the best dishes of my life and also the fastest.

That's it. Cucina espressa, as well as povera—one more reminder that the best food in the world is both simple and local.

– Christopher Kimball

Passatelli in Brodo

Start to finish: 1¼ hours (30 minutes active) Servings: 4 to 6

In the ancient village of Monteveglio, Paolo Parmeggiani taught us how to make homemade passatelli in brodo, a simple and flavorful dumpling soup that exemplifies cucina povera, or peasant cooking. Parmeggiani, owner of the small restaurant/hotel Trattoria del Borgo, demonstrated the dish—made with stale bread, cheese, eggs, broth and little else. Passatelli are small, squiggly dumplings, made by extruding dough through smallish holes, that are simply poached and served in chicken broth. We found that in lieu of a traditional passatelli maker, a potato ricer with ³⁄₁₆-inch perforations works well for extruding the dough. Another alternative is to use a cooling rack with a ³⁄₈-inch wire grid (instructions are included in the recipe). To make passatelli dough, Italian cooks use stale bread processed into breadcrumbs, but since we rarely have leftover bread, we start with fresh bread and dry it in the oven. Homemade chicken broth is a cornerstone of this dish, but if store-bought is the only option, be sure to use low-sodium, and you may wish to boost its flavor by dropping a chunk of Parmesan rind into the broth as it heats.

Don't use pre-grated Parmesan or domestic Parmesan-like cheese. With so few ingredients in the passatelli, using true Parmigiano-Reggiano is essential for flavor. Purchase it in a chunk, not pre-grated, as the cheese loses freshness once it's grated. Plus, if you buy a chunk, you will have a piece of rind to simmer in the broth as a flavor booster.

7 ounces stale country-style bread, cut or torn into rough 1-inch pieces (about 5 cups)

3 large eggs

2 teaspoons, plus 1 tablespoon extra-virgin olive oil, divided, plus more to serve

4 ounces Parmesan cheese (without rind), cut into rough 1-inch chunks, plus finely grated Parmesan to serve

¼ teaspoon grated nutmeg, plus more to serve

Kosher salt and ground black pepper

2 quarts homemade chicken broth (facing page; see headnote)

Heat the oven to 300°F with a rack in the middle position. Distribute the bread on a rimmed baking sheet. Toast, stirring occasionally, until dried and crisped but not browned, about 20 minutes. Cool completely.

In a 2-cup liquid measuring cup or medium bowl, whisk together ½ cup water, the eggs and the 2 teaspoons oil. In a food processor, process the Parmesan chunks until finely ground, about 20 seconds. Add the cooled toasted bread, the nutmeg and ¼ teaspoon each salt and pepper. Process until powdery, about 1 minute. With the machine running, slowly add the egg mixture; process until smooth, about 1 minute. Let rest in the processor for 5 minutes; the mixture will thicken as it stands.

Process for another 10 seconds. The mixture will be thick but smooth and resemble mashed potatoes. Scrape it into a medium bowl, cover with plastic wrap and let rest at room temperature for 15 minutes or refrigerate for up to 1 hour; the mixture will thicken further as it stands.

Line a rimmed baking sheet with kitchen parchment and brush the parchment with the remaining 1 tablespoon oil; set aside. In a large saucepan over medium-high, bring

the broth to a boil. Transfer one-third of the dough to the hopper of a ricer with ³⁄₁₆-inch perforations. Press the dough directly over the saucepan of simmering broth until it forms rough 2 to 3-inch lengths, then shake the ricer to release the dough into the broth. (Alternatively, place a rack with a ³⁄₈-inch wire grid across the pot of simmering broth. Scoop one-third of the dough onto the center of the rack, then use a silicone spatula to press the dough through the wires, allowing the dumplings to fall into the broth; rap the rack to release the last bits of dough into the saucepan.)

Cook the passatelli until it floats to the surface, then continue to cook for 1 minute. Using a slotted spoon, scoop out the passatelli, letting it drain, then transfer to the prepared baking sheet. Cook the remaining dough in 2 more batches in the same way, then remove the pot from the heat. Let the passatelli rest for 10 to 20 minutes; it will firm up as it cools.

Return the broth to a simmer over medium-high, then taste and season with salt and pepper. Divide the passatelli among individual bowls and ladle in the broth. Top each serving with grated Parmesan and grated nutmeg, then drizzle with oil.

Homemade Chicken Broth

In an 8- to 12-quart pot, combine **4 pounds chicken backs**, **4 quarts water** and **1 teaspoon salt**. Bring to a vigorous simmer over high, then reduce to low. Simmer gently, uncovered, for 4 hours; adjust the heat as needed to maintain a steady but gentle bubbling action. Set a fine-mesh strainer over a large (at least 5-quart capacity) heatproof container. Transfer the contents of the pot to the strainer; discard the solids. Strain the broth in batches, if needed. Let the broth cool until barely warm to the touch, then refrigerate, uncovered, until fully chilled. Scrape the congealed fat off the surface of the chilled broth; discard the fat or reserve for another use. The broth is ready to use, or can be refrigerated in airtight containers for up to a week or frozen for a few months.

Pallotte Cacio e Ova

Pecorino "Meatballs" in Tomato Sauce

Start to finish: 50 minutes Servings: 4 to 6

At Checchino dal 1887, a restaurant in Rome's Testaccio neighborhood, we were introduced to pallotte cacio e ova, or cheese and egg balls, a dish that transforms simple ingredients into hearty, comforting sustenance. A generous amount of pecorino Romano, plus eggs, breadcrumbs and a few aromatics are combined to form a dough-like mixture. We also add some nutty Parmesan to balance pecorino's funkiness. Formed into spheres and fried in olive oil, the meat-free "meatballs" are toothsome and umami-rich from the cheeses, but also boast a fritter-like crispness and browning on their exteriors. After frying, the "meatballs" are finished in a quick-simmered four-ingredient (not counting the salt and pepper) tomato sauce that balances their savoriness. For minimal knife work, we use a food processor to first make the breadcrumbs, then to blitz together the cheese, garlic and basil. Pallotte cacio e ova makes a fine first course, or a satisfying dinner that happens to be vegetarian.

Don't use pre-grated cheeses for this recipe, as they are too dry and dusty. Pecorino and Parmesan, each purchased in a chunk, are essential not only for best flavor but also for achieving the right texture and degree of moistness in the "meatball" mixture. When selecting pieces, make sure to take the rind into account, as it will need to be trimmed before use.

To make the sauce, in a large saucepan over medium-high, combine the oil and garlic. Cook, stirring, until the garlic is lightly browned, 2 to 3 minutes. Add the tomatoes with juices, basil sprigs, 1 cup water and ½ teaspoon salt. Bring to a simmer, then reduce to medium and cook, stirring occasionally, until slightly thickened, about 10 minutes. Taste and season with salt and pepper. Remove from the heat and cover to keep warm.

Meanwhile, to make the meatballs, in a food processor, process the bread until broken down into fine crumbs, about 30 seconds. Transfer to a large bowl. To the food processor, add the pecorino, Parmesan, basil, garlic and oregano; process until the ingredients are finely chopped, about 1 minute. Add the cheese mixture to the breadcrumbs along with the eggs and ¼ teaspoon each salt and pepper. Using a silicone spatula, stir until evenly moistened and homogeneous. Pinch off a 1-tablespoon portion and roll it between your hands into a ball, or pallotte, then place on a large plate. Form the remaining mixture in the same way; you will have about 20 balls.

In a 12-inch skillet over medium, heat the oil until shimmering. Add the pallotte and cook, occasionally turning them with a slotted spoon, until golden

FOR THE SAUCE:

1 tablespoon extra-virgin olive oil

2 medium garlic cloves, smashed and peeled

14½-oz can whole peeled tomatoes, crushed by hand

2 basil sprigs

Kosher salt and ground black pepper

FOR THE "MEATBALLS":

5 slices hearty white sandwich bread (about 7 ounces), crusts removed, torn into pieces

4 ounces pecorino Romano cheese (without rind), cut into rough 1-inch chunks, plus finely grated pecorino, to serve

1 ounce Parmesan cheese (without rind), cut into rough 1-inch chunks

⅓ cup lightly packed fresh basil, plus chopped fresh basil to serve

2 medium garlic cloves, smashed and peeled

½ teaspoon dried oregano

3 large eggs, beaten

Kosher salt and ground black pepper

½ cup extra-virgin olive oil

brown all over, 5 to 7 minutes; transfer to a paper towel–lined plate as they are done.

When all the "meatballs" have been fried, remove and discard the garlic and basil sprigs from the sauce. Re-cover, then return the sauce to a simmer over medium. Gently lower the pallotte into the sauce, then cook, gently stirringly, until heated through, 2 to 3 minutes. Divide the pallotte among serving bowls and spoon the sauce over and around them. Serve sprinkled with chopped basil and additional pecorino.

Pasta without the pasta

Antico Falcone is not your typical Roman restaurant. It's on the quiet side, with large half-moon windows high up on the wall, sienna-colored floor tiles and blank white walls. It is a clean, modern respite from the hustle and bustle of one of the world's busiest tourist cities, and the food is vastly superior to the huge plates of pasta being served to value-seeking tourists.

I recently returned to Antico Falcone in my search for the perfect cacio e pepe, but during lunch, another dish caught my attention: palline al verde, an exquisite, simple preparation of spinach-ricotta balls briefly poached in water and served with a bright, barely cooked tomato sauce. It is classic Italian—simplicity married to excellence.

Back in the kitchen, chef Mimmo Galal (born in Egypt in 1962 and cooking at the restaurant since 1987), gave me a cooking lesson. The dish belongs to the tradition of pasta filling served without a pasta wrapping, often referred to as "gnudi." The batter is straightforward: ricotta, spinach, whole eggs, salt and Parmesan. Galal rolls out golf ball-sized portions by hand, dredges them in flour, and then poaches them in simmering water for just 90 seconds. A quick-cooked tomato sauce is ladled onto a plate, followed by the palline. Almost lighter than air, freshly sauced and with a punch of Parmesan, this recipe makes the A-list.

But back at Milk Street, we encountered a problem. Our palline fell apart in the poaching water, probably due to the consistency of our store-bought ricotta. Draining the ricotta of excess liquid helped, as did squeezing out as much moisture as possible from the spinach. With a bit of flour, we finally had a light texture that held together. We also added some pecorino to the

"Almost lighter than air, freshly sauced and with a punch of Parmesan, this recipe makes the A-list."

Parmesan to bolster flavor, and we found that a one-hour stay in the fridge was helpful to keep the palline intact. For cooking time, 90 seconds proved insufficient, since the centers emerged undercooked and pasty. A full 8 to 10 minutes seemed better, or until a skewer inserted into the center meets resistance. (One reason the cooking time is extended is that we cook all 20 palline at one time; Antico Falcone prepares this dish to order.)

Although we often think of a traditional Italian tomato sauce as an all-day, long-simmered affair, the Romans often opt for a can of tomatoes and the simplest of preparations. A little EVOO, two cloves of garlic, a small can of whole tomatoes and some basil, and in 10 minutes of simmering, you are good to go. And please note that the whole garlic cloves are cooked in the oil for just two minutes and then discarded! This is a classic Italian technique shared by every cook I have ever worked with in Italy, despite the naysayers who claim that slam-bang garlic flavor is the cornerstone of Italian cooking. It ain't!

–Christopher Kimball

Palline al Verde

Spinach and Ricotta Dumplings

Start to finish: 1¾ hours Servings: 4 to 6

At Trattoria Antico Falcone in Rome, palline al verde—which translates as "green balls"—were small dumpling-like orbs of ricotta, Parmesan and an abundance of spinach. Since the only binder was egg, their texture was delicate and creamy, and their flavor was fresh and light, complemented by a simple tangy-sweet tomato sauce. A dredging of flour just before the palline were cooked created a barely-there coating that helped hold the dumplings together as they simmered and gave the sauce a surface to cling to. When re-creating the dish, we found it necessary to also add a little flour to the dumpling mixture to accommodate the quality of the ricotta sold in U.S. supermarkets. Store-bought frozen spinach, squeezed dry to remove excess moisture, offers convenience without sacrificing flavor or texture. Antico Falcone offers palline al verde as a first course, but with crusty bread and a leafy salad alongside, we think it makes an excellent light main.

Don't skip the step of refrigerating the dumplings before dredging them in flour and forming them into balls. They are easier to shape when chilled and will hold together better when simmered.

To make the dumplings, wrap the spinach in a kitchen towel and squeeze to wring out as much moisture as possible. It should release about 1½ cups water and you should have 7 to 8 ounces squeezed spinach; discard the water.

In a food processor, pulse the spinach until finely chopped, 10 to 12 pulses. Add the ricotta, egg, Parmesan, pecorino, nutmeg and ½ teaspoon each salt and pepper. Pulse to combine, about 10 pulses. Transfer to a medium bowl. Stir in ½ cup flour.

Mist a large plate or a pie plate with cooking spray. Moisten your hands with water, then form a generous tablespoon of the spinach mixture into a ball and place on the plate. Repeat until all of the mixture has been shaped; you will have about 20 balls. Refrigerate uncovered for 30 minutes to 1 hour.

Meanwhile, make the sauce. In the food processor, process the tomatoes with juices until smooth, about 30 seconds. In a medium saucepan over medium, cook the oil and garlic, stirring occasionally, until the garlic is lightly browned, about 2 minutes; remove and discard the cloves. Add the tomatoes along with ¼ cup water and ½ teaspoon each salt and pepper. Bring to a simmer, then reduce to medium-low and cook, uncovered and stirring occasionally, until thickened slightly, about 10 minutes. Remove from the heat and stir in the basil. Taste and season with salt and pepper, then cover to keep warm.

In a large pot over high, bring 4 quarts water to a boil. While the water heats, put the remaining

FOR THE DUMPLINGS:

Two 10-ounce boxes frozen chopped spinach, thawed

1 cup whole-milk ricotta cheese

1 large egg

2 ounces Parmesan cheese, finely grated (1 cup)

1 ounce pecorino Romano cheese, finely grated (½ cup)

½ teaspoon freshly grated nutmeg

Kosher salt and ground black pepper

¾ cup all-purpose flour, divided

FOR THE SAUCE AND SERVING:

14½-ounce can whole peeled tomatoes

1 tablespoon extra-virgin olive oil

2 medium garlic cloves, smashed and peeled

Kosher salt and ground black pepper

¼ cup lightly packed fresh basil, chopped

Parmesan cheese, finely grated, to serve

¼ cup flour in a wide, shallow bowl or a pie plate. Remove the ricotta-spinach balls from the refrigerator. Using your hands, drop one into the flour and toss to lightly coat. Lift it out and gently shake off any excess flour, roll between the palms of your hands, then return it to the plate. Flour the remaining portions in the same way.

Stir 1 tablespoon salt into the boiling water. Using a slotted spoon and adding only a few at a time, carefully lower all of the dumplings into the water. Gently stir to prevent sticking, then cook until a skewer inserted into the center of the dumplings meets some resistance, about 10 minutes; the dumplings will begin to rise to the surface after about 2 minutes. Adjust the heat as needed to maintain a gentle simmer. Meanwhile, return the sauce, partially covered, to a simmer over medium.

When the dumplings are done, use the slotted spoon to transfer them to a clean plate. Spoon about ¼ cup sauce onto each of 4 to 6 shallow serving bowls, then top with the dumplings. Sprinkle with Parmesan and serve right away.

Conchiglie Ripiene con Radicchio al Forno
Baked Stuffed Shells with Radicchio and Sausage

Start to finish: 1¾ hours, plus cooling Servings: 6

Radicchio, a red and white member of the chicory family, is a favorite vegetable in the Veneto region of Italy. In her kitchen in Treviso, home cook Alessandra Bianchi showed us how to make conchiglie ripiene con radicchio al forno. She stuffed parcooked pasta shells with a filling of radicchio sautéed with shallots before covering them with besciamella (the Italian version of French béchamel) and baking them until browned and bubbly. In our version, we include a little Italian sausage in the filling to make the dish rich and satisfying enough to be a main. Be sure to use jumbo shells for this recipe, boil them until they're just shy of al dente (they will finish cooking in the oven) and drizzle them with a little oil after draining to prevent them from sticking together.

Don't worry if the stuffed shells don't look perfect when they're placed in the baking dish. Under the besciamella and cheeses and after baking, their appearance won't matter.

In a small bowl, combine the sausage with ⅓ cup water. Stir with a fork until well combined. In a large pot over medium, heat the oil until shimmering. Add the sausage and shallot; cook, stirring occasionally and breaking the meat into small pieces, until the sausage is no longer pink and begins to brown, 8 to 10 minutes.

Add the wine and cook, stirring occasionally, until the liquid is reduced by about half, 2 to 3 minutes. Add the radicchio and ½ teaspoon each salt and pepper. Cook, stirring, until the radicchio is wilted, 2 to 3 minutes. Transfer to a medium bowl; reserve the pot. Stir half of the Parmesan into the mixture, then taste and season with salt and pepper.

In the now-empty pot over high, bring 4 quarts water to a boil. Stir in the pasta and 1 tablespoon salt, then cook, stirring occasionally, until just shy of al dente. Reserve ½ cup of the cooking water, then drain; set aside. Drizzle the shells with 1 tablespoon oil and toss gently to coat. Heat the oven to 425°F with a rack in the middle position.

In a medium saucepan over medium, melt the butter. Whisk in the flour, then cook, whisking constantly, for 2 minutes. While whisking, gradually add the milk and bring to a simmer. Add the nutmeg, and ¼ teaspoon each salt and pepper, then reduce to low. Cook, whisking often, until the sauce thickens, reduces slightly and no longer tastes of raw starch, 10 to 15 minutes. Remove from the heat, then whisk in the reserved pasta water and ¼ cup of the remaining Parmesan.

Spread 1 cup of the sauce in a 9-by-13-inch baking dish. Spoon the filling into the shells, dividing it evenly (generous 1 tablespoon each) and placing the shells filled side up in a single layer in the baking dish.

8 ounces sweet Italian sausage, casing removed

1 tablespoon extra-virgin olive oil, plus more for drizzling

1 large shallot, minced

½ cup dry white wine

2 medium heads radicchio (1 pound total), bruised outer leaves removed, cored and chopped (about 6 cups)

Kosher salt and ground black pepper

2 ounces Parmesan cheese, finely grated (1 cup), divided

8 ounces jumbo shell pasta (20 to 24 shells)

4 tablespoons salted butter, cut into 4 pieces

¼ cup all-purpose flour

2 cups whole milk

½ teaspoon freshly grated nutmeg

2 ounces fontina cheese, shredded (½ cup)

Ladle the remaining besciamella
evenly over the top; it's fine if the
shells peek through the sauce.
Sprinkle evenly with the fontina and
remaining Parmesan. Bake until the
cheese is bubbling and browned, 30
to 35 minutes. Cool on a wire rack
for 15 minutes before serving.

PIZZA and PANE

The bun that tastes like an Italian grinder

Pio di Benedetto's shop—a claustrophobic corner market in Naples' Piazza Guglielmo Pepe—was a jumble of jarred capers, bagged polenta and canned tomatoes. Side-by-side pictures of Jesus and Sophia Loren watched over a cascade of mortadella and cheeses. Outside, a cranky elderly man sold produce heaped over the hood and windshield of a blue Fiat Panda, cherry-red tomatoes strung between roof rack poles. The car seemed as old and cantankerous as he.

And everywhere—outside and in, mounded on baking sheets, piled in a display case, perched on delivery boxes and wooden stools—there were panini napoletani, a bready local breakfast di Benedetto bakes at home to sell in his shop, Salumeria Pio. Except the buns felt somehow out of place, irregular and lumpy oversized mounds of lightly browned dough with meaty bits poking through. Rather scone-like, they looked like something better paired with English tea than Italian salumi.

The taste, however, made the provenance clear. Rich, savory and moist, with salty spikes of cheese and cured meat. So intensely craveable I found a quiet spot outside to enjoy a whole-bag-of-potato-chips moment with it. The texture was scone-adjacent, but the flavor channeled the spirit of an Italian grinder.

Turns out, my confusion wasn't misplaced. Panini napoletani traditionally are made by topping a sheet of yeasted dough with bits of cured meats and cheese. It then is rolled, sliced and baked much like a stromboli. The buns di Benedetto baked looked nothing like that, but the taste was spot on.

Sipping a beer at the bold hour of 10 a.m., di Benedetto explained that he has run the shop for 55 years, since he was 15. He started baking when he was 18 and the panini napoletani followed soon after. As a rushed young shopkeeper, he didn't have time for the folding and fuss of the classic technique. So he improvised, dumping together the dough ingredients and whatever bits of hard salami, prosciutto and cheese were kicking around the shop, then mixing, mounding and baking.

Part of what made di Benedetto's buns so good—beyond their dump-and-stir ease—was that despite their richness, they remained light. With all that fat—he used lard in the dough, which then was studded with fatty bits of meat and ample hunks of provolone cheese—I expected them to land like a bread bomb in my stomach.

And they probably would have. Except di Benedetto had a simple trick that kept them lighter. Rather than simply add chopped bits of prosciutto to the dough, he first lightly cooked the meat to render and discard much of the fat that otherwise would have bled into the dough during baking, weighing down the finished bun.

> "The texture was scone-adjacent, but the flavor channeled the spirit of an Italian grinder."

It's a trick we borrowed when we re-created di Benedetto's buns. We found it easiest to microwave the prosciutto, as well as a bit of salami, for about a minute. It was just enough to lightly crisp the meat—for a pleasant textural contrast—and render the fat, which we could simply pour off before mixing. The result packed intense meaty-cheesy flavor without feeling heavy.

A savory Italian scone, indeed!

— J.M. Hirsch

Panini Napoletani
Neapolitan Salami-Provolone Buns

Start to finish: 2 hours (35 minutes active), plus cooling Makes twelve 3-inch buns

Naples shopkeeper Pio di Benedetto taught us that cooking the meat briefly before adding it to the dough is the secret to these rich but light cheesy buns. Di Benedetto bakes and sells his much-simplified version of a regional favorite, panini napoletani, at the tiny Salumeria Pio in Naples. The richly flavored buns typically are made from yeasted dough layered with meat and cheese, then rolled, sliced and baked. But di Benedetto takes a simpler approach and mixes the meat and cheese right into the dough. For our adaptation, we use salami and prosciutto, and we briefly microwave the meats. Instead of lard, we opt for butter, though you can substitute an equal amount of lard for 4 tablespoons of the butter. In Naples, di Benedetto sells his buns as a breakfast item, but they're also great served with braised beans or hearty greens. Leftovers keep and reheat well. Store in an airtight container in the refrigerator for up to two days; rewarm on a baking sheet tented with foil in a 350°F oven for 15 to 20 minutes.

Don't finely chop the cured meats. Chop them only roughly so they have presence in the baked breads. After microwaving, be sure to cool the meats to room temperature.

170 grams (6 ounces) thinly sliced salami, roughly chopped

113 grams (4 ounces) thinly sliced prosciutto, roughly chopped

488 grams (3¾ cups) all-purpose flour, plus more for dusting

1 tablespoon instant yeast

2 teaspoons ground black pepper

170 grams (12 tablespoons) cold salted butter, cut into ½-inch cubes

227 grams (8 ounces) provolone cheese, preferably aged provolone, cut into ¼-inch cubes

1¼ cups warm water (100°F to 110°F)

In a large microwave-safe bowl, combine the salami and prosciutto. Microwave on high, uncovered, until the meats just begin to crisp, about 1 minute, stirring once halfway through. Pour off and discard any fat in the bowl; cool to room temperature.

Line 2 rimmed baking sheets with kitchen parchment. In a food processor, combine the flour, yeast and pepper; pulse until well combined, about 12 pulses. Scatter in the butter, then pulse until the mixture resembles coarse sand, 10 to 12 pulses. Empty the mixture into the large bowl containing the meats, then add the provolone. Using a silicone spatula, fold until the ingredients are evenly distributed. Drizzle the water over the mixture, then fold with the spatula until the mixture comes together in a cohesive, evenly moistened dough.

Using a ½-cup dry measuring cup, scoop the dough into 12 even portions, lightly packing the dough into the cup and placing 6 on each prepared baking sheet, evenly spaced; the dough should easily invert out of the cup in a puck-like shape. Cover each baking sheet with a kitchen towel and let rise at room temperature for 1 hour.

Meanwhile, heat the oven to 425°F with a rack in the middle position. Uncover 1 baking sheet and bake until the buns are golden brown, 25 to 27 minutes. Remove from the oven and, using a wide metal spatula, transfer the buns to a wire rack. Bake the second batch in the same way. Cool to room temperature.

The bruschetta of my dreams

If I were an astronaut, I would dream of landing on an alien world, a landscape out of a 1950s science-fiction comic, complete with dinosaurs and mysterious humanoids. But as a cook, I dream of walking down a small side street in a dusty medieval town only to stumble across a jewel of an eatery, displaying some as-yet-undiscovered revelation about the culinary arts.

I am thrilled to say that this is no daydream—it actually happened last summer during a trip to Umbria, when I came across the restaurant Silene, the brainchild and passion of Nicoletta Franceschini. I found it on a small street, in a small town, Foligno, which felt half-abandoned in the summer heat, with silent courtyards and empty cobblestone alleys.

Once described as a "woodland sprite," Franceschini combines a diminutive charm blessed with a creative force that appears unworldly. Her cooking would be a slam-dunk three Michelin stars in New York or Paris. The interior cool and flower-decked, with pale green walls and a floral wallpaper that would be spot-on for the set of "A Midsummer Night's Dream," Silene transports one to the inner dream world of the chef.

My hours in the kitchen with Franceschini offered many lessons. Yes, she often works with ingredients beyond the reach of most—eel stock, nettle-infused dough and fermented strawberry—but it is the simplicity of her touch that impresses most, as with her honey-roasted fig and prosciutto bruschetta. Lesson One: A hint of garlic flavors oil; it remains in the background. Lesson Two: Fresh herbs are essential tools in the culinary quiver, not helter-skelter add-ons. Lesson Three: Be bold with your combinations of sweet, sour, crunch, soft, bright, fruity and meaty.

The bruschetta begins with frying three cloves of garlic and rosemary briefly in olive oil and then removing them. The bread is then fried, but just on the outside; the interior must remain soft. Plump green figs are roasted with local honey and herbs (marjoram and lemon verbena). Then the fruit and sauce is spooned over the toasted bread that has been draped with prosciutto.

Here at Milk Street, we readily accept our more prosaic culinary skills, using the broiler to toast bread and cook the figs. Lemon zest and arugula provide the pop of freshness at the end, rather than harder-to-find fresh marjoram and verbena.

We eagerly tip our toques to a chef whose skills transcend ours but nonetheless provide inspiration for a homemade bruschetta that is still a dream.

–Christopher Kimball

"Plump green figs are roasted with local honey and herbs."

Bruschetta con Prosciutto e Fichi Arrostiti

Honey-Roasted Fig and Prosciutto Bruschetta

Start to finish: 25 minutes Servings: 4 to 6

At Silene Piccolo Ristorante in the central Italian town of Foligno, we tried a savory-sweet take on bruschetta that inspired this honey-tossed fig rendition. Chef Nicoletta Franceschini roasts plump green figs with local honey, fragrant herbs and garlic, then spoons the fruit and its juices over prosciutto-topped toasts. As for the bread, Franceschini fries slices of country-style boule in garlic-enriched olive oil. To simplify and streamline, we toast our bread all at once under the broiler, then repurpose the baking sheet for the figs. We also rub the warm toasts with a garlic clove to re-create the allium notes of Franceschini's seasoned oil. If you can't find fresh figs, a ripe but firm Bosc pear, unpeeled and sliced lengthwise about ¼ inch thick, will work well in their place. The final touch is a few leaves of peppery, lemon-dressed arugula, which brings bright freshness and a pop of color.

Don't scatter the figs across the surface of the baking sheet. Gather them with the cut sides facing up in the center to minimize the spread of juices, which will easily scorch under the broiler.

Heat the broiler with a rack positioned about 6 inches from the element. Generously brush both sides of each bread slice with oil and place in a single layer on a broiler-safe rimmed baking sheet. Broil until golden brown on both sides, 2 to 3 minutes, flipping the slices about halfway through and rotating the baking sheet as needed for even toasting. Remove from the oven and lightly rub the garlic clove all over one side of each toast. Cut each toast in half crosswise and transfer to a platter; set aside. Reserve the baking sheet for the figs.

In a medium bowl, whisk together the honey, oil and ½ teaspoon each salt and pepper. Add the figs and rosemary, then gently toss until evenly coated. Place the figs cut sides up on the reserved baking sheet, gathering them in the center (if using a pear, there's no need to position the slices in a certain way, but do gather them in the center). Tuck the rosemary into the figs, then drizzle with the honey mixture remaining in the bowl. Wipe out and reserve the bowl. Broil until softened and lightly caramelized, 3 to 5 minutes. Meanwhile, in the reserved bowl, combine the arugula and lemon juice; toss and set aside.

Drape a few pieces of prosciutto over each toast, dividing them evenly. Place the figs on top of the prosciutto, dividing them evenly; discard the rosemary. Drizzle the bruschette with any juices on the baking sheet. Top with the arugula and sprinkle with lemon zest and flaky sea salt (if using).

Four 1-inch-thick slices from a country-style boule

2 tablespoons extra-virgin olive oil, plus more for brushing

1 medium garlic clove, smashed and peeled

2 tablespoons honey

Kosher salt and ground black pepper

4 ounces fresh figs, stemmed and quartered, or 1 ripe but firm Bosc pear, unpeeled, halved, cored and sliced lengthwise about ¼ inch thick

1 sprig rosemary

2 cups lightly packed baby arugula

1 teaspoon grated lemon zest, plus 1 teaspoon lemon juice

4 ounces thinly sliced prosciutto, each slice torn into 3 or 4 pieces

Flaky sea salt (optional)

Bruschetta con Verdure Saltate e Pecorino

Bruschetta with Wilted Greens and Pecorino

Start to finish: 35 minutes Servings: 2 to 4

For this crisp-tender take on bruschetta, we dip the bread in egg before toasting it, another riff on the inventive cooking we encountered in chef Nicoletta Franceschini's Umbrian restaurant. Franceschini fried her bruschetta in olive oil and finished by topping the bread with bitter greens sautéed with garlic, followed by shaved pecorino and more olive oil. The egg soak lends the bread a softness and richness reminiscent of French toast. For our adaptation, we dip only one side of each bread slice, creating a textural contrast of custard on one side and crisp on the other. Rustic country-style bread works best here, as its sturdy crumb easily supports the toppings. Look for a boule rather than an elongated loaf, and cut slices from the center, where the loaf is the tallest. Offer one piece of bruschetta as a first course for four, or two pieces per person as a light meal for two.

Don't skip the step of toasting the bread before dipping it in egg. Untoasted, the slices will be too soft, even after frying, to support the toppings.

In a 12-inch skillet over medium, heat 1 tablespoon oil until shimmering. Add the bread and toast, turning occasionally, until golden brown on both sides, 4 to 5 minutes. Transfer to a plate; set aside.

In the same skillet, combine 1 tablespoon of the remaining oil, the garlic and pepper flakes. Cook over medium, stirring occasionally, until the garlic is lightly browned, about 1 minute. Add the greens and cook, tossing with tongs, until wilted, 1 to 2 minutes. Add ¼ cup water, cover and cook, stirring occasionally, until the stems are tender, 3 to 4 minutes. Taste and season with salt and pepper; transfer to a plate and set aside. Wipe out the skillet.

In a pie plate or wide, shallow bowl, beat the eggs and ½ teaspoon each salt and black pepper until well combined. In the skillet over medium, heat the remaining 1 tablespoon oil until shimmering. While the pan is heating, place the bread slices in the egg mixture and let soak until the bottoms are well coated, about 30 seconds; dip only one side of each slice and do not fully saturate the bread (you may not use all the egg mixture).

Add the bread, egg-dipped side down, to the skillet and cook until lightly browned, 1 to 2 minutes. Flip the pieces and cook until the second sides are heated through, about 1 minute. Place the bread on a platter, egg side up. Top with the greens, evenly dividing them. Using a vegetable peeler, shave pecorino onto each portion, then drizzle with additional oil.

3 tablespoons extra-virgin olive oil, divided, plus more to serve

Two ¾-inch-thick slices from a country-style boule (see headnote), halved crosswise

2 medium garlic cloves, thinly sliced

¼ teaspoon red pepper flakes

1 bunch (about 8 ounces) dandelion greens, trimmed and chopped into 2-inch pieces

Kosher salt and ground black pepper

2 large eggs

Pecorino Romano cheese, for shaving

Rome's reinvented panzanella

Conspiracy theories abound regarding the many supposed mysteries hidden at the Vatican in Rome. But it never occurred to me that one of those well-kept secrets would be the recipe for a bread salad so light it is named for a cloud.

When I met him in 2022, Angelo Arrigoni had been tending his nearly century-old bakery, Panificio Arrigoni, much of his life. It sat on an alleyway corner just steps from the Holy See, an area once so steeped in baking that circular stones were embedded in building exteriors along the street so people could use them to measure the bread they bought and ensure it had been baked to regulation size.

Arrigoni's grandfather opened the bakery during the late 1920s and at one point provided bread for the pope. A single window revealed stacks of wheaty loaves, crispy-cheesy flatbreads, tomato-flecked pizzette and packets of biscuits, all of them heaped tantalizingly along a white marble counter that drew you down the long, narrow shop, the far end dominated by a massive oven.

I'd likely have passed by the otherwise nondescript entryway had it not been for an unusual sight in that window. A heap of what I wanted to call flatbreads, yet they were decidedly not flat. Rather, they were puffs. Pizza-sized puffs of cracker-thin bread, almost comically balloon-like. I'd never seen a bread like it in Italy.

Arrigoni called them — gently burnished, crisp and light as air — pane di nuvola, or cloud bread. As far as he knew, his was the only bakery in

"I'd never seen a bread like it in Italy."

Rome, possibly in the country, that made it. For good reason. Pane di nuvola was the result of a happy accident by his grandfather not long after the shop opened.

Apparently, he had some spare bread dough that otherwise would have gone to waste. On a whim, he rolled it out thin and baked it as an unadorned pizza crust. But what emerged from the oven was more of a pillow than a pizza. Maybe it was a humid day, or maybe he'd been a bit liberal with the water when mixing. Either way, the dough had been slightly overhydrated.

In the oven, that extra moisture turned to steam that puffed the dough. And unlike Middle Eastern pita, this bread was so thin and was in the heat just long enough that it crisped and held its form.

It didn't take Arrigoni's grandfather long to make use of this novelty, which was too cracker-like to tear and too bulbous to top with anything beyond a brush of olive oil. Italians are loath to waste bread, even hard or stale loaves. Hence, Tuscan panzanella, which tosses hunks of stale bread with juicy tomatoes and dressing for a robust salad.

The grandfather apparently cracked a hole in the top of the bread—revealing a hollow interior—then filled the loaf with a mix of well-dressed bitter greens, tomatoes, raisins, pine nuts and cheese. A panzanella rebuilt inside out.

Pane di nuvola stuffed with salad became a family and local staple.

Arrigoni's longtime baker, Theresa Araya, demonstrated the blissfully simple recipe, yet another variation on the ancient algorithm of flour, water, yeast and salt. After rising, the dough was rolled wonderfully thin, then slid into the oven for just minutes. When it emerged, puffed and cracker-crisp, she sloshed olive oil over it with a paintbrush in a pail.

"It gets wet when you put the salad in it" just as a traditional panzanella would, Arrigoni said. "But that's why you eat it immediately. And that's not a problem, because everyone devours it."

– J.M. Hirsch

Panzanella Nuvola di Roma

Roman Cloud Bread

Start to finish: 2 hours (45 minutes active) Servings: 4

We learned this unique take on Italian bread and salad, called panzanella nuvola di roma, from Angelo Arrigoni of Panificio Arrigoni, a bakery that for decades operated just outside the Vatican. The crisp yet pleasantly chewy, cracker-thin flatbreads are known as nuvola or "cloud" bread, a nod to their airy texture and puffy shape. Once cooled, the rounds are cracked open, creating a delicious bowl for bitter greens, often accented by resinous pine nuts and salty, nutty Parmesan cheese. Some bakery patrons sliced off a "wedge," yielding a portion of bread with salad inside; others simply tore the bread by hand and used it to scoop up salad. We found that a blend of bitter greens and sturdy romaine hearts, plus thinly sliced fennel, stood up best to our punchy lemon-anchovy dressing. The breads can behave somewhat unpredictably in the oven. Occasionally even within the same batch, three will puff impressively while the fourth... not so much. If you end up with a bread or two that puff less, rather than crack it open and fill it with salad, simply break it in half or quarters and serve the pieces alongside. For make-ahead convenience, the baked breads will keep at room temperature for a few hours, but the salad won't hold, so assemble it just before serving.

Don't worry if you don't have a baking steel or stone. An overturned baking sheet works well as a flat surface for baking the breads. A hot oven is important for proper puffing, so after slipping a dough round into the oven to bake, quickly close the oven door to prevent excessive heat loss.

To make the bread, in a medium bowl, combine the flour, yeast and salt; stir with a wooden spoon. Add the water and stir, scraping the sides of the bowl, until a shaggy, slightly floury dough forms. Turn the dough out onto the counter and knead by hand until well developed and elastic, about 8 minutes. The dough will be quite sticky to start but will become less so with kneading; do not add more flour. Shape the dough into a ball; the surface will not be perfectly smooth. Wash and dry the bowl, then lightly coat it with oil. Return the dough to the bowl, turning to coat with the oil.

Cover with plastic wrap and let rise at room temperature until doubled in bulk, 1 to 1½ hours.

About 30 minutes into rising, position an oven rack about 6 inches from the element. Place a baking steel or stone or an inverted baking sheet on the rack and heat the oven to 450°F.

When the dough has doubled in bulk, lightly dust the counter with flour and turn the dough out onto it. Using a knife, divide the dough into 4 pieces. Form each into a loose ball, then cover the balls with a kitchen towel; let rest for 15 minutes.

FOR THE BREAD:

274 grams (2 cups) bread flour, plus more for dusting

1 teaspoon instant yeast

1 teaspoon table salt

¾ cup plus 1 tablespoon warm water (100°F to 110°F)

Extra-virgin olive oil

FOR THE SALAD:

2 small garlic cloves, finely grated

2 or 3 oil-packed anchovy fillets

Kosher salt and ground black pepper

⅓ cup extra-virgin olive oil

3 tablespoons lemon juice

1 romaine heart, cut crosswise into ½-inch pieces

4 cups lightly packed baby arugula, or radicchio cut into bite-size pieces, or a combination

1 small fennel bulb, trimmed, halved and thinly sliced

⅓ cup pine nuts, toasted

1 ounce Parmesan cheese, finely grated (½ cup), plus more to serve

Lightly flour the counter and set 1 ball on top; keep the remaining portions covered. Using a rolling pin, roll the ball into a thin round about 8 inches in diameter, dusting with flour as needed; it's fine if the dough does not form a perfect circle. Lightly dust a pizza peel with flour, then transfer the dough to the peel; reshape the round if needed. Slide the round onto the baking steel and quickly close the oven door. Bake until the bread is puffed and deep golden brown in spots, 8 to 10 minutes.

Using tongs, gently grip the bread and transfer to a wire rack. Shape and bake the 3 remaining dough balls in the same way. (The breads will hold well at room temperature for a few hours.)

When you are ready to serve, make the salad. In a large bowl, combine the garlic, anchovies and 1 teaspoon salt. Using a fork, mash to a paste. Whisk in the oil, lemon juice and ½ teaspoon black pepper. Add the romaine hearts, arugula, fennel, pine nuts and Parmesan; toss well. Taste and season with salt and pepper.

If desired, lightly brush the breads with oil. Place each bread on a serving plate. Using the blunt side of the blade of a chef's knife, crack open each bread. Fill each bread with a quarter of the salad, allowing it to spill onto the plates. Sprinkle with additional Parmesan and serve right away.

Italy's best tomato focaccia

The focaccia emerge from the oven—a truck-sized stone behemoth that radiates with breathtaking intensity—so quickly, the bakers at Panificio Fiore exhaust their shelves of cooling racks, forcing them to line the pans along the white tiled floor as they use a 14-foot peel to rapid-fire reload and bake the next batch.

The century-old wood-fired oven can hold 48 focaccia at once, baking them in just over 10 minutes. Even then, making hundreds a day, the workers can't keep pace with the lunch line that twists out the tiny shop and down one of the many winding stone alleys of Bari, a thin strip of a city along the Adriatic Sea on the heel of the Italian boot. Over and again, they hand the focaccia to Antonio Fiore, whose grandfather opened the shop in 1940.

Standing at the front counter, customers blurting orders at him, Fiore tosses each foot-round focaccia onto a concave stainless steel slab—designed to allow excess olive oil to drip away—then uses a long serrated knife to cut wedges to order, wrapping them in parchment before handing over the still-warm hunks dotted with crushed tomatoes and glistening whole green olives.

In the midst of the rush, he hands me a thick wedge, oil staining the paper and slicking my fingers. It is shockingly crispy and lightly crunchy on the bottom—almost shattering—yet the top remains airy-chewy and tender, with bursts of brine and juicy sweet tomato. It is unlike any focaccia I've eaten, all too often singularly and unappealingly dense and doughy, lacking texture or definition. Fiore's is rich with contrasts, fried in parts, baked in others.

With each crunchy-chewy bite I understand all the more why his focaccia was named the best in all of Italy. Less clear was how he managed to make it so good. And so different.

Tucked amongst the arches of Pontifical Basilica di San Nicola, Panificio Fiore occupies a former crypt that dates to at least 1508. Its white stone walls and columns are plastered with pictures of the church's namesake St. Nicholas.

A long glass display case offers a dozen varieties of focaccia, many with wedges already hacked out. Bianca (just olives); cipolle e pomodoro (onion and tomato); melanzane e pomodoro (eggplant and tomato); patate, pomodoro e carciofi (potato, tomato and artichoke); and pomodoro, formaggio e rucola (tomato, cheese and arugula) among them. But the most popular—and that which the bakers today labor at—is pomodoro e olive, or tomato and olives.

Focaccia is the street food of Bari, a meal intended to be eaten immediately; it is fresh for only a few hours. Fiore complains that other bakers make more and make them faster, but that's not traditional—and you can taste their shortcuts. To show me the right way, he guides me into the

> "I understand all the more why his focaccia was named the best in all of Italy."

kitchen, where waves of heat and yeast wash over you.

As Fiore rattles off the main ingredients—flour, yeast, water, salt and olive oil—nothing strikes me as unusual, nothing that can account for the delicious push-and-pull of tender-crispy that makes his focaccia so memorably good. Turns out, the difference isn't in the what, but in the how. Particularly, how long and how much.

On one side of the room, dough rises in containers the size of trash cans. The bakers—all of them family—hoist the buckets of dough, dumping it in large, almost oozing piles onto metal tables for portioning. The dough is tender and flabby and barely can be handled. That's the first clue—the ratio of water to dry ingredients clearly is higher than normal.

A typical focaccia dough uses water equal to about 56 percent of the weight of flour used. Fiore's recipe clocks in at more than 90 percent water to flour. That difference is critical because wet doughs produce weaker gluten, the protein that gives most baked goods their structure. Weak gluten tears easily, especially when all that excess moisture in the dough turns to steam in the oven. The combination creates an airy, open and more tender crumb.

An equally important difference turns out to be timing. While a typical focaccia might rise for one to two hours, Fiore's rises for four hours, during which the dough rises, falls, then rises again, a process that leaves it looking and feeling blown out. This produces more gas than a shorter rise. Though some of that gas depletes over time—resulting

in less dramatic oven spring when the focaccia first hits the hot oven—the remaining gas, combined with the steam and gluten structure, creates more and larger air pockets in the dough.

The source of the crisp bottom—not merely browned, as with a pizza, but almost crackling—becomes clear as the dough is portioned into dark metal pans. Olive oil so copious it sloshes up the side of the dough goes into the pan first, effectively frying the bottom of the focaccia as the top bakes.

Back at Milk Street, adapting the recipe mostly was a matter of logistics. In the heat of Fiore's kitchen, four hours is plenty for

rising. But in significantly cooler home kitchens, we needed to let the dough go for about six hours to get similar results. And without the benefit of a wood-fired oven that can crank upward of 600°F, we needed to bake our focaccia a bit longer.

We also needed a substitute for the tomatoes. Lightly crushed cherry tomatoes offered the best flavor in place of the almost iridescent Sicilian tomatoes Fiore used. Halving them, then lightly mashing them removed some of the juices that otherwise pooled unappealingly on the surface of the focaccia. The result? Italy's best focaccia a little closer to home.

– J.M. Hirsch

Focaccia Pomodoro e Olive

Tomato-Olive Focaccia

Start to finish: 7¼ hours (40 minutes active), plus cooling Servings: 12

At Panificio Fiore in Bari, Antonio Fiore showed us how this focaccia bakes up impossibly tender thanks to an unexpectedly high hydration level. To achieve a light, open-crumbed texture, the dough must be wet—so wet, in fact, it verges on a thick, yet pourable batter. Resist the temptation to add more flour than is called for. Shaping such a sticky, high-hydration dough by hand is impossible. Instead, the dough is gently poured and scraped into the oiled baking pan; gravity settles it into an even layer. If you have trouble finding Castelvetrano olives, substitute any large, meaty green olive. To slice the baked focaccia for serving, use a serrated knife and a sawing motion to cut through the crust and crumb without compressing it. If desired, serve with extra-virgin olive oil for dipping. For convenience, the dough can be prepared and transferred to the baking pan a day in advance. After it has settled in the pan, cover tightly with plastic wrap and refrigerate. The next day, prepare the toppings. Uncover, top the dough with the olives and tomatoes and let stand at room temperature for 45 minutes, then finish and bake as directed.

Don't disturb the dough during its rise. And when transferring the dough to the baking pan, handle it gently. The goal is to retain as much gas in the dough as possible so the focaccia bakes up with an airy texture. Don't use a baking dish made of glass or ceramic; neither will produce a crisp, browned exterior, and glass is not safe to use in a 500°F oven.

502 grams (3⅓ cups) bread flour

5 teaspoons instant yeast

1 teaspoon white sugar

2 cups water, cool room temperature

8 tablespoons extra-virgin olive oil, divided

1¾ teaspoons table salt, divided

130 grams (1 cup) cherry tomatoes, halved

138 grams (1 cup) Castelvetrano olives, pitted and halved (see headnote)

1 teaspoon dried oregano

¾ teaspoon ground black pepper

In a stand mixer with the dough hook, mix the flour, yeast and sugar on medium until combined, about 30 seconds. With the mixer on low, drizzle in the water, then increase to medium and mix until the ingredients form a very wet, smooth dough, about 5 minutes. Turn off the mixer, cover the bowl and let stand for 10 minutes. Meanwhile, coat the bottom and sides of a large bowl with 2 tablespoons of oil; set aside.

Sprinkle 1 teaspoon of salt over the dough, then knead on medium until smooth and elastic, about 5 minutes; the dough will be wet enough to cling to the sides of the bowl. Using a silicone spatula, scrape the dough into the oiled bowl. Dip your fingers into the oil pooled at the sides of the bowl and dab the surface of the dough until completely coated with oil. Cover tightly with plastic wrap and let stand at room temperature for 5½ to 6 hours; during this time, the dough will double in volume, deflate, then rise again (but will not double in volume again).

After the dough has risen for about 4½ hours, heat the oven to 500°F with a baking steel or stone on the middle rack. Mist a 9-by-13-inch metal baking pan with cooking spray, then pour 2 tablespoons of the remaining oil in the center of the pan; set aside.

When the dough is ready, gently pour it into the prepared pan, scraping the sides of the bowl with a silicone spatula to loosen; try to retain as much air in the dough as possible. The dough will eventually settle into an even layer in the pan; do not spread the dough with a spatula, as this will cause it to deflate. Set aside while you prepare the tomatoes.

In a medium bowl, use a potato masher to lightly crush the tomatoes. Scatter the olives evenly over the dough, then do the same with the tomatoes, leaving the juice and seeds in the bowl. If the dough has not fully filled the corners of the pan, use your hands to lightly press the toppings to push the dough into the corners. Let stand uncovered at room temperature for 20 minutes.

Drizzle the dough with the remaining 4 tablespoons oil, making sure each tomato is coated. Sprinkle evenly with the oregano, remaining ¾ teaspoon salt and the pepper. Place the pan on the baking steel or stone and bake until golden brown and the sides of the focaccia have pulled away from the pan, 20 to 22 minutes. Cool in the pan on a wire rack for 5 minutes. Using a wide metal spatula, lift the focaccia from the pan and slide it onto the rack. Cool for at least 30 minutes before serving.

In Naples, we tasted the fire in the pizza

If you want to really get the pulse of Italy, at least southern Italy, you need to go to Naples. It is crowded, dirty, edgy and without happy-go-lucky tourists wandering the sidewalks, gelatos in hand. It's not far from Rome in kilometers, but it's a galaxy away in terms of culture.

I had traveled down to Naples for one reason—to get a close-up look at how Neapolitan pizza is really made. Not the New York version, but the real deal. L'antica Pizzeria da Michele was the obvious choice since it was founded in 1870 and serves just two basic styles—marinara and margherita. The sidewalk wait was long, about 45 minutes, and this was March, not the height of the season. Inside was small, one room in the front next to the wood-fired oven, and another off to the side.

Fortunately, our table was in front and I had a direct line of sight into the oven and to the two pizza makers who were stretching and topping the rounds of dough. The first thing I noticed is that everyone was using a knife and fork. At first, I thought this was a matter of Italian style—maybe self-respecting Italians even in Naples did not eat pizza out of hand. But when we were served our first pizzas, the reason became clear. The centers of the pizzas were soggy, not crisp, due to the watery fresh mozzarella. The other thing I noticed was the cooking time. Our pizzas were cooked in about 75 seconds, each round being turned almost constantly so no one edge was overcooked. It made me wonder if a somewhat slower oven, or cooking the pizzas a bit farther away from the hot coals, would have solved the problem.

Of course, the "problem" may have been me. I arrived at Michele's preferring a crisp bottom crust or, at least, not a soggy one, but the locals did not seem to mind. I was left with an unanswered question: Is Neapolitan pizza defined by the fresh mozzarella and the soggy center, or is this simply the way they do it at Michele's? A quick glance at YELP generated some skepticism. Many reviewers called out burned crusts and soggy bottoms but, again, this may be more cultural than absolute. I found the flavor of the pizza and the ingredients exceptional and after a couple of bites, the soggy center was no bother. What I liked was the char of the crust married to the sweet, fresh tomato topping and the milky flavor of the mozzarella. Just like Naples, it ain't perfect but it is the essence of great pizza and a great city. You can taste the fire in the pizza and feel the burning pulse of the city in this raggedy, out-on-the-sidewalk town. What more could one ask?

–Christopher Kimball

> "I found the flavor of the pizza and the ingredients exceptional."

Impasto Pizza
Pizza Dough

*Start to finish: 4¼ hours (40 minutes active) Makes about 2½ pounds dough
(enough for four 10-inch pizzas)*

This pizza dough is a wet, high-hydration dough (about 76 percent hydration). It also starts with a preferment—which, in this case, is a mixture of bread and semolina flours, a little sugar, yeast, salt and water that's left to stand for an hour at room temperature, during which time it becomes active and bubbly. The preferment then is mixed with more bread flour, olive oil, salt and water and allowed to rise for about 1½ hours. The end result is a pizza crust with a rustic, open crumb; a chewy-crisp texture; and bubbles that char in the oven, forming the spotting that's characteristic of high-end pizzeria pies. The flavor is wheaty and complex yet clean, not yeasty and boozy like drier doughs made with an abundance of yeast. For make-ahead and storage convenience, there are a couple good stopping points in this recipe. After 30 minutes of room-temperature rising, the dough can be refrigerated for up to 24 hours. Or, after dividing into four portions, the dough can be allowed to rise at room temperature for 30 minutes, then refrigerated for up to 48 hours. For topping and baking instructions, refer to specific pizza recipes, but keep in mind you will need a peel for shuttling the pies into and out of the oven and a baking stone or steel. Before baking, we heat the oven and steel (or stone) for an hour at 500°F or 550°F to build up heat, but prior to shaping and topping pies, we switch the oven to broil. The upper heating element browns and chars the surface of the pizza while the hot steel crisps the bottom crust.

Don't be shy about flouring the counter as you portion and shape the dough. This dough is wet—almost pourable—but as long as it and the work surface is floured, it's very workable. It's much more compliant than lower-hydration doughs and does not snap back with the same vigor, so it's easy to shape into rounds.

To make the preferment, in the bowl of a stand mixer, stir together both flours, the sugar, yeast, salt and 1 cup water. Cover and let stand at room temperature for 1 hour; the mixture will resemble a thick, bubbly batter.

To make the dough, to the preferment, add the flour, oil, salt and 1 cup water; stir to roughly combine. Attach the bowl and dough hook to the mixer. Mix on low until well combined, about 2 minutes, then increase to medium-low and mix until an elastic, webby dough forms, 8 to 10 minutes; scrape the sides of the bowl and push the dough off the hook a few times during mixing. Scrape the sides of the bowl and gather the dough in the center of the bowl. Cover and let rise at room temperature until doubled, about 1½ hours. (If making ahead, let rise for about 30 minutes, then refrigerate for up to 24 hours.)

FOR THE PREFERMENT:

137 grams (1 cup) bread flour

85 grams (½ cup) semolina flour

2 teaspoons white sugar

¾ teaspoon instant yeast

¼ teaspoon table salt

FOR THE DOUGH:

411 grams (3 cups) bread flour, plus more for dusting

1½ tablespoons extra-virgin olive oil

1½ teaspoons table salt

Generously flour the counter and a rimmed baking sheet. Using floured hands and a bowl scraper or silicone spatula, scrape the dough out onto the counter; if the dough was refrigerated, it's fine to work with it while it is cold. The dough will be very sticky. Dust with flour, then use a floured metal bench scraper or chef's knife to divide the dough into 4 portions. Flour the cut sides of each piece of dough.

Form each portion into a taut ball by cupping your hands around the base of the dough, slightly cradling it. Rotate and drag the dough along the counter, allowing the base to catch on the surface to create tension that pulls the dough into a tighter round. Repeat a few more times, until the dough forms a relatively uniform ball. Transfer to the baking sheet, spacing the portions evenly. Dust the dough balls with flour, then

cover with a kitchen towel. Let rise at room temperature until doubled, 1 to 1½ hours if the dough was room temperature before portioning, or about 2 hours if it was refrigerated. (If you intend to save any portions for baking in the next day or two, let rise for only 30 minutes, then transfer to a 3- to 4-cup plastic container with a tight-fitting lid and refrigerate for up to 48 hours). The dough now is ready to shape and bake.

Pizza Margherita

Start to finish: 5 hours (40 minutes active)   Makes two 10-inch pizzas

The Associazione Verace Pizza Napoletana establishes regulations on pizza bearing the name "Neapolitan" or "Napoletana." So though pizza alla margherita is an Italian classic and our version attempts to re-create the pizza we tasted in Naples, it is not Neapolitan. It is, however, a top-notch homemade pie. Fresh mozzarella cheese is key. After slicing it, be sure to pat the pieces dry to remove excess moisture that can lead to a soggy crust. Our pizza dough recipe makes enough for four 10-inch pies, but you will need only two portions for this recipe. You may wish to use the other two portions to make pizza alla marinara (p. 291), or, to make four pizza margherite, simply double the toppings below.

Don't forget to heat the baking steel or stone for at least an hour before baking, and be sure to turn the oven to broil before shaping the dough.

All-purpose flour, for dusting the counter

Two portions pizza dough (p. 286)

Semolina flour, for dusting the pizza peel

⅔ cup tomato sauce for pizza (facing page), divided

4 ounces fresh mozzarella cheese, cut into ¼-inch-thick slices, then torn or cut into 1- to 2-inch pieces, patted dry, divided

12 to 14 fresh basil leaves

Extra-virgin olive oil, to serve

At least 1 hour before baking, heat the oven to 500°F (or 550°F if that's your oven's maximum temperature), with a baking steel or stone on the middle rack.

When you are ready to shape the dough, heat the oven to broil (use the low setting if your oven offers multiple broiler settings). Generously dust the counter with all-purpose flour and set one portion of dough on top. With your hands, slightly flatten the dough, then with your fingertips, gently press it into an 8-inch round of relatively even thickness. Flip the dough over and press into a 10-inch round, working from the center outward and leaving a ½-inch border around the perimeter; occasionally flip the dough to ensure the bottom is not sticking to the counter.

Dust a baking peel with semolina, then transfer the round to the peel and, if needed, reshape into a 10-inch round; gently shake the peel to ensure the dough slides freely. Spread half of the tomato sauce evenly on the dough, leaving a ½-inch border. Sprinkle evenly with half of the mozzarella.

Slide the pizza onto the baking steel or stone and bake until the crust is spottily browned and the cheese is melted, 5 to 8 minutes. Using the peel, transfer the pizza to a cutting board. Brush away any residual semolina on the peel.

Shape, top and bake the second portion of dough in the same way. While the second pizza is baking, tear 6 to 8 basil leaves into pieces and scatter them over the baked pizza, then drizzle with oil. Cut into slices and serve.

When the second pizza is done, remove it from the oven and finish it in the same way as the first. Cut into slices and serve.

Tomato Sauce for Pizza

Start to finish: 5 minutes Makes 1½ cups

In a blender, puree a **14½-ounce can whole peeled tomatoes** until smooth, 15 to 30 seconds. Transfer to a small bowl or container. Stir in **1 tablespoon extra-virgin olive oil** and **¾ teaspoon table salt**. Set aside until ready to use. (In an airtight container, the sauce can be refrigerated for up to 5 days or frozen for a few months.)

Pizza alla Marinara

Start to finish: 5 hours (40 minutes active) Makes two 10-inch pizzas

Pizza alla marinara is said to be the oldest type of tomato-topped pizza. A simple, cheese-free pie, it's made by scattering sliced garlic and dried oregano onto the tomato layer, then drizzling with olive oil—in that order, according to standards established by the Associazione Verace Pizza Napoletana. Some consider anchovies an acceptable addition, others call them heretical. We're in favor of the savory depth they add when mashed into a paste and stirred into the tomato sauce, but you can omit them if you like. Our pizza dough recipe makes enough for four 10-inch pies, but you will need only two portions for this recipe. If you wish to make four pizze alla marinara, this recipe is easy to double, or if you need to satisfy those who request cheese on their pizza, use the extra dough to make pizza margherite (p. 288).

Don't be afraid to generously dust the counter with flour when shaping the pies. The high-hydration dough is very wet, so a liberal use of flour will minimize sticking.

3 or 4 oil-packed anchovy fillets, patted dry

1 cup tomato sauce for pizza (p. 289)

All-purpose flour, for dusting the counter

Two portions pizza dough (p. 286)

Semolina flour, for dusting the pizza peel

2 garlic cloves, thinly sliced, divided

½ teaspoon dried oregano, divided

Extra-virgin olive oil, for drizzling

At least 1 hour before baking, heat the oven to 500°F (or 550°F if that's your oven's maximum temperature), with a baking steel or stone on the middle rack.

When you are ready to shape the dough, heat the oven to broil (use the low setting if your oven offers multiple broiler settings). In a small bowl and using a fork, mash the anchovies to a smooth paste; stir in the tomato sauce.

Generously dust the counter with all-purpose flour and set one portion of dough on top. With your hands, slightly flatten the dough, then with your fingertips, gently press it into an 8-inch round of relatively even thickness. Flip the dough over and press into a 10-inch round, working from the center outward and leaving a ½-inch border around the perimeter; occasionally flip the dough to ensure the bottom is not sticking to the counter.

Dust a baking peel with semolina, then transfer the round to the peel and, if needed, reshape into a 10-inch round; gently shake the peel to ensure the dough slides freely. Spread ½ cup tomato sauce evenly on the dough, leaving a ½-inch border. Sprinkle evenly with 1 sliced garlic clove and ¼ teaspoon oregano, then drizzle with oil.

Slide the pizza onto the baking steel or stone and bake until the crust is spottily browned and the sauce is bubbling and darkened, 5 to 8 minutes. Using the peel, transfer the pizza to a cutting board. Brush away any residual semolina on the peel.

Shape, top and bake the second portion of dough in the same way. While the second pizza is baking, drizzle the first one with oil, then cut into slices and serve.

When the second pizza is done, remove it from the oven. Drizzle with additional oil, cut into slices and serve.

Farinata di Ceci
Chickpea Flatbread with Rosemary

Start to finish: 30 minutes Servings: 4 to 6

Chickpea flour adds crisp, light texture to this flatbread, a savory pancake of sorts that we ate at the Cascina Lana winery in Piedmont. Farinata di ceci is an unleavened pancake-like flatbread made from a simple batter of chickpea flour, water and sometimes olive oil. In Piedmont, Karin Vitale, a cook at Cascina Lana winery, prepared a massive tractor tire–sized, rosemary-infused farinata that she cooked outdoors in a wood-fired oven. She travels, with her oven, to fairs around the region preparing farinata, which is sliced and served with various toppings, prosciutto and Gorgonzola among the favorites. For our version, we use a 10-inch cast-iron skillet to achieve deep, even browning. A nonstick skillet will work, but because the cooking oil tends to pool on a nonstick surface, the browning will be more uneven than in cast iron. Chickpea flour with a fine, even grind that feels smooth, not nubby and granular, is best for this recipe. Bob's Red Mill, a brand widely available in supermarkets, and Anthony's, sold online, both work well. Warm water in the batter hydrates the flour more quickly than room-temperature liquid. If desired, the recipe can easily be doubled to yield eight farinata.

Don't forget to add another 1 tablespoon oil before cooking each flatbread. The oil both prevents sticking and promotes browning. If at any point the oil begins to smoke, reduce the heat to avoid scorching. Be sure to cover the farinata with a kitchen towel after transferring from the skillet to the plate. The towels will trap in enough steam to keep the flatbreads soft and pliable, but not so much that they turn limp and soggy.

1½ cups chickpea flour (see headnote)

Kosher salt and ground black pepper

1½ cups warm water (100°F)

¼ cup extra-virgin olive oil, plus 4 tablespoons, for cooking

½ teaspoon minced fresh rosemary

2 to 4 ounces thinly sliced prosciutto

2 to 4 ounces Gorgonzola cheese, crumbled

In a large bowl, whisk together the chickpea flour, 1 teaspoon salt and ¼ teaspoon pepper. Whisk in half the water until smooth. While whisking, slowly add the remaining water. Whisk in the ¼ cup oil until incorporated but small beads of oil remain visible, then add the rosemary and whisk until combined.

In a 10-inch cast-iron skillet over medium-high, heat 1 tablespoon oil until shimmering. Pour ½ cup of the batter into the center of the skillet, then tilt the pan so the batter covers the surface. Cook until the bottom is well browned, 1½ to 2 minutes. Using a thin metal spatula, carefully flip the flatbread. Cook until the second side is dark spotty brown, another 1½ to 2 minutes. Transfer to a large plate and cover with a kitchen towel.

Using 1 tablespoon of the remaining oil, cook the remaining batter in the same way, stacking the flatbreads on the plate. Reduce the heat if the oil begins to smoke or if the flatbreads begin to cook too quickly.

To serve, cut each flatbread into 4 wedges. Serve warm, with the prosciutto and Gorgonzola on the side for topping as desired.

Erbazzone

Savory Greens Tart with Pancetta and Parmesan

Start to finish: 2¼ hours (1¼ hours active), plus cooling Servings: 8

In Bologna, home cook Paola Tassi made us her version of erbazzone, inspiring this rich and savory tart. Erbazzone, a speciality of the Emilia-Romagna region, typically features a filling of wild greens and pancetta in a pork fat-enriched crust. In the filling, we tested everything from spinach to broccoli rabe, but preferred a duo of Swiss chard and lacinato kale for their combination of textures and flavor. Beet greens work well in place of chard—just be sure to cook the mixture a few minutes extra to ensure the sturdier beet greens are fully tender. As for the crust—we opted for butter over pork fat, but to mimic the savoriness of lard, we added a little grated Parmesan cheese to the dough. We also experimented with shaping methods, including a double-crusted tart formed in a pie plate and a more svelte version in a French-style fluted pan. Our favorite was a rustic, freeform, crostata-like iteration. This gave each slice an ideal crust to filling ratio. More importantly, its open top allowed steam from the greens to evaporate in the oven, creating an evenly browned tart with no soggy bottom.

Don't roll the dough too thin. A sturdy base is essential for supporting the mound of braised greens. Also, be sure to strain and press the greens after cooking them. You don't need to be aggressive, but removing extra moisture will make for a crisp bottom crust.

To make the crust, in a food processor, combine the flour, Parmesan and ¼ teaspoon kosher salt; pulse 3 or 4 times. Scatter about 42 grams (3 tablespoons) butter over the flour mixture and process until well incorporated, 15 to 20 seconds. Scatter in the remaining butter, then pulse until broken into pieces no larger than small peas, 10 to 12 pulses. Drizzle the ice water over the mixture, then pulse until curdy clumps form, 12 to 15 pulses.

Turn the dough out onto the counter. Gather and press it firmly into a disk about 6 inches in diameter. Wrap tightly in plastic, smoothing out the edges and forming the disk into a neat round.

Refrigerate at least 30 minutes while you prepare the filling (or up to 2 days). Heat the oven to 425°F with a rack in the middle position.

To make the filling, in a large pot over medium-high, combine the oil, pancetta, onion, chard stems, pepper flakes and ½ teaspoon black pepper. Cook, stirring occasionally, until well browned, 5 to 7 minutes. Add the chard leaves and kale a handful at a time, stirring until wilted after each. Add ½ cup water and ¼ teaspoon salt, then scrape up any browned bits. Cover, reduce to medium-low and cook, stirring occasionally, until the greens are wilted and tender, 7 to 9 minutes.

FOR THE CRUST:

260 grams (2 cups) all-purpose flour, plus more for dusting

1 ounce Parmesan cheese, finely grated (½ cup)

Kosher salt

226 grams (16 tablespoons) cold salted butter, cut into ½-inch cubes

½ cup ice water

FOR THE FILLING:

1 tablespoon extra-virgin olive oil, plus more for brushing

4 ounces pancetta, chopped

1 medium red onion, finely chopped

1 medium bunch (about 8 ounces) Swiss or rainbow chard, stems finely chopped, leaves roughly chopped, reserved separately

¼ teaspoon red pepper flakes

Kosher salt and ground black pepper

1 medium bunch (about 8 ounces) lacinato kale, stemmed and roughly chopped

2 ounces Parmesan cheese, finely grated (1 cup), plus more for sprinkling

4 scallions, thinly sliced

Drain the mixture in a colander set in the sink. Using a spatula or spoon, press the greens to remove excess moisture. Return the mixture to the pot, then stir in the Parmesan and scallions. Taste and season with salt and black pepper.

Remove the chilled dough from the refrigerator. If it is too firm to roll out, let it stand at room temperature 5 to 10 minutes. Lightly flour a sheet of kitchen parchment that will fit onto a rimmed baking sheet. Unwrap the dough and set it on the parchment. Using a rolling pin, roll it into a 14- to 15-inch circle. Slide the parchment with the dough onto a rimmed baking sheet.

Mound the filling in the center of the dough, leaving a 2-inch border around the edge; it's fine if the filling is still slightly warm. Working in one direction around the circumference of the dough, fold the edge toward the center and up onto but not entirely covering the filling, pleating it at intervals as you go. Gently press the pleats so they remain in place.

Brush the dough liberally with oil. Bake until the crust is golden brown, 30 to 35 minutes, rotating the baking sheet halfway through. Cool on the baking sheet on a wire rack for about 30 minutes. Slide a wide metal spatula under the tart to loosen it from the parchment and transfer to a platter. Serve warm or at room temperature.

FRUTTI
DI MARE

With spaghetti and clams, the sauce is in the shell

The bigoli emerges from the bronze die thick, rough and hot to the touch, snaking itself into coils that slink over the cook's outstretched hand to form bundles of fresh pasta he arranges one after another in a tray. It's one of the sexiest things I've ever seen, pasta so fresh and extruded with such pressure that it steams.

I'm at Perduto, a canal-side restaurant in Venice where the pasta is made in 6-kilo batches each morning in the front window. Of course, this being Venice, by that time the tables outside already are full. Here, the drinking and eating start early, Aperol spritzes and wine lining up by 9 a.m.

Inside, the staff mounds a long copper and marble bar with cicchetti, savory nibbles destined to be nestled onto crostini or polenta. At Perduto, a space that has been home to one restaurant or another since at least the 1800s, most of those nibbles involve seafood of some sort—plump grilled squid, octopus salad, baccalà mantecato (a pâté made from dried cod).

Walk down the bar and the tables cluster. Because the kitchen is small, cooks spill into the serving area, dining tables becoming prep space. Garlic chopped here, seafood shelled there, salting sliced tomatoes to the side. The result is a delicious onslaught of aromas that makes you want everything on the menu.

And that pasta in the window? It is for bigoli con vongole, or the dish we know better as spaghetti and clams (bigoli being the rougher, thicker

"The oil, starch and clam juice emulsify, creating a thick sauce that coats."

Venetian cousin of spaghetti). It's why I've come to Perduto. And though the dish is ridiculously simple, I quickly learn that, as with so many Italian recipes we think we know, it's the small details we overlook that matter most.

Chef Gianpiero Turdo offers to walk me through the recipe, the whole thing taking just 15 minutes. A fast and very active 15 minutes!

Turdo begins by warming olive oil, garlic and parsley in a large skillet. When we can smell the cloves, he discards them. They've done their job of flavoring the oil. He then adds several cups of the local and so very fresh caparossoli clams. As they start to sizzle, he adds a splash of white wine, then pops on a cover.

The pasta then goes into boiling water for a spare four minutes. The pasta isn't even halfway done, but the clams have popped open, smelling sweet and briny. Turdo scoops out the partially cooked bigoli and heaps it over the clams along with ladlefuls of the starchy water it was cooking in.

That's when the tossing begins. Holding the skillet firmly by the handle, he jerks it back and forth, turning the water, pasta, clams and their juices into a delicious tangle. It's that movement—many minutes of it—that is the secret ingredient to this dish. The oil, starch and clam juice emulsify, creating a thick sauce that coats.

The dish is done. And as I fork up those tender, thick strands and plump clams, I find it shocking how so few and such simple ingredients can combine into a dish of wonderful briny-savory-sweet complexity.

—J.M. Hirsch

Spaghetti alle Vongole
Spaghetti with Clams

Start to finish: 35 minutes Servings: 4

At Perduto, a canal-side restaurant in Venice, chef Gianpiero Turdo taught us to make the regional pasta classic: bigoli con vongole (bigoli with clams). When boiling the pasta, we drain it when it is not quite al dente. The noodles will finish cooking in the reduced clam juices, a technique that infuses the spaghetti with the sweet briny notes of the clams. The al dente pasta, garlic, wine, parsley and briny clams were a seamless blend of complementary flavors and the deliciousness of the dish belied the ease with which it came together. Bigoli is a long, thick, round extruded noodle, sometimes made with whole-wheat flour, sometimes with eggs. At Perduto, the bigoli are house made. In the U.S., easier-to-find spaghetti or bucatini are good substitutes. We prefer littleneck clams for this recipe, but Manila clams also work. Whichever variety you use, scrub the clams well to remove as much grit as possible.

Don't use more than 2 quarts of water to cook the pasta and don't forget to reserve about 2 cups of water before draining the spaghetti. The pasta water needs to be extra-starchy so that when some is added at the end of cooking, it gives the sauce body and clingability.

12 ounces spaghetti or bucatini

Kosher salt and ground black pepper

3 tablespoons extra-virgin olive oil, plus more to serve

4 medium garlic cloves, smashed and peeled

¼ teaspoon red pepper flakes

1 cup dry white wine

3 pounds littleneck or Manila clams, scrubbed

½ cup finely chopped fresh flat-leaf parsley

Lemon wedges, to serve

In a large pot, bring 2 quarts water to a boil. Stir in the pasta and 1½ teaspoons salt, then cook, stirring occasionally, until just shy of al dente. Reserve about 2 cups of the cooking water, then drain; set aside.

In a large Dutch oven over medium-high, combine the oil and garlic; cook, stirring until the garlic is lightly browned, about 2 minutes. Add the pepper flakes and cook, stirring, until fragrant, about 30 seconds. Remove and discard the garlic. Stir in the wine, bring to a simmer and cook until reduced to about ¼ cup, 6 to 8 minutes.

Stir in the clams, cover and cook, stirring occasionally; as the clams open, transfer them to a large bowl. When all clams have opened, simmer the juices in the pot until reduced by half. Discard any unopened clams.

Add the pasta and any accumulated clam juices (but not the clams themselves) in the bowl to the pot. Cook, constantly stirring and tossing, until the pasta is al dente, 2 to 3 minutes, adding reserved pasta water as needed so the noodles are lightly sauced.

Off heat, stir in the parsley, then taste and season with salt and pepper. Return the clams and any remaining juices to the pot; toss to combine. Serve drizzled with additional oil and with lemon wedges on the side.

Zuppa di Pesce
Italian Seafood Stew

Start to finish: 1 hour 10 minutes Servings: 4

In Ancona, the capital of the Marche region on Italy's Adriatic coast, we learned two similar types of fisherman's stew. Chef Raffaele Attili at Trattoria La Cantineta demonstrated his recipe for guazzetto and chef Corrado Biló at Trattoria La Moretta taught us brodetto. Both were tomato based and featured four or more types of seafood. We combined our favorite attributes of each to create our version of seafood stew. Be sure to use a firm, meaty white fish that won't flake apart in the broth. Swordfish is a good option, as is monkfish. We especially like scallops in this dish. Seek out "dry" sea scallops, ones that have not been treated with sodium tripolyphosphate (STPP), a preservative that forces them to retain water. Dry scallops have a creamy pinkish hue, and a sweeter and purer flavor. If not available, shrimp are delicious, too. Serve with crusty bread for dipping.

Don't use canned diced tomatoes, which are processed with calcium chloride that keeps their texture firm. Canned whole tomatoes that are crushed by hand better integrate into the broth and meld with the other ingredients.

3 tablespoons extra-virgin olive oil

1 small carrot, peeled and finely chopped

1 small celery stalk, finely chopped

2 tablespoons chopped fresh flat-leaf parsley, plus more to serve

1 tablespoon tomato paste

1 medium garlic clove, minced

¼ to ½ teaspoon red pepper flakes

¼ cup dry white wine or dry vermouth

14½-ounce can whole peeled tomatoes, crushed by hand

Kosher salt and ground black pepper

1 pound boneless, skinless firm white fish steaks or fillets, such as swordfish or monkfish (see headnote), cut into 1- to 1½-inch pieces

8 ounces dry sea scallops (see headnote), side tendons removed, or 8 ounces large (21/25 per pound) shrimp, peeled and deveined

1 pound small hardshell clams (about 1½ inches in diameter) or mussels, scrubbed

Lemon wedges, to serve

In a large Dutch oven over medium, heat the oil until shimmering. Add the carrot, celery and parsley; cook, stirring occasionally, until slightly softened, about 4 minutes. Add the tomato paste, garlic and pepper flakes; cook, stirring, until fragrant, about 1 minute. Add the wine and cook, scraping any browned bits, until syrupy, about 1 minute. Add the tomatoes with juices, ½ cup water and ½ teaspoon salt. Bring to a simmer, then cover partially, reduce to medium-low and cook, stirring occasionally, until slightly thickened and the aromatics have fully softened, 15 to 17 minutes.

Stir in the fish, cover and cook until a skewer inserted into the largest piece meets a little resistance, 10 to 15 minutes. Increase to medium-high, then scatter the scallops over the surface, followed by the clams. Cover and cook until the clams have opened, about 5 minutes, stirring once about halfway through.

Stir again, then discard any clams that have not opened. Taste and season with salt and pepper. Serve sprinkled with additional parsley and with lemon wedges.

Gamberi alla Toscana con Fagioli Bianchi

Tuscan-Style Shrimp with White Beans

Start to finish: 25 minutes   Servings: 4

With its miles of coastline and reputation as the home of mangiafagioli—or bean eaters—it's no surprise that shrimp and white beans are a classic pairing in the cuisine of Tuscany. In this quick, easy recipe, the two are the stars, but with so few supporting ingredients, it's important to use a dry white wine that's good enough to drink on its own. Serve warm or at room temperature with a leafy salad and crusty bread to round out the meal.

Don't forget to cover the skillet and lower the heat after adding the shrimp. This will allow the shrimp to cook gently and without risk of scorching and toughening.

In a 12-inch skillet over medium-high, heat the oil until shimmering. Add the onion, rosemary, pepper flakes and ½ teaspoon salt; cook, stirring occasionally, until the onion is translucent, 4 to 6 minutes. Stir in the beans, then add the wine and cook, uncovered and stirring occasionally, until the pan is dry, 5 to 7 minutes.

Stir in the shrimp. Cover, reduce to medium-low and cook until the shrimp are opaque throughout, 4 to 5 minutes; stir once about halfway through.

Off heat, taste and season with salt and black pepper. Remove and discard the rosemary sprig. Stir in the parsley and serve drizzled with additional oil.

3 tablespoons extra-virgin olive oil, plus more to serve

1 medium yellow onion, finely chopped

1 sprig fresh rosemary

½ teaspoon red pepper flakes

Kosher salt and ground black pepper

Two 15½-ounce cans butter beans or cannellini beans, rinsed and drained

¾ cup dry white wine

1 pound extra-large (21/25 per pound) shrimp, peeled and deveined

1 cup lightly packed fresh flat-leaf parsley or fresh basil, roughly chopped

In Lido, we learn the
real taste of Venice

A web of water and arched bridges, the stitching that tethers the cluster of islands that is Venice. On the main island it's easy to be dazzled, ocher- and sunflower-colored buildings splashing sunlight onto canals where narrow stairwells descend to waves lapping luminescent green.

Of course, the real Venice is beyond the postcard pretty. Grab a water taxi to the outer islands and you're in Venice's version of the suburbs. It's how I find myself in Lido, a narrow barrier island a world away from the throngs of tourists.

Here, there are cars, yet the streets are quiet. The pacing is calmer, the views of the water less obstructed. And it's here that I meet Marika Contaldo Seguso, a cookbook author who documents the city's culinary traditions, and her husband, a 23rd-generation glassmaker whose family has been in the craft on neighboring Murano island since 1397.

Seguso begins my education on Venetian cooking with a history lesson. Location being everything, much of the cuisine begins with the bounty of the lagoon, which also determined what would become the dominant flavor profile of so many foods. That is, sweet and sour.

It's a gentle push and pull credited to the long history of Venetians using vinegar and sugar to preserve seafood. It's not a bold—albeit delicious—flavor stroke like Vietnamese caramel shrimp. Rather, it's a more gentle contrast that lends subtle complexity to the dish. To demonstrate, Seguso offers to teach me scampi alla busara, or prawns poached in tomatoes.

The cooking is simple; the flavors are anything but. In a large skillet, she heats oil with garlic cloves and shell-on prawns just long enough for both to flavor the fat. The garlic then is discarded, the prawns are set aside. A splash of white wine sizzles, then chopped tomatoes, torn fresh basil and red pepper flakes are added.

The sauce cooks down until it is thick and almost jammy, the taste bright and sharp. Seguso then adds a hint of white sugar—maybe 2 teaspoons—just enough to round out the flavor of the tomatoes and underline their sweetness without dulling their tang. When she is happy, spaghetti cooked just shy of al dente in a bare amount of water is added.

The starchy water that clings to the pasta as she forks it into the skillet helps thicken the sauce further. Eventually, the prawns return to the pan to finish cooking in the gentle heat of the sauce and pasta. The result is rich, sweet, tangy and briny with flavors that run deeper than the simple ingredients suggest.

It's a craveable combination, and one that makes me glad to have slipped free of the clamoring crowds.

—J.M. Hirsch

"The result is rich, sweet, tangy and briny with flavors that run deeper than the simple ingredients suggest."

Scampi alla Busara

Spaghetti with Shrimp, Tomatoes and White Wine

Start to finish: 45 minutes Servings: 4 to 6

In Venice, cookbook author Marika Contaldo Seguso taught us to make a regional classic, scampi alla busara, that inspired this dish. Large, sweet, shell-on prawns are bathed in a sauce made with fresh tomatoes and flavored with a splash of white wine, smashed garlic cloves and a sprinkling of pepper flakes. She paired her scampi alla busara with al dente pasta. We adapted Seguso's recipe using shelled shrimp in place of the prawns; to build flavor into our sauce, we briefly simmer the shrimp tails in the wine reduction, then remove them before the tomatoes are added.

Don't use more than 3 quarts of water to boil the spaghetti. The aim is for the pasta water to be extra-starchy, as some of it is reserved (don't forget to set aside about 1 cup before draining) and used near the end of cooking to give the sauce some clingability. Also, don't boil the spaghetti until al dente. Drain it when it's just shy of al dente, as it will finish cooking directly in the sauce.

In a large pot, bring 3 quarts water to a boil. Add the spaghetti and 2 teaspoons salt; cook, stirring occasionally, until just shy of al dente. Reserve about 1 cup of the cooking water, then drain the pasta and return it to the pot; set aside.

In a 12-inch skillet over medium, heat 2 tablespoons of the oil until shimmering. Add the garlic and shrimp tails, then cook, stirring occasionally, until the garlic begins to brown, 3 to 4 minutes. Add the wine, bring to a simmer and cook, stirring, until it has reduced by about half, 2 to 3 minutes. Using tongs or a slotted spoon, remove and discard the garlic and shrimp tails.

Into the wine reduction, stir the tomatoes, half of the basil, the sugar, pepper flakes and ½ teaspoon each salt and black pepper. Bring to a simmer over medium-high, then reduce to medium and simmer, stirring occasionally, until the tomatoes are softened and jammy and the juices have fully evaporated, 12 to 15 minutes.

Add the shrimp and cook, stirring occasionally, until they begin to turn pink, about 2 minutes. Pour the mixture over the spaghetti in the pot, then add the remaining 2 tablespoons oil and ½ cup of the pasta water. Cook over medium, tossing with tongs, until the sauce clings to the spaghetti and the shrimp are cooked through, 3 to 4 minutes; add more cooking water 1 tablespoon at a time if the mixture looks dry.

Off heat, taste and season with salt and pepper, then stir in the remaining basil. Serve drizzled with additional oil.

1 pound spaghetti

Kosher salt and ground black pepper

4 tablespoons extra-virgin olive oil, divided, plus more to serve

4 medium garlic cloves, smashed and peeled

1½ pounds extra-large shrimp (21/25 per pound), peeled (tails removed and reserved) and deveined

⅓ cup dry white wine

2 pounds ripe plum tomatoes, cored and chopped

1 cup lightly packed fresh basil, torn, divided

2 teaspoons white sugar

½ teaspoon red pepper flakes

Pasta alla Marinara al Cucchiaio
Pasta with Shellfish and Tomatoes

Start to finish: 40 minutes   Servings: 4 to 6

We encountered ditaloni alla marinara al cucchiaio at chef Corrado Biló's restaurant Trattoria la Moretta in the coastal city of Ancona. The dish translates quite simply as "seafood ditaloni with a spoon," and Biló told us his inspiration was a pasta dish loaded with seafood, yet easily eaten with a spoon. Ditaloni, a smallish ridged tube pasta, is not easy to find in the U.S., so for our adaptation, we chose medium shells—an appropriate shape for a seafood dish—or mezzi rigatoni. For a variety of flavor and texture, we use a trio of shellfish: calamari (shrimp is a fine alternative), scallops and mussels (or clams). It's worth seeking out dry sea scallops—that is, ones that have not been treated with sodium tripolyphosphate (STPP), a preservative that causes them to retain water. Dry scallops have a pinkish hue and a clean, sweet flavor.

Don't forget to cover the Dutch oven after adding the mussels. The lid traps heat in the pot for faster and more even cooking.

Add the tomatoes with juices to a blender; process until smooth, 15 to 30 seconds. Set the tomatoes aside. In a Dutch oven, bring 2 quarts water to a boil. Add the pasta and 1½ teaspoons salt, then cook, stirring occasionally, until just shy of al dente. Reserve ¾ cup of the cooking water, then drain. Set the pasta and cooking water aside.

In the same pot over medium, combine the oil, onion, garlic, pepper flakes, half the parsley and ½ teaspoon salt. Cover and cook, stirring, until the onion has softened, 8 to 10 minutes. Add the wine and cook, uncovered and stirring, until reduced by half, 3 to 4 minutes. Add the tomatoes, the reserved pasta water and ½ teaspoon each salt and black pepper. Bring to a simmer and cook, uncovered and stirring, until

a wooden spoon drawn through leaves a trail, 8 to 10 minutes.

Stir in the mussels, cover and cook until most have opened, 2 to 3 minutes; stir once about halfway through. Using a slotted spoon, transfer the mussels to a medium bowl, discarding any that have not opened. Stir the calamari and scallops into the sauce. Cook, uncovered and stirring, until the calamari begins to turn opaque, about 2 minutes.

Add the pasta and cook, stirring occasionally, until the scallops and calamari are opaque throughout and the pasta is al dente, 2 to 3 minutes. Stir in the mussels and accumulated juices. Off heat, taste and season with salt and black pepper, then stir in the remaining parsley. Serve drizzled with additional oil.

14½-ounce can whole peeled or diced tomatoes

8 ounces medium shell pasta or mezzi rigatoni

Kosher salt and ground black pepper

1 tablespoon extra-virgin olive oil, plus more to serve

½ small yellow onion, finely chopped

4 medium garlic cloves, thinly sliced

½ teaspoon red pepper flakes

½ cup finely chopped fresh flat-leaf parsley, divided

½ cup dry white wine

1 pound mussels or small hard-shell clams (about 1⅓ inches in diameter), scrubbed

8 ounces cleaned calamari, tubes cut into ½-inch rings, or small (41/50 per pound) shrimp, peeled and deveined

8 ounces dry sea scallops (see headnote), side tendons removed, cut into ½-inch chunks

Gnocchi allo Zafferano, Gamberi e Cozze

Gnocchi with Saffron, Shrimp and Mussels

Start to finish: 40 minutes   Servings: 4 to 6

At Trattoria la Moretta, located in Ancona, the capital of Italy's Marche region, chef Corrado Biló pairs gnocchi with a seafood ragù made from large prawns and clams with smaller pieces of chopped mixed seafood. Our goal was to mimic the sweet, briny flavors but make the dish more amenable to home cooking. We found that starting with a quick mussel broth built a flavorful base, while adding saffron, like Biló did, gave the sauce floral, earthy notes and a warm golden hue. Either uncooked homemade gnocchi (p. 250) or store-bought gnocchi (which is precooked) works well here. For pasta fans, we also tested the recipe using a 9-ounce package of fresh fettuccine, and the results were great. Cook the pasta according to package instructions and add it in the same way you would the gnocchi.

Don't pour the gnocchi into a colander; instead, use a slotted spoon to lift them from the water and place them directly in the skillet.

In a large pot over medium, combine the oil, scallion whites, garlic, thyme sprigs and pepper flakes (if using). Cook, stirring, until the garlic is softened and fragrant, about 3 minutes. Add the wine and bring to a boil over medium-high. Stir in 1 cup water and return to a boil. Scatter in the mussels, then cover and cook, stirring once halfway through, until most of the mussels have opened, 4 to 6 minutes.

Using a slotted spoon or wire skimmer, transfer the mussels to a rimmed baking sheet to cool; discard any that have not opened. Strain the broth through a fine-mesh strainer into a 12-inch skillet; discard the garlic and thyme sprigs. Wipe out the pot and fill with 3 quarts water, then bring to a boil over medium-high.

While the water heats, bring the broth in the skillet to a simmer over medium-high. Add the saffron and simmer, stirring occasionally, until reduced to about 1 cup, 5 to 7 minutes. Meanwhile, remove the mussels from the shells; discard the shells. If the water is not yet boiling, cover the skillet and reduce the heat to low.

When the water in the pot reaches a boil, add the shrimp to the skillet. Cook over medium, stirring occasionally, until the shrimp have just turned opaque, about 2 minutes. Meanwhile, in the boiling water, cook the gnocchi according to the gnocchi recipe or package instructions. Using the slotted spoon, gently transfer the gnocchi to the skillet. Add the mussels, then cook over medium, swirling the pan and gently folding with a silicone spatula, until well combined, about 1 minute. Off heat, stir in the lemon juice, chopped thyme and scallion greens. Taste and season with salt and black pepper.

2 tablespoons extra-virgin olive oil

3 scallions, thinly sliced, whites and greens reserved separately

2 medium garlic cloves, smashed and peeled

2 large sprigs thyme, plus ½ teaspoon chopped fresh thyme, reserved separately

¼ to ½ teaspoon red pepper flakes (optional)

½ cup dry white wine

2 pounds mussels, scrubbed

¼ teaspoon saffron threads, crumbled

12 ounces medium-large (31/40 per pound) shrimp, peeled (tails removed) and deveined

1 pound uncooked homemade gnocchi or store-bought gnocchi (see headnote)

2 teaspoons lemon juice

Kosher salt and ground black pepper

Pasta con Acciughe e Pomodorini
Pasta with Tomatoes, Anchovies and Garlic

Start to finish: 35 minutes Servings: 4 to 6

At Trattoria La Cantineta in Ancona chef Raffaele Attili taught us to make tagliolini ai sardoncini, in which he paired pasta with a simple but intensely flavored sauce of tomatoes, garlic and anchovies. (Sardoncini are sardines, but Attili opted for anchovies.) For our version, we blend a can of whole or diced tomatoes with their juices. Don't use canned crushed or pureed tomatoes. These products have a thicker, heavier consistency than whole or diced tomatoes. A generous amount of oil-packed anchovies disintegrates into the quick-cooking sauce and lends richness. In the finished dish, the sauce should cling tightly to the pasta with little pooling on the bottom.

Don't forget to reserve some water before draining the pasta. Depending on the consistency of your sauce, you may not need any of it, but if the sauce is too thick to nicely coat the noodles, you'll need some to thin it.

14½-ounce can whole peeled tomatoes or diced tomatoes

1 pound spaghetti

Kosher salt and ground black pepper

2 tablespoons extra-virgin olive oil, plus more to serve

4 medium garlic cloves, minced

¼ teaspoon red pepper flakes

About 20 oil-packed anchovies (from a 2-ounce tin), patted dry and roughly chopped

½ cup finely chopped fresh flat-leaf parsley, divided

⅓ cup dry vermouth

Add the tomatoes with juices to a blender; process until smooth, 15 to 30 seconds. Alternatively, add the tomatoes to a medium bowl and blend with an immersion blender until smooth. Set the tomatoes aside.

In a large pot, bring 4 quarts water to a boil. Stir in the pasta and 1 tablespoon salt, then cook, stirring occasionally, until just shy of al dente. Reserve ½ cup of the cooking water, then drain and return the pasta to the pot.

Meanwhile, in a 12-inch skillet over medium, cook the oil and garlic, stirring, until lightly golden, 1 to 2 minutes. Add the pepper flakes, anchovies and half the parsley; cook, stirring, until the anchovies are mostly broken down,

about 1 minute. Add the vermouth and cook, stirring, until reduced by half, 1 to 2 minutes.

Add the tomatoes and ½ teaspoon each salt and black pepper. Bring to a simmer, then reduce to medium-low and cook, uncovered and stirring occasionally, until slightly thickened, 5 to 6 minutes. If the pasta is not yet done, set aside off heat.

Add the sauce to the pasta in the pot. Cook over medium, tossing, until the pasta is al dente, 2 to 3 minutes. Add reserved pasta water 1 tablespoon at a time, if needed, so the sauce clings to the pasta. Off heat, toss in the remaining parsley. Taste and season with salt and black pepper. Serve drizzled with additional oil.

Zuppa di Lenticchie di Castellucio con Gamberi
Lentil Soup with Lemony Shrimp

Start to finish: 1 hour Servings: 4 to 6

At Vittoria Ristorante, a 100-year-old eatery in Marche, chef Sunni Martelli taught us to make her grandmother's lentil and shrimp soup. The coastal region is known for its seafood, while lentils are a nod to its neighbor, Umbria. To make the lentils creamy and tender, Martelli cooked them like risotto, adding liquid slowly and in stages. She used the Castelluccio variety, which are grown in the Umbrian village of the same name, but French lentils du Puy also work well. Puy lentils may take a little longer to cook, so be sure to taste them for doneness. Serve the soup with crusty bread.

Don't add the shrimp before the lentils are tender. The saucepan is removed from the heat as soon as the shrimp are added to ensure that they do not overcook. If your lentils are not already tender, they won't finish cooking during this period.

In a medium saucepan over medium-high, bring 2 quarts water to a simmer; cover and reduce to low to keep warm. In a large saucepan over medium-high, heat the oil until shimmering. Add the lentils, carrots, celery and ½ teaspoon salt. Cook, stirring, until the vegetables are softened, 3 to 5 minutes. Add the garlic, pepper flakes and thyme. Cook, stirring, until fragrant, about 30 seconds.

Add the wine and cook, stirring, until most of the liquid is absorbed, 1 to 2 minutes. Add 2 cups of the hot water and bring to a boil over medium-high. Reduce to medium and simmer, stirring often, until about half the liquid is absorbed, 5 to 7 minutes. Add another 2 cups hot water and cook until about half of the liquid is absorbed,

another 5 to 7 minutes. Add the remaining water, the bay and ½ teaspoon salt; return to a simmer over medium. Cook, uncovered and stirring occasionally, until the lentils are fully tender and the soup has thickened slightly, about 30 minutes.

Meanwhile, in a medium bowl, toss the shrimp with the lemon zest and ¼ teaspoon each salt and black pepper; set aside. Once the lentils are fully tender, stir in the shrimp. Remove from heat and let stand, uncovered, until the shrimp are cooked through, about 5 minutes. Remove and discard the thyme sprigs and bay. Stir in the lemon juice, then taste and season with salt and black pepper. Ladle into bowls, drizzle with additional oil and sprinkle with parsley.

¼ cup extra-virgin olive oil, plus more to serve

1¼ cups Castelluccio lentils (see headnote) or lentils du Puy, rinsed and drained

2 medium carrots, peeled and finely chopped

2 medium celery stalks, finely chopped

Kosher salt and ground black pepper

3 medium garlic cloves, finely chopped

¼ to ½ teaspoon red pepper flakes

4 sprigs fresh thyme

½ cup dry white wine

1 bay leaf

1 pound extra-large (21/25 per pound) shrimp, peeled (tails removed) and deveined

1 teaspoon grated lemon zest, plus 1 tablespoon lemon juice

Finely chopped flat-leaf parsley, to serve

Ceci e Vongole

Chickpeas and Clams

Start to finish: 30 minutes Servings: 4 to 6

Giancarlo Suriano, founder of Suriano, a purveyor of Calabrian ingredients, taught us his version of ceci e vongole, a quick one-pot dish of chickpeas and clams. Calabrian chilies are fruity and not too spicy; Fresno chilies are a good substitute, and even red pepper flakes will do in a pinch. Canned chickpeas are easy and work well, but for the best flavor, cook your own dried chickpeas (p. 87) and use 3 cups cooked chickpeas plus 1 cup of cooking liquid. If you prefer mussels, they work well in place of clams; the cooking time remains the same. Whichever you use, be sure to discard any that do not open after cooking.

Don't add the clams until the broth is boiling, then quickly cover the pot. Clams cook best when blasted with heat and steam, so keep the lid on until ready to stir.

In a large Dutch oven over medium, combine the oil, garlic, chili, rosemary and ¼ teaspoon pepper; cook, stirring, until the garlic has softened and the mixture is fragrant, about 4 minutes. Stir in the tomato paste, then add the chickpeas and 1 cup water. Bring to a boil over medium-high. Scatter the clams into the pot, cover and cook until most of the clams have opened, 5 to 7 minutes, stirring once about halfway through.

Stir once again, then remove and discard the rosemary and any clams that have not opened. Stir in the lemon juice, then taste and season with salt and pepper. Serve drizzled with additional oil and with crusty bread.

¼ cup extra-virgin olive oil, plus more to serve

3 medium garlic cloves, thinly sliced

1 medium Fresno chili, stemmed, seeded and chopped, or ¼ teaspoon red pepper flakes

4-inch sprig rosemary

Kosher salt and ground black pepper

2 teaspoons tomato paste

Two 15½-ounce cans chickpeas, rinsed and drained (see headnote)

3 pounds small hard-shell clams (1 to 1½ inches diameter), such as littleneck or Manila, scrubbed

1 tablespoon lemon juice

Crusty bread, to serve

Spaghetti con Tonno, Olive Verdi e Pomodorini

Spaghetti with Tuna, Green Olives and Tomatoes

Start to finish: 45 minutes Servings: 4 to 6

This pasta dish is a riff on one we learned from home cook Eleonora Fratini Martini in the Marche region of Italy. She transformed canned tomatoes into a complexly salty, umami-rich sauce using anchovies, tuna and tons of olives. Like Martini, we use green olives; they are firmer and more buttery than black ones and give the sauce a meaty quality. We found that olive oil–packed tuna—plus a splash of its packing oil in place of the anchovies—yielded our desired level of brininess. Be sure to avoid tuna packed in water. It lacks the flavor and richness of oil-packed tuna and has a drier, mealier texture. Also, look for tuna with no added salt, which will give you better control over the salinity of the finished dish.

Don't use diced canned tomatoes. They are too firm and won't break down properly in the sauce. They also often have skins attached, which makes for an unpleasant texture in the finished dish.

¼ cup extra-virgin olive oil, plus more to serve

4 garlic cloves, thinly sliced

2 tablespoons tomato paste

14½-ounce can whole peeled tomatoes, crushed by hand

Kosher salt and ground black pepper

1½ cups pitted green olives, chopped

5-ounce can olive oil–packed tuna (preferably unsalted), drained, oil reserved, flaked into bite-size pieces

1 pound spaghetti, fettuccine or linguine

1 cup lightly packed fresh flat-leaf parsley, finely chopped

In a large pot, boil 4 quarts water. Meanwhile, in a 12-inch skillet over medium, combine the oil, garlic and tomato paste. Cook, stirring often, until the garlic is softened and fragrant and the tomato paste darkens, about 2 minutes. Stir in the tomatoes with juices, ½ teaspoon salt and ¼ teaspoon pepper. Cook, stirring occasionally, until thickened, 3 to 5 minutes. Add the olives, tuna and 3 tablespoons of the reserved tuna oil. Stir well, then remove from heat.

While the sauce is cooking, add the pasta and 1 tablespoon salt to the boiling water. Cook, stirring occasionally, until the pasta is just shy of al dente. Reserve 1 cup of the cooking water, then drain. Return the pasta to the pot.

Add the sauce to the pasta and cook over medium-high, tossing, until al dente, 3 to 5 minutes; add reserved pasta water as needed so the sauce clings to the noodles. Off heat, stir in the parsley. Taste and season with salt and pepper. Serve drizzled with additional oil.

CARNE

Naples is known for its pizza.
We went for the meatballs

In bold heaps and gilded piles, Christmas spills from doorways along Via San Gregorio Armeno, a cobblestone alley dedicated to a peculiar Neapolitan tradition—the assembling of elaborate, often offbeat home Nativity scenes. Dozens of artisans craft and sell miniature characters: Joseph, Mary, Jesus, the Magi, of course, but also lesser-known attendees at the birth of Christ—the pizza maker, the butcher with charcuterie, the nonna making meatballs. It is Naples, after all.

That last character amused me most as I wound my way past the shops, down toward the Gulf of Naples and into yet another, less festive alley. I'd come to Italy to learn this city's way with meatballs. I'd been told one bite would change the way I thought about this simple red sauce dish. That seemed a stretch. But then again, if they were good enough for Jesus...

Down that new alley, I was greeted by yet more heaps and piles. This time in the windows of Trattoria La Tavernetta. Mounds of eggplant, mushrooms, peppers and zucchini, all glistening, charred and doused in olive oil. Next to them, taped to the glass, a photocopied handwritten menu for the day. Lasagna classica Napoletana al forno. Penne al pomodoro. Calamari fritti. Fettuccine alla Bolognese. And, of course, polpette al sugo. Simply, meatballs with sauce.

Walk into Tavernetta—all white tiles and red brick arches—and you quickly realize family is as foremost as food. Five sisters, their parents and their grandmother, Maria Grazia Cibelli. At 74, she holds forth in the tiny kitchen, assembling that lasagna, carefully layering one sheet of noodles, one ladle of ragù, one handful of tiny meatballs at a time. She was so good a cook at home, she opened a restaurant back in the '70s. Her family followed her.

I sit at one of the restaurant's nine tables and order as many dishes as it will hold. House wine is poured from a chilled carafe. The room hushes unexpectedly. Enza Vittozzi, one of the sisters, offers an impromptu performance. Still in her apron and standing nearly motionless beneath the archway that separates dining room from kitchen, she opens her mouth. Her voice builds and expands, reverberating. "Ave Maria" washes over the room, wine glasses vibrating, the song a presence itself. A classically trained opera singer. The family restaurant is Enza's side gig between performances. Today it also serves as her stage.

As applause erupts, the food arrives. Cibelli's lasagna is rich, sweet and meaty, those tiny meatballs tucked between layers of cheese and pasta. Pasta Genovese, a tangle of caramelized onions and noodles, all studded with bits of beef that add seasoning more than substance. A simple broccoli, mostly leaves, blanched, browned and bathed in a mix of red pepper flakes, olive oil and bold garlic.

"Based on size alone, I expect them to be dense and heavy, but instead they are deceptively light."

But without question the meatballs are the star of the impressive spread. Two massive orbs of ground beef set in a shallow pool of ragù, red and glistening. They are served as often with pasta as without. Today, they stand alone. One bite and I understand their inclusion in the Nativity. Based on size alone, I expect them to be dense and heavy, but instead they are deceptively light. My fork cleaves them easily. They are so tender, I can't believe they hold their shape. The taste is meaty, savory, rich and balanced by the sweet, smooth ragù. Plenty of wine and these meatballs are all I need.

Credit for the meatballs goes to another sister, Rosa Vittozzi. She walks me through the recipe, but it is so minimalist—and the ingredients so common—it's hard to understand how they combine to make meatballs so different from and so much better than any I've ever had. Cheese, eggs, parsley, bread and beef hardly represent a dramatic departure from the norm. So Rosa invites me to return a few mornings later to watch her make them.

When I arrive that day by 10:30 a.m., the restaurant already is a fluster of activity. Piles of produce are scattered across the dining room tables, the sisters having turned the space into prep areas. Rosa has spread the meatball ingredients over several. In a large pot, the soft, white innards of numerous sourdough loaves soak in water. In a large metal tray, eggs have been cracked over a mound of ground beef. Parsley and grated pecorino Romano and Parmesan cheeses round it out.

A handful at a time, over and again, she plucks large hunks of bread from the water and squeezes them like a sponge before adding them to the meat and eggs. Soon, the beef is obscured by the bread. So much bread. Surely too much bread. Then she adds the cheeses and parsley and begins to knead. When the mixture is uniform, she grabs a tennis ball of it and, with hands so fast they blur, rolls it between her palms, at times making it almost levitate.

With all that bread I was certain the meatballs would collapse, but she hardly was gentle with them. From here, they can be pan-fried or roasted before finishing in a ragù of little more than olive oil, tomato sauce and fresh basil. When I taste them, again the tenderness amazes me. Despite their size, I eat two without the usual meat bomb belly feeling.

As I continue to eat meatballs across Naples, I learn that the volume of bread indeed is what sets them apart. Rosa uses a mixture that called for 25 percent bread,

but some cooks go as high as 40 percent. All of which explains why they are so tender and moist. And despite my concerns, the bread (helped by the eggs) acts a binder, helping them keep their shape even through multiple stages of cooking.

Back at Milk Street, this was an easy adaptation. We stuck close to Rosa's recipe, including her simple ragù. The one glitch? We struggled to get consistent results when soaking and squeezing the bread. We suspect Rosa's years of practice make it easy for her. For us the easy part was getting it wrong—with bread too moist or squeezed too dry. We also found that bread variety mattered greatly in how it retained water.

Our simple solution—panko breadcrumbs. The coarse white crumbs held moisture consistently and evenly, and required no squeezing. And we noticed no difference between the meatballs made with them and those with bread. The only thing we couldn't replicate? Enza's generous helping of "Ave Maria."

—J.M. Hirsch

Polpette Napoletane con Ragù

Neapolitan Meatballs with Ragù

Start to finish: 50 minutes Servings: 6 to 8

In Naples, Rosa Vittozzi, part of the family-run Trattoria La Tavernetta, showed us how to make meatballs Neapolitan style—generously sized and ultra-tender from a high ratio of bread to meat. For our version, we opted to use Japanese panko breadcrumbs. Panko, which has a neutral flavor and a light and fluffy but coarse texture, greatly streamlines the meatball-making process, eliminating the need to remove the crusts from fresh bread, cut and measure, soak in water, then squeeze out excess moisture. Panko only needs to be moistened with water and it's ready to use. Neapolitans serve their meatballs with a basic tomato sauce they refer to as "ragù." We use pecorino liberally in this recipe: a chunk simmered in the sauce, as well as grated both in and over the meatballs. Though not traditional, pasta is a fine accompaniment. Or offer warm, crusty bread alongside.

Don't be shy about mixing the panko-meat mixture with your hands. It takes a few minutes to work the mixture together until homogeneous. Your hands are the best tools for this. Don't bake the meatballs without first allowing them to chill for 15 to 20 minutes; this helps them hold their shape. And after baking, make sure to let the meatballs rest for about 10 minutes before adding them to the sauce; if the timing is off and the sauce is ready before the meatballs have rested, simply remove the pot from the heat and let it wait.

Heat the oven to 475°F with a rack in the middle position. Line a rimmed baking sheet with kitchen parchment and mist with cooking spray. In a large Dutch oven over medium-high, heat 2 tablespoons of the oil until shimmering. Add the onion and ¼ teaspoon salt, then cook, stirring occasionally, until softened, about 5 minutes. Add the garlic and 1 teaspoon of the pepper flakes; cook, stirring, until fragrant, about 30 seconds. Remove from the heat, then transfer half of the onion mixture to a large bowl.

In a medium bowl, combine the panko and 1¼ cups water; press the panko into the water and let stand until fully softened, about 5 minutes. Mash with your hands to a smooth paste, then add to the bowl with the onion mixture. Using a fork, mix until well combined and smooth. Stir in the grated cheese, beaten eggs, remaining 2 tablespoons oil, ¾ teaspoon salt and 2 teaspoons black pepper. Add the meat and mix with your hands until completely homogeneous.

Using a ½-cup dry measuring cup, divide the mixture into 8 portions. Using your hands, shape each into a compact ball and place on the prepared baking sheet, spacing them evenly apart. Refrigerate uncovered for 15 to 20 minutes. Re-shape the meatballs if they have flattened slightly, then bake until lightly browned, about 20 minutes. Let cool on the baking

4 tablespoons extra-virgin olive oil, divided, plus more to serve

1 large yellow onion, finely chopped

Kosher salt and ground black pepper

6 medium garlic cloves, finely grated

1½ teaspoons red pepper flakes, divided

6½ ounces (2½ cups) panko breadcrumbs

3 ounces pecorino Romano cheese, 2 ounces finely grated (1 cup), 1 ounce as a chunk, plus more grated, to serve

1 large egg, plus 1 large egg yolk, beaten together

1½ pounds 90 percent lean ground beef

Two 28-ounce cans whole peeled tomatoes

6 to 8 large basil leaves

sheet set on a wire rack for about 10 minutes.

While the meatballs cook, in a food processor or blender, puree the tomatoes with their juices one can at a time, until smooth, about 30 seconds, transferring the puree to a large bowl. Return the Dutch oven to medium and heat the remaining onion mixture, stirring, until warmed through, about 2 minutes. Stir in the tomatoes, remaining ½ teaspoon pepper flakes, the basil and the chunk of cheese. Bring to a simmer over medium-high and cook, stirring occasionally, until slightly thickened, about 15 minutes. Taste and season with salt and pepper.

Using a large spoon, carefully transfer the meatballs to the sauce, then, using 2 spoons, turn each to coat. Bring to a gentle simmer, then reduce to medium-low, cover and cook for 5 minutes. Remove the pot from the heat and let stand, covered, for about 5 minutes to allow the meatballs to firm up slightly. Remove and discard the pecorino chunk. Serve with additional grated cheese.

A long, slow walk for pasta alla Genovese

It seemed like a good idea at the time—a hike with three of my kids from Ravello down to the Amalfi Coast in March. Instead of a week in Rome, with the hectic circus of trattorias, fine dining, afternoon stops at gelaterias, a hushed tour of the Vatican and a walkabout at the Villa Borghese, we decided to bring our walking shoes and backpacks to cover as much ground as possible to feel Italy in our bones (and our feet).

The week started with one night at a nice hotel on the coast, all peach-hued walls, flower vases and long corridors. From there, a van would drop us at our starting point in the Valle delle Ferriere (valley of the iron-works), from which we would wind our way up into the mountains, all slaggy rock and plunging views down the terraced mountainsides to the valleys below, dotted with red-tiled cottages.

We climbed endless stone steps, passing panniered donkeys—true beasts of burden—and treaded carefully on rough-hewn paths on the sides of outcroppings with only spindly wooden railings for safety. One evening, back in Ravello, we inched our way through the fog to Trattoria da Cumpa' Cosimo off a cobblestone street for a true family meal: sturdy wooden tables, worn menus, rustic bread and equally sturdy pasta dishes with decent wine, all served in the local dialect.

Over time, the landscape softened. We passed olive groves, walked through a small dense forest, stopped for caffè, and picked up a hitchhiker (a small black mutt) along the way. We caught glimpses of the sea and the coast, brightly speckled with pastel homes painted onto the steep coastal mountains. With sore feet and well-earned appetites, we finally reached the town of Amalfi and made our way to a white-washed modern eatery, where I had my first taste of pasta alla Genovese.

"Richly satisfying without culinary somersaults."

This is not a pesto and it was not invented in Genoa. (The origins are unclear, though some suggest it was a dish brought by sailors who docked at the namesake port city.) It is a long-cooked onion sauce often served over a thick tubular pasta such as paccheri. The Genovese I was served at lunch also had thin slices of what looked to be brisket—enough to give the dish some backbone without being a stomach bomb. I loved it because it was typically Italian—pounds of onions cooked for hours with some meat thrown in if you have it: richly satisfying without culinary somersaults.

Later, we came across this same recipe at A' Cucina Ra' Casa Mia in Naples. For their meat they use short ribs, so we followed suit back at Milk Street.

We call for 3 pounds of onions—a mandoline makes short work of the slicing—and cook them in a low oven with a classic soffritto for an hour and a half along with the beef, pepper flakes and a Parmesan rind if you have one; then uncover and cook for an additional 90 minutes. Like a long hike, pasta alla Genovese is slow but deeply satisfying.

–Christopher Kimball

Pasta alla Genovese

Start to finish: 3¾ hours (40 minutes active) Servings: 6 to 8

Don't be fooled by the name of this dish. This is not pasta with Genovese basil pesto, nor is it from Genoa. Rather, the sauce is an onion-based ragù and a classic in the Neapolitan culinary repertoire. (How the sauce acquired its name is unknown, but we were told in Naples that some believe it comes from the Genovese sailors who visited Naples for trade. The theory goes that either they made this dish while in town or—more likely—locals made it for them.) Some versions of pasta alla genovese are meat-free, others include a small amount of beef or veal as a flavoring, but never as a key ingredient. Taking a cue from A' Cucina Ra' Casa Mia in Naples, we use boneless beef short ribs in ours. We combine beef, cut into chunks, with carrots, celery and an abundance of onions in a Dutch oven and put the pot into the oven, where the heat is slow and steady, until the meat is tender enough to fall apart when prodded with a fork. Slicing 3 pounds of onions by hand is a good opportunity to hone your knife skills, but if you prefer, they can be sliced on a mandoline. The ragù can be made up to three days ahead, then reheated gently before tossing with just-cooked pasta.

Don't be concerned that there's so little liquid in the pot after adding the onions and beef. In the covered pot warmed by the oven heat, the vegetables and meat release moisture that becomes the braising liquid. For the second half of cooking, don't forget to uncover the pot. This allows some of that liquid to evaporate for a richer, more concentrated flavor and consistency.

Heat the oven to 325°F with the rack in the lower-middle position. In a large Dutch oven over medium, heat the oil until shimmering. Add the pancetta and cook, stirring occasionally, until lightly browned, about 3 minutes. Add the carrots and celery, then cook, stirring occasionally, until the vegetables begin to soften, 3 to 5 minutes. Add the wine and cook, scraping up any browned bits, until reduced by about half, about 3 minutes. Add the onions, beef, pepper flakes, Parmesan rind (if using), ½ teaspoon salt and 1 teaspoon black pepper, then stir to combine. Cover, transfer to the oven and cook for 1½ hours.

Remove the pot from the oven and stir. Return to the oven, uncovered, and cook until stewy and the meat falls apart when pressed with a fork, about another 1½ hours. Tilt the pot to pool the cooking liquid to one side, then use a wide spoon to skim off and discard as much fat as possible. Remove and discard the Parmesan rind (if used). Cover and set aside while you cook the pasta.

In a large pot, bring 4 quarts water to a boil. Stir in the pasta and 1 tablespoon salt, then cook, stirring occasionally, until al dente. Reserve about 1 cup of the cooking water, then drain the pasta.

2 tablespoons extra-virgin olive oil, plus more to serve

3 to 4 ounces pancetta, chopped

2 medium carrots, peeled and finely chopped

2 medium celery stalks, chopped

1 cup dry white wine

3 pounds yellow onions, halved and sliced

1½ pounds boneless beef short ribs, trimmed and cut into 2-inch chunks

¾ teaspoon red pepper flakes

2-inch piece Parmesan rind (optional), plus 2 ounces Parmesan cheese, finely grated (1 cup)

Kosher salt and ground black pepper

1 pound rigatoni pasta

½ cup finely chopped fresh flat-leaf parsley

Add the pasta to the Dutch oven
and toss to combine with the sauce,
adding about ½ cup of reserved
pasta water. Add the parsley and
half the grated Parmesan, then toss
again; add more reserved water as
needed so the sauce coats the pasta.
Taste and season with salt and black
pepper. Serve with the remaining
Parmesan.

For better pasta sauce, throw away your garlic

Winding, twisting up Via Roma, there is a persistent, gentle breeze that pulls the dry salt of the Tyrrhenian Sea up from the coast and over the cobblestones of the main street of Gragnano, a tiny hillside town in the shadows of rumbling Mount Vesuvius. It is by design.

Once, this avenue would have been draped in pasta, row upon row of wooden racks, noodles drying in a wind the street was built to capture and channel. Today, the dozens of pasta factories that once crowded Gragnano—where even the graffiti is spaghetti—have dwindled, and the pasta, still considered some of the best in Italy, is dried indoors.

Alfonso Cuomo is the 10th generation of his family in the business—Pastificio Cuomo. Young and energetic as he discusses pasta's potential to reinvigorate his community, he is one of my guides during a weeklong exploration of the simple—and surprisingly speedy—pastas of the Neapolitan region.

He starts by showing me the massive building, parts crumbling, where his relatives once made pasta one step, one floor at a time. Whole grains loaded from the roof, working their way downward as they were milled, mixed, kneaded and cut before landing at the street to dry. Today, the whole operation consumes just a few rooms.

In his shop kitchen, pasta—a thick, twisty spiral called vesuviotti that's meant to resemble a volcano—is close to boiling. Cuomo is demonstrating a simple pasta sauced with broccoli and sausage. But the first step puzzles

"A wonderful technique that allows garlic to infuse a dish without overwhelming it."

me. He heats a generous glug of olive oil in a skillet, then tosses in several whole cloves of garlic. A few minutes later, he throws them away, leaving just the oil in the pan. A wonderful technique that allows garlic to infuse a dish without overwhelming it.

It's how we learned that real Italian cooks throw away their garlic!

Into this garlic-infused oil, he crumbles sausage packed with fennel seeds and chili flakes. Garlic—though there is none left in the pan—anise and spice saturate the air. Once the meat is browned, he adds heaps of gently bitter broccoli leaves he'd earlier sautéed in olive oil.

The pasta has barely cooked, but he pulls it out, splashing it and some of its starch-rich water into the skillet with the sausage and greens. It finishes cooking in the pan, quickly absorbing any liquid and all the flavor. In minutes, the broccoli and sausage have thickened into a peppery-meaty sauce that clings hard to the pasta.

Cuomo's recipe did require a few substitutions. Much as we loved it, vesuviotti pasta obviously was out. But we got a similar texture from orecchiette, the small cup-like shape helping to catch the sauce. Broccoli leaves are common in Italy, but rare here. We got a similar flavor with finely chopped broccoli rabe. Finally, none of the sausage we tried had the same bold flavors of fennel and chili we'd had in Gragnano, but this was easily fixed by adding fennel seeds and red pepper flakes.

The result is rustic, rich and delicious.

– J.M. Hirsch

Pasta con Friarielli e Salsiccia

Pasta with Sausage and Broccoli Rabe

Start to finish: 30 minutes   Servings: 4

In the hillside town of Gragnano, pasta maker Alfonso Cuomo showed us this simple dish featuring garlic-infused oil that adds flavor without being overwhelming. If you can't find orecchiette, campanelle is a good substitute; it cooks in just about the same time. Adding the broccoli rabe in two stages gives the dish textural interest, as some pieces will be fully tender and almost saucy, while others retain a bit of bite. To crush the fennel seeds, pulse a few times in a spice or coffee grinder or use a mortar and pestle. Once everything is in the skillet, the pan will be filled to the brim; the easiest way to stir is with two spatulas and a gentle tossing motion.

Don't skip mixing water into the sausage. The water loosens the sausage, making it easier to break into pieces while cooking so that it's more evenly distributed in the finished dish.

In a medium bowl, combine the sausage with ⅓ cup water. Stir with a fork until well combined; set aside. In a large pot, bring 2 quarts water to a boil. Add 1½ teaspoons salt and the orecchiette, then cook, stirring occasionally, for 5 minutes; the pasta should be tender at the edges but still quite firm at the center. Drain in a colander set in a large heat-safe bowl; reserve the cooking water and pasta separately.

In a 12-inch skillet over medium, heat 1 tablespoon of oil and the garlic cloves. Cook, stirring, until the garlic begins to brown, about 2 minutes. Remove and discard the garlic, then add the sausage. Cook over medium-high, stirring occasionally and breaking the meat into small pieces, until the sausage is no longer pink and begins to brown, about 3 minutes. Add the fennel seeds, pepper flakes, half of the broccoli rabe and ½ cup of the reserved cooking water, then stir to combine. Cover and cook, stirring occasionally, until the rabe is just tender, about 3 minutes.

Stir in another 1½ cups of the reserved cooking water, the remaining broccoli rabe and the pasta, then bring to a simmer. Cover and cook, stirring occasionally, until the rabe is tender and the pasta is al dente, another 3 to 5 minutes, adding more cooking water as needed so the sauce clings to the pasta.

Off heat, stir in the Parmesan and the remaining 1 tablespoon oil, then taste and season with salt and black pepper. Serve with additional Parmesan and oil.

12 ounces hot Italian sausage, casing removed

Kosher salt and ground black pepper

12 ounces orecchiette pasta

2 tablespoons extra-virgin olive oil, divided, plus more to serve

6 medium garlic cloves, smashed and peeled

2 tablespoons fennel seeds, crushed

½ teaspoon red pepper flakes

1 bunch broccoli rabe, trimmed and finely chopped (about 8 cups), divided

1 ounce Parmesan cheese, grated (½ cup), plus more to serve

In Bologna, even the humble
cutlet gets dressed up for dinner

Over the years, I have been given dozens of cooking lessons, from scallion pancakes in Taipei to tlayudas in Oaxaca. None of them, however, started with a glass of bubbly, a chef's apron and a bear hug until I showed up at Trattoria Bertozzi, a small eatery owned by Fabio Berti and Alessandro Gozzi on the outskirts of Bologna, the capital of Italy's Emilia-Romagna region.

Nothing much happens in Emilia-Romagna without prosciutto, Parmesan and a glass of pignoletto—and for good reason. The local sparkling wine is soft not bitter, inviting not aggressive, and asks to be paired with good food and lively conversation, even at 10 a.m. But this was late afternoon, before evening service, so a chilled bottle appeared immediately, toasts were made, and then I was asked to cook dinner under the watchful eye of Gozzi.

The dish was the classic cotoletta alla Bolognese, a veal cutlet coated in egg and breadcrumbs, sautéed in plenty of hot oil, coated with prosciutto and grated Parmesan, placed into a fresh skillet with a bit of broth and butter, then simmered covered for two to three minutes, removed, and the sauce reduced. Simplicity often belies complexity, and this recipe is a case in point: hot oil for browning, umami powerhouses (prosciutto and Parmesan), steam for melting the cheese, and a quick pan sauce reduction to finish.

Back at Milk Street, we did not have pignoletto, but we did have the other ingredients, though we switched out veal for chicken. (I pray that Berti and Gozzi will forgive this transgression in the spirit of international relations.) We also reduced the amount of cooking oil so that the entire recipe can be made in one skillet. After the initial browning, butter, garlic and water are added to finish cooking; the sauce is reduced with the cutlets in the pan, and a dash of lemon juice completes the dish.

My evening at Trattoria Bertozzi taught me that the Italian kitchen may be more casual than the French "brigade," but the cooking is no less purposeful or delicious.

–Christopher Kimball

"Simplicity often belies complexity, and this recipe is a case in point."

Cotoletta alla Bolognese

Bolognese-Style Chicken Cutlets

Start to finish: 35 minutes   Servings: 4

The classic Italian cotoletta alla Bolognese is a breaded veal cutlet that is pan-fried, then topped with salty, savory sliced prosciutto and Parmigiano-Reggiano cheese. In an unusual twist, the ham-and-cheese layered cutlets are cooked in a simple pan sauce just long enough to melt the Parmesan; the bottom crust softens but the surface retains its toastiness. For our version, we slice boneless, skinless chicken breasts in half horizontally to create cutlets about ½ inch thick that do not require pounding. To balance the saltiness of the prosciutto and cheese, we make a simple lemony, butter-enriched pan sauce and serve the cutlets with lemon wedges for squeezing.

Don't use pre-shredded Parmesan cheese. Freshly shredded true Parmesan (Parmigiano-Reggiano) had the best texture when melted. (To shred the cheese, use the small holes on a box grater; a wand-style grater yields a fine, fluffy texture that makes the cheese difficult to divide among the cutlets.) Finally, when adding the water to the pan, be sure to pour it around the cutlets, not on top of them.

Two 8- to 9-ounce boneless, skinless chicken breasts

1 large egg

¾ cup plain dry breadcrumbs

Ground black pepper

2 tablespoons extra-virgin olive oil

4 tablespoons salted butter, cut into 4 pieces

4 medium garlic cloves, smashed and peeled

4 thin slices prosciutto

3 ounces Parmesan cheese, shredded on the small holes of a box grater (1½ cups)

2 tablespoons lemon juice, plus lemon wedges to serve

Using a chef's knife, slice each chicken breast in half horizontally, creating a total of 4 cutlets, each about ½ inch thick. In a wide bowl, beat the egg well. In a wide, shallow dish (such as a pie plate), stir together the breadcrumbs and ½ teaspoon pepper. One at a time, coat the cutlets in egg on both sides, letting any excess drip off, then coat both sides with crumbs, pressing to adhere. Place the cutlets in a single layer on a large plate and refrigerate uncovered for 10 to 15 minutes.

In a 12-inch skillet over medium-high, heat the oil until shimmering. Add the cutlets in a single layer and cook until golden brown, about 2 minutes. Using tongs, flip the cutlets, then add the butter and garlic, placing them in the spaces between the cutlets; swirl the skillet until the butter is melted. Pour ½ cup water around the edges of the skillet; do not pour directly onto the cutlets. Working quickly with the pan still over medium-high, lay 1 prosciutto slice onto each cutlet, then sprinkle with the Parmesan, dividing it evenly. Cover and cook until the Parmesan is melted, about 2 minutes.

Uncover and cook until about ¼ cup of liquid remains in the pan, about 30 seconds. Using a metal spatula, transfer the cutlets to a serving platter. Off heat, remove and discard the garlic from the skillet, then stir in the lemon juice. Spoon the sauce over the cutlets and serve with lemon wedges.

In Rome, we learned the dirty secret to the best pasta

Claudia Rinaldi cautioned me when I arrived at her apartment on the outskirts of Rome. "The first thing you need to know about pasta alla zozzona is what the word means," she said. "It's a Roman word for dirty."

That didn't deter me. Translate it as you like, I wanted it. In fact, I'd come to Italy almost entirely to learn how to make pasta alla zozzona, a dish until a few weeks before I'd never heard of.

But the descriptions I'd read sounded transcendent, a fusion of two of the region's most important—not to mention best-known and most delicious—pasta dishes: pasta alla carbonara and pasta all'Amatriciana. So perhaps a pasta primer is in order.

Carbonara is a rich dish in which pasta is sauced with a mix of eggs, crisped guanciale (or sometimes pancetta), ample pecorino Romano cheese and plenty of black pepper. Amatriciana uses a similar formula, but replaces the eggs with tomatoes. Zozzona marries elements of both, and tosses in some Italian sausage for good measure.

"It's a dirty mess of delicious stuff," Rinaldi said.

Indeed. A more forgiving translation is leftovers, which also likely is an explanation of how the dish came to be. The bits and pieces of zozzona are Italian pantry staples, the sorts of things easily thrown together with pasta on any given weeknight.

Rinaldi blitzed through the recipe, browning sausage and pancetta while the pasta cooked, then adding tomatoes—canned are just fine, even in Italy—and simmering them down until thick. Eggs, cheese and pepper were next, all melding in the skillet. The result was rich, bright and deeply satisfying. I could have eaten many bowls of this.

Though wonderfully simple, it took learning the recipe a second time to identify the almost effortless techniques that elevate these common ingredients into something spectacular.

I was at Mamma Angelina, a family restaurant at the edge of the city. Chef-owner Andrea Dell'Omo doesn't have zozzona on his menu, but he should. He offered to teach me his version and it easily was one of the best things I've eaten. Ever.

As he made it, three things stood out. First, he cooked his pasta in what seemed barely enough water. This is vital. People assume the creaminess of sauces such as this come from the cheese and eggs. And it does. But it also comes from the starch that leaches from the pasta into the cooking water, and that starchy water is a key ingredient in the sauce.

Second, he didn't simply add tomatoes to the dish. He cooked them in the same skillet used to cook the sausage and guanciale. The juices deglazed the pan, pulling meaty richness into the sauce. And he cooked

"It's a dirty mess of delicious stuff."

down the tomatoes, concentrating their sweet acidity to coat, rather than drip off, the pasta.

Finally, and most importantly, he knew when to crank up the heat (when browning the meats) and when to kill the flame (when adding the slurry of eggs, cheese, pepper and pasta water). Doing the latter over heat turns the mixture into scrambled eggs. I tasted versions from less talented cooks and trust me, scrambled egg pasta is not a good thing.

Call it dirty pasta. Call it leftover pasta. I don't care. I'll have another serving.

–J.M. Hirsch

Rigatoni alla Zozzona

Start to finish: 40 minutes Servings: 4 to 6

Rigatoni alla zozzona is a classic Roman pasta dish—a mashup of cheesy, porky, egg-rich carbonara and spicy, tomatoey Amatriciana. At Mamma Angelina, a trattoria in Rome, chef Andrea Dell'Omo taught us his version. The sauce requires only a handful of simple ingredients, almost no knifework and comes together speedily. It begins with spicy Italian sausage and cured pork cooked in olive oil; Dell'Omo used guanciale (pork jowl), but pancetta is equally good and easier to source. Canned crushed tomatoes simmer into a savory-sweet sauce. Eggs beaten with pecorino and a little reserved pasta water are added at the end; gentle residual heat cooks everything just enough so it has a rich velvetiness.

Don't boil the pasta until al dente. Drain it when it's just shy of al dente, as it will finish cooking directly in the sauce. Also, be sure to reserve some of the cooking water before draining the pasta; you will need it to make the sauce. Finally, don't add the ¼ cup reserved pasta water to the egg mixture before the water has had a chance to cool slightly. If it's scalding hot, it will curdle the eggs.

1 pound rigatoni

Kosher salt and ground black pepper

3 tablespoons extra-virgin olive oil, divided, plus more to serve

4 ounces pancetta or guanciale, chopped

8 ounces hot Italian sausage, casings removed

14½-ounce can crushed tomatoes (1½ cups)

1 large egg, plus 2 large egg yolks

1 ounce finely grated pecorino Romano cheese (½ cup), plus more to serve

In a large pot over medium-high, bring 3 quarts water to a boil. Add the pasta and 1 tablespoon salt, then cook, stirring occasionally, until just shy of al dente. Reserve about 2 cups of the pasta cooking liquid, then drain; set aside.

In the same pot over medium-high, combine 1 tablespoon oil and the pancetta. Cook, stirring, until it has rendered some of its fat and begins to brown, about 2 minutes. Add the sausage and cook, breaking it into small pieces, until browned, about 3 minutes. Using a slotted spoon, transfer half of the pancetta-sausage mixture to a small bowl; set aside.

Into the pancetta-sausage mixture in the pot, stir the tomatoes. Bring to a simmer over medium and cook, stirring, until thickened, 6 to 8 minutes. Stir in 1 cup of the reserved pasta water, then the pasta. Cook, stirring and tossing, until the pasta is al dente, 3 to 5 minutes. Meanwhile, in a small bowl, whisk together the remaining 2 tablespoons oil, the egg and yolks, pecorino, 1 teaspoon pepper and ¼ cup of the reserved pasta water.

Remove the pot from the heat. Add the egg mixture and reserved pancetta-sausage mixture. Stir until the sauce thickens slightly and clings to the pasta, about 2 minutes. If needed, add reserved cooking water 1 tablespoon at a time to adjust the consistency. Taste and season with salt. Serve sprinkled with additional pepper and cheese and drizzled with additional oil.

Brasato al Barolo
Barolo-Braised Beef Short Ribs

Start to finish: 5 hours (50 minutes active) Servings: 4 to 6

Brasato al Barolo, or beef braised in Barolo wine, is a classic dish from Piedmont in northern Italy. Customarily, the beef is a roast that is slow-cooked, then sliced and served like a pot roast. The cooking liquid, rich with the essence of wine, beef and aromatics, becomes a sauce. For a more elegant take on the dish—one that can be the center of a special-occasion dinner—we opted for bone-in beef short ribs. Short ribs start out tough but are well marbled; slow, gentle braising renders them succulent and tender. Seek out meaty ribs—English cut (not flanken-style), if ordering from a butcher—that ideally are 4 to 5 inches in length so each rib is a single serving. The braise is named for the wine used in its making—Barolo, a deep, complex Piedmontese wine made from Nebbiolo grapes that lend generous tannins and acidity. But it isn't cheap, so you might consider Barbaresco or Nebbiolo d'Alba, though any decent dry red wine works. The beef requires a few hours of braising, so instead of stovetop simmering, which demands a watchful eye and burner adjustments, we rely on the steady, even heat of the oven. The ribs won't fit comfortably in a Dutch oven, so you will need a roasting pan, one that measures about 13 by 16 inches, plus heavy-duty, extra-wide foil to cover it. Polenta is a traditional accompaniment to beef in Barolo, but mashed potatoes would be equally delicious.

Don't forget to lower the oven temperature after removing the aromatics from the oven. The aromatics brown at 475°F, but 325°F is the temperature for braising the ribs. Also, when reducing the wine, don't simmer it vigorously. Allowing it to reduce slowly, at just below a simmer, preserves its nuances and results in a smoother, brighter flavor.

½ ounce dried porcini mushrooms

¾ cup boiling water

4 ounces pancetta, chopped

2 tablespoons extra-virgin olive oil

8 ounces cremini mushrooms, trimmed and chopped

2 large yellow onions, halved and thinly sliced

2 medium carrots, peeled and chopped

2 medium celery stalks, chopped

4 medium garlic cloves, smashed and peeled

2 tablespoons tomato paste

750-ml bottle Barolo wine (see headnote)

2 cups low-sodium beef broth

3 bay leaves

3 thyme sprigs

1 large rosemary sprig

6 pounds bone-in beef short ribs, trimmed, each 4 to 5 inches long (see headnote)

¼ cup all-purpose flour

3 tablespoons salted butter, room temperature

Kosher salt and ground black pepper

3 tablespoon finely chopped fresh flat-leaf parsley

Heat the oven to 475°F with a rack in the lower-middle position. In a small bowl, combine the porcini mushrooms and boiling water; set aside. Meanwhile, in a large roasting pan, combine the pancetta, oil, cremini mushrooms, onions, carrots, celery, garlic and tomato paste. Using your hands, rub the paste into the other ingredients. Roast, without stirring, until deeply browned, about 40 minutes.

While the aromatics are roasting, in a large saucepan over medium, bring the wine to a bare simmer, then reduce to medium-low to maintain a bare simmer (it should steam, with only a few bubbles occasionally breaking the surface), until reduced to about 1½ cups, about 30 minutes. Remove from the heat and add the broth, bay, thyme and rosemary. Using a fork, transfer the porcini from their soaking liquid to the wine mixture, then pour the mushroom soaking liquid through a fine-mesh strainer into the wine mixture.

When the aromatics are deeply browned, remove the roasting pan from the oven; reduce the oven temperature to 325°F. Bring the wine mixture to a simmer over medium-high. Nestle the short ribs meaty side down in the aromatics in the roasting pan, then add the wine mixture. Cover tightly with extra-wide, heavy-duty foil; if the pan has fixed raised handles, be sure to get a good seal around the base of the handles. Transfer to the oven and cook for 3½ hours.

Remove the roasting pan from the oven and carefully remove the foil, allowing the steam to vent away from you; reserve the foil. Using tongs, flip each rib meaty side up. Return the pan, uncovered, to the oven and cook until a skewer inserted into the ribs meets no resistance, 45 minutes to 1 hour. Using tongs, transfer the ribs to a platter and tent with the reserved foil. Let rest for 20 minutes.

While the ribs rest, set a fine-mesh strainer over a large saucepan. Scrape the contents of the roasting pan into the sieve; press on the solids to extract as much liquid as possible, then discard the solids. Tilt the pan to pool the liquid to one side, then use a wide spoon to skim off and

discard as much fat as possible; you should have about 3 cups defatted liquid. Bring to a simmer over medium-high, then reduce to medium and cook until reduced to about 2½ cups, about 5 minutes. Meanwhile, in a small bowl, mix the flour and butter until homogeneous.

With the liquid simmering over medium-low, whisk in the butter-flour mixture a spoonful at a time. Return to a simmer and cook, whisking often, until the sauce no longer tastes starchy and is thick enough to coat the back of a spoon, about 5 minutes. Off heat, taste and season with salt and pepper.

Uncover the short ribs and pour on about half of the sauce. Sprinkle with the parsley. Transfer the remaining sauce to a serving bowl and serve on the side.

Make-Ahead Instructions

Follow the recipe to braise the short ribs. When the ribs are fully tender, after removing the roasting pan from the oven, flip each piece meaty side down, then let cool completely. Re-cover the pan with the foil and refrigerate for up to 48 hours. To finish, use a spoon to remove and discard the solidified fat on the surface of the braising liquid and bring to room temperature. Put the pan, covered with foil, in a 350°F oven until the ribs are heated through, 20 to 30 minutes. Continue with the recipe to strain the cooking liquid (you will not need to skim the fat off the liquid after straining) and make the sauce.

Straccetti di Manzo

Steak Salad with Balsamic and Parmesan

Start to finish: 45 minutes (25 minutes active) Servings: 4 to 6

Straccetti di manzo, which translates roughly from the Italian to "little rags of beef," is a trattoria staple. The version we enjoyed at Armando al Pantheon in Rome inspired our riff on the dish. The cooking here is minimal and quick, making this ideal for a weeknight dinner, but the beef must be thinly sliced. We freeze the meat for about 20 minutes to firm it a bit, which allows a sharp knife to glide through the grain. After a quick sear in a hot skillet, the steak slices go directly onto a bed of peppery arugula and sweet-tart tomatoes. Balsamic vinegar, reduced as it deglazes the pan, and shaved Parmesan are the finishing touches. We prefer tri-tip steak for this recipe, as it has great flavor and a tender texture.

Don't dress the arugula and tomatoes too far in advance or they will wilt and turn soggy. Wait until after the beef is sliced before tossing the veggies with the oil, lemon juice and salt. Also, don't stir the beef during the first three minutes of cooking. Allowing it to cook undisturbed will give the meat a chance to develop flavorful browning.

Place the steak on a plate and freeze, uncovered, until partially frozen, about 20 minutes. Using a sharp knife, slice the beef against the grain on the diagonal no thicker than ¼ inch. Sprinkle with salt and black pepper; toss to coat. On a deep, wide platter, toss the arugula and tomatoes with 1 tablespoon of the oil, the lemon juice and ¼ teaspoon salt.

In a 12-inch skillet over medium-high, heat the remaining 1 tablespoon oil until barely smoking. Add the garlic and pepper flakes; cook, stirring, until fragrant, about 30 seconds. Add the beef in an even layer; cook without stirring until only a little pinkness remains and some liquid has been released, about 3 minutes. Stir, redistribute in an even layer and cook until no longer pink, about 1 minute. Using tongs, place the steak on the vegetables, leaving the garlic in the pan.

Add the balsamic to the pan and bring to a simmer over medium-high; cook, scraping up any browned bits, until slightly reduced, about 1 minute. Discard the garlic; pour the balsamic over the steak. Shave Parmesan over the top, then finish with additional oil and black pepper.

1½ pounds beef tri-tip steak

Kosher salt and ground black pepper

5-ounce container baby arugula

1 pint cherry or grape tomatoes, halved

2 tablespoons extra-virgin olive oil, divided, plus more to serve

1 tablespoon lemon juice

2 medium garlic cloves, smashed and peeled

½ teaspoon red pepper flakes

¼ cup balsamic vinegar

Parmesan cheese, for shaving

Whatever happened to
saltimbocca alla Romana?

Walking the streets of Rome, you may miss the nasoni, 19th-century water fountains that are just over a meter high and made of cast iron. (The name means "big nose," which describes the curved pipe that delivers the continuous stream of water.) To drink from these fountains, place your finger at the end of the pipe, and a jet of water shoots upward from a small hole on top of the pipe. Free drinking water is the right of every Roman citizen.

In addition to the Roman ruins and the nasoni, the recipes that make up the core of Roman cooking also seem to be a basic right, since the local chefs seem perfectly happy to include them on almost every menu. One of my favorite classic Roman recipes is not a pasta dish; it is saltimbocca alla Romana. A thin veal cutlet is topped with prosciutto and a fresh sage leaf, lightly floured and then cooked quickly in a skillet with white wine and oil and/or butter.

Elio Mariani, chef and co-owner with his siblings at Checchino dal 1887, gave me a personal cooking class, starting with the rump-cut cutlets that he seasoned with a pinch of salt and a mixture of dry and minced fresh sage (to evenly flavor the meat). He started cooking the cutlets in a butter/oil mixture over medium heat, prosciutto side down to start. Near the end of cooking, which only takes a few minutes, he added a splash of white wine to deglaze the pan and to add flavor as it reduced. (Checchino backs up on Monte Testaccio, a massive pile of ancient broken amphorae—the shards are called cocci—which make up the far wall of the wine cellar.)

We made a couple of changes back at Milk Street. We cooked fresh sage leaves and two smashed garlic cloves in oil to start and then removed them. This flavored the oil—plus, we crumbled the fried sage leaves over the finished cutlets. We also pressed the prosciutto to the cutlets (we use chicken breasts, not veal) without using toothpicks to fasten, which worked well. No additional flour was added to the sauce.

One last minor point—when we added the white wine, we poured it around the perimeter of the skillet, not directly onto the cutlets to avoid disturbing the coating.

–Christopher Kimball

> "The recipes that make up the core of Roman cooking also seem to be a basic right."

Chicken Saltimbocca

Start to finish: 30 minutes Servings: 2 to 4

We modeled our chicken version of classic saltimbocca on the technique shown to us by chef Elio Mariani at Checchino dal 1887 in Rome, as well as by Mimmo Galal, a chef at Trattoria Antico Falcone in Rome. Following his lead, we simply lay the prosciutto slices on the cutlets, relying on the tackiness of the meat to hold them together, thereby eliminating the need for the typical toothpick fasteners. Dusting the prosciutto-topped chicken with flour prior to cooking assists with browning and lends just a little body to the white wine that's added at the end, yielding a light, bright sauce to complement the savoriness of the cutlets. Just ¼ inch thick, the cutlets are lightning-quick to cook. If the ones you purchase are thicker, place them between two sheets of plastic wrap and use a meat pounder to pound them to ¼ inch. Another option is to purchase two 8- to 10-ounce boneless breasts, split each one horizontally, then pound them. Each cutlet is a modest but ample single serving, or for heartier portions, offer two per person. If you're a saltimbocca classicist, see the veal version below. Turkey cutlets also are delicious, so we include a recipe that uses them as well.

Don't pour the wine directly onto the cutlets in the skillet. Pour it around the perimeter of the pan, so the prosciutto doesn't become soggy from the moisture.

¼ cup all-purpose flour

Kosher salt and ground black pepper

4 thin slices prosciutto

Four 5- to 6-ounce chicken breast cutlets, each ¼ inch thick (see headnote)

2 tablespoons extra-virgin olive oil

2 medium garlic cloves, smashed and peeled

8 to 10 fresh sage leaves

½ cup dry white wine

In a pie plate or large, shallow bowl, whisk together the flour and ½ teaspoon each salt and pepper. Lay a slice of prosciutto on each cutlet and, using the palm of your hand, press to adhere; it's fine if the prosciutto does not fully cover the cutlet. One at a time, dredge the cutlets in the flour mixture, turning to coat. Shake off any excess and place in a single layer on a large plate.

In a 12-inch skillet over medium, combine the oil and garlic, then add the sage, scattering the leaves so they lay flat in a single layer. Cook, occasionally, flipping the sage and garlic, until the sage is crisped and the garlic is lightly browned, about 1 minute. Remove the pan from the heat and, using tongs, transfer the sage to a small plate; remove and discard the garlic. Return the pan to medium and add the cutlets, prosciutto side down, in a single layer; cook, without disturbing, until golden brown on the bottoms, 1 to 2 minutes. Using tongs, flip and cook until the second sides are golden brown, about 2 minutes.

Remove the skillet from the heat and pour the wine around the perimeter of the pan; don't pour it directly onto the cutlets. Return to medium and cook, occasionally shaking the pan, until the liquid is slightly reduced, 2 to 3 minutes. Transfer the cutlets to a platter. Taste the sauce and season with salt and pepper, then drizzle it onto the cutlets and crumble the fried sage over the top.

Turkey Saltimbocca

Purchase 4 turkey breast cutlets (about 1 pound total weight) instead of chicken cutlets; the cutlets will likely be about ½ inch thick. One at a time, place them between 2 sheets of plastic wrap and pound with a meat pounder to an even ¼-inch thickness. Follow the recipe using the turkey cutlets in place of the chicken cutlets.

Veal Saltimbocca

Purchase 1 pound ¼-inch-thick veal cutlets and as many prosciutto slices as you have cutlets; you will likely have more than 4 cutlets, which will require cooking in 2 batches. Follow the recipe to top the cutlets with the prosciutto, cutting the prosciutto as needed to fit on the veal, then dredge the cutlets in flour. Cook the sage and garlic as directed; transfer the sage to a small plate, then remove and discard the garlic. Return the pan to medium and add half of the cutlets, prosciutto side down, to the pan in a single layer; cook, without disturbing, until golden brown on the bottom, 1 to 2 minutes. Using tongs, flip and cook until the second sides are golden brown, about 2 minutes; transfer to a platter. Add another 1 tablespoon extra-virgin olive oil to the pan, heat over medium until shimmering and cook the remaining cutlets in the same way. When they are done, return the first batch to the pan, placing the cutlets prosciutto side up. Remove the pan from the heat and pour in the wine around the perimeter of the pan; don't pour it directly onto the cutlets. Return to medium and cook, occasionally shaking the pan, until the liquid is slightly reduced, 2 to 3 minutes. Transfer the cutlets to the platter. Taste the sauce and season with salt and pepper, then drizzle it onto the cutlets and crumble the fried sage over the top.

Bringing home porchetta

Standing in Grutti, it's not the imposing 13th-century fortress or the adjacent St. Agnes Church that you notice first. Nor the yellow-green patchwork of fields that unfold over the valley behind them, rolling and rising toward a mountainous backdrop.

It's the wind you notice. Because in this map-speck Umbrian village of 500 people, it carries a heady blend of crisp-skinned pork dancing with something herbal and rich—maybe allium. It's a smell at once of winter and summer.

I'd come to Umbria for porchetta, a roasted whole-hog tradition with pre-Roman roots. This is food without subtlety—a massive pig boned, slathered and stuffed with herbs by the handful, fresh fennel and chopped meats, then roasted on a spit until the skin crackles and the fat drips alluringly.

Porchetta defines this region, even more so than barbecue does the American South. Handwritten signs advertise it on butcher shop windows in every town and at roadside stands along the serpentine roads between.

Most of those signs point to Grutti. In these parts, the town is synonymous with porchetta.

At least four families here make their living entirely from porchetta—sold by the sandwich or kilo—at weekly markets in ancient town squares across central Italy. Some began a century ago with a cart and a donkey. The original food trucks.

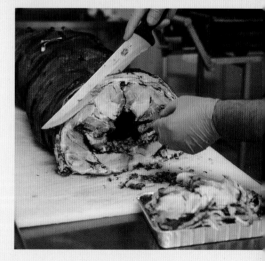

They have an eager audience. Every kind of family celebration somehow involves porchetta, says Elisa Benvenuta, deputy mayor of the municipality that includes Grutti. "There's not a wedding or a christening or a birthday without it."

She leads me on a short walk from the castle to the workshop owned by her cousins, fourth-generation porchetta masters who butchered their first hogs at age 11. Inside, Luca Benedetti is busy slicing the rib bones out of an upturned 200-pound pig splayed on a stainless-steel table. By the time he's finished, the rib meat stands out as a row of neatly parallel ridges.

The boning process is a brutal business, a blend of precise cuts and unsettling pops and scrapes that gives life to that old political saw about not wanting to see how the sausage is made. Luca says boning matters mostly for presentation and convenience; that morning they served hundreds of people in Perugia, competing with eight other porchetta stands.

He rubs a heavy layer of salt and pepper onto the meat, enough to tickle every nose in the room, and cups his hand to funnel it into deep cuts in the thickest parts. He then reaches for a forest-green blend of wild rosemary and fennel foraged from the valley. Later, his Uncle Mauro will pull out bunches of the herbs so I can smell them separately and then together, a lesson on aromatics that brings me back to childhood holiday dinners.

> "Porchetta defines this region, even more so than barbecue does the American South."

A thick coating of the herbs, mixed with chopped garlic, goes into the cavity next, then a stuffing of seasoned liver and other offal. Luca immediately wraps the beast around a metal rod and sews it all together with a curved 8-inch needle that his grandfather fashioned from the prong of a beach umbrella in the 1970s. "They were once made out of good steel, so they are the best things to use," he says. "These are the secrets."

The pig, head still on, slides into a blazing industrial oven for two hours to crisp the skin. Then the heat is lowered; the pig bastes in its own juices for another eight hours.

Too long to wait for a taste. Instead, Mauro turns to a half-consumed porchetta and takes great care to assemble sandwiches with slices of each part of it. The key is to get a bit of everything—crunchy skin, juicy rib, fatty belly and green, mineraly stuffing—in one bite.

We eat silently, chewing and nodding in approval as I marvel at how a day-old roast on a dry roll could be this satisfyingly moist. Maybe that's why it's been made more or less that same way since the Etruscans dominated this area 2,500 years ago, according to academics who have pored over medieval texts.

Despite the historic pedigree, porchetta is hardly stuck in the past. It's actually surging in popularity because of both a shift toward the Slow Food movement and a changing society. Busy working parents often grab a kilo of porchetta on their lunch break from which to build an easy family dinner. "Now the Italians have become like the Americans," Mauro says. "Everyone is always running and hectic and stressed."

A few miles away in San Terenziano, where a new yearly festival called the Porchettiamo is gaining steam, Maurizio Biondini is leading the street food evolution of what was once derided as a bricklayers' sandwich. He and a friend built his hipster food cart, Focaracceria Umbra, with an antique motorcycle and a pop-up carnival stand.

Maurizio also learned butchering at 11, and inside the climate-controlled warehouse where he ages ham legs into prosciutto and cheeks into guanciale, he displays all the traditional techniques of slicing and stuffing and roasting a porchetta. Except he serves his on buttery unsalted focaccia—an iconoclastic move in itself—with pecorino cheese and creamy lard flavored with truffles, spicy peppers or thyme. The warm sandwich melts together into an unctuous decadence of herbs and fat, but Maurizio stays modest.

"I'm not the best," he says. "I'm different."

He invites me to dinner with his in-laws back in Grutti, where his father has a butcher shop. We sit next to the overlook under an arbor of grape leaves as the valley begins turning the same roasted orange as the setting sun. The table fills with fried zucchini blossoms and sage leaves, melon wrapped with Maurizio's prosciutto, then handmade tagliatelle with wild asparagus and eventually a sword's length of charred pork ribs, loin and liver wrapped in bay leaves. It's all washed down with wine from bottles whose labels have long worn off.

Nearly everything on the table comes from the valley below, as it has for thousands of years.

—Albert Stumm

Porchetta al Finocchio e Rosmarino

Fennel-Rosemary Porchetta

Start to finish: 1½ days (30 minutes active) Servings: 8

Porchetta is a roasted whole hog tradition from the Italian region of Umbria. Turning it into a home cook–friendly pork roast proved challenging. After testing recipes with pork loin (too dry) and pork belly (too fatty), we settled on a boneless pork butt roast. Traditional porchetta is succulent and complex because almost all parts of the pig are used. For our scaled-down version, we added pancetta (seasoned and cured pork belly that has not been smoked), which lent a richness to the filling and helped baste the roast from the inside out. Fennel is a key flavor of the dish. We used ground fennel seeds in a seasoning rub and, while the roasted pork rested, we used the time (and the flavorful fond in the pan) to roast wedges of fresh fennel. Be sure to buy a boneless pork butt, not a boneless picnic roast; both are cut from the shoulder, but the butt comes from higher up on the animal and has a better shape for this recipe. Porchetta leftovers make great sandwiches, thinly sliced and served on crusty bread or ciabatta rolls. Leftover roasted fennel is perfect for sandwiches, as well.

Don't cut short the porchetta's resting time. The roast is much easier to slice after it rests for the full hour.

To prepare the roast, remove any twine or netting around the pork. Locate the cut made to remove the bone, then open up the roast. Using a sharp knife, continue the cut until the roast opens like a book; do not cut all the way through, as the meat must remain in one piece. Using the tip of a paring knife, make 1-inch-deep incisions into the pork, spaced about 1 inch apart; do not cut all the way through the meat. Set aside.

In a food processor, pulse the pancetta until coarsely chopped, about 15 pulses. Add the butter, rosemary, oregano, garlic, pepper flakes, ½ cup of the ground fennel and 1 teaspoon salt. Process until the mixture forms a spreadable paste, about 1 minute, scraping the bowl as needed. Spread the paste evenly over the interior of the pork, pressing the paste into the cuts. Roll the roast into a tight cylinder, then set it seam side down.

Cut 7 to 9 pieces of kitchen twine, each 28 to 30 inches long. In a small bowl, stir together the remaining 2 tablespoons ground fennel, 1½ teaspoons salt, the brown sugar and pepper. Rub this mixture over the top and sides of the roast. Using the twine, tie the roast at 1-inch intervals; you may not need all of the twine. Trim the ends of the twine. Wrap the roast tightly in plastic, transfer to a large baking dish and refrigerate for at least 24 hours or up to 48 hours.

Heat the oven to 300°F with a rack in the middle position. Set a roasting rack in a roasting pan and

FOR THE ROAST:

7- to 8-pound boneless pork butt

8 ounces pancetta, cut into ½-inch cubes

4 tablespoons (½ stick) salted butter, room temperature

1 cup (1½ ounces) lightly packed fresh rosemary leaves

1 cup (1 ounce) fresh oregano leaves

20 garlic cloves, peeled

1 tablespoon red pepper flakes

½ cup plus 2 tablespoons ground fennel, divided

Kosher salt

2 tablespoons packed light brown sugar

2 teaspoons ground black pepper

FOR THE SAUCE:

¾ cup pan juices

⅓ cup lemon juice

2 tablespoons extra-virgin olive oil

2 teaspoons ground black pepper

1 teaspoon ground fennel

pour 4 cups water into the pan. Unwrap the roast and set it fat-side up on the rack. Roast until the center registers 195°F, 6 to 7 hours.

Transfer the roast to a carving board and let rest, uncovered, for 1 hour. Reserve the liquid in the pan.

Meawhile, make the sauce. Pour the liquid in the roasting pan into a fat separator; if making roasted fennel (see recipe below), do not wash the roasting pan. Let the liquid settle for 5 minutes. In a medium bowl, whisk together ¾ cup of the juices, the lemon juice, ¼ cup water, the olive oil, pepper and ground fennel.

Cut the pork into thin slices, removing the twine as you slice. Serve with the pan sauce.

Roasted Fennel

Start to finish: 50 minutes Servings: 8

Heat the oven to 450°F with a rack in the middle position. In the roasting pan used to cook the porchetta, combine the fennel, oil and ½ teaspoon salt. Stir until the fennel is evenly coated.

Roast for 20 minutes, then stir. Roast for another 10 minutes, then add the water and scrape up the browned bits on the bottom of the pan. Continue to roast until tender and lightly browned, about another 10 minutes.

4 large fennel bulbs, trimmed, halved, cored and cut lengthwise into 1-inch wedges

¼ cup extra-virgin olive oil

Kosher salt

½ cup water, if needed

Hold the tomatoes, please!

I am beginning to think that "authentic" is a matter of personal opinion and experience, rather than something well baked into the historical record. Take pollo alla cacciatora, or "hunter's chicken," which is usually described as chicken cooked in a rustic tomato sauce. Italians in the Renaissance were hunting game, not chicken, and the actual preparation had few rules, since it depended entirely on what was available locally. And tomatoes—and tomato sauces—were not all that popular until the 19th century in Italy, even though they had been "discovered" in the 16th century.

So imagine my delight when I met Chef Umberto at Piatto Romano in Rome, who prepared a rabbit cacciatore that used no tomatoes and relied instead on white wine, anchovies, vinegar, garlic and herbs. Vastly superior to the tomato sauce version, it also has a higher claim to authenticity, given the absence of tomatoes.

Start with a cut-up chicken or rabbit, brown it well and remove it from the pan, and then make a soffritto with anchovies, garlic, chilies and olive oil. Add the browned meat back to the pan, along with three large sprigs of rosemary and then a bottle of white wine. Cook in an oven and finish with more wine and vinegar. (Umberto used a whopping 250 grams—or about 1 cup—of vinegar, which seemed bold.) It was bright and lively and celebrated the flavor of the game.

Our version was close to what Umberto had demonstrated, but we cooked the white wine down in the skillet before adding back the chicken, which helped concentrate the sauce. We also reduced the vinegar to ¼ cup, although the vinegar used in Italy may well be lower in acid and therefore less potent.

We also finished the dish in a 450°F oven, and since the chicken pieces were not submerged in sauce, the skin browns and crisps beautifully.

Even in Rome, tomato sauce ain't everything!

–Christopher Kimball

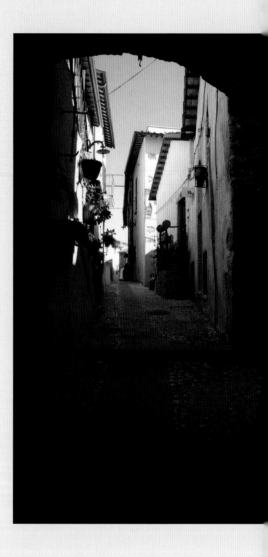

"It was bright and lively and celebrated the flavor of the game."

Pollo alla Cacciatora Romana

Roman-Style Chicken Cacciatora

Start to finish: 50 minutes (30 minutes active) Servings: 4 to 6

Cacciatora, it turns out, is not always a chunky, tomato-heavy braise. At Piatto Romano in Rome, we learned how to make the Roman version—an elegant, minimalist dish bright with the acidity of white wine and vinegar and heady with rosemary, garlic and anchovies, not a tomato in sight. We adapted Piatto Romano's rabbit cacciatora, opting for chicken and making a few simplifications. With so few ingredients, deeply searing the bone-in, skin-on pieces is necessary for developing rich flavor. To preserve the chicken's browning during braising, the pieces are only partially submerged in liquid and cooked, uncovered, to completion in a 450°F oven; the dry heat keeps the skin crisp and caramelized even as the liquid simmers in the bottom of the pan. (You will need an oven-safe 12-inch skillet for this recipe.) We like this cacciatora with a starchy side, such as crusty bread, polenta or mashed potatoes.

Don't forget to lower the heat before adding the wine. This helps prevent fiery flare-ups if the wine splashes out of the skillet.

2½ to 3 pounds bone-in, skin-on chicken thighs or breasts, trimmed and patted dry

Kosher salt and ground black pepper

2 tablespoons extra-virgin olive oil

6 to 8 oil-packed anchovy fillets, patted dry

6 medium garlic cloves, minced

Three 5-inch rosemary sprigs, plus 1 teaspoon minced fresh rosemary, reserved separately

¼ teaspoon red pepper flakes

750-ml bottle dry white wine, such as pinot grigio or frascati

¼ cup white wine vinegar

Heat the oven to 450°F with a rack in the middle position. If the chicken breasts are larger than about 12 ounces each, cut them in half crosswise. Season the chicken all over with salt and pepper.

In a 12-inch oven-safe skillet over medium-high, heat the oil until shimmering. Add the chicken skin-side down and cook, until golden brown on both sides, 8 to 10 minutes, flipping the pieces halfway through. Transfer to a large plate; set aside.

To the skillet over medium, add the anchovies, garlic, rosemary sprigs and pepper flakes. Cook, stirring, until the anchovies have broken down and the mixture is fragrant, about 1 minute. Reduce to low, then slowly add the wine. Bring to a simmer over medium-high and cook, scraping up the browned bits,

until the wine has reduced by about half, 8 to 10 minutes.

Return the chicken skin side up to the pan and add the accumulated juices. Transfer to the oven and cook until a skewer inserted into the thickest part of the chicken meets no resistance, 12 to 15 minutes.

Remove the skillet from the oven (the handle will be hot) and set it on the stovetop. Transfer the chicken, skin side up, to a deep platter. Remove and discard the rosemary sprigs from the skillet. Add the minced rosemary and vinegar to the liquid in the skillet; bring to a simmer over medium-high. Cook, stirring, until reduced by about half, about 5 minutes. Remove from the heat, then taste and season with salt and black pepper. Spoon the sauce over and around the chicken.

Polpettine alla Cacciatora

Roman-Style Meatball Cacciatora

Start to finish: 1 hour, plus chilling Servings: 4

At Piatto Romano restaurant in Rome, we learned that the local way to make cacciatora doesn't involve tomatoes. Rather, the sauce has a base of white wine and is infused with rosemary and garlic, plus anchovies that lend umami but whose flavor otherwise fades into the background. White wine vinegar added at the finish brightens the profile. This recipe is our version of Piatto Romano's polpettine alla cacciatora that pairs meatballs, well-seared to develop flavor-building browning, with the bold yet bright sauce. Though the restaurant uses only beef to make their meatballs, we preferred the more tender texture we got by including ground pork. Polenta or warm, crusty bread are good accompaniments.

Don't cook the meatballs immediately after shaping them. Refrigerating them for at least an hour will firm them up so they hold together better in the skillet.

In a large bowl, whisk together ¼ cup water, the breadcrumbs, eggs, grated garlic, parsley and ½ teaspoon each salt and black pepper. Add the beef and pork, then mix with your hands until thoroughly combined. Divide into 20 portions (about 2 tablespoons each) and place on a large plate. Using your hands, form each into a smooth ball. Refrigerate, uncovered, for 1 hour (the meatballs can be refrigerated up to 12 hours, covered).

In a 12-inch skillet over medium, heat the oil until shimmering. Add the meatballs and cook, turning occasionally, until browned on all sides, about 10 minutes. Return the meatballs to the plate and set aside.

To the fat remaining in the skillet, add the sliced garlic, the anchovies, rosemary sprigs and pepper flakes. Cook over medium, stirring, until the anchovies have broken down and the mixture is fragrant, about 1 minute. Reduce to low, then add the broth, followed by the wine. Bring to a simmer over medium-high and cook, scraping up the browned bits, until the liquid has reduced by about half, 5 to 8 minutes.

Add the meatballs and any accumulated juices to the pan, along with ½ cup water. Cook, uncovered and occasionally swirling the pan, until the center of the meatballs reach 160°F, 7 to 10 minutes.

Remove and discard the rosemary sprigs. Add the minced rosemary and vinegar; cook, stirring, until the sauce is slightly thickened and reduced, about 2 minutes. Remove from the heat, then taste and season with salt and black pepper. Serve sprinkled with additional chopped parsley.

¼ **cup plain fine dried breadcrumbs**

2 large eggs

1 medium garlic clove, finely grated, plus 6 medium garlic cloves thinly sliced, reserved separately

3 tablespoons finely chopped fresh flat-leaf parsley, plus more to serve

Kosher salt and ground black pepper

1 pound 80 percent lean ground beef

8 ounces ground pork

2 tablespoons extra-virgin olive oil

6 to 8 oil-packed anchovy fillets, patted dry

Three 5-inch rosemary sprigs, plus 1 teaspoon minced fresh rosemary, reserved separately

¼ **teaspoon red pepper flakes**

1 cup low-sodium beef broth

2 cups dry white wine, such as pinot grigio or frascati

1 tablespoon white wine vinegar

The ancient pasta sauce that gets better the less you do to it

Sometimes the most important cooking technique is benign neglect. Or to put it more politely, knowing when to step away from the stove and let time, heat and ingredients mingle with minimal input from us.

That's certainly the case with ragù cilentano, a tomato paste-looking sauce I first learned of somewhat by chance in the kitchen at Tenuta Nonno Luigi, a restaurant in the town of Bellosguardo in Italy's Campania region.

The restaurant's name roughly means Grampa Luigi's Place. And perched on a rambling hillside of olive trees and bushes of lavender and rosemary, the yard littered with antique green glass wine casks, it does have that feel.

Chef Giuseppe Croce was teaching me his ethereal take on onion rings—imagine onions sliced paper thin, barely breaded, fried until crackling, then drizzled with balsamic syrup—when I noticed a pot of something thick and red on the stove.

A local dish drawn from cucina povera and of no real interest, he assured me. I took a smell, then dabbed a spoon into it for a taste. It was an explosion, an intense, paste-like tomato sauce studded with bits of beef, pork and plenty of other this-and-that hunks of meat. I assured him it was of very real interest.

With a shrug, he dropped a handful of freshly made pasta into boiling water. When it was nearly finished, he scooped it out and into a skillet, adding a generous scoop of that thick sauce and a equally generous splash of the pasta cooking water.

With a few flips of the skillet, the sauce loosened and coated the pasta. In a minute, the tangle was mounded on a plate and topped with grated aged ricotta. The taste was so deep and so rich, it almost was hard to believe.

"The taste was so deep and so rich, it almost was hard to believe."

Ragù cilentano, it turns out, is an ancient recipe, a byproduct of the working poor who managed the farmlands of local nobility. They had two things in abundance—tomatoes and the scraps of meat deemed unfit for their bosses—and one thing in short supply—time to fuss at the stove over dinner. Together, those factors collaborated to create an amazing sauce.

Croce explained that the only way for the workers to get a meal on the table was to combine the ingredients in the morning—tomatoes, maybe some onions and herbs, and those stray bits of meat—and let it cook down, untended for many hours while they worked the fields. By evening, they had a rich sauce easily stored and thinned for serving as needed.

That simplicity made it an easy recipe to adapt. Since most of us don't work the fields, we enhanced the tomatoes with tomato paste to mimic the reduction that would have played out over a day. And in the spirit of the original recipe, we moved the cooking into the more even heat of the oven, where the sauce could cook down without attention from us.

Finally, since we've long lost our taste for scavenging for meat scraps from nobility, we opted to use beef short ribs and pancetta, both of which can handle a long simmer and deliver big, bold meaty flavor.

Because any dish that gets better for being ignored deserves a place on our table.

—J.M. Hirsch

Ragù Cilentano

Slow-Cooked Short Rib Ragù with Pasta

Start to finish: 3¼ hours (40 minutes active) Servings: 6

At Tenuta Nonno Luigi, a restaurant in the town of Bellosguardo in Italy's Campania region, chef Giuseppe Croce taught us how he makes ragù cilentano, a unique dish not well known outside of the area. The tomato-centric sauce gets its deliciously intense flavor and thick, lush consistency from multi-hour cooking (six hours, in the case of Croce's ragù) with various types of meat—traditionally only small amounts of scraps, he explained—that melt into and merge with the tomatoes as the ingredients slowly concentrate. To adapt his recipe, we limited the meats to two: pancetta for its salty, porky flavor and short ribs that lend deep, beefy richness. We also use tomatoes in two forms: sweet-tart canned whole tomatoes and tomato paste for depth and umami. For convenience as well as steady, even cooking, we simmer the sauce in the oven so no careful monitoring is needed. The ragù pairs especially well with sturdy, thick, chewy pasta shapes such as cavatelli or orecchiette. The finished sauce can be cooled and stored in an airtight container in the refrigerator for up to three days; rewarm it in a covered saucepan over medium before tossing it with just-cooked pasta.

Don't add more salt and pepper at the start of cooking than the recipe calls for. As the ingredients reduce, the flavors become concentrated. It's best to adjust seasoning at the very end, after the ragù has been tossed with the pasta. When the sauce is done, don't skim off all of the fat that rises to the surface; a little fat delivers flavor and pasta-coating silkiness.

1 tablespoon extra-virgin olive oil

4 ounces pancetta, chopped

1 medium yellow onion, chopped

3 tablespoons tomato paste

½ cup dry white wine

1 pound boneless beef short ribs, cut into 1-inch chunks

28-ounce can whole peeled tomatoes, crushed by hand

Kosher salt and ground black pepper

1 pound cavatelli or orecchiette pasta

½ cup chopped fresh basil

1 ounce Parmesan cheese, finely grated (½ cup), plus more to serve

Heat the oven to 350°F with a rack in the lower-middle position. In a Dutch oven over medium, combine the oil, pancetta and onion. Cook over medium, stirring occasionally, until the onion is lightly browned, 4 to 5 minutes. Add the tomato paste and cook, stirring, until it starts to darken and stick to the bottom of the pot, 1 to 2 minutes. Add the wine and cook, scraping up any browned bits, until reduced by half, about 1 minute. Stir in the beef, tomatoes with juices, ½ cup water and ½ teaspoon each salt and pepper. Bring to a simmer over medium-high, cover, transfer to the oven and cook for 2 hours.

Remove the pot from the oven, uncover and stir, scraping the sides of the pot. Return to the oven uncovered and cook until a skewer inserted into a piece of beef meets no resistance, about 30 minutes. Remove from the oven. If desired, skim off and discard some of the fat from the surface, but leave some for flavor. Cover to keep warm while you cook the pasta.

In a large pot, bring 4 quarts water to boil. Add the pasta and 1 tablespoon salt; cook, stirring occasionally, until al dente. Reserve ½ cup of the cooking water, then drain the pasta.

Add the pasta to the ragù and cook over medium, stirring, until the pasta is well coated in sauce and everything is heated through; if it looks dry, stir in reserved cooking water as needed. Off heat, stir in the basil and cheese, then taste and season with salt and pepper. Serve with additional cheese.

Panino di Manzo con Rucola e Salsa al Marsala
Open-Face Steak Sandwiches with Arugula and Marsala Sauce

Start to finish: 40 minutes Makes 4 toasts

We took some liberties with the filetto alla borbonica that Angelo di Antonio, chef at Ristorante Colle Santamaria in Civitella del Tronto, demonstrated for us. The layered dish, said to be created for King Frederick II of Naples, has a bread base topped with a thinly cut beef steak, on which sits a hefty slice of mozzarella and a couple anchovy fillets, usually arranged in the sign of the cross. A marsala pan sauce is obligatory. We opted for a medium-rare, inch-thick ribeye steak, cut into thin slices after cooking for piling onto mozzarella-topped bread that's been broiled to make the cheese melty. This recipe calls for a generous amount of marsala—1½ cups—so avoid supermarket marsala "cooking wine," which contains added sugar, salt, preservatives and no flavor nuances.

Don't over-reduce the sauce. You might be inclined to simmer it until it's syrupy and glaze-like, but stop short of taking it that far. The correct yield is about ¾ cup; the consistency may be a bit "loose" and the amount may seem overly abundant, but this is intentional so there is ample sauce to pool on the plate and soak into the bread.

Season the steak on both sides with salt. In a 12-inch skillet over medium-high, heat the oil until barely smoking. Add the steak, reduce to medium and cook until well browned on the bottom, 5 to 6 minutes. Flip the steak and cook until the second side is well browned and the center registers 120°F for medium-rare, another 5 to 6 minutes. Transfer to a plate, reserving the skillet. Heat the broiler with a rack positioned about 6 inches from the element.

To the now-empty skillet, add the marsala and anchovies. Cook over medium-high, scraping up any browned bits, until reduced by about half, 5 to 7 minutes. Stir in 1 tablespoon vinegar, along with any accumulated steak juices. Taste the sauce and season with salt and pepper, then remove the pan from heat.

While the sauce simmers, place the bread in a single layer, cut sides up, on a broiler-safe rimmed baking sheet. Top with the mozzarella, dividing it evenly; the cheese will not cover the entire surface of the bread slices. Broil until the bread is browned at the edges and the cheese has softened, 2 to 3 minutes; rotate the baking sheet as needed for even toasting. Remove from the oven and transfer the bread to a platter or individual plates.

In a small bowl, toss the arugula with the remaining 1 tablespoon vinegar. Transfer the steak to a cutting board, then slice it thinly (about ¼ inch thick). Divide the meat evenly among the bread slices. Top with the arugula, then spoon on the sauce. Drizzle with additional oil and sprinkle with Parmesan.

1-pound beef ribeye steak

Kosher salt and ground black pepper

1 teaspoon extra-virgin olive oil, plus more to serve

1½ cups dry marsala wine

4 oil-packed anchovies, patted dry and minced

2 tablespoons white balsamic vinegar, divided

1 ciabatta loaf (about 11-by-4½ inches), halved crosswise, each piece split horizontally, for a total of 4 pieces, or two ciabatta rolls, split horizontally

8 ounces fresh mozzarella cheese, sliced about ¾ inch thick

2 cups lightly packed baby arugula

Finely grated Parmesan cheese, to serve

Orecchiette con Salsiccia e Rucola

Orecchiette with Sausage and Arugula

Start to finish: 30 minutes Servings: 4 to 6

A ragù of ground pork and wild fennel that we ate at Osteria Sa Domu Sarda in Cagliari, Sardinia, served as the inspiration for this quick and easy pasta dish. Dry vermouth and citrusy lemon zest perfectly balance the richness of the Italian sausage and the pepperiness of baby arugula. Orecchiette, a coin-sized, saucer-shaped pasta, is ideal for catching flavorful bits of sausage, scallions and fennel seeds; if you can't find orecchiette, small shells and cavatelli work well, too.

Don't forget to reserve 1 cup of the pasta cooking water before draining the pasta. You will need it to build the sauce.

In a large pot, bring 4 quarts water to a boil. Add 1 tablespoon salt and the pasta, then cook, stirring occasionally, until just shy of al dente. Reserve 1 cup of cooking water, then drain. Return the pasta to the pot.

While the pasta cooks, in a 12-inch skillet over medium-high, heat the oil until shimmering. Add the sausage and cook, breaking it into small chunks, until well browned, 6 to 8 minutes. Using a slotted spoon, transfer to a paper towel–lined plate, then pour off and discard all but 1 tablespoon of the fat.

To the fat in the pan, add the scallion whites, garlic and fennel seeds. Cook over medium, stirring,

until the scallions are softened, 2 to 3 minutes. Add the vermouth and cook, scraping up any browned bits, until most of the liquid evaporates, about 1 minute. Stir in the reserved cooking water, the lemon zest and half of the scallion greens. Bring to a simmer and cook until slightly thickened, 1 to 2 minutes.

Pour the mixture over the pasta, then add the sausage. Cook over medium, stirring, until heated through, 1 to 2 minutes. Add the arugula and toss to wilt. Off heat, stir in the Parmesan. Serve sprinkled with the remaining scallion greens and drizzled with oil; offer additional Parmesan on the side.

Kosher salt

1 pound orecchiette pasta

1 tablespoon extra-virgin olive oil, plus more to serve

1 pound sweet or hot Italian sausage, casing removed

2 bunches scallions, sliced, white and green parts reserved separately

4 medium garlic cloves, chopped

2 teaspoons fennel seeds

¼ cup dry vermouth or white wine

1 teaspoon grated lemon zest

5-ounce container baby arugula, roughly chopped

1½ ounces Parmesan cheese, finely grated (¾ cup), plus more to serve

Real Italians really do
eat spaghetti and meatballs

Giovanni Iezzi strums his fingers across the taut wire guitar strings, filling his sawdust-caked workshop with a delicate, vibrating twang. "Che melodia," he says, then strums the instrument again. "Che melodia!" What a melody!

Except Iezzi isn't a musician and the shoebox-sized instrument he's holding isn't a guitar, at least not in the conventional sense. It's a chitarra—which, confusingly, translates from Italian as guitar—one he spent the last 45 minutes crafting for me from bits of beechwood, a few bolts, a handful of tiny brass nails and fiber-thin wire made just for this purpose.

I'd come to Pretoro—a medieval Italian village of about 800 people tucked into and up the hills of Abruzzo, a mountainous region wedged between Rome and the Adriatic Sea—to better understand the chitarra, a romantic, if somewhat clunky, almost harp-like tool used to make a rough-hewn, square-sided, spaghetti-like pasta of the same name.

But the real—and most delicious—lesson I'd learn in those hills is the unexpected and hidden truth about that most American—and supposedly least Italian—of classic Italian-American dishes we all grew up with: spaghetti and meatballs.

Predictably, we've got it all wrong.

Conventional wisdom holds that spaghetti and meatballs is an Italian-American creation. Real Italians—those living in Italy, that is—don't know it and don't eat it. Bathing meatballs in tomato sauce, then ladling them onto platters of spaghetti simply isn't done. And that's true. From a certain point of view.

To understand that, we need to look at immigration patterns. During the late 1800s and early 1900s, several million Italians left Italy to immigrate to the United States. Most of them were from southern Italy, places like Naples and Sicily. Their culinary norms came to define what we consider "real Italian" cooking, even if those norms didn't persist in the U.S.

For context, pasta in much of Italy—however sauced—is a primo, or first course. There may be meat in the sauce, but it mostly is as a flavoring, not the main event. A bit of guanciale for richness, for example. Meat, including marinara-drenched meatballs, is served separately as a secondo, or main course. East is East, and West is West, and never the twain shall meet.

Things changed as Italians adapted to life in the U.S. Meat and money were more abundant than in the old country. And most culinary historians credit New York's Italian community with marrying large, Neapolitan-style meatballs to the pasta course. But that's not really where the story begins. Because real Italians, it turns out, very much eat pasta and meatballs.

Like most people in Abruzzo, Iezzi grew up eating a dish called pasta alla chitarra con pallottine, or to put it less lyrically, pasta made on a chi-

> "Each mouthful is a balance of thick noodles and tender meatballs."

tarra and served with tiny balls of meat. He never thought it would become his life's work.

His father was a woodworker who made mortai e pestelli, or elaborately decorated wooden mortars and pestles. Iezzi followed him into the trade, but focused on chairs, which he sold at markets around the region. That is, until online shopping and chain stores cut into his business so severely it no longer was viable. That was about 20 years ago.

Making chitarras started as a fun challenge. He didn't know anyone else doing it, yet plenty of people used them to make the region's signature pasta, best described as thick spaghetti with squared edges. Demand built and hit especially hard during the pandemic. Today, he builds 1,500 chitarras a month and says it's never enough.

"I'd like to make many other things, but I just don't have the time," he says. "No one else wants to do this."

A chitarra basically is a rectangular box without a top or bottom. Two sturdy end pieces are held in place by four horizontal rails, and the wire is wrapped in parallel lines end to end across the top and bottom, narrower spacing on one side, wider on the flip. The difference allows the cook to decide how wide to make their pasta, spaghetti thin or fettuccine thick.

A different, antiquated machine helps Iezzi router, cut, trim or plane each piece of the chitarra, a 15-step process to assemble. The most cumbersome part is the stringing of the wire, all done by hand. It's a lot of work, and it's a dying art; his children won't continue the business. "In five or six years when I have to

stop, all of these machines will be thrown out," he says.

The origins of the chitarra are a bit muddled, but most date its creation to the mid-1800s, a time when Germans introduced thin steel wire to Italy and some clever folks there figured out how to use it to cut pasta (until then, it mostly had been cut by hand with a knife or rolling pin etched with dozens of ridges and grooves).

And the name, despite its musical affinity, probably actually

comes from the French "carrer," or to square. However created and named, the chitarra took off, becoming so culturally important in Abruzzo it was part of a woman's dowry in marriage.

Which explains the pasta. The meatballs? Also a muddle. But Abruzzo has a long tradition of raising sheep for milk and meat, and meat is consumed more often here—and more abundantly—than further south. Abruzzo also enjoys a long coastline, adding ample

seafood to the cuisine. All of which at least partly explains why pasta here is paired more often and more abundantly with meat and seafood than in other regions.

Maria di Marino is equal parts curt and cozy. Standing at her kitchen table in front of her flickering fireplace—her husband sitting nearby, patiently waiting for his lunch—she started her pasta by using the side of her hand to cut the sign of the cross into the mound of flour on the table. "I do that to make sure it comes out good," she explains.

She is 88, a retired teacher and is showing me how to make chitarra pasta using the chitarra her mother had cooked with since long before di Marino was born. So it's got some mileage on it. In short order, six eggs and 600 grams of flour come together into a golden-hued dough. After a brief rest—for herself and the dough—she divides it in half and begins rolling.

Four hundred kilometers north in Bologna, cooks are instructed to roll their pasta so thin you could see Basilica di San Luca through it. And they take that seriously. Here in Pretoro, just a few hundred yards from Iezzi's workshop, if you want to see the local church, you'll do better to look through di Marino's window. Pasta in Abruzzo is rolled much thicker.

When the mound of dough has been rolled to the size of a large pizza, di Marino cuts it into 6-inch-wide sheets, just shy of the width of her mother's chitarra. One at a time, she lays each sheet over the chitarra's thinly spaced wires, then presses and rolls a wooden pin over it. It doesn't happen as quickly as you expect, but in about

10 seconds, lines appear on the pasta. A few seconds later, those lines become perforations. A few seconds more and the perforations become cuts.

When di Marino strums the chitarra with her fingertips, thick noodles fall onto the table. Perfectly formed, squared off strands of thick pasta. She repeats the process with each sheet until she has a heaped mound of pasta substantial enough to feed us all. Meanwhile, a simple tomato sauce simmers in a terra cotta pot on the stove.

Honestly, it seems like a fussy, time-consuming way to make pasta. Surely, a knife would make faster—if slightly irregular—work of it. But after it's boiled and sauced, the rationale becomes evident. The chitarra produces pasta with a particularly coarse texture, even more so than pastas extruded through bronze dies. Those rough edges are exceptionally good at catching sauce and holding it tight. They also excel at leaching starch, the secret to perfectly thickened sauces.

The value of all this is clear when di Marino brings sauce and pasta together. The result is hearty and satisfying in ways that seem too good to be true. Equal parts tender and robust, the pasta drags the sauce with it. No pooling at the bottom of the bowl. Those who enjoy sopping up excess sauce with a hunk of bread will be sorely disappointed. I'm OK with that.

To see how all this plays out with meatballs and marinara, I headed to Pescara, a city along Abruzzo's coast. Luisa Carinci—whose home is stacked with antique cooking equipment, including weathered pasta boards and mul-

tiple chitarras—explains that she grew up eating pasta alla chitarra con pallottine. So did her husband. "I had to learn it even if I didn't want to," she said with a laugh.

To make the meatballs, Carinci used ingredients that should feel familiar to any Italian food-loving American—ground beef, eggs, breadcrumbs, grated Parmesan cheese, nutmeg, salt, pepper and parsley. It came together quickly and without fuss. Same for the sauce. A soffritto of celery, carrot and onion cooked in olive oil, then crushed tomatoes and not much else.

The forming of the meatballs is where things diverged. Carinci

pinched off tiny bits of the meat mixture, forming each into a gumball. Unlike large Neapolitan meatballs, which are meant to be eaten solo with a fork and knife, pallottine—which also go by a confusing array of other names, including polpettine—are intended to be forked up with mouthfuls of pasta. And for that to work, they need to be small.

Some people make them even smaller, Carinci explained. But she prefers them to be about ½ inch or so each. Otherwise, you might as well just make ragù, and we're in the wrong region for that.

Now where Americans might fuss over how to brown the meat-balls, the Abruzzesi prefer to just get on with it. They are dumped directly into that simple marinara to simmer for a few minutes. And because they are so small, a few minutes is plenty. This clearly matters. The short cooking time is enough to infuse the sauce with meaty flavor, but brief enough to leave the meatballs tender and light, rather than the dry and tough golf balls we know best.

Now back to that marriage of rough cut pasta and saucy meat-balls. The best versions I ate in Abruzzo did this in a skillet over medium heat. That mattered, too, as this gave the sauce additional time to reduce and the pasta a chance to release more starch into it. The result was thickly sauced noodles studded with tender, tiny meatballs.

When I tasted it all together—dusted, of course, with a bit of grated Parmesan—I won't lie... It was like your favorite childhood spaghetti and meatballs, except they'd matured in very delicious ways. True to Carinci's promise, it was easier to eat, each mouthful a balance of thick noodles and tender meatballs, each sized just right for the other.

It was immediately recogniz-able and also entirely new. All of which makes me very happy to know that real Italians really do eat spaghetti and meatballs.

—J.M. Hirsch

Pasta alla Chitarra con Pallottine
The Original Spaghetti and Meatballs

Start to finish: 1½ hours Servings: 6 to 8

In Teramo, a town in the Abruzzo region of central Italy, we learned from several home cooks and restaurant chefs how to make a local specialty: pasta alla chitarra con pallottine, the ancestor of Italian-American spaghetti and meatballs. Pasta alla chittara, the pasta used in Italy, is a long strand shape that's squared off instead of round like spaghetti, and the meatballs are marble-sized orbs that get tangled in the pasta and are so small they don't require cutting at the table (pallottine translates as "pellets" or "small balls"). Pasta alla chitarra is available in many supermarkets, but if you're not able to find it, bucatini works nicely, as does spaghetti, but ideally, use a brand that is die-cut, which leaves the noodles with a rough, porous surface that better grips the sauce. Meatloaf mix, a combination of ground pork, beef, and veal, is ideal for tender, flavorful meatballs. If the meat counter doesn't offer meatloaf mix, 8 ounces each of ground pork and 80 percent lean ground beef can be used in its place. Browning a portion of seasoned meat mixture, which includes both egg and Parmesan, along with the aromatics, creates drippings in the pot that lend the sauce rich, deep, meaty flavor.

Don't be tempted to make the meatballs larger. They don't need to be perfectly round or uniform in size, but they should be small enough so they integrate into the strands of pasta. Also, be sure to drain the pasta when it's still very underdone. Taste a piece; it should be tender only at the exterior and still quite firm at the core. The pasta will finish cooking directly in the sauce, resulting in noodles that have absorbed flavor and that are perfectly slicked with sauce.

1 large egg

1 pound meatloaf mix (see headnote)

1½ ounces Parmesan cheese, finely grated (¾ cup), divided, plus more to serve

4 tablespoons finely chopped fresh flat-leaf parsley, divided, plus more to serve

¾ teaspoon freshly grated nutmeg

Kosher salt and ground black pepper

¼ cup plus 2 tablespoons extra-virgin olive oil, divided, plus more to serve

1 small yellow onion, finely chopped

1 small carrot, peeled and finely chopped

1 small celery stalk, finely chopped

2 tablespoons tomato paste

28-ounce can whole peeled tomatoes, crushed by hand

½ teaspoon white sugar

1 pound chitarra, bucatini or spaghetti (see headnote)

In a medium bowl, beat the egg with a fork. Add the meatloaf mix, ¼ cup Parmesan, 2 tablespoons parsley, the nutmeg, 1 teaspoon salt and ¾ teaspoon pepper. Using your hands, mix and knead the mixture until homogeneous; set aside.

In a large Dutch oven over medium-high, heat the ¼ cup oil until shimmering. Add the onion, carrot, celery, tomato paste, ⅓ cup of the meatball mixture, the remaining 2 tablespoons parsley and 1 teaspoon salt. Cook, stirring occasionally, until the vegetables are tender and the mixture is brown and sticking

to the pot, 8 to 10 minutes. Add the tomatoes with juices, the sugar, 1 cup water and ½ teaspoon pepper. Bring to a simmer, scraping up the browned bits. Reduce to medium-low, cover partially and cook, stirring occasionally, until a spoon drawn through the mixture leaves a trail, 30 to 35 minutes.

While the sauce simmers, line a rimmed baking sheet with kitchen parchment. Form the remaining meatball mixture into ½-inch balls (about ½ teaspoon each) and place on the baking sheet. Refrigerate, uncovered, until ready

to use. Fill a large pot with 4 quarts water and bring to a boil.

When the sauce is ready and the water is boiling, use your hands to add the meatballs several at a time to the sauce. Cover, reduce to medium-low and cook, stirring occasionally and gently. Meanwhile, to the boiling water, add the pasta and 1 tablespoon salt. Cook, stirring occasionally, until the noodles are tender on the exterior but still very firm in the center, about 5 minutes. Reserve about ½ cup of the cooking water, then drain.

Uncover the sauce and meatballs and bring to a simmer over medium. Add the pasta, the remaining ½ cup Parmesan, the remaining 2 tablespoons oil and ¼ cup reserved cooking water. Cook, tossing to combine, until the sauce has thickened and the pasta is al dente, 3 to 5 minutes; add reserved pasta water as needed so the sauce clings to the noodles. Off heat, taste and season with salt and pepper. Serve sprinkled with additional Parmesan and parsley and drizzled with additional oil.

DOLCE

In Italy, lemons transform the basic Bundt cake

For Salvatore Aceto, lemons are not a fruit. Or rather, not merely a fruit. They are poetry. They are love. His life bears this out.

The sixth-generation lemon farmer met and married his wife in his lemon grove, a terraced farm richly green and yellow from some 2,700 trees tucked tight to Italy's Amalfi hillside. Ask for a tour and his narrative about the region's unique sfusato Amalfitano lemons will be punctuated with soliloquies about the lemon juice—not blood—he says runs through his veins.

And then there is the lemon cake. The torta al limone his mother taught his wife, Giovanna.

"I married her just for the lemon cake," Salvatore says, quite seriously.

It's understandable. As so much of the food of Amalfi is—lemon risotto, lemon pesto, lemon liqueur, even pasta is boiled with lemon—Giovanna's cake is unsparingly saturated with citrus. Multiple tablespoons of zest go into the batter, perfuming the kitchen as it bakes. But it is the finishing flourish that puts this cake over the top.

Using nearly a cup of lemon juice, Giovanna makes a golden syrup that is poured over the just-baked cake while it's still in the pan. The already moist cake slowly absorbs the lemony syrup, becoming even more tender and glistening when it later is turned out of the pan and sliced.

The result is a ridiculously tender cake with bold, bright flavor that wants for nothing. And it makes clear Salvatore's love for his lemons. And his wife.

—J.M. Hirsch

"The result is a ridiculously tender cake with bold, bright flavor that wants for nothing."

Torta al Limone

Amalfi-Style Lemon Cake

Start to finish: 1 hour (25 minutes active), plus cooling Servings: 10 to 12

Giovanna Aceto, whose family owns a generations-old lemon farm on the Amalfi Coast, showed us how to make torta al limone, a simple lemon cake popular throughout the region. Naturally, Aceto used farm-grown lemons, a variety called sfusato Amalfitano that mature to the size of softballs; the fruits are wonderfully fragrant and have a subtle sweetness. Lucky for us, in recipes such as torta al limone, regular supermarket lemons work perfectly well, as their tartness can be offset by adding a little more sugar. Lemon zest perfumes the cake, then a lemon syrup is poured on after baking to keep the crumb moist and add a layer of tangy-sweet flavor. We use a Bundt pan as a substitute for the conical fluted pan that Aceto uses for her torta. The fastest, simplest way to prep the Bundt pan is with baking spray, which is similar to cooking spray, but with added flour. Alternatively, mix 2 tablespoons melted butter and 1½ tablespoons flour, then brush the mixture onto the pan, making sure to coat all the peaks and valleys.

Don't forget to grate the zest before juicing the lemons; grating is much easier when the fruits are whole. Also, don't allow the cake to cool for more than about 10 minutes before the first application of syrup. Absorption is better and more even when the crumb is warm. But after pouring on the second half of the syrup, don't let the cake cool for longer than 30 minutes or it may be difficult to remove it from the pan.

428 grams (2 cups) white sugar, divided

2 tablespoons grated lemon zest, plus ¾ cup lemon juice

260 grams (2 cups) all-purpose flour

2 teaspoons baking powder

½ teaspoon table salt

198 grams (14 tablespoons) salted butter, room temperature

3 large eggs, room temperature

½ cup whole milk, room temperature

Heat the oven to 350°F with a rack in the middle position. Mist a 12-cup nonstick Bundt pan with baking spray. In a small saucepan, combine 214 grams (1 cup) of the sugar and the lemon juice. Cook over medium-high, stirring, until the sugar dissolves, 4 to 5 minutes. Pour into a 2-cup glass measuring cup or small bowl; you should have about 1¼ cups syrup. Cool while you make and bake the cake.

In a medium bowl, whisk together the flour, baking powder and salt. In a stand mixer with the paddle attachment, beat the remaining 214 grams (1 cup) sugar and the lemon zest on medium until fragrant, 1 to 2 minutes, scraping the bowl once or twice. Add the butter and beat on medium-high until the mixture is light and fluffy, scraping the bowl as needed, 3 to 5 minutes.

With the mixer running on low, add the eggs one at a time, beating until combined after each addition and scraping down the bowl as needed. Increase to medium and beat until well aerated, about 3 minutes. With the mixer running on low, add about one-third of the flour mixture followed by about half of the milk. Next, add about half of the remaining flour mixture, then the remaining milk and finally the remaining flour mixture. Mix on low until just combined, about

1 minute. Fold the batter a few times with a spatula to ensure no pockets of flour remain; the batter will be thick.

Scoop the batter into the prepared pan and spread in an even layer. Bake until golden brown and a toothpick inserted into the cake about 2 inches from the edge comes out clean, 35 to 40 minutes.

Cool in the pan on a wire rack for 10 minutes. Poke the cake with a toothpick every ½ inch or so, inserting the toothpick as deep as possible into the cake. Slowly pour half of the syrup evenly over the cake, then let stand for about 5 minutes to allow the syrup to soak in.

Slowly pour the remaining syrup onto the cake, then cool for

30 minutes. If the cake looks stuck to the sides in any spots, including the center tube, carefully loosen those areas by inserting a thin-bladed knife between the cake and the pan. Invert the cake onto a platter, lift off the pan and cool to room temperature.

Torta Caprese
Caprese Chocolate and Almond Torte

Start to finish: 1 hour 10 minutes (20 minutes active) Servings: 10

This flourless chocolate cake from Capri, (where it is called torta Caprese), gets its rich, almost brownie-like texture from ground almonds and a generous amount of egg. Before grinding the nuts, we toast them to intensify their flavor and accentuate the deep, roasted notes of the chocolate. We preferred the cake made with bittersweet chocolate containing 70 to 80 percent cocoa solids. You can, of course, use a lighter, sweeter bittersweet chocolate, but the cake will have less chocolate intensity. Serve slices warm or at room temperature dolloped with unsweetened whipped cream.

Don't forget to reduce the oven to 300°F after toasting the almonds. Also, don't overbake the cake or its texture will be dry and tough. Whereas most cakes are done when a toothpick inserted at the center comes out clean, a toothpick inserted into this one should come out with sticky, fudgy crumbs, similar to brownies.

217 grams (2⅓ cups) sliced almonds

5 large eggs

2 teaspoons vanilla extract

8 ounces bittersweet chocolate (see headnote), roughly chopped

199 grams (1 cup) packed dark brown sugar

½ teaspoon table salt

Heat the oven to 350°F with a rack in the middle position. Spread the almonds in an even layer on a rimmed baking sheet and toast in the oven until golden brown, 8 to 10 minutes, stirring once about halfway through. Cool to room temperature.

While the almonds cool, reduce the oven to 300°F. Mist the bottom and sides of a 9-inch round cake pan with cooking spray, line the bottom with a round of kitchen parchment, then mist the parchment. Crack the eggs into a liquid measuring cup and add the vanilla; set aside.

In a food processor, process 186 grams (2 cups) of the almonds until finely ground, 20 to 30 seconds. Add the chocolate and pulse until the chocolate is finely ground, 10 to 15 pulses. Add the sugar and salt, then process until well combined, about 30 seconds, scraping the bowl as needed. With the machine running, gradually pour in the egg mixture. Continue processing until the batter is smooth and homogeneous, about another 15 to 20 seconds. Remove the blade and scrape the bowl.

Pour the batter into the prepared pan, then sprinkle evenly with the remaining 31 grams (⅓ cup) almonds. Bake until the center feels firm when gently pressed and a toothpick inserted at the center comes out with moist, fudgy crumbs attached, 30 to 35 minutes.

Let cool in the pan on a wire rack for 30 minutes. Run a knife around the sides of the cake, then invert onto a rack. Peel off the parchment and reinvert the cake onto a platter. Serve warm or at room temperature.

Crema al Mascarpone

Mascarpone Mousse

Start to finish: 20 minutes   Servings: 4

The Italian dessert known as zabaione, a rich concoction of whipped egg yolks, sugar and sweet wine, is a classic for a reason, but it can be heavy and too sweet and/or boozy. This five-ingredient mascarpone mousse we encountered in Milan is both lighter and simpler. Unlike zabaione, which uses only yolks and is cooked over a double boiler, the mousse, known as crema al mascarpone, uses egg whites as well, making it airy and light. It requires no cooking and comes together in minutes. Just be sure the mascarpone is softened to cool room temperature so it combines easily with the egg yolks. A hand mixer makes easy work of whipping the egg whites, but you also could use a whisk and a little elbow grease. Serve the mousse as soon as it's made, or cover and refrigerate for up to 45 minutes. A dusting of cocoa adds visual appeal as well as a hint of chocolate flavor; fresh berries or crisp cookies also are excellent. Note that the eggs are not cooked.

Don't forget to thoroughly clean the bowl and beaters or whisk that you'll be using to whip the whites. Any residual fat will prevent the whites from attaining the proper loft.

In a medium bowl, whisk together the egg yolks and 1 tablespoon of sugar until smooth and pale yellow in color. Add the mascarpone and whisk until well combined, then whisk in the rum; set aside.

In a medium bowl, combine the egg whites and the remaining 2 tablespoons sugar. With a hand mixer on medium-high, whip until they hold soft peaks when the beaters are lifted, 1 to 2 minutes; do not overwhip.

With a silicone spatula, fold about a third of the whipped whites into the mascarpone mixture until just a few streaks remain. Fold in the remaining whites, taking care not to deflate the mixture. Serve right away or cover with plastic wrap and refrigerate for up to 45 minutes. Dust with cocoa just before serving.

2 large eggs, separated

3 tablespoons white sugar, divided

8-ounce container mascarpone cheese (1 cup), softened

4 teaspoons dark rum

Cocoa powder, to serve

Torta Barozzi

Italian Flourless Chocolate Torta

Start to finish: 1 hour (30 minutes active), plus cooling Servings: 8 to 10

Pasticceria Gollini in Vignola, not far from Modena, is home to the sumptuous flourless chocolate cake known as torta Barozzi. Created in 1886 by pastry chef Eugenio Gollini and named for Jacopo Barozzi da Vignola, a 16th-century architect, the much-loved sweet continues today to be produced according to a closely guarded secret recipe. Impostor recipes abound, as professional and home bakers alike have attempted to re-create the dessert, and we ourselves set out to devise a formula. It's well known that torta Barozzi is made without wheat flour (and is therefore gluten free). Instead, a combination of ground peanuts and almonds—along with whipped egg whites—deliver a structure that's somehow rich and dense yet remarkably light. We found that we could skip the peanuts, as almond flour alone worked well. To achieve a complex chocolatiness, we use both cocoa powder and bittersweet chocolate (ideally, chocolate with about 70 percent cocoa solids). Instant espresso powder accentuates the deep, roasty, bitter notes and a dose of dark rum lifts the flavors with its fieriness. Serve with lightly sweetened mascarpone or whipped cream, or with vanilla gelato.

Don't use natural cocoa. The recipe will still work, but the cake will be lighter in color and not quite as deep in flavor as when made with Dutch-processed cocoa. Take care not to overbake the cake. Remove it from the oven when a toothpick inserted at the center comes out with a few sticky crumbs clinging to it. After 30 to 45 minutes of cooling, the cake is inverted out of the pan; don't worry about re-inverting it. True torta Barozzi is left upside down for cutting and serving; we do the same with ours.

141 grams (10 tablespoons) salted butter, cut into 10 pieces, plus more for the pan

6 ounces bittersweet chocolate, chopped

21 grams (¼ cup) Dutch-processed cocoa powder, plus more for dusting

1 tablespoon instant espresso powder

4 large eggs, separated, room temperature

161 grams (¾ cup) white sugar, divided

100 grams (1 cup) almond flour

½ teaspoon table salt

3 tablespoons dark rum

Heat the oven to 350°F with a rack in the middle position. Butter an 8-inch square pan, line the bottom with a parchment square and butter the parchment.

In a medium saucepan over medium, melt the butter. Remove from the heat and add the chocolate, cocoa and espresso powder. Let stand for a few minutes to allow the chocolate to soften, then whisk until the mixture is smooth; cool until barely warm to the touch.

In a large bowl, vigorously whisk the egg yolks and 107 grams (½ cup) of the sugar until lightened

and creamy, about 30 seconds. Add the chocolate mixture and whisk until homogeneous. Add the almond flour and salt, then whisk until fully incorporated. Whisk in the rum; set aside.

In a stand mixer with the whisk attachment or in a large bowl with a hand mixer, whip the egg whites on medium-high until frothy, 1 to 2 minutes. With the mixer running, gradually add the remaining 54 grams (¼ cup) sugar, then beat until the whites hold soft peaks, about 2 minutes. Add about a third of the whipped whites to the

yolk-chocolate mixture and fold
with a silicone spatula to lighten
and loosen the base. Scrape on the
remaining whites and gently fold
in until well combined. Transfer to
the prepared pan and gently shake
or tilt the pan to level the batter.

Bake until the cake is slightly
domed and a toothpick inserted
at the center comes out with a few

crumbs attached, 30 to 35 minutes.
Cool in the pan on a wire rack for 30
to 45 minutes; the cake will deflate
slightly as it cools.

Run a paring knife around the
inside edge of the pan to loosen the
cake, then invert onto a platter; if
needed, peel off and discard the
parchment. Cool completely. Dust
with cocoa before serving.

The sultry, six-ingredient
side of tiramisù

No liquor. No cooking. A shockingly minuscule amount of sugar. And maybe a side of prostitution? This clearly was not the tiramisù we know.

I was in Treviso, a canal-cut city in northeastern Italy where the dessert was born. And I quickly learned how easy it is to make a bad tiramisù. The good news is that it's even easier to make an excellent one. The lesson? Simplicity is best.

I got my first lesson in tiramisù assembly—for truly, that best describes the process, as no cooking or baking occurs in the traditional making of this treat—from the folks at Camelia Bakery, which was voted to have the city's best tiramisù. I could and probably should have simply stopped there. They earned that honor and every sample I tried after disappointed.

That's even more impressive when you realize Camelia Bakery—which looks a bit like an English tea shop—has been around only since 2015. Few question that tiramisù was created in Treviso, but how long ago is another matter.

Some say it's a relatively modern creation, perhaps dating only to the middle of the last century. Others tell of a saucier origin dating to an 1800s brothel where it was served as an aphrodisiac. For years after, it supposedly was eaten at home only on the down-low, lest diners share in the shame of its scandalous past.

Whatever the truth, classic tiramisù should contain only six ingredients, Linda Maria Botter, daughter of now-deceased owner of Camelia Bakery, Camelia Botter, told me—biscuits, coffee, sugar, mascarpone, egg yolks and cocoa powder. The magic is in selecting only the best of those ingredients and finding just the right ratios of each.

To show how it's done, baker Camilla Conzera combined egg yolks and cane sugar in a stand mixer, emphasis on the eggs. In fact, three times as many eggs as sugar by volume. While many cooks opt to gently heat this mixture—known as zabaione—traditional tiramisù never does, favoring the cleaner, richer and lighter taste of raw.

Once the eggs and sugar were whipped glossy, firm and boldly yellow, Conzera added massive amounts of mascarpone, probably three times the total volume of the eggs and sugar. She then whipped the mixture again, creating a light, airy cream-like treat that mounded in thick, shiny swirls in the mixer bowl.

Next, the biscuits. Conzera explained that only savoiardi biscuits—what we know as lady finger cookies—are acceptable. But unlike the spongy varieties we often get here, these are lightly crispy outside, almost glistening with a faint dusting of granulated sugar, and ever so slightly chewy at the center. And they always are snapped in half before use to

> "The magic is in selecting only the best of those ingredients and finding just the right ratios of each."

allow them to better absorb the cooled espresso they get dunked in for just the briefest of seconds.

For assembly, I expected a trifle-like project, something layered in a bowl and large enough to feed a crowd. But in Treviso single servings—sometimes stacked on small plates, more often layered into small cups—are the norm.

Conzera scooped some of the filling into a piping bag, then began, squirting about ¼ cup of the mixture into the bottom of a cup. She then soaked two savoiardi

halves for just a second or two in espresso, then set them into the filling. Over them, another ¼ cup of filling, followed by another four savoiardi halves, then a final layer of cream.

But hold off on the finishing sprinkle of cocoa powder. In classic tiramisù, Botter told me, the biscuits must be perfectly soft with no crunch. And that requires at least a 12-hour rest in the refrigerator before it is ready to serve. Only then does it get an aggressive dusting of cocoa.

When I tasted one that had been properly rested, it honestly was a bit shocking. It was utterly rich and creamy, but not cloying thanks to the bare amount of sugar used. The pleasant bitterness of the cocoa powder perfectly balanced the indulgence of the mascarpone. And, as promised, the biscuits offered a deliciously spongy burst of coffee, but no crunch.

A few bites in and I understood how one might consider this an aphrodisiac, fact or fiction.

—J.M. Hirsch

Tiramisù

Start to finish: 30 minutes, plus chilling Servings: 6

In Treviso, where tiramisù was born, we were shown how to make the dessert by Linda Maria Botter of Camelia Bakery, whose tiramisù was voted best in the city. The lesson: Simplicity is best. Many recipes start with cooking a zabaione, a yolk-rich custard that requires careful monitoring, so it was a revelation that raw egg yolks and sugar simply whipped until voluminous make a lighter, better tiramisù. Mascarpone gently whisked into the base completes the filling. Espresso is the classic soaking liquid for the lady fingers, but we found strong brewed coffee to be equally good. Avoid espresso made from instant powder; it tastes thin and flat. The lack of rum is not an oversight; it's not common in Italy. The type of lady fingers to use here have the texture of dry sponge cake. On package labels, they sometimes are called savoiardi biscuits; you will need one 7-ounce package. In Treviso, tiramisù often is assembled in individual portions. We offer the option to make six servings in 8-ounce ramekins or a family-style version in an 8-inch square dish. This is an ideal make-ahead dessert. Once assembled, it will keep in the refrigerator for up to two days. Note: the egg yolks in this recipe are not cooked.

Don't remove the mascarpone from the refrigerator until ready to use it. Cold mascarpone is less likely to "break" during mixing. For the same reason, do not overmix once the mascarpone is added. Keep the speed on low and the timing to a minimum. Lastly, soak the lady fingers in coffee for only one to two seconds. The cookies become soggy if overmoistened.

7 large egg yolks

71 grams (⅓ cup) white sugar

Two 8-ounce containers mascarpone cheese (2 cups), cold

3 cups strong brewed coffee or espresso (see headnote), room temperature

24 to 26 lady fingers, if assembling in an 8-inch square dish, or 18 lady fingers, broken in half, if making individual portions (see headnote)

Cocoa powder, preferably Dutch-processed, for dusting

In a stand mixer with the whisk attachment, beat the egg yolks and sugar on high until the mixture is pale, fluffy, doubled in volume and falls in a thick ribbon when the whisk is lifted, about 10 minutes. Reduce to low and, with the machine running, add the mascarpone a large spoonful at a time. After all the mascarpone has been added, scrape the bowl. Mix on low for another 10 to 20 seconds just until homogeneous; do not overmix. Pour the coffee into a medium bowl.

To assemble in an 8-inch square dish, soak a lady finger in the coffee for no more than a couple seconds, then place in the bottom of an 8-inch square baking dish. Repeat until the bottom of the dish is fully lined. Spoon on half of the mascarpone mixture, then spread in an even layer. Gently rap the dish against a folded towel or potholder placed on the countertop so the layers settle. Cover the mascarpone with another layer of coffee-dipped lady fingers (you may not use all of the coffee or cookies). Scrape on the remaining mascarpone mixture and spread in an even layer.

To assemble individual portions, you will need six 8-ounce ramekins. Soak 2 lady finger halves in the coffee for no more than a

couple seconds and place in the bottom of a ramekin. Spoon on ¼ cup mascarpone mixture. Repeat the process 2 more times for a total of 3 layers each of lady fingers and mascarpone mixture. Gently rap the ramekin against a folded kitchen towel or potholder placed on the countertop so the layers settle.

Cover and refrigerate for at least 6 hours or up to 2 days. Remove from the refrigerator just before serving. Uncover. Spoon cocoa into a fine-mesh strainer and sift a generous layer onto the tiramisù. Serve right away.

The ancient Italian crumb-topped ricotta and jam tart you've probably never heard of

I was expecting a typical Roman meal at Armando al Pantheon, just a half block from Rome's Pantheon—a neighborhood where the food, to be honest, is often mediocre. I appreciate the dedication to the unchanging Roman menu, but too many dishes are not prepared with the love and attention one finds outside of Rome. On this occasion, however, I was pleasantly surprised.

Founded in 1961 by Armando Gargioli, the restaurant is small, paneled in dark wood with a tile floor, with booths and small tables seating no more than 30 guests. The menu is a far cry from trattoria standards. Yes, you can find the classic pastas—gricia, amatriciana and carbonara—but the anti-pasti include filetto di aringa (herring with beans), polpettine di farro (spelt balls with black truffle sauce), an excellent and simple straccetti di manzo (thin strips of beef served with arugula and vinegar) and faraona stufata (guinea fowl stew).

And for dessert, they offer torta antica roma, one of the recipes that I had on my must-try list. It arrives on the table as a thin wedge of tart, barely an inch high, with a mottled crumb topping and a thin layer of ricotta and jam sandwiched in the middle. (This recipe is not to be confused with the classic cherry-ricotta crostata from Pasticceria il Boccione, opened in 1815 in the Jewish quarter. That is a heavier offering, a pastry enclosed cheesecake, which I purchased the next day. It was delicious, but heartier and more old-school.) Other versions of this dessert use a top pastry crust, not a crumble, and the ricotta and cherry jam layers often switch places depending on the whim of the baker.

Since the chef at Armando al Pantheon would not part with his recipe, I asked my guide, Arianna Pasquini, if she could help. I paid for an excursion to Armando to suss out the dessert, and she commented that the pastry

> "Nuts are also a key ingredient, as is butter and, of course, sugar."

dough was probably sbrisolona, a cake-cookie hybrid from Mantua that has a crumby texture. Sbrisolona is made with wheat flour but also commonly includes cornmeal, polenta or semolina. Nuts are also a key ingredient, as is butter and, of course, sugar.

We tested many variations and ended up with a flour-cornmeal combination (semolina flour also works) along with ground slivered almonds, lemon zest, an egg, leavener, vanilla, sugar, etc. The good news is that although this is a sticky dough, you do not have to roll it out—just press it into the bottom of a springform pan and bake for about a half hour. The ricotta is enriched with egg, poppy seeds and sugar and chilled. Cooled for 15 minutes but still warm, the baked crust is filled with the ricotta mixture, topped with jam, and then topped again with crumbled dough, the same dough used for the bottom crust. The crust goes back in the oven for 35 to 40 minutes.

So there you have it, a truly Roman dessert. A no-roll, down-to-earth tart with intriguing layers of taste and texture: a pastry dough base, ricotta, jam, and a crumbled cookie-like topping. It is the epitome of great Italian cooking—familiar, simple ingredients, where good taste is more important than good looks. A French pastry chef might opine that this tart appears too working-class, but Roman cooks would smile and say, "If the food is properly prepared, it always looks good on the plate!"

–Christopher Kimball

Torta Antica Roma

Ricotta and Cherry Jam Tart

Start to finish: 2 hours (50 minutes active), plus cooling Makes one 9-inch tart

At Armando al Pantheon, a trattoria in Rome, we ended our meal with a slice of torta antica roma—a rustic tart inspired by the traditional Roman combination of ricotta and cherries. The base was a tender, buttery, almost cakey crust, and the topping was a crumby mixture of the same composition. Sandwiched between was a layer of jam on a bed of ricotta dotted with poppy and sesame seeds. For our adaptation, we devised a dough that gets flavor and texture from almonds that are ground in the food processor, plus a small measure of semolina (or cornmeal). Lemon zest brings brightness and baking powder adds a little lift and lightness. Sour cherry jam, with its balance of sweet and sour, is best in this tart; some brands might specify Morello cherries, a variety of the fruit, on the label. If sour cherry jam is not available, good-quality strawberry jam is a better option than sweet cherry jam. Covered tightly, leftovers will keep in the refrigerator for up to three days; bring to room temperature before serving.

Don't use part-skim ricotta, as it lacks richness and has a grainy texture. Also, after making the crust mixture and transferring half to the pan, be sure to refrigerate the remainder, which will become the crumb topping. If it's kept at room temperature, it won't hold its shape during baking and will melt into the filling. Lastly, don't spread the ricotta and jam layers all the way to the edges or the filling will caramelize against and stick to the pan, making it tricky to remove the tart for serving.

Heat the oven to 350°F with a rack in the middle position. Mist a 9-inch springform pan with cooking spray.

To make the crust and topping, in a small bowl, whisk together the egg and vanilla. In a food processor, combine the almonds, white sugar and lemon zest. Process until the nuts are roughly chopped, about 15 seconds. Add both flours, the baking powder and salt; pulse to combine, about 5 pulses. Scatter the butter over the top, then pulse until the butter has been reduced to pea-sized bits, about 10 pulses. Drizzle the egg mixture over the top, then pulse until the mixture is evenly moistened and resembles damp sand; it will not form a cohesive dough.

Transfer half of the mixture to the prepared springform pan, then distribute in an even layer and lightly press it; do not firmly compact the mixture. Transfer the remainder to a medium bowl and refrigerate uncovered until needed. Bake the crust until golden brown, 25 to 30 minutes.

FOR THE CRUST AND TOPPING:

1 large egg

2 teaspoons vanilla extract

65 grams (½ cup) slivered almonds

71 grams (⅓ cup) white sugar

2 teaspoons grated lemon zest

163 grams (1¼ cups) all-purpose flour

57 grams (⅓ cup) semolina flour or 48 grams (⅓ cup) fine yellow cornmeal

½ teaspoon baking powder

½ teaspoon table salt

85 grams (6 tablespoons) salted butter, cut into ½-inch cubes, room temperature

FOR THE FILLING AND FINISHING:

15- or 16-ounce container whole-milk ricotta

1 large egg yolk

1 tablespoon poppy seeds

1 teaspoon vanilla extract

¼ teaspoon almond extract (optional)

320 grams (1 cup) sour cherry jam (see headnote)

1 teaspoon grated lemon zest

Powdered sugar, to serve

Meanwhile, make the filling.
In a medium bowl, combine the
ricotta, egg yolk, poppy seeds,
vanilla and almond extracts (if
using); fold with a silicone spatula
until well combined. Cover and
refrigerate until ready to use. In a
small bowl, stir together the jam
and lemon zest; set aside.

When the crust is done, transfer
to a wire rack and cool for about 15
minutes; leave the oven on.

Scrape the ricotta mixture onto
the still-warm crust and spread
in an even layer, leaving a ¼-inch
border at the edge. Dollop the jam
onto the ricotta and gently spread
in an even layer to cover the ricotta
layer; try not to mix the jam into
the cheese. Remove the topping
mixture from the refrigerator.
Scoop up a handful, firmly squeeze
it until it forms a cohesive clump,
then crumble and break the clump
into bits, scattering them over

the tart; aim for a mixture of fine
crumbles and pebbly, pistachio-
sized pieces. Continue adding the
remaining topping in the same way,
distributing it in an even layer; it
will not fully cover the tart. Bake
until the jam is bubbling at the
edges and the crumb topping is light
golden brown, 35 to 40 minutes.

Transfer to a wire rack and cool
for about 30 minutes. Remove the
pan sides and cool completely. Before
serving, dust with powdered sugar.

Bonet alla Piemontese
Italian Chocolate Custard with Amaretti

Start to finish: 3½ hours (25 minutes active) Servings: 6 to 8

Amaretti are crisp, airy Italian cookies with an almond flavor. In this elegant dessert from Italy's Piedmont region, the cookies are crushed, then soaked and baked into a cocoa-enriched custard. A layer of caramel on the bottom of the pan becomes a sauce once the dessert is unmolded, similar to crème caramel or flan. During baking, the amaretti crumbs rise to the surface of the custard and form a cake-like layer that, after inverting, becomes the base of the dessert. Coffee heightens the chocolatey flavor and a bit of dark rum adds a subtle bite that balances the sweetness. If you can't find amaretti, substitute an equal amount of Stella D'oro Almond Toast. To crush the cookies, place them in a heavy-duty zip-close bag and bash them gently with a rolling pin. Either Dutch-processed or natural cocoa works in this recipe.

Don't let the custard mixture cool before baking or the timing will be off. The baking time may also be affected by the temperature of the water in the water bath, so make sure to use room-temperature, not hot or boiling, water. Don't be surprised if a little caramel remains in the pan after the custard is unmolded; this is normal.

107 grams (½ cup) plus 71 grams (⅓ cup) white sugar, divided

1½ cups heavy cream

½ cup brewed coffee

100 grams (1 cup) finely crushed amaretti cookies, plus crushed amaretti cookies, to serve

28 grams (⅓ cup) unsweetened cocoa powder

½ teaspoon table salt

3 large eggs, plus 3 large egg yolks

2 tablespoons dark rum

Heat the oven to 350°F with a rack in the middle position. In a medium saucepan, combine ¼ cup water and 107 grams (½ cup) sugar. Cook over medium, occasionally swirling the pan, until the sugar has dissolved, 3 to 4 minutes. Increase to medium-high and cook, gently swirling the pan, until the caramel is lightly smoking and dark amber in color, about 4 minutes. Carefully pour it into a 9-by-5-inch metal loaf pan and gently tilt to coat the bottom of the pan; set aside.

Pour the cream and coffee into the now-empty pan and bring to a bare simmer over medium. Add the crushed amaretti and whisk until the crumbs are softened, about 1 minute. Remove from the heat and set aside.

In a large bowl, whisk together the remaining 71 grams (⅓ cup) sugar, the cocoa and the salt. Whisk in the eggs, yolks and rum. While whisking, gradually add the hot cream mixture. Pour the mixture into the caramel-lined loaf pan, then set the pan in a 9-by-13-inch baking dish.

Pour enough room-temperature water into the outer baking dish to come about halfway up its sides, then carefully transfer to the oven. Bake until the center of the custard jiggles slightly when the loaf pan is gently shaken and a paring knife inserted at the center of the custard comes out mostly clean, 50 to 55 minutes.

Carefully remove the loaf pan from the water bath and set on a wire rack. Remove the baking dish from the oven and discard the water

bath. Let the custard cool to room temperature, then cover with plastic wrap and refrigerate until cold, at least 2 hours or up to 1 day.

To serve, fill a 9-by-13-inch baking dish with about 1 inch of hot tap water. Uncover the loaf pan, place in the baking dish and let stand for about 5 minutes. Run a paring knife around the inside of the pan to loosen the custard. Invert onto a serving platter, then lift off the pan. Garnish with additional crushed amaretti. Cut into slices and serve.

Fregolotta
Italian Almond Crumb Cookie

Start to finish: 50 minutes (25 minutes active), plus cooling Servings: 4 to 6

Fregolotta is a Venetian cookie akin to buttery streusel topping. The cookie is baked into a slab and allowed to cool before it is broken into rustic shards or coarse crumbs for serving. Offer pieces of fregolotta alongside coffee, tea or dessert wine, or crumble it onto bowls of ice cream or gelato. In an airtight container, fregolotta will keep for up to a week.

Don't worry if the almonds are not in uniform pieces after chopping. Uneven bits add to the charm of the cookie. For the crispest texture, make sure to allow the fregolotta to cool completely before serving.

184 grams (1¼ cups) whole almonds

3 large egg yolks

2 tablespoons whole milk

130 grams (1 cup) all-purpose flour

214 grams (1 cup) white sugar

¼ teaspoon table salt

85 grams (6 tablespoons) cold salted butter, cut into ½-inch cubes

Heat the oven to 350°F with a rack in the lower-middle position. Place the almonds in a 9-by-13-inch metal baking pan and toast in the oven until lightly browned, 5 to 7 minutes, stirring once. Transfer the nuts to a cutting board and cool; reserve the pan and leave the oven on. Meanwhile, in a small bowl, whisk together the egg yolks and milk.

When the almonds are cooled, roughly chop them and add them to a large bowl along with the flour, sugar and salt; stir to combine. Scatter the butter over the top and, using your fingers, rub the butter into the dry ingredients until the mixture resembles coarse crumbs. Drizzle on the yolk-milk mixture and stir with a silicone spatula until it resembles a combination of pebbles and sand; it should not form a cohesive dough.

Mist the bottom and sides of the reserved baking pan with cooking spray. Transfer the mixture to the reserved pan and distribute in an even layer but do not compress or compact it.

Bake until light golden brown, 25 to 30 minutes. Cool in the pan on a wire rack for about 10 minutes. Using a metal spatula, carefully pry the fregolotta out of the pan and transfer directly to the rack; it's fine if it breaks during removal. Cool to room temperature. To serve, break the fregolotta into pieces of the desired size.

Biscotti di Mandorle e Agrumi
Almond and Citrus Biscotti

Start to finish: 1½ hours (30 minutes active), plus cooling Makes about 28 biscotti

In Tuscany, Antonio Mattei Premiata Fabrica di Biscotti is a bakery that has been churning out the twice-baked cookies for more than a century and is credited with their creation. Their biscotti are classic and simple, just flour, sugar, eggs, almonds and pine nuts. Meanwhile, Tuscan cookbook author Giulia Scarpaleggia includes citrus zest, butter and honey for richer flavor and chewier texture in her homemade biscotti. This recipe bridges the two. While the biscotti are great the day of baking, their flavor and texture are best the following morning—perfect for dunking in coffee or tea.

Don't skip the step of rubbing the orange and lemon zests into the sugar. This draws out the zests' essential oils and evenly distributes them.

293 grams (2¼ cups) all-purpose flour, plus more for dusting

1 teaspoon baking powder

½ teaspoon table salt

214 grams (1 cup) white sugar

1 tablespoon grated lemon zest

1 tablespoon grated orange zest

2 tablespoons honey

2 large eggs

147 grams (1 cup) whole almonds

Heat the oven to 350°F with a rack in the middle position. Line a rimmed baking sheet with kitchen parchment. In a small bowl, combine the flour, baking powder and salt. In a large bowl, combine the sugar and both zests. Using your fingers, rub the zest into the sugar until fragrant. Add the honey and eggs, then beat with a hand mixer on medium until slightly thickened and almost doubled in volume, about 1 minute (alternative, whisk vigorously by hand for about 2 minutes).

Add the flour mixture and, using a silicone spatula, stir and fold, mashing the mixture against the bowl, until the dry ingredients are evenly moistened. Add the almonds; lightly flour your hands and knead gently until they are evenly distributed.

Lightly flour the counter, then turn the dough out onto it and divide in half. Moisten your hands with water and roll one portion into a log 14 inches long and 2 inches wide. Place the log on one side of the prepared baking sheet. Shape the remaining dough in the same way and place on the other side of the baking sheet, spacing the logs about 4 inches apart.

Bake until the logs are deep golden brown and have spread into flat, fissured loaves that are firm on the surface and appear dry in the cracks, about 30 minutes, rotating the baking sheet halfway through. Cool on the baking sheet on a wire rack for 20 minutes; immediately after removing from the oven, reduce the temperature to 275°F.

Using a wide metal spatula, carefully transfer the loaves to a cutting board; reserve the baking sheet and its parchment. Using a serrated knife and a gentle sawing motion, cut each still-warm loaf on the diagonal into ½-inch-thick slices.

Place the biscotti cut side up in a single layer on the reserved baking sheet. Bake until firm and dry, 30 to 35 minutes, rotating the baking sheet about halfway through. Cool on the baking sheet on a wire rack for about 10 minutes. Transfer the biscotti directly to the rack and cool completely.

Index

ACKNOWLEDGMENTS

Writing a cookbook can be an intimidating endeavor requiring the bringing together of disparate ingredients to achieve a delicious result. Here, those ingredients are the talented people in and around Milk Street working to create a singular well-conceived concept, from recipe idea and development through photography, editing and design. Many hands and minds make this possible.

In particular, I want to acknowledge J.M. Hirsch, my tireless editorial director and co-author; Michelle Locke, our relentlessly organized books editor; our exacting food editors Dawn Yanagihara and Ari Smolin; and Matthew Card, creative director of recipes; for leading the charge on conceiving, developing, writing and editing all of this.

Also, Jennifer Baldino Cox, our art director, and the entire design team who captured the essence of Milk Street. Special thanks to our travel photographer, Christopher Warde-Jones; our recipe photographer, Joe Murphy; our designers, Gary Tooth and Ashley Prine, and all the stylists, art directors and photographers who have worked so hard to make Milk Street look so good.

Likewise, our talented kitchen crew, including kitchen director Wes Martin; our recipe development director Courtney Hill; recipe developers Rose Hattabaugh and Hisham Ali Hassan; our culinary support team, Kevin Clark, Elizabeth Mindreau and Hector Taborda; and the many cooks whose talent, skill and dedication have created the thousands of recipes that are the heart of Milk Street. Also Deborah Broide, Milk Street director of media relations, has done a spectacular job of sharing with the world all we do.

We also have a couple of folks to thank who work outside of 177 Milk Street. Michael Szczerban, editor, and everyone at Little, Brown and Company have been superb and inspired partners in this project. And my long-standing book agent, David Black, has been instrumental in bringing this project to life both with his knowledge of publishing and his friendship and support. Thank you, David!

Finally, a sincere thank you to my business partner and wife, Melissa. She has nurtured the Milk Street brand from the beginning so that we ended up where we thought we were going in the first place.

And, last but not least, to all of you who have supported the Milk Street project. Each and every one of you has a seat at the Milk Street table.

—Christopher Kimball

ABOUT THE AUTHORS

Christopher Kimball is founder of Christopher Kimball's Milk Street, a food media company dedicated to changing the way we cook. It produces three television shows: *Christopher Kimball's Milk Street*, *My Family Recipe* and *Milk Street Cooking School*. It also produces a public radio show and podcast heard by more than 500,000 listeners weekly. Kimball founded *Cook's Magazine* in 1980, the *Who's Who of Cooking in America* in 1983, and *Cook's Illustrated* in 1993. Through 2016, Kimball was host and executive producer of *America's Test Kitchen* and *Cook's Country* television shows. He also hosted *America's Test Kitchen* radio show on public radio. Kimball is the author of numerous cookbooks, including *The Cook's Bible*, *The Dessert Bible*, and *The Kitchen Detective*. He also wrote *Fannie's Last Supper* and the Christopher Award–winning *Dear Charlie*, a collection of personal essays.

J.M. Hirsch is a James Beard Award–winning food and travel writer. He is editorial director of Christopher Kimball's Milk Street and author of six cookbooks, including *Freezer Door Cocktails: 75 Cocktails That Are Ready When You Are*, *Pour Me Another: 250 Ways to Find Your Favorite Drink* and *Shake Strain Done: Craft Cocktails at Home*.

Christopher Kimball's Milk Street is located at 177 Milk Street in downtown Boston and is dedicated to changing the way America cooks, with new flavor combinations and techniques learned around the world. It is home to Milk Street TV, a three-time Emmy Award–winning public television show, a James Beard Award–winning bimonthly magazine, an award-winning public radio show and podcast, a cooking school and global culinary tour provider and an online store with more than 1,000 hard-to-find ingredients, tools and pantry products from around the world. Milk Street's cookbooks include the James Beard–winning *Milk Street Tuesday Nights*, the IACP-winning *Milk Street Vegetables*, *Milk Street 365*, *Milk Street Simple* and *Milk Street Cookish*. Milk Street also invests in nonprofit outreach, partnering with FoodCorps, the Big Sister Association of Greater Boston and the Boys & Girls Clubs of Dorchester.